SECOND EDITION

AN INVITATION TO
ENVIRONMENTAL
SOCIOLOGY

Sociology for a New Century

A Pine Forge Press Series

Founding Editors: Charles Ragin, Wendy Griswold, Larry Griffin

Sociology for a New Century brings the best scholarship in key areas to today's students in a series of short texts authored by research leaders in the social sciences. Each book addresses its subject from a comparative, historical, and global perspective, and, in doing so, connects social science to the wider concerns of students who are seeking to make sense of our dramatically changing world.

- *An Invitation to Environmental Sociology, Second Edition,* Michael M. Bell
- *Global Inequalities,* York Bradshaw and Michael Wallace
- *Economy/Society: Markets, Meanings, and Social Structure,* Bruce G. Carruthers and Sarah L. Babb
- *How Societies Change,* Daniel Chirot
- *Ethnicity and Race: Making Identities in a Changing World,* Stephen Cornell and Douglas Hartmann
- *The Sociology of Childhood, Second Edition* William Corsaro
- *Cultures and Societies in a Changing World, Second Edition,* Wendy Griswold
- *Crime and Disrepute,* John Hagan
- *Gods in the Global Village: The World's Religions in Sociological Perspective,* Lester R. Kurtz
- *Waves of Democracy: Social Movements and Political Change,* John Markoff
- *Development and Social Change: A Global Perspective, Third Edition,* Philip McMichael
- *Women and Men at Work, Second Edition,* Irene Padavic and Barbara F. Reskin
- *Aging, Social Inequality, and Public Policy,* Fred C. Pampel
- *Constructing Social Research: The Unity and Diversity of Method,* Charles C. Ragin
- *Making Societies: The Historical Construction of Our World,* William G. Roy
- *Cities in a World Economy, Second Edition,* Saskia Sassen
- *Gender, Family and Social Movements,* Suzanne Staggenborg
- *Law/Society: Origins, Interactions, and Change,* John R. Sutton

SECOND EDITION

AN INVITATION TO
ENVIRONMENTAL
SOCIOLOGY

MICHAEL MAYERFELD BELL
University of Wisconsin—Madison

with
Michael S. Carolan

PINE FORGE PRESS
An Imprint of Sage Publications, Inc.
Thousand Oaks • London • New Delhi

For information, address:

 Pine Forge Press
A Sage Publications Company
2455 Teller Road
Thousand Oaks, California 91320
(805) 499–4224
E-mail: sales@pfp.sagepub.com

Sage Publications Ltd
1 Oliver's Yard
55 City Road
London EC1Y 1SP
United Kingdom

SAGE Publications India Pvt. Ltd.
B-42, Panchsheel Enclave
Post Box 4109
New Delhi 110 017 India

Printed in the United States of America

Library of Congress Cataloging-in-Publication Data

Bell, Michael, 1957-
An invitation to environmental sociology / Michael Mayerfeld Bell.— 2nd ed..
   p. cm.
Includes bibliographical references and index.
ISBN 0-7619-8775-4 (pbk.)
  1. Environmentalism. 2. Environmental responsibility. 3. Environmental ethics. I. Title.
GE195.B46 2004
363.7—dc222   2004004543

04   05   06   07   08   10 9 8 7 6 5 4 3 2

Acquiring Editor:	Jerry Westby
Editorial Assistant:	Vonessa Vondera
Production Editor:	Sanford Robinson
Copy Editor:	Pam Suwinsky
Typesetter:	C&M Digitals (P) Ltd.
Indexer:	Molly Hall
Cover Designer:	Janet Foulger

Brief Table of Contents

For my father
Moses David Bell (1923–1996)
Writer, scholar, teacher
Washtub-bass player extraordinaire
A lover of people and the land
He fished without hooks

Detailed Table of Contents

Preface

Outside, the first real snows of winter are falling. It is a week before the solstice, and the days will soon be at their shortest and darkest. Summer is long past, and now the harvest is too. The world has gone to bed, and the blizzard is providing the blanket. It is the season of endings, and here I am, writing the very last part of this book—its beginning.

The preface to a book is generally the last part an author writes, as I noted in the preface to the first edition. It may seem an odd practice, to end by beginning. But it is appropriate to my main message: that social and environmental interactions are best understood as a kind of ecological dialogue, an unfinalizable conversation in which one interchange leads to another. And it is equally appropriate to this time of year, for what does the winter solstice tell us but that every ending is a beginning, a new moment in the ever-unfolding round of existence.

I take comfort in this thought. The current condition of the environment, and our dialogue with it, is depressing to most students of environmental sociology. When I consider the—at best—ambiguous improvements in that condition and dialogue since the first edition of this book appeared in 1998, I cannot deny that I too sometimes feel disheartened and discouraged. But to participate in a dialogue is to experience potentiality. We *can* change, particularly if we act as a *we*, as a community that invites into the conversation all its social and environmental constituents. Thus the title of my book: *An Invitation to Environmental Sociology*.

In this second edition, I try to widen the invitation. As with the first edition, my goal has been to present environmental sociology with a style that both engages and challenges the reader. I have sought to be accessible without sacrificing attention to troubling issues and difficult concepts. My model once again has been Peter Berger's classic *Invitation to Sociology*. This second edition also follows the organizational scheme of the first, with chapters grouped into three parts: the material, the ideal, and the practical. Each of the original eight chapters of the book return, although they have all been updated, several have been substantially reorganized, and the writing and argument throughout has gotten another polish. Plus the book's invitation has been widened with two new chapters: one on body and health at the end of Part I, on the material side of ecological dialogue; and one on risk and rationality at the end of Part II, on the ideal side. These are both areas of greatly increased interest and research among environmental sociologists. The new chapters also give me an opportunity to better develop some of the book's main themes, especially environmental inequality and environmental justice, and to introduce some concepts that are new to the book.

For readers familiar with the first edition, perhaps it would be helpful to provide a summary of the changes, chapter by chapter. Here goes.

Chapter 1: Environmental Problems and Society. The section on "the environmental predicament" has been extensively updated with current research on the status of sustainability, environmental justice, and the rights and beauty of nature. The biggest changes are to the sections on global warming, water shortages, who gets the bads and goods, and species loss.

Chapter 2: Consumption and Materialism. There are few changes to this chapter. Most significant is a new example of the relationship between positional goods and species loss (the declining population of toothfish, popular for sushi), and updated discussions on disappearing leisure time and the weak relationship between wealth and international comparisons of reported happiness.

Chapter 3: Money and Machines. This chapter has one new section, on the interrelationship of markets and states, which introduces the distinction between "negative regulation" and "positive regulation," helpful for understanding governmental regulation of environmental impacts. I rewrote the section on technology as culture, and now use Y2K as the central example. The sections on livestock confinement and on automobiles have also been updated with the results of recent studies and debates.

Chapter 4: Population and Development. Aside from updating population and development statistics, and adding a brief discussion of biotech rice to the history of efforts to increase rice production and a paragraph on labor time in the discussion of women and development, this chapter is virtually unchanged.

Chapter 5: Body and Health. This entirely new chapter uses several extended case studies—the Bhopal disaster; mercury poisoning among the Ojibway of Grassy Narrows, Ontario; the explosion of the AZF fertilizer factory in Toulouse, France, in 2001; environmental racism in the United States; the health impacts of pesticides around the world—to introduce environmental sociological work on the body and health, stressing issues of inequality. I also introduce a new concept here, the "invironment," the zone of the body's perpetual interaction with the environment. The chapter concludes with a sociological critique of the utilitarian perspective on environmental justice (or what by that point in the chapter I am calling "invironmental justice"). I try here to merge the sociological eye with that of political philosophy, gaining some depth perception through the work of John Rawls, Amartya Sen, and Ronald Dworkin.

Chapter 6: The Ideology of Environmental Domination. I made very few changes to this chapter. Most of those few were oriented toward updating the discussion of ecofeminism, especially recent efforts to move beyond the debate over the essentialism many have worried about in some ecofeminist writings.

Chapter 7: The Ideology of Environmental Concern. This chapter does have some significant changes. Foremost, I removed the section on Beck's theory of the "risk society," and replaced it with a section on "ecological modernization theory," a perspective that in part builds on Beck's work. My discussion of Beck can now be found in Chapter 9, the new chapter on risk. Also, I made substantial changes to the discussion of environment concern, drawing on the latest studies and surveys. Plus there is a new postscript to the chapter, based on a family story my mother (who still shows up in the beginning of the chapter) recently told me.

Chapter 8: The Human Nature of Nature. The only change of note in this chapter is I have added an overview of Latour's "actor network theory."

Chapter 9: The Rationality of Risk. Aside from the discussion of Beck's "risk society" theory, which was formerly in the chapter on environmental concern, the material in this chapter is all new. The basic framework of the chapter is the exploration of the tension between "rational" conceptions of risk and the democracy of knowledge. Along the way, I introduce readers to cultural aspects of risk and the sociology of disasters, focusing on the work of Mary Douglas, Aaron Wildavsky, Kai Erikson, and Charles Perrow. The main examples I discuss are Mad Cow Disease, traffic deaths, the 1972 Buffalo Creek flood, Three Mile Island, and the debate over genetic modification. The chapter concludes with a discussion of the precautionary principle and the importance of open and trusting dialogue, versus claims to authoritativeness, in issues of risk and uncertainty.

Chapter 10: Organizing the Ecological Society. This chapter has changed somewhat. I've added a new concept, what I call "virtual environmentalism"—how social reorganization can make it possible to be environmental without *having* to be environmental. There's a new section that applies the concept of the "dialogue of solidarities" to the management of grazing land in two Moroccan villages. The section on new urbanism has been recast as a section on "smart growth" (but with a bit of new urbanism still in the mix). And my little confessional in the beginning of the chapter has been updated to reflect my current circumstances. Otherwise, it's pretty much the same.

This second edition would not have come about without its own ecology of dialogue and help. Central to that ecology was Michael Carolan, my former graduate student and now colleague. I was under enormous time constraints in completing this revision, because of foolishly promising too much to too many people. (Maybe I've learned my lesson now. Sure hope so.) Mike saved the day by helping write the new chapter on risk and rationality, and providing some important background support for the new chapter on the body and health. I owe him a lot. Thanks, Mike.

There is a second, expanded edition of my family too now, as Eleanor joined us and the world shortly after I completed the work on the first edition of the book. She and her brother Sam were amazingly tolerant of my late nights and blurry eyes this past fall. They cheered me up and cheered me on all the way through. And their mother, my wife Diane Bell Mayerfeld, shouldered way more than her share of family responsibilities so that I could get this done. She did plenty of cheering up and cheering on too. And you should have heard the cheering when I finished. (Maybe you did.)

And my heartfelt thanks go to Jerry Westby, the new editor at Pine Forge Press, and his henchmen with the long raincoats and violin cases. Jerry exhibited far more good humor than I deserved, given how dreadfully late I was with this manuscript.

Ben Penner and Sanford Robinson at Pine Forge also exuded good spirits and gentle growls in just the right proportions. Pam Suwinsky did a marvelous job with the copy editing for this edition, and was inordinately patient with my last-minute ways. Nonetheless, it was a great relief when the big Cadillac that was parked across the street most of the fall finally drove away.

I also need to give yet another round of thanks to Steve Rutter, the founding publisher of Pine Forge Press, who played such a central role in the first edition of this book. Without his sense of what the first edition could be, it never would have been successful enough to warrant this second edition. And I would also like once again to thank Wendy Griswold, one of the founding editors of *Sociology for a New Century,* the series in which this book was born. Wendy recruited me to write the first edition, and gave me much wise editorial guidance as I struggled with the early drafts.

Through both editions, it has been a rare pleasure to work with a publisher like Pine Forge Press that supports both engaging and challenging writing. Many textbooks try to present the "medium" view of an academic field—or worse, a smoothed-over view—in an effort to create a text that goes down easy. Scholarly works, although they may take a strong and novel position, are generally written in language accessible to only a small club of experts. Neither approach inspires broad public interest and participation in the life of the mind. Pine Forge Press seeks to transcend the traditional boundary between the textbook and the scholarly monograph, offering works that are readable and accessible to students but nonetheless original and intellectually challenging syntheses of academic fields.

In other words, while I hope my book is accessible and interesting to students, I also offer it as a work of scholarship. The principal scholarly contribution of the book is the concept of "ecological dialogue," a concept that I believe can serve as one useful framework for understanding environmental sociology. But I do not present ecological dialogue as the last word on the subject of environmental sociology. Rather, I can only hope that the concept stimulates students and other readers to consider closely the issues of environmental sociology and to contribute to reasoned discussion about them. That will be enough. Let the end of this book lead to many more new beginnings. Thus we may find that changing social and environmental interactions is not only possible, but that we've already done it.

MMB
Madison, Wisconsin

CHAPTER 1

Environmental Problems and Society

Without self-understanding we cannot hope for enduring solutions to environmental problems, which are fundamentally human problems.

—Yi-Fu Tuan, 1974

"**P**ass the hominy please."

It was a lovely brunch, with fruit salad, home-made coffee cake, a great pan of scrambled eggs, bread, butter, jam, coffee, tea—and hominy grits. Our friends Dan and Sarah had invited my wife and me and our son over that morning to meet some friends of theirs. The grown-ups sat around the dining room table, and the kids (four in all) careened from their own table in the kitchen to the pile of toys in the living room, and often into each other. Each family had contributed something to the feast before us. It was all good food, but for some reason the hominy grits (which I had never had before) was the most popular.

There was a pleasant mix of personalities, and the adults soon got into one of those excited chats that leads in an irreproducible way from one topic to another, as unfamiliar people seek to get to know each other a bit better. Eventually the inevitable question came my way: "So what do you do?"

"I'm an environmental sociologist."

"Environmental sociology. That's interesting. I've never heard of it. What does sociology have to do with the environment?"

The point of this book is to answer that question—a question I'm often asked—and in a more complete way than the 2-minute answers the dynamics of casual conversation generally allow. But let me begin with the 2-minute answer.

Environmental sociology is the study of community in the largest possible sense. People, other animals, land, water, air—all of these are closely interconnected. Together they form a kind of solidarity, what we have come to call *ecology*. As in any community, there are also conflicts in the midst of the interconnections. Environmental sociology studies this largest of communities with an eye to understanding the origins of, and proposing solutions to, these all-too-real social and biophysical conflicts.

Environmental problems are not only problems of technology and industry, of ecology and

1

biology, of pollution control and pollution prevention. They are also social problems. Environmental problems are problems *for* society—problems that threaten our existing patterns of social organization. Environmental problems are as well problems *of* society—problems that challenge us to change those patterns of organization. It is people who create environmental problems, and it is people who must resolve them. And for that we need, among other disciplines, sociology.

One of sociology's most basic contributions to the study of environmental problems is to point out the pivotal role of social inequality. Not only are the effects of environmental problems distributed unequally across the human community, social inequality is deeply involved in causing those problems. Social inequality is both a product and a producer of pollution, overconsumption, resource depletion, habitat loss, risky technology, and rapid population growth. As well, social inequality influences how we envision what our environmental problems are. And most fundamentally, it can influence how we envision nature itself, for inequality shapes our social experiences, and our social experiences shape all our experience.

Which returns us to the question of community. Social inequality cannot be understood apart from the communities in which it takes place. We need, then, to make the study of community the central task of environmental sociology. Ecology is often described as the study of natural communities. Sociology is often described as the study of human communities. Environmental sociology is the study of both together, the single commons of the Earth we humans share, sometimes grudgingly, with others—other people, other forms of life, and the rocks and water and soil and air that support all life. Environmental sociology is the study of this, the biggest community of all.

A Panorama of the Book

That's the 2-minute answer. But clearly the topic of environmental sociology is vast. Not even a

book the length of this one can cover all of it, at least not in any detail. In the pages to come, we will take a series of field trips into this vast landscape, pausing here and there for a closer look at various significant features of the terrain. Rather than attempting some sort of sociological aerial photography, the book intensively investigates a few topics on the ground and occasionally scales a high overlook for a panoramic view. Such an approach, I believe, will lead to the most balanced understanding of environmental sociology.

For the most part, this first chapter presents several such panoramic views—of environmental sociology, of the environmental predicament, and, in this section, of the book itself. After this introduction, the book falls into three parts:

The Material: How consumption, the economy, technology, development, population, and the health of our bodies shape our environmental situation

The Ideal: How culture, ideology, moral values, risk, knowledge, and social experience influence the way we think about and act toward the environment

The Practical: How we might better resolve environmental conflicts, taking both the material and the ideal into account.

Of course, it is not possible to fully separate these three topics. The deep union of the material, the ideal, and the practical is one of the most important truths that environmental sociology has to offer. The parts of the book represent only a sequence of emphases, not rigid conceptual boundaries. A number of themes running throughout the book help unite the parts:

- The dialogic, or interactive and unfinished, character of causality in environmental sociology
- The interplay of material and ideal factors
- The connections between the local and the global

- The central role of social inequality in environmental conflicts
- The power of the metaphor of community for understanding these social and ecological dynamics
- The important influence of democratic institutions and commitments in our environmental practices

By approaching environmental sociology in this way, I hope to bridge a long-standing dispute among scholars about the relationship between environment and society. *Realists* argue that environmental problems cannot be understood apart from the threats posed by society's current ecologic relations. They believe that social scientists can ill afford to ignore the material truth of environmental problems. *Constructionists* do not necessarily disagree, but they emphasize the influence of social life in how we conceptualize those threats, or the lack of those threats. Constructionists focus on the ideological origins of environmental problems—including their very definition *as* problems (or as non-problems). A realist might say, for example, that the ozone hole is a dangerous consequence of how we currently organize social life. A constructionist might say that in order to recognize the danger—or even the existence—of the ozone hole, we must wear the appropriate conceptual and ideological eyeglasses. Simply put, realists and constructionists disagree over whether the purpose of environmental sociology is to understand environmental problems or environmental "problems."[1]

Fundamentally, the realist-constructionist debate is over *materialist* versus *idealist* explanations of social life. (I mean "materialist" here in the philosophical sense of emphasizing the material conditions of life, not in the sense of material acquisitiveness. And I similarly mean "idealist" in the philosophical sense of emphasizing the role of ideas, not in the sense of what is the best or highest.) The tension between materialist and idealist explanations is itself a centuries-old philosophical dispute, one that perhaps all cultural traditions have grappled with in one way

or another. An ancient fable from India expresses the tension well. A group of blind people encounters an elephant for the first time. One person grabs the elephant's tail and says, "An elephant is like a snake!" Another grabs a leg and says, "An elephant is like a tree!" A third grabs an ear and says, "An elephant is like a big leaf!" To the materialist, the fable shows how misinformed all three blind people are, for a sighted person can plainly see how the "snake," "tree," and "big leaf" connect together into what an elephant really is. To the idealist, the fable says that we all have our ideological blindnesses, and there is no fully sighted person who can see the whole elephant—that we are all blind people wildly grasping at the elusive truth of the world.

The approach to this ancient debate I take is that the material and the ideal dimensions of the environment depend upon and interact with each other. What we believe depends on what we see and feel, and what we see and feel depends on what we believe. It is not a matter of either/or; rather, it is a matter of both-together. Each side helps constitute and reconstitute the other, in a process that will never, we must hope, finish. I term this mutual and unfinalizable interdependence *ecological dialogue*.[2] Throughout the book I consider the interplay, the constant conversation, between the material and ideal dimensions of this never-ending dialogue. (See Figure 1.1.)

Let me also make it clear that this book takes an activist position with regard to environmental problems and the way we think about them. We often look to scholars to provide an unbiased perspective on issues that concern us, and we sometimes regard an active commitment to a political position as cause for suspicion about just how scientific that perspective is. Yet, as many have argued, it is not possible to escape political implications.[3] Everyone has concerns for and interests in the condition of our world and our society. Such concerns and interests are what guide us all every day, and scholars are no different from anyone else in this regard. Nor should they be any different. Such concerns and interests are not necessarily a problem for scholarship.

Figure 1.1   Ecological dialogue.

On the contrary, they are the whole reason *for* scholarship.

This does not mean that anything goes—that any perspective is just as academically valid as any other because all knowledge is only opinion and we are all entitled to our own opinions. Scholarship is opinion, of course, but it is a special kind of opinion. What scholarship means is being critical, careful, honest, open, straightforward, and responsible in one's opinions—in what one claims is valid knowledge. One needs to reason critically and carefully, to be honest about the reasons one suggests to others, to be open to the reasons others suggest, to be straightforward about one's political reasons, and to be responsible in the kinds of reasons one promotes. Being honest, open, and straightforward with each other about our careful, critical reasons is the only academically responsible thing to do.[4]

Therefore, it is best for me to be straightforward about why I think environmental sociology is an important topic of study: I believe there are serious environmental problems that need concerted attention, and soon. And I believe environmental issues are closely intertwined with a host of social issues, most of them at least in part manifestations of social inequality and the challenges inequality poses for community. Addressing these intertwinings, manifestations, and challenges is in everyone's interests. We will all benefit, I believe, by reconsidering the present state of ecological dialogue.

My perspective, particularly the focus on social inequality, coincides more closely with the current politics of the left than the right. Yet issues of the environment cut across traditional political boundaries, as Chapter 8 discusses. The evidence and arguments that I offer in this book should be of interest to anyone committed to careful, critical reasoning. In any event, we should not let political differences stop us from engaging in dialogue about ecological dialogue.

Nevertheless, you, the reader, should be aware that I indeed have a moral and political perspective and that it unavoidably informs what I have written here. Keep that in mind as you carefully and critically evaluate what is in this book. But it is also your scholarly responsibility to be open to the reasoning I present and to have honest reasons for disagreeing.

The Environmental Predicament

Let us now turn to some of the reasons that lead many people to believe there is cause for considerable concern about the current condition of ecological dialogue: the challenges to *sustainability, environmental justice,* and the *rights and beauty of nature.* These, the three central environmental issues, will already be well known to some readers. Still, it is appropriate to pause and review them here, as these considerations underlie the rest of the book.

Sustainability

How long can we keep doing what we're doing? This is the essential question of sustainability. The length of the list of threats to environmental sustainability is, at the very least, unnerving. True, much is unknown, and some have exaggerated the dangers we face. Consequently, there is considerable controversy about the long-term consequences of humanity's continuing transformation of the Earth, as Chapter 9 discusses in some detail. But much relevant evidence has been gathered, and some have underestimated the dangers involved. It is therefore prudent that we all pay close attention to the potential challenges to sustainability.

Global Warming. Perhaps the greatest uncertainty (and controversy) surrounds an issue that poses one of the greatest potential environmental threats: global warming. There is considerable evidence that the world is heating up. When averages are calculated for the entire globe, the

10 warmest years on record (through 2003) have all occurred since 1990.[5] And the trend is upward: The 1970s were hotter than the 1960s, the 1980s were hotter than the 1970s, the 1990s were still hotter, and the 2000s are looking to be hotter yet. (See Figure 1.2.) At this writing, the hottest five years on record are, in descending order, 1998, 2002, 2003, 2001, and 1997.[6] In every year since 1977, the annual average world temperature has been at least 14 degrees Celsius (57 degrees Fahrenheit), a level hardly ever reached in the past 200 years.[7]

These weather records show that there was a grain of truth to an earlier generation's stories about having to walk to school through 3 feet of chilling snow, barefoot and uphill both ways. Eighteenth- and nineteenth-century images of the whole town out for a skating party or of Hans Brinker and his silver skates on the frozen canals of the Netherlands are more than merely romantic. It really was colder back then. Winters were longer, blizzards were stronger, and glaciers used to come down farther out of the mountains. 1963 was the last year Dutch canals froze enough that the "Tour of Eleven Towns," once an annual event with thousands of participants, could be skated—until it was moved to the northern coast of Finland in 1977.[8] There are reports that Long Island Sound, the body of salt water between Long Island and the Connecticut coast, used to freeze over some winters and people would drive 15 miles across the ice with a team and wagon. That hasn't happened in 150 years.[9]

It's not warming up everywhere. Different places are experiencing different changes, which is why the issue is often called "global climate change" rather than "global warming." But overall, the heat is on, globally. If this warming trend continues over the next 100 years, say most climatologists and oceanographers, we will see some major environmental changes. Climatic zones will shift, rainfall patterns will change, and weather conditions will become more variable. In addition, average sea level will rise 1–2 feet—and possibly higher—as glaciers and the ice caps melt and as ocean water heats up and expands.[10]

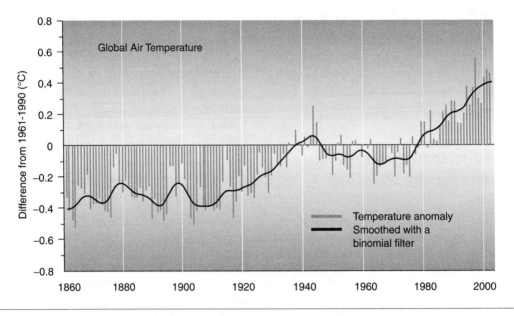

Figure 1.2   A warming world: Average global air temperature, 1866–2002.

(Ocean water will not heat up and expand by much, but the incredible volume of water in the oceans means that even a slight expansion leads to a considerable rise in sea level.)

The predicted consequences would be dramatic, to say the least. Some forests may die off because of newly unfavorable growing conditions. Some urban areas will experience increased drinking water shortages and heat waves. Warmer temperatures and changes in rainfall patterns could increase the incidence of disease, as the new conditions would likely be more hospitable to mosquitoes, ticks, rodents, bacteria, and viruses. The incidence of damaging storms is also likely to increase. Extensive regions of low-lying coastal land (where much of the world's human population lives) would be in grave danger of flooding during storm surges—or even under water. It is not inconceivable that whole countries, such as the low-lying Pacific Island nations of Tuvalu and Kiribati, could in time be washed away. In view of the threat, the New Zealand government has already made plans for accepting immigrants displaced from Tuvalu.[11]

The consequences for agriculture would be complex. Some prime agricultural areas will likely be stricken with drier conditions. For example, farmers in Iowa, the leading corn-producing region in the United States, might have to switch over to wheat and drought-tolerant corn varieties, which would mean overall declines in food production per acre.[12] On the other hand, some regions will likely receive more rain. Yet many of these regions do not have the same quality of soil as, say, Iowa. To add to the complexity, carbon dioxide (the gas implicated as the principal cause of global warming, as I discuss in a moment) can stimulate growth in some crop plants; one study has found a 17 percent yield boost in soybeans.[13] However, this stimulation may not result in actual increased crop yields because of other limiting factors, such as low rainfall, poor soil conditions, and the existence of other pollutants in the air.[14]

No one knows exactly what the overall effects would be. Nevertheless, it's scary stuff. Indeed, the predictions seem to be coming true already. For instance, meteorologists worry that we are seeing an increase in heat waves and resulting fatalities: The spell of four days that peaked around 100 degrees Fahrenheit between July 12 and 15, 1995, blamed for 739 deaths in Chicago.[15]

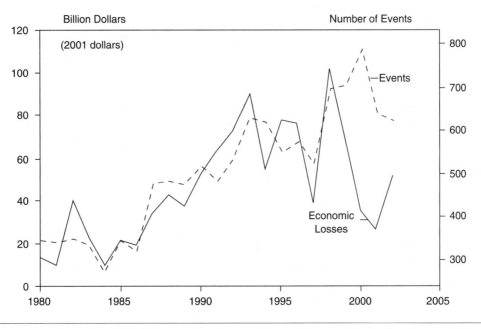

Figure 1.3   The price of global warming: Economic losses from weather-related natural disasters worldwide, 1980–2002.

The 2002 heat wave from April to May in India, which killed 1,000 people.[16] The even more horrific 2003 heat wave in Europe estimated to have killed an astounding 14,802 people in France, plus many dozens in other European countries.[17]

The occurrence of devastating storms and hurricanes is also way up—the global rate now is four times what it was in the 1960s—and the insurance industry is quite worried about the upsurge in claims that has resulted.[18] During the 1990s, worldwide economic losses from catastrophic weather events averaged $71 billion each year, three times the 1980s rate, fives times the 1970s rate, and eight times the 1960s rate.[19] In 1998, the worst year yet, worldwide losses topped $100 billion.[20] Most worrisome of all, weather-related deaths are on the rise, despite better forecasting.[21] (See Figure 1.3.)

Meteorologists are becoming increasingly alarmed about the successive break-offs of ever-larger chunks of Antarctica's ice shelves, such as the Rhode Island-sized patch of the Larsen B Ice Shelf that disintegrated during February 2002.[22] At the North Pole, there isn't as much ice to begin with, but we're showing worrisome signs of

losing what there is. By 1997, the winter extent of the Arctic ice cap had declined 6 percent since 1978, and its thickness in summer had dropped 42 percent since the 1950s, from 10.2 feet to 5.9 feet, and possibly more now.[23] There are now commonly sizable stretches of open water in the Arctic ice cap during the summer, including a 10-mile-by-3-mile-wide stretch quite close to the North Pole itself in 2001, although scientists say this summer open water may have been going on for some time.[24] But the northern ice cap is clearly retreating and thinning. Some Norwegian scientists predict that in 50 years we may have no Arctic ice cap at all at the height of Northern Hemisphere summer.[25]

As well, warmer world weather has been implicated in the resurgence of cholera in Latin America in 1991 and pneumonic plague in India in 1994, and in the outbreak of a hantavirus epidemic in the U.S. Southwest in 1994. Scientists are wondering if global warming is a factor in about 10 other diseases that resurged or reemerged in the 1990s.[26] Increased allergy complaints may be due to global warming, one study suggests.[27]

On a possibly more positive note, regions north of 45 degrees north latitude turned greener between 1981 and 1991. These areas are greening up about a week earlier in spring, staying green a few days longer in the fall, and experiencing about a 10 percent increase in plant growth, perhaps helping crops by lengthening the growing season.[28] But the existence of this effect is yet more evidence that the world is indeed warming.

Not all climatologists agree that we are seeing the first stages of human-induced global warming, though almost all do.[29] George W. Bush's administration was famously (some say infamously) doubtful about its reality at first, and created worldwide controversy when it decided to pull the United States from the Kyoto Protocol for reducing global warming; 178 other nations nevertheless signed on in July 2001. But in June 2002, the Bush Administration released a report that called global warming due to human activities "very likely." The report also suggested that "some of the goods and services lost through the disappearance or fragmentation of natural ecosystems are likely to be costly or impossible to replace."[30]

But even among critics, there hasn't been much doubt for a while that the world is heating up.[31] The questions most dissenters have asked are *Why?*, *Will it continue?*, and *Does it matter?* Perhaps such variations in world climate are normal processes of nature. More sun spots. Changes in the Earth's orbit. Changes in the amount of reflective particles in the atmosphere, maybe because of more (or less) volcanism. Perhaps. Indeed, these processes undoubtedly are important influences on climate trends. But there is now nearly global agreement with the United Nations Intergovernmental Panel on Climate Change, which wrote in 1996 that "the balance of evidence suggests a discernable human influence on global climate."[32] In 2002, that same panel concluded that "there is new and stronger evidence that most of the warming observed over the last 50 years is attributable to human activities."[33]

The biggest culprit: the release of extra carbon dioxide into the atmosphere. Like a greenhouse,

extra carbon dioxide traps more heat that would otherwise radiate away—about 1.4 watts of energy per square meter over the past 150 years.[34] Here's how it works: The energy we get from the sun travels here in the form of light, not heat. When sunlight reaches the Earth's surface, some of that energy is absorbed and converted into heat. This heat then radiates back out. Our atmosphere lets much of this radiant heat energy pass into outer space, but, like the glass on a greenhouse, blocks the passage of some of it. No problem here. The greenhouse-like effect of the atmosphere keeps the world in its usual temperature range of 0 to 100 degrees Fahrenheit. If our atmosphere didn't trap some heat, the Earth would be as cold as the moon. But heat does not pass through carbon dioxide as easily as it passes through some of the other constituents of the atmosphere. Thus, extra carbon dioxide increases the amount of heat trapped by the atmospheric greenhouse, as if someone had closed off the vents at the apex of the greenhouse roof.

Carbon dioxide is not the only "greenhouse gas," however, nor is it pound for pound the worst. Methane adds another climate "forcing," as climatologists say, of about 0.7 watts per square meter over the past 150 years. Chlorofluorocarbons (CFCs) contribute a forcing of 0.35 watts per square meter, even though a far smaller amount of CFCs than carbon dioxide have been released into the atmosphere. There are other human-caused forcings, too. Nitrous oxide adds a 0.15 watt forcing, and ozone in the lower atmosphere adds 0.5 watts.

Then there's what climatologists call "black carbon"—more prosaically known as soot. Black carbon is not exactly a gas. But it packs a 0.8 watt climate forcing, number two after carbon dioxide. It absorbs the sun's incoming rays, rather than blocking radiation on the way back out, and it makes snow dirtier, so it reflects less of the sun's energy back into space. The dirtier snow also melts faster because of soot's absorption of light energy, again lessening the ability of snow to reflect away the sun's rays. In fact, one recent study concludes that black carbon is the number

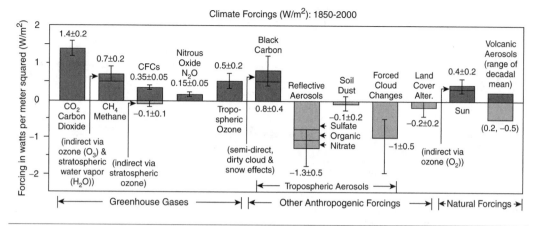

Figure 1.4   The contributions of various "climate forcings" to global climate change.

one culprit in global warming, even ahead of carbon dioxide, because the concentration of its effects in the snowy high latitudes lends more "efficacy" to its forcing.[35] All told, then, these other forcings add up to two times as much as carbon dioxide—and perhaps three times as much, when we take into account the climatic efficacy of black carbon.[36] (See Figure 1.4.)

And they've all been on the rise. For example, carbon dioxide is up to 368 parts per million in the atmosphere from 270 in the mid-eighteenth century. Methane now registers 1,750 parts per billion, up from about 700.[37] Why are they on the rise? The jump in these gases closely correlates with the acceleration of the Industrial Revolution around 1850, when we started burning fossil fuels and clearing forests at a huge rate. (See Figure 1.5.) Fossil fuels and trees are great banks of carbon, and burning them is a process of oxidization that releases energy. The energy moves the machines of an industrialized world, and the oxidized carbon—that's carbon dioxide—joins the atmosphere. Large amounts of nitrous oxide, smog, and black carbon particulates go with it. By now, we have pumped many an oil and gas field dry, mined out many a coal seam, and dug out many a peat bog, all to stoke the fires of industrial technology. And we have cleared much of the world's forest land, usually by burning, to grow crops for a rapidly expanding population.

Then add in CFCs from refrigerants, aerosol cans, and certain industrial processes, and methane from a variety of sources including the decomposition of our vast garbage mounds and the digestive tracks of our livestock.

Plus there is evidence that the changes in the landscape wrought by both agriculture and urbanization are having a big impact on the global climate. Ever wonder why the downtowns of cities seem so hot at night, even after the sun has gone down? The lack of trees and the abundance of blacktop creates what climatologists call the "urban heat island" effect. As well, agriculture has changed the land surface such that more of the sun's energy is absorbed. According to one preliminary study, half of global warming might be due to land use changes alone.[38]

The good news is that, as Figure 1.5 shows, the rate of growth in greenhouse gas climate forcings has been declining since 1990—in part because of international environmental cooperation, but also because of the collapse of the economies of the former Eastern bloc countries, reducing their carbon dioxide emissions. Still, this graph is of the *rate of growth* in forcings, not the *amount* of forcings. We continue to force the climate, and push our luck, more and more every year.

You could think of these various climate forcings as acting like extra blankets on a warm night, gradually stifling the planet. I say "on a

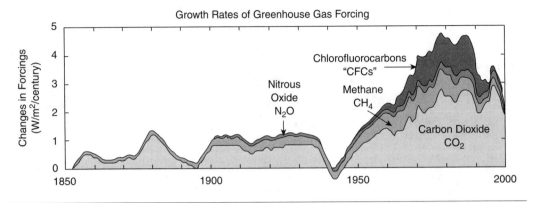

Figure 1.5   Greenhouse gases on the rise: Increases in the rate of growth in atmospheric additions of greenhouse gases.

warm night" because solar radiation is also on the rise (but at a smaller rate than early critics of global warming claimed), adding in a 0.4 watt per square meter forcing. All told, the roughly 1,000 scientists from 120 countries that comprise the Intergovernmental Panel on Climate Change estimate that average temperatures will rise 1.4 to 5.8 degrees Celsius by the year 2100. This is an enormous average increase when you consider that an average drop of 6 degrees Celsius caused the ice ages, covering much of the northern latitudes with a mile-thick sheet of ice.[39] Climate is a touchy thing. A few degrees average change one way or the other can make quite a difference. In this case, we could be on the verge of many centuries of generally lousy sleeping weather—and circumstances much more ominous than that.

At the very least, the connection between global warming and the various climate forcings is something to think about on a hot summer evening as you ponder whether you should crank the air conditioner up another notch, causing your local utility to burn just that much more carbon-based fuel, and to release that much more smog and soot to generate the necessary electricity.[40] You could be making matters worse.

The Two Ozone Problems. There are several other threats to our atmosphere. While perhaps not quite as drastic in their potential consequences as global warming, they are plenty drastic enough

for considerable concern. Two of these threats involve ozone, although in quite different ways.

Ozone forms when groups of three oxygen atoms bond together into single molecules, which chemists signify as O_3. Most atmospheric oxygen is in the form of two bonded oxygen atoms, or O_2, but a vital layer of O_3 in the upper atmosphere helps protect life on the Earth's surface from the effects of the sun's ultraviolet radiation. Ultraviolet light can cause skin cancer, promote cataracts, damage immune systems, and disrupt ecosystems. Were there no ozone layer in the upper atmosphere, life on Earth would have evolved in quite different ways—if indeed it had begun at all. In any event, current life forms are not equipped to tolerate much more ultraviolet radiation than the surface of the Earth currently receives. We badly need the upper atmosphere ozone layer.

In 1974, two chemists, Mario Molina and Sherwood Rowland, proposed that chlorofluorocarbons—which, as we have seen, are also a potent global warming forcer—could be reacting with the ozone layer and breaking it down. Molina and Rowland predicted that CFCs could ultimately make their way into the upper atmosphere and attack the integrity of the ozone layer. In 1985, scientists poring over satellite imagery of the atmosphere over Antarctica discovered (almost accidentally) that the ozone layer over the South Pole had, in fact, grown dangerously depleted.

Many studies later, we now know that this "ozone hole," as it has come to be called, is growing in overall size. We also know that it changes in size with the seasons, has a much smaller mate over the North Pole, and stretches to some degree everywhere on the planet except the tropics. In fact, it's really not a hole. It is more accurate to say that, outside the tropics, the ozone layer is *depleted,* particularly over the South Pole. At times, the layer depletes to as low as 25 percent of the levels observed in the 1970s.[41] Most worrisome is that the area of high depletion might spread to heavily populated areas. In 2000, as of this writing the year of the biggest ozone depletion event, the high depletion area passed over the tip of South America for nine days. It nearly got there again in 2003, as of this writing the year with the second worst ozone "hole." Australians and New Zealanders have yet to experience this, but they're plenty worried. Levels of depletion there are already worse than in other populated regions, skin cancer rates are the highest in the world, and classes in "sun health" have become an essential feature of the school curriculum.[42] And in Punta Arena, Chile, the world's most southerly city, skin cancer rates shot up 66 percent between 1994 and 2001.[43]

Just as there is no "proof" that increased atmospheric carbon dioxide causes global warming, there is also no proof that CFCs are causing the depletion of the ozone layer. But the drama of Rowland's and Molina's prediction (although even they had underestimated the degree of depletion), the seriousness of the likely consequences, and measurements that consistently show ultraviolet radiation on the increase have galvanized the world into unusually cooperative action.[44] In 1987, the major industrial countries signed the first of a series of agreements, known as the Montreal Protocol, to reduce the production of CFCs. As a result of these agreements, CFC production for use in these countries ended on December 31, 1995, and will end throughout the world after 2010. By 1996, annual CFC production had already fallen to about 150,000 tons—down from more than 1,000,000 tons in

late 1980s—although it has declined only slightly since then.[45] (See Figure 1.5.)

It will be many decades until the depletion is repaired, however. The ozone-damaging chlorine that CFCs contain remains resident in the atmosphere for some time, and the HCFCs (hydrochlorofluorocarbons) industrial countries first turned to as a substitute also damage the ozone layer to some extent. Plus, like CFCs, HCFCs are a potent greenhouse gas. Chlorine-free "greenfreeze" refrigerants do not damage the upper atmosphere ozone layer and don't contribute to global warming. Greenfreeze technology now dominates the refrigerator market in Europe and is taking hold in South America, Japan, China, and elsewhere. But greenfreeze is just now reaching the North American market, and at this writing is not yet available in its refrigerators. Meanwhile, an extensive black market in CFCs has arisen in North America.[46] Thus, the current expert view is that ozone depletion will be with us until the middle of the century at least.[47]

But the reduction of CFC production is nevertheless an astounding success story—not least for Rowland and Molina, who received the 1995 Nobel Prize in chemistry for their work, along with Paul Crutzen for his important earlier studies of the ozone layer. Given the unusual level of international cooperation that led to the Montreal Protocol, it is particularly appropriate that this Nobel Prize went to a Mexican (Molina), an American (Rowland), and a Dutch scientist (Crutzen).

Much less progress, however, has been made on resolving the other ozone problem: ozone at ground level. Hardly a city in the world is free of a frequent brown haze above which only the tallest buildings rise. (See Figure 1.6.) Ozone is the principal component of this brown smog that has become an unpleasantly familiar feature of modern urban life.

Ground-level ozone forms when sunlight glares down on a city's dirty air. As a result of fossil fuel combustion, cars and factories discharge large volumes of a whole array of nitrogen oxide compounds. NO_X (pronounced "knocks") is the

Figure 1.6   Late afternoon air pollution settles in the hills behind New Haven, Connecticut. The air pollution from major cities often seeps out into the surrounding countryside.

usual term for this varied nitrous mixture. In sunlight, NO_X reacts with volatile organic compounds (or VOCs) to produce ozone. (VOCs are also produced during fossil fuel combustion, as well as off-gassing from drying paint and from various industrial processes.) If the day is warm and still, this ozone will hug the ground. Because it needs sunlight to form, scientists often call the resulting haze "photochemical smog."

Although we need ozone up high to protect us from the sun, down low in the inhabited part of the atmosphere ozone burns the lung tissue of animals and the leaf tissue of plants. This can kill. It is hard to come up with precise figures, but current estimates are that photochemical smog and other forms of outdoor air pollution cause 50,000 to 188,000 premature deaths in the United States every year; worldwide, the figures are probably four times as much.[48] Smog alerts have become an everyday feature of big city life in all industrial countries. Walking and bicycling are increasingly unhealthful and unpleasant— driving people even more into their cars and causing even more smog. Mexico City is the

worst; unhealthy levels of ozone, as defined by the World Health Organization, occur there more than 300 days each year.[49] When it drifts out of the city into the countryside, smog also reduces crop production and damages forests. An ongoing study in Illinois has found that soybeans suffer a 20 percent yield loss due to ozone, and a 1994 study found that worldwide it is responsible for yield reductions on the order of a few percentage points—not an insignificant amount in a hungry world.[50]

To put the matter simply, there's too much ozone down low, not enough up high, and no way to pump ozone from down here to up there.

Particulates and Acid Rain. Big cities and their surrounding suburbs also face the hazard of fine particulates in the air. These particles are microscopic—the definition of "fine particulates" is particles 2.5 microns (one-fortieth the diameter of a human hair) or smaller in size—and they penetrate deeply into lung tissue. In contrast to the brownish color of photochemical smog, fine particulates envelop cities with a whitish smog.

About half of these particulates are basically dust, mainly released because of poor fuel combustion in cars, trucks, power plants, wood stoves, and outdoor burning, or kicked up by traffic, construction, and wind erosion from farms. Most of the rest are tiny pieces and droplets of sulfates, nitrates, and VOCs formed in the atmosphere following the burning of fossil fuels, such as the coal used for electric generation—what are called "secondary" particulates.[51] Ammonium and ammonium compounds also contribute significantly to secondary fine particulate pollution, mainly due to emissions from livestock and fertilizers.

According to a 1996 study by the Natural Resources Defense Council, some 64,000 Americans a year suffer premature death because of fine particulates; a 1991 study by the U.S. Environmental Protection Agency found a similar result.[52] Another study found that in American cities with the most fine particulates, residents are 15 to 17 percent more likely to die prematurely.[53] Fine particulates smaller than 10 microns in diameter are the most dangerous ones.

And then there's acid rain. This is an issue that has largely dropped from sight, after a flurry of concern in the 1970s and early 1980s over sharp declines in the populations of some fish and frogs and extensive signs of stress and die-back in many forests. But acid rain is still falling from the sky, despite substantial efforts to reduce acidifying emissions of sulfur dioxide and NO_X (which also have other dangerous impacts, as we have seen). These pollutants combine with water in the atmosphere to acidify rain, resulting in direct damage to plant tissues, as well the leaching of nutrients from soil and the acidification of lake waters, which in turn affect most wildlife—particularly in areas with normally acidic conditions, where ecosystems have less capacity to buffer the effects of acid fallout. When things get bad enough, lakes die and trees refuse to grow, like the miles of blasted heath that surround the old nickel smelters in Sudbury, Ontario. The situation is especially severe in northern Europe, where more than 90 percent of natural ecosystems have been damaged by acid rain, and where

a year 2000 survey by the European Union found that 22 percent of all trees in Europe have lost 25 percent or more of their leaves.[54] Conditions are also quite worrisome in much of Canada and in the forests of the northeastern United States.

In fact, the situation seems to be getting worse. Between 1992 and 1999, the condition of trees in Europe did improve in 15 percent of the test sites, but deteriorated in a further 30 percent.[55] Similarly in the United States, a 2000 review of the scientific literature by the federal government's General Accounting Office found that the condition of lakes in New England and the Adirondack Mountains of New York was either stable or getting worse, but none seemed to be improving.[56] Some 43 percent of Adirondack lakes are expected to be acidic by 2040—up from the 19 percent observed to be acidic in 1984.[57] In Taiwan, the Central Weather Bureau has registered increasingly severe acid rain events in recent years.[58] There does, however, seem to be some slight improvement in the condition of Canadian lakes and forests—but only slight.[59]

Why after so many years of effort does acid rain still threaten? Technological improvements, international treaties, and domestic legislation have all contributed to a sharp decline in sulfur emissions in most countries. But we have made little overall progress in reducing nitrogen emissions. Industry's nitrogen emissions have been reduced, but these advances have been overwhelmed by increased emissions from automobiles and trucks as the world comes to rely ever more on these highly polluting forms of transportation.[60] Plus there is evidence that the ability of sensitive ecosystems to handle acid rain has been damaged such that slight improvement in the acidity of rain often does not result in any improvement in the condition of lakes and forests.[61]

Acid rain is still a big problem.

Threats to Land and Water. There's a well-known saying about land: They aren't making any more of it. The same is true of water. And in a way, there is less of both each year as the expansion of industry, agriculture, and development erodes and pollutes what we have, reducing the world's capacity to sustain life.

Consider soil erosion in the United States. Soil erodes from American cropland 16 times faster than it can form anew through ecological processes.[62] Despite decades of work in reducing soil erosion, largely in response to the lessons of the Dust Bowl, it still takes a bushel of soil erosion to grow a bushel of corn.[63] The Conservation Reserve Program, implemented by the U.S. Congress in 1985 and reauthorized in 1996, resulted in significant improvements by offering farmers 10-year contracts to take the most erodable land out of production. Many farmers have also switched to much less erosive cropping practices. Consequently, soil lost to water erosion dropped from 1,700 million tons each year to 1,150 million tons, and soil lost to wind erosion dropped from 12 tons per hectare to 11 tons.[64] But those numbers are still way too high, most observers in and out of agriculture agree.

Elsewhere, the situation is equally grim. Soil erosion exceeds replacement rates on a third of the world's agricultural land.[65] Worldwide, almost a quarter—23 percent—of the world's cropland, pasture lands, forests, and woodlands have been become degraded.[66] True, fertilizers can make up for some of the production losses that come from eroded soils, at least in the short term, but only at increased cost to farmers and with increased energy use from the production of fertilizer and the application of it to fields—and increased water pollution as the fertilizer washes off into streams, rivers, and groundwater.

Soil erosion is only one of many serious threats to farmland. Much of the twentieth century's gains in crop production was due to irrigation. But irrigation can also salinize soils. Because most irrigation occurs in parched regions, the abundant sunlight of dry climates evaporates much of the water away, leaving salts behind. In China, nearly half of the cropland is irrigated, and 15 percent of the irrigated land is affected by salinization. In the United States, only about 10 percent of cropland is irrigated, but almost a quarter of it has experienced salinization. In Egypt, virtually 100 percent of cropland is irrigated, and almost a third of it is affected by salinization.[67]

Irrigation can also waterlog poorly drained soils. Clearing of land is doing the same thing in Australia. Once the land is cleared of its native woodland and bush, rates of transpiration—the pumping of water through the leaves of plants, enabling plants to "breathe"—slow down. Water tables in the dry wheat belt of western Australia are rising by up to 1 meter a year, waterlogging these poorly drained soils. This in turn can lead to salinization as waterlogged soils bake in the sun. One estimate suggests that 33 million hectares of land have been degraded by salinization in Australia, resulting in an annual loss of $200 million (in Australian dollars) worth of farm production.[68] Thus over-irrigation can turn soils both swampy and salty at the same time.

Irrigation of cropland, combined with the growing thirst of cities, is leading to an even more fundamental problem: a lack of water. The Global Water Policy Project categorizes 36 nations around the world as "water-stressed"—that is, they do not have sufficient water resources to provide for their population's agricultural, industrial, and residential needs.[69] How do they survive? Mainly by importing food, a strategy that leaves them dependent on world markets. Even in countries not classified as water-stressed, the situation is increasingly dire. Take the United States and Mexico. By the time it reaches the ocean in the Gulf of California, the Colorado is probably the world's most famous non-river, for not a running drop remains after the farms and cities of the United States and Mexico have drunk their fill. Further development in the regions dependent on the Colorado River will require water from other sources—and it is not obvious where those generally dry territories can easily find other sources—or greatly improved efficiency in current water use.

In the Murray-Darling Basin of Australia, the country's richest agricultural region, the story is much the same. Now only a fifth of the water that enters the basin's rivers is still there by the time the Murray reaches the sea, and the comparative trickle of water that remains is salty and prone to bacterial blooms and fish kills.[70] Perhaps the most dramatic example of overuse of water sources is the Aral Sea in central Asia—once the world's fourth largest lake. Diversion for irrigation has reduced the Aral's surface area by 60 percent and its water volume by nearly 80 percent. Salinity has quadrupled, former fishing ports lie miles inland, thousands of square miles of lake bottom have turned to desert, the original fish are gone (as well as half the bird and mammal species), and the region's economy has collapsed.[71]

Not only surface water, but groundwater too is being rapidly depleted. Over-irrigation can lead to rising water tables and the waterlogging of soils in some regions, but the more general problem is falling water tables from the depletion of groundwater stocks. Around the world, extraction of groundwater for cities and farms is exceeding replenishment rates. Recent production gains in agriculture in India have relied heavily on irrigation from groundwater, but now, because of what one observer has called a "race to the bottom of the aquifer," local villagers are being forced to pump from as deep as 700 feet.[72] Water levels are dropping in some 90 percent of wells in the Indian state of Gujarat.[73] In the dry Great Plains of the United States, farmers pump the famous Ogallala Aquifer far faster than it recharges from precipitation, endangering 15 percent of U.S. corn and wheat production and 25 percent of U.S. cotton production. Nearly a fifth of the Ogallala's water reserves have already been pumped out, and the taps have had to be turned off in many places.[74] In the north China plain, a major grain-producing area, water tables have been dropping at the rate of 3–5 feet each year, due to overdraw for irrigation.[75] In some regions, the lowering of water tables is causing major land subsidence. Downtown Mexico City has dropped nearly 25 feet.[76] Some parts of the Central Valley of California have dropped as much.[77] Venice has dropped just 10 centimeters

because of pumping of the freshwater aquifer beneath it, but for a city at the water line that is an alarming figure.[78]

Overextraction can degrade the quality of the groundwater that remains. The main threat here again is salinization, either through the overapplication of irrigated water applied to the land's surface or through the invasion of seawater into shrinking groundwater aquifers. Ten percent of wells in Israel have already been abandoned because of seawater invasion, and many more will soon have to be given up.[79] In the Indian state of Gujarat, half the hand-pumped wells are now salty.[80] When irrigated water is overapplied, the salinization of the soil can be carried down into the aquifer, as the water percolates down past crop roots. In many areas, only some 30–40 percent of irrigated water actually reaches crops, with the rest being lost through evaporation and percolation, promoting salinization of groundwater. In the lower Indus River Valley of India and Pakistan, the situation is so bad that engineers have installed an expensive system of pumps and surface drains to carry some of the salinized groundwater away to the sea.[81]

Much of the freshwater that remains is badly polluted. "The amount of water made unusable by pollution," Donella Meadows, Denis Meadows, and Jorgen Randers have noted, "is almost as great as the amount actually used by the human economy."[82] In fact, we are very close to using, or making unusable, all the easily accessible freshwater—freshwater that is close to where people live (as opposed to rivers in the Arctic, say) and that can be stored in rivers, lakes, and aquifers (as opposed to the huge amounts of freshwater lost to the sea during seasonal floods, which cannot be easily stored).[83] The remaining margin for growth in freshwater use is disturbingly narrow.

Cleaning up water pollution is one way to increase that vital margin, and industrial water pollution has diminished in many areas, particularly in the wealthier countries. We have also made progress in controlling agricultural water pollution. But we still have a long way to go. Since

1950, farmers across the world have upped their use of commercial fertilizers eightfold and their use of pesticides thirty-two-fold, although trends have been leveling off and even dropping somewhat recently.[84] In the United States, the development of stronger pesticides for a number of years led to substantial drops in the number of pounds of pesticides farmers applied. But since the late 1980s, the U.S. trend has been up once again, with about a 10 percent increase since that time.[85] The resulting runoff continues to threaten the safety of many drinking water supplies and has had severe impacts on the ecological viability of many lakes, rivers, and streams. We all need something to eat and something to drink, but our efforts at maintaining food production through the use of agricultural chemicals are putting us in the untenable position of trading one for the other: food to eat for water to drink.

Or are we trading them both away? In addition to the threats to agricultural production caused by soil erosion, salinization, waterlogging, and water shortages, we are losing considerable amounts of productive farmland to the expansion of roads and suburbs, particularly in the wealthiest nations. Cities need food; thus, the sensible place to build a city is in the midst of productive agricultural land. And that is just what people have done for centuries. But the coming of the automobile has made possible (although not inevitable) the sprawling forms of low-density development so characteristic of the modern city. The result is that cities now gobble up not only food but also the best land for growing it. The problem is worst in the United States, which has both a large proportion of the world's best agricultural land and also some of the world's most land-consuming patterns of development. Some 86 percent of fruit and vegetable production and 63 percent of dairy production comes from urban counties or from counties adjacent to urban counties. Each year, some 1.2 million acres of agricultural land was lost to development between 1992 and 1997, an area the size of Delaware.[86] Given that the United States has almost a billion acres of agricultural land,

this may not seem worth worrying about. But in most cases, it is our best land that we are losing, and in the places where we most need it: close to where people live.

Then factor into the calculation the effects of global warming, photochemical smog, and acid rain on crop production. Add some major issues I have not even mentioned: increased resistance of pests to pesticides, declining response of crops to fertilizer increases, the tremendous energy inputs of modern agriculture, loss of genetic diversity, desertification due to overgrazing, pesticide residues in food. No wonder that increases in agricultural production have been falling behind increases in human population. Total grain production has flattened out since 1996; the peak year was 1998.[87] Plus there are more people to feed. The result is that, after decades of steady increases, world grain production per person per year has declined from the historical high of 346 kilograms in 1984 to 294 kilograms in 2002, the first year below 300 kilograms since 1972.[88]

The land fares ill, and there is less to eat and less to drink.

Environmental Justice

On the morning of January 4, 1993, 300,000 Ogoni rallied together. The protesters waved green twigs as they listened to speeches by Ken Saro-Wiwa, a famous Ogoni writer, and others. With such a huge turnout, the Ogoni—a small African ethnic group, numbering only half a million in all—hoped that finally someone would pay attention to the mess that Shell Oil Company has made of their section of Nigeria. Leaking pipelines. Oil blow-outs that shower on nearby villages. Disrupted field drainage systems. (Much of Ogoniland has to be drained to be farmed.) Fish kills. Gas flares that foul the air. Water so polluted that even wearing clothes washed in it causes rashes. Acid rain from the gas flares so bad that the zinc roofs people in the area favor for their houses corrode away after a year.

Meanwhile, the profits have flowed overseas to Shell and to the notoriously corrupt Nigerian government. The Ogoni have gotten only the pollution.[89]

Such open protest by the relatively powerless is a courageous act. And for the Ogoni, the consequences were swift and severe. During the next two years, Nigerian soldiers oversaw the ransacking of Ogoni villages, the killing of about 2,000 Ogoni people, and the torture and displacement of thousands more.[90] Much of the terror was carried out by people from neighboring regions whom the soldiers forced or otherwise enticed into violence so that the government could portray the repression as ethnic rivalry.[91] The army also sealed the borders of Ogoniland, and no one was let in or out without government permission. Ken Saro-Wiwa and other Ogoni leaders were repeatedly arrested and interrogated. Finally, the government trumped up a murder charge against Saro-Wiwa and eight others and, despite a storm of objection from the rest of the world, executed them on November 10, 1995.[92] The torture and killing of protestors continues, for example with the shooting by police of Friday Nwiido on June 15, 2001, a few weeks after Nwiido had led a peaceful protest against the April 29, 2001, oil blow-out that rained Shell's crude onto the surrounding countryside for nine days.[93]

The Ogoni experience is a vivid example of a common worldwide pattern: Those with the least power get the most pollution.

The Ogoni experience is also an outrage, as virtually the entire world (aside from Nigeria's rulers) agrees.[94] This outrage is a reminder of another of the three central issues of environmentalism: the frequent and tragic challenges to environmental justice. There is a striking unevenness in the distribution of environmental benefits and environmental costs—in the distribution of what might be termed *environmental goods* and *environmental bads*.[95] Global warming, sea level rises, ozone depletion, photochemical smog, fine particulate smog, acid rain, soil erosion, salinization, waterlogging, desertification, loss of genetic diversity, loss of farmland to

development, water shortages, water pollution—these have a potential impact on everyone's lives. But the well-to-do and well-connected are generally in a better position to avoid the worst consequences of environmental problems—and, often, to avoid the consequences entirely.

Who Gets the Bads? Take the hazardous waste crisis, for instance. Wealthy countries are now finding that there is more to disposing of garbage than simply putting it in a can on the curb. One response has been to pay others to take it. We now have a lively international trade, much of it illegal, in waste too hazardous for rich countries to dispose of at home.

There has been considerable protest about this practice. In 1988, Nigeria even went so far as to commandeer an Italian freighter with the intent of loading it up with thousands of barrels of toxics that had arrived from Italy under suspicious circumstances and shipping it back to Europe. After a heated diplomatic dispute, the waste—which in fact turned out to originate in 10 European countries and the United States—was loaded on board the *Karin B.*, a West German ship, and sent back to Italy. But harbor officials in Ravenna, Italy, where the waste was supposed to go, refused the load because of vigorous local opposition to it. The *Karin B.* was later refused entry in Cadiz, Spain, and banned from French and British ports, where it also tried to land. Months later it was finally accepted into Italy.[96]

In 1989, in response to diplomatic crises like these, 105 countries signed the Basel Convention, which is supposed to control international toxic shipments. Yet loopholes are large enough, and enforcement lax enough, that these shipments still go on. Nor do international conventions control domestic companies like COINTERN of Mexico, which dumped 20,000 tons of illegal waste near the Mexican town of Guadalcazar between 1989 and 1993. Nor do international conventions stop foreign companies from merely relocating their most hazardous production practices to poorer countries—like Metalclad,

Inc., of Illinois, which purchased the Guadalcazar site, promising to clean up the dump, but only if the Mexican government would allow Metalclad to reopen the dump afterward.[97] When local people and government officials tried to stop them, Metalclad filed a successful suit in international court, using a provision of the North American Free Trade Agreement. They were even awarded $16.7 million in damages.[98]

Toxic wastes are typically local in their effects, and it is typically the local communities that are least politically empowered—whether because of class, race, ethnicity, nationality, or rural location—that receive the bulk of them.[99] So too for the siting of hazardous industrial facilities. These are realities painfully well known to the people of Bhopal, Minamata, Toulouse, and Love Canal, and the thousands of communities subjected to lesser-known local toxic disasters. Although individually smaller, these disasters are collectively just as significant as the better-known ones, and perhaps more significant.[100]

Toxic wastes have an impact not only where people live but also where they work. Consider the cumulative effects of pesticides and toxic chemicals on those who work with them every day. Many of our industrial practices expose workers—generally those on the production line, as opposed to those in the front office—to environmental hazards. Increasingly, the wealthy countries are exporting these kinds of jobs overseas, where workers have less choice over their conditions of employment, and then importing the goods back home (but still scooping up the profit in between). Exporting hazardous jobs does not lessen the degree of environmental inequality involved, however. Indeed, the inequality often increases because of lax environmental regulation in poorer countries.

But all this seems to take the place far away—until a toxic disaster happens in your own community. The growing placelessness of the marketplace makes it easy to overlook the devastating impact untempered industrialism can have on the daily lives of the farm worker applying alachlor in the field and the factory worker running a noisy machine on a dirty and dangerous assembly line. When we shop, we meet a product's retailers, not the people who made it, and the products themselves tell no tales.

Who Gets the Goods? Environmental justice also concerns patterns of inequality in the distribution of environmental goods. These patterns are usually closely associated with inequality in the distribution of wealth. Thus, those who are concerned about environmental justice often point to the huge inequalities in average income between countries. Here are the numbers, based on gross domestic product (GDP) per capita in 2001 in U.S. dollars.[101]

The average annual income in the world is $5,120. In contrast, the average income in the world's 24 wealthiest countries is $26,510. In the United States, it is $34,280—and the United States is not the world's richest country. That distinction goes to Luxembourg at $39,840 per capita, and $48,560 in per capita buying power when we take into account the lower cost of living there. (The United States ranks as the second richest country in the world in per capita buying power.)

With all that income flowing up top, hardly any is left for those on the bottom. The people of the 49 poorest nations average just $430 per capita per year—hardly more than a dollar a day. The 53 million people of the Democratic Republic of the Congo have the lowest average: just $80 per capita per year. The situation is hardly better for the people of Ethiopia and Burundi: just $100. In Sierra Leone it's $140. True, the cost of living is unusually low in those countries. That $80 annual income in Congo buys about what $630 buys in the United States. But even $630 is not very much. And because Sierra Leone's cost of living is higher than the Democratic Republic of the Congo's, a $140 annual income in Sierra Leone buys only about what $460 buys in the United States, making Sierra Leone the world's poorest nation, according to these figures—still hardly more than a dollar a day.[102] Imagine living on so little.

Moreover, despite the many advances in technology and the change to a more market-oriented world economy, income inequality has dramatically increased in recent decades. In 1960, the fifth of the world's people living in its richest countries commanded 30 times as much of the world's income as the fifth of people living in the poorest countries—a figure that, in most people's view, was bad enough.[103] Roughly 100 years earlier, in 1879, it was 7 to 1.[104] But today, that richest fifth commands *68* times as much of the world's income as the poorest fifth.[105]

These figures are all based on the populations of whole countries. But there are also substantial levels of inequality *within* countries. Typically, the income differential between the richest 20 percent and poorest 20 percent within a country is 6 to 1 or less.[106] In many poor and middle income countries, however, the numbers are far higher. The situation is most extreme in Sierra Leone, where the richest fifth command 57.6 times the income of the poorest fifth. In another half-dozen countries, such as Brazil and South Africa, the ratio is 30 to 1 or higher.[107] In 13 other countries, it is 15 to 1 or higher.

Although there is usually less inequality in wealthy countries, some do exceed the world norm. In Germany, the ratio of richest to poorest 20 percent is 8 to 1. In the United States, it is 9 to 1. Interestingly, the situation in the United States represents a historical reversal. In the 1920s (the first decade for which these figures are available), the United States was one of the most economically egalitarian countries, giving America the image of the land of opportunity. In comparison, most European countries, such as Britain, were more wealth stratified at the time. Today European countries are all less stratified, in most cases much less so—such as the 4 to 1 figures for the Scandinavian countries and the 5 to 1 and 6 to 1 figures for France, Belgium, Switzerland, Spain, and the Netherlands.[108] The lowest figure in the world is for Japan, 3.4 to 1.[109]

Inequality within countries means that the 68 to 1 ratio of income between the fifth of people living in the richest countries and the fifth living in the poorest understates the level of global inequality. If the richest fifth of the world population from all countries, rich and poor, were put together, their income would likely total 150 times that of the poorest fifth of the world's population.[110] (See Figure 1.7.)

Consequently, taking the world's population as a whole, the number of very poor people is staggering. Some 1.2 billion live on less than $1 a day. Some 2.8 billion—nearly half the world—live on less than $2 a day.[111] One could try to put the matter in more positive terms and point out that the percentage of the world's population now living on less than $1 a day is smaller than it was in the 1980s—24 percent versus 28 percent. But the *number* of people living in poverty remains about the same, and the difference between top and bottom has continued to widen, as we have seen.[112] And if we compare today with 1960, the percentage has remained quite similar while the number has roughly doubled.[113]

The wealth of the world's richest people is equally staggering. During the peak of the late 1990s' economic expansion, in 1999, the wealth of the 200 richest people in the world hit about $1 trillion. That's a cool $5 billion each, about double what they had in 1994. Now consider the wealth of the 582 million people living in the world's 43 poorest countries. As their assets are so minimal, we can roughly speaking consider their annual income the same as their wealth. That income for all of them together amounts to $156 billion, less than a sixth of the wealth of the 200 richest.[114] Now let's make a simple (and generous) assumption about the 2.8 billion living on less than $2 a day—that they each make the full $2 a day, giving them a combined annual income (and, again, roughly speaking a combined wealth) of $1.022 trillion. Two hundred people, as wealthy as 2.8 billion. In fact, the assets of the three wealthiest people in the world exceed $146 billion.[115] Three people, wealthier than 582 million.

While only one of them is Bill Gates, the wealth of the average person in the rich countries leads to a substantial global *consumption gap*. The average person in the rich countries consumes

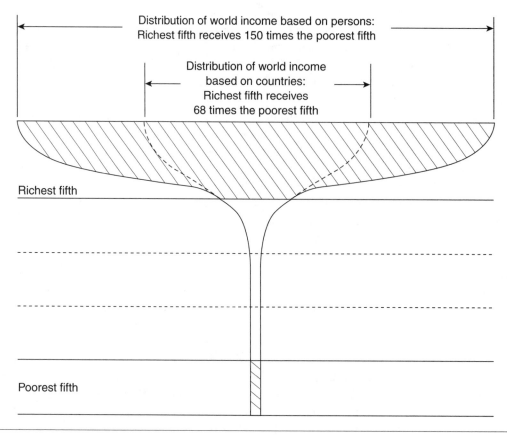

Distribution of world income based on persons:
Richest fifth receives 150 times the poorest fifth

Distribution of world income
based on countries:
Richest fifth receives
68 times the poorest fifth

Richest fifth

Poorest fifth

Figure 1.7   The champagne glass of world wealth distribution. The fifth of world population from the world's richest countries receives about 68 times the income of the fifth of world population from the poorest countries. When calculated on the basis of the richest fifth of persons from all countries versus the poorest fifth from all countries, the ratio of income disparity likely rises to 150 to 1.

three times as much grain, fish, and freshwater; six times as much meat; 10 times as much energy and timber; 13 times as much iron and steel; and 14 times as much paper as the average resident of a developing country. And that average person from a rich country uses 18 times as much in chemicals along the way.[116] These consumption figures are lower than the 68 to 1 income differential because the comparison here is between the roughly 20 percent of the world that lives in industrial countries and the roughly 80 percent who don't—not the richest fifth of countries and the poorest fifth. If the 60 percent in the middle were removed from the calculations, the consumption gap for many of these items would probably reach or exceed the 68 to 1 ratio of wealth. (For some items, however, it would not— even a very wealthy person can eat only so much grain, fish, and meat.)[117]

Along with the consumption gap comes an equally significant *pollution gap*. The wealthy of the world create far more pollution per capita than do the poor. For example, in the rich countries, per capita emissions of carbon dioxide are 12 times higher than in poor countries.[118] Moreover, the rich countries are also more able to arrange their circumstances such that effects of the pollution they cause are not as significantly felt locally, as with the export of toxic wastes.

The consequences of these differentials are serious indeed. Roughly 900 million people in the low- and middle-income countries suffer malnutrition, about 14 percent of the total world population.[119] Thirty-four percent of the children in the developing countries are underweight for their age, a figure that reaches as high as 66 percent in Bangladesh, one of the world's poorest nations. Because of rampant malnourishment, adults face a reduced capacity to work and children grow up smaller, have trouble learning, and experience lifelong damage to their mental capacities.[120]

Many of the world's poor find it difficult to protect themselves from environmental bads. All told, 1 billion people do not have shelter that adequately protects them from such environmental hazards as rain, snow, heat, cold, filth, and rats and other pests. One hundred million have no shelter at all.[121] Moreover, the world's poor are more likely to live on steep slopes and in low-lying areas that are prone to landslides and floods. More than a billion lack access to safe drinking water.[122] Two and a half billion do not have adequate sanitation.[123] The poor are also typically relegated to the least productive farmland, undermining their capacity to provide themselves with sufficient food (as well as income). Compounding the situation are the common associations between poor communities and increased levels of pollution and toxic waste and between poverty and environmentally hazardous working conditions.

It is also possible to have too much of the good things in life. The world over, 1 billion people—and counting—are overweight, more than the number who do not have enough food. Some 300 million people are obese.[124] And the diseases associated with too much food are increasing as well: diabetes (especially type II), hypertension, heart disease, stroke, and many forms of cancer. In the United Kingdom, two-thirds of men and half of women are either overweight or obese. The prevalence of obesity in the United Kingdom

tripled between 1980 and 1998 to 21 percent of women and 17 percent of men.[125] The situation in the United States is even worse, with some 65 percent of all adults overweight or obese in 2000. Obesity in the United States has doubled since 1980 to 31 percent.[126] Other wealthy countries have experienced weight rises as lifestyles have become more sedentary and calorie intake has increased.

But the problem of overweight is not limited to the wealthy nations. Weight problems are increasing dramatically in poorer nations, as people increasingly take up more sedentary lives there, and as food consumption shifts more into the marketplace and away from home production, making healthier foods less readily available for the poor. The problem is particularly pronounced in urban areas. In urban Samoa, 75 percent of adults are obese—not just overweight, but obese. In some cities in China, 20 percent or more are obese.[127] Yet the world's wealthy are generally better able to protect themselves from the consequences of high weight. Medical treatments for diabetes, circulation problems, and cancer are far less accessible for the poor.

Considering these stark facts, it comes as no surprise that people in the wealthy countries live an average of almost 28 years longer than those in the poor countries, despite great advances in the availability of medical care—78.1 years versus 50.4 years.[128] In 14 very poor countries, the average person has no better than a 50 percent chance of reaching age 40.[129] In the least developed countries, 24 percent won't even make it to age 5.[130]

Within-country differences in income have a substantial impact on the quality of life of the poor, even in rich countries. In the United States, some three and half million Americans experience a period of homelessness during the year, about a third of them children, according to a 2000 study.[131] A 2001 survey of 27 cities by the U.S. Council of Mayors found that requests for emergency shelter services were up in 22 of them.[132] Although conditions have substantially improved in the European Union since the mid-1990s, some 390,000 people in Germany are still homeless, plus about 200,000 in Italy and about 165,000 in the United Kingdom, according to a 2002 study.[133] Thirty million Americans—about 11 percent of the U.S. population—live in conditions of "food insecurity," the U.S. Department of Agriculture's term for households that face difficulty meeting basic food needs for all its members. About a third of these households reported experiencing involuntary hunger at some point during the year. Rates of food insecurity are twice as high for black and Hispanic households as they are for white households. And as of 2001, the trend is getting worse, not better.[134] A 2001 study revealed that 7 million Americans receive food assistance from emergency food pantries and other sources in any given week.[135] Almost 60 percent of food assistance agencies in that study reported that the number of people using their services is going up.[136]

Food, shelter, longevity—these are the most basic of benefits we can expect from our environment. And yet people's capabilities to attain them are highly unequal. As Tom Anthanasiou has observed, ours is a "divided planet."[137]

The Rights and Beauty of Nature

"A thing is right when it tends to preserve the integrity, stability, and beauty of the biotic community. It is wrong when it tends otherwise."[138] These are probably the most famous lines ever written by Aldo Leopold, one of the most important figures in the history of the environmental movement. His words direct our attention to a broader sense of our community and, in a way, to a broader sense of equality and inequality. Understood in this way, environmental justice concerns not only the rights of humans but the rights of nonhumans—of animals, plants, and even the land. Leopold also directs our attention to a word that is certainly one of the hardest of all to define but is no less significant for that difficulty: *beauty*. (Indeed, the difficulty of defining beauty may be much of what makes it so significant.)

Threats to the integrity, stability, and beauty of the biotic community are manifold. Take the loss of species. (See Figure 1.8.) For example, of the 9,800 known species of birds, two-thirds are in decline.[139] Some 12 percent are threatened with extinction, and another 8 percent seem likely to become so soon.[140] Many have already gone; the passenger pigeon, the dodo, the ivory-billed woodpecker, and the 11 species of moa are only some of the best known. Since 1800, 103 have gone extinct.[141] With its moa and other species that developed without pressure from mammalian predators, New Zealand has perhaps been the hardest hit; about half the bird species of the North and South Islands have disappeared in the past 800 years.[142]

Estimates of extinction rates for all species vary widely because we still do not have a good count of how many there are, or ever were. Many species are still unknown or survive in such low numbers that they are hard to study. But even the low estimates are staggering. Perhaps the most widely regarded account, based entirely on individual assessments for each species, is the "Red List" of the World Conservation Union, a 140-nation organization. The 2003 Red List currently registers 12,257 species of plants and animals as threatened with extinction. In addition to the 12 percent of bird species, the list includes 24 percent of mammal species, 3 percent of fish, 4 percent of reptiles, and 3 percent of amphibians. But while information is available on all bird and almost all mammal species, only a fraction of the known species of fish, reptiles, and amphibians have been assessed by the World Conservation Union—less than 6 percent. Of those that have been assessed, some 49 percent of fish, 62 percent of reptiles, and 39 percent of amphibians show up on the 2003 Red List. Very few of the world's 298,000 identified plant and lichen species and 1,190,000 identified invertebrate species have been assessed—just 3 percent of the plants and lichens and 0.3 of the invertebrates—so it is very hard to calculate reliable extinction figures for them.[143]

The overall extinction rate is thus in the realm of educated guesswork, given the spotty data we

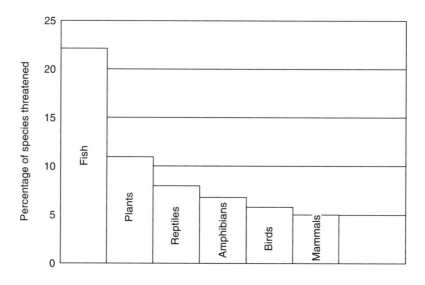

Figure 1.8   The hole in the gene pool: Percentage of known species threatened in the United States.

have. Richard Leakey, the famous paleontologist, is one who has made a try. He suggests that we could lose as many as 50 percent of all species on Earth in the next 100 years, largely because of very high rates of extinction among invertebrates, the group we know the least about. (For example, some 72 percent of the insect species that the IUCN has assessed are threatened.) If Leakey's anywhere near right, that would put the current period of extinction on the same scale as the one that did in most dinosaurs and much of everything else 65 million years ago, and four earlier ones that had a similar effect on the Earth's biota. That's why Leakey and Roger Lewin call the current period the "sixth extinction."[144] Some biologists have placed the current rate of extinction for all species at between 4,000 and 36,000 each year, somewhere between one every 10 minutes and one every 90 minutes.[145] If so, that means it is likely that another species went extinct since you began reading this chapter. When we add in the extinction of subspecies and varieties, the decreasing diversity of planetary life is even more dramatic.

Of course, species have always come and gone, as Charles Darwin famously observed in his theory of natural selection. But the rate of these losses has greatly increased since the beginning of the Industrial Revolution. Some have disappeared because of habitat loss, as forestlands have been cleared, grasslands plowed, and wetlands drained and filled. Some have suffered from pollution. Some have found themselves with no defenses against animals, plants, and diseases that humans have brought, often unintentionally, from other regions of the world. The Earth is a single, gigantic preserve for life, and we have not been honoring its boundaries and protecting its inhabitants.

The loss of species is an instrumental issue of sustainability. The leaking global gene pool means a declining genetic resource base for the development of new crops, drugs, and chemicals. In addition, most ecologists suspect that decreased diversity destabilizes ecosystems, ecosystems that we too need to survive. But the ethical and aesthetic impact of the loss of so many forms of life may be as great, if not greater.

The loss is not only one of forms of life but also forms of landscape. Take deforestation, an issue that has received much attention recently. The world has lost about half of its original

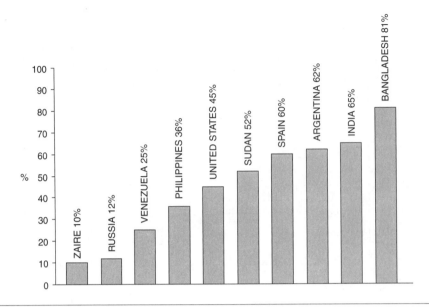

Figure 1.9   The human footprint in 10 countries: Percentage of land area converted from natural ecosystems.

forestland. Substantial degradation and fragmentation afflicts another 30 percent.[146] Some 4.2 percent of the world's forests were lost between 1990 and 2000 alone, 94 percent in the tropics.[147] Indonesia has lost 40 percent of its forests since 1950. Rwanda and Burundi each lost 39 percent between 1990 and 2000 alone.[148] (See Figure 1.9.)

Deforestation presents a challenge for sustainability. The loss of trees promotes global warming as trees are converted into atmospheric carbon dioxide and forest habitat is converted into agricultural land. Yet deforestation also has an aesthetic impact, destroying the beauty of forests and the spiritual value of wooded wilderness. Forests can regrow, of course, but the most recent data finds that is only happening at about 22 percent of the rate of deforestation.[149] Forests can also be replanted, but here again the rate is far below the rate of loss. Some 161 million acres of natural forest were cut down in the 1990s, and 31 million acres were replanted. Half of that replanting was on land where the natural forests were cut down to make way for trees more desired by the timber industry.[150] These replanted forests are poor substitutes for the woods they replace, at least in terms of biodiversity—the ecological

equivalent of exchanging the paintings in the Louvre for a permanent display of engineering blueprints.

There's another loss too—the disappearance of a kind of quiet intimacy with the Earth, the sense of being connected to the land and to each other through land. (See Figure 1.10.) It is a common complaint that modern technology removes us from contact with a greater, wilder, and somehow realer reality. This removal, it should be said, has been the whole point of modern technology, but some have come to wonder whether our lives are emptier because of it. A romantic concern, perhaps. But do we want a world without romance?

And finally, there's the question of our right to make such great transformations in the world. Nothing lasts forever, of course. Over millions of years, even a mountain is worn away by erosion. Wind, rain, ice, and changes in temperature constantly sculpt the land, and the shape of Earth's surface constantly changes as a result. But geologists now recognize humans to be the most significant erosive force on the planet.[151] Agriculture, forest cutting, road building, mining, construction, landscaping, and the weathering

Figure 1.10   The beauty of nature: Sunset on the Connecticut coast.

effects of acid rain—all these have resulted in enormous increases in the amount of sediment that rivers carry into the oceans. We wield the biggest sculptor's chisel now. Perhaps it is our right. If so, then it is also our responsibility.

Although I have not covered the question of the rights and beauty of nature in much detail, let me conclude here. These issues are certainly no less worthy of our consideration than those of sustainability and environmental justice, it seems to me. But I'm exhausted just thinking about the others, and I imagine you are too. Maybe that's the most difficult environmental problem of all. There are so many of them.

The Social Organization of Environmental Problems

These matters seemed quite remote at that lovely brunch as we loaded up our plates with fruit salad, coffee cake, scrambled eggs, bread, butter, and those great hominy grits. Remote but ironic. Here I was amid a group of three families whose incomes, although not unusually high by Western standards, are sufficient to command a brunch that two centuries ago would have been seen as lavish even by royalty. And what was I doing? Once I had finished explaining environmental sociology, I was reaching for seconds.

My point is not that there is something wrong with pigging out every once in a while. Nor is it that consumption is necessarily a bad thing. (To live is to consume.) Rather, I tell this story to highlight how social circumstances can lead to the sidelining of concern and action about environmental consequences.

Everything we do has environmental implications, as responsible citizens recognize today. The adults at the brunch were genuinely interested in my explanation of environmental sociology for just that reason. But the currents of social life quickly washed over the momentary island of recognition and concern that my explanation had created. (One does not dwell long on any topic at a party.) Soon we were all reaching for more of the eggs from chicken-factory hens; the fruit salad with its bananas raised on deforested land and picked by laborers poorly protected from pesticides; the coffee cake made with butter and milk from a dairy herd likely hundreds of energy-consuming miles away; the grits made from corn grown on an Iowa farm at the price of one bushel of soil erosion for one bushel of grain. Meanwhile, the conversation moved on to other matters. And soon we guests would be getting into our cars and driving home, spewing smog and greenhouse gases all along the way.

A completely ordinary brunch. But do you refuse to invite friends over because you cannot easily get environmentally friendly ingredients for the dishes you know how to prepare? Do you refuse a host's food because it was produced in a damaging and unjust manner? And do you refuse an invitation to brunch because the buses don't run very regularly on a Sunday morning, because a 20-minute ride in the bike trailer in below-freezing weather seems too harsh and long for your 5-year-old, and because no one nearby enough to carpool with is coming to the party? Do you refuse, especially when you have your own car sitting in the driveway, as is almost certainly the case in the United States?

Likely not.

What leads to this sidelining of environmental concern and action is the same thing that manufactures environmental problems to begin with: the *social organization of daily life*—how we as a human community institute the many structures and motivations that pattern our days. Caught in the flow of society, we carry on and carry on and carry on, perhaps pausing when we can to get a view of where we're eventually headed, but in the main just trying to keep afloat, to be sociable, and to get to where we want to go on time. Our lives are guided by the possibilities our social situation

presents to us and by our vision of what those possibilities are—that vision itself being guided in particular directions by our social situation. That is to say, it is a matter of the social organization of both our material conditions and the ideas we bring to bear upon them. Yet the environmental implications of those conditions and those ideas are seldom a prominent part of how we socially organize our situation. Instead, that organization typically depends most on a more immediate presence in our lives: Other people.

We need, I believe, to consider the environment as an equally immediate (and more social) presence in our lives. That does not mean we need to be always thinking about the environmental consequences of what we do. As an environmental sociologist, I cannot expect this—especially when I don't always think about environmental consequences myself. People have lots and lots of other concerns. Nor should it be necessary to think constantly about environmental consequences. Rather, what is necessary is to think carefully about how we as a community organize the circumstances in which people make environmentally significant decisions. What is necessary is to create social situations in which people take the environmentally appropriate action, even when, as will often be the case, they are not at that moment consciously considering the environmental consequences of those actions. What is necessary is to reorganize ourselves so what we daily find ourselves doing compromises neither our social nor our environmental life.

The challenge of environmental sociology is to illuminate the issues such a reorganization must consider.

PART I

The Material

CHAPTER 2

Consumption and Materialism

I buy, therefore I am.

—Graffito seen in New Haven,
Connecticut, mid-1980s

Wladziu Valentine Liberace did not lead a modest life. At the time of his death in 1987, the famous Las Vegas entertainer owned more than 30 cars, including a Model A Ford, an English taxi, and two Rolls Royces. One Rolls was covered in mirrored tiles. The second was painted in patriotic red, white, and blue, and Liberace would sometimes start his shows by driving it onto the stage. Liberace made his money playing the piano. He had 18 of these, including ones played by Chopin, Brahms, Schumann, Liszt, and Gershwin—not to mention a vast collection of miniature pianos. Onstage, Liberace favored long capes, dazzling jewelry, and lots of gold lamé. One of his capes reportedly weighed more than 100 pounds, and the Neptune costume that he wore at the 1984 World's Fair in New Orleans weighed 200 pounds. It took 47 trunks to stow all the outfits he took on tour. (Liberace liked changing clothes.) The Liberace Museum of Las Vegas needs three buildings to display it all.[1]

We are not all Liberaces. Nor would we likely be even if we all earned $50,000 a week, as Liberace did at the height of his career. Few of us are so unabashedly materialistic. But it is certainly the case that, aside from the poor, nearly everyone today consumes more than is necessary to survive, and some of us a lot more. Yet we are not satisfied.

Why? What do we want it all for? This is an important sociological question, for it relates to all three of the central issues of environmentalism: sustainability, environmental justice, and the rights and beauty of nature. Can society and the Earth sustain a world of Liberaces? Can some people consume like Liberace without impoverishing others and without damaging nature?

One common answer to the question of why we consume so much more than we need is that people are greedy. In the words of Mahatma Gandhi, "The world has enough for everybody's need, but not enough for everybody's greed."[2] There is much wisdom in Gandhi's aphorism. Better sharing of the world's resources would go a long way toward resolving the three central issues of environmentalism, and this is a theme that subsequent chapters continually return to.

But Gandhi was also implying something else, both in this statement and in the way he lived his remarkable life: It is possible to change our feelings of greed if we make an effort to do so. "Greed" is socially highly variable. There are those who make $50,000 a week and give quite a bit of it away. (Even Liberace gave some away.) There are also people who truly have no interest in wealth. The variability of greed indicates that it is not an immutable natural fact. How we arrange our social lives can markedly influence the character of the "greed" we feel within ourselves. The kinds of goods that our greed desires vary markedly across time and culture. It is also important to see that the motivations behind the pursuit of material pleasures are complex.

This chapter begins the exploration of the material dimensions of environmental sociology by considering the *social psychology of consumption* and the complex and variable pleasures that underlie it.

The Material Basis of the Human Condition

We have bodies. We need to eat, we need shelter, and we generally need some kind of clothing. Certain inputs and outputs are essential to all living bodies, which means that no body can exist without interacting with its environment. As Karl Marx, the controversial nineteenth-century philosopher, observed, "The worker can create nothing without *nature,* without the *sensuous external world.* [By *sensuous* Marx meant what we learn of through our senses.] It is the material on which his labor is manifested, in which it is active, from which and by means of which it produces."[3] But can there be any controversy here? Who could long deny—and yet still live—that we must produce our livelihood from what Marx called the "sensuous external world," or what is commonly termed today the "environment"?

Marx also observed that "the mode of production of material life conditions the social, political and intellectual life process in general."[4] In other words, there are many ways that societies can arrange material production from the environment, and these arrangements have great consequences for how we live, even how we think. Our ecology is our economy, and our economy is our society.

You don't have to be a Marxist to appreciate the centrality of material forces in social life. Marx's basic idea is probably as widely accepted as any idea could be. Bill Clinton—an occasional liberal, perhaps, but certainly no Marxist—put it well with the famous motto of his 1992 U.S. presidential campaign: "It's the economy, stupid." Or, as we might put the point more generally, "It's the material, stupid."

Ecological Dialogue

But we must be wary of the simplistic clarity of a purely materialist perspective. *Material* factors always depend upon *ideal* factors. The converse is equally true. Our ideals are shaped by the material conditions of our lives, and our material conditions are shaped by our ideals. You can only do what you can do. But what you can do is as much a matter of what you know, believe, and value—all ideal factors—as it is a matter of what your material circumstances are. Moreover, what your material circumstances are depends in large measure on what you know, believe, and value. If you don't know about germs, you are far more likely to do things that leave you vulnerable to their effects. And what you know, believe, and value depends on your material circumstances. If you live in the Arctic, you are likely to know quite a bit about ice and snow. It's a dialogue—a constant interplay of factors that condition and influence each other, a never-ending conversation between the material and ideal dimensions of social life.[5]

The concept of dialogue provides an alternative to the mechanical, hammer-and-nails notion

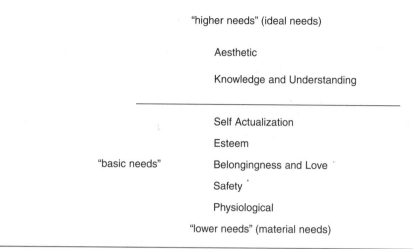

"higher needs" (ideal needs)

Aesthetic

Knowledge and Understanding

Self Actualization

Esteem

"basic needs"   Belongingness and Love

Safety

Physiological

"lower needs" (material needs)

Figure 2.1   Maslow's hierarchy of needs.

of causality that the social sciences for many years attempted to borrow from that ultimate materialist science, physics. In social life, causality is rarely, if ever, a one-way street, and the material is rarely, if ever, all that is involved. (In fact, mechanical materialism probably isn't even good physics, as physicists themselves increasingly argue.)[6] Rather than a mechanical realm of linear causes and effects, social life is an interactive phenomenon in which causes cause effects and effects effect causes, blurring the boundary between them. When we call something in social life a "cause" or an "effect" we are intellectually, and artificially, arresting this constant interplay for a moment. A material cause or effect and an ideal cause or effect are all mere intellectual "moments" in the endless *ecological dialogue.* (See Figure 1.1.)

Social analysis does have to enter the dialogue somewhere, though. In order to be able to understand the interactiveness of the world, you have to be able to distinguish that which is interacting. In order to understand connection, overlap, and mutual constitution, you must be able to see *difference.* Otherwise there will be nothing to connect, overlap, and mutually constitute. In this part of the book we enter the ecological dialogue from the material side of things. In the next part,

we will enter from the ideal side. Although we enter the dialogue from these different sides, these different moments, in each chapter of each part we will be inevitably drawn over from the material to the ideal and from the ideal back to the material. But we have to start somewhere.

The Hierarchy of Needs

One of the most famous explanations of the relationship between the material and the ideal is psychologist Abraham Maslow's theory of the *hierarchy of needs.* This hierarchy, Maslow argued in a famous 1943 paper, is relatively fixed and universal across cultures.[7] At the bottom of the hierarchy are the "basic needs," beginning with a foundation in physiological needs and moving up to needs for safety, belongingness and love, esteem, and self-actualization. Above the basic needs are additional needs for knowledge and understanding and for aesthetic satisfaction. (See Figure 2.1.)

Why this hierarchy? Isn't knowledge and understanding, for example, a pretty basic need? Maslow argues that some needs have to be satisfied before we will direct our efforts toward others, and that these are therefore the most basic. When a person's "belly is chronically full," wrote Maslow, "at once other (and higher) needs emerge and these, rather than physiological hungers, dominate the organism. And when these in turn are satisfied, again new (and still higher) needs emerge, and so on."[8]

Maslow made several key observations about the hierarchy of needs:

- Our efforts to gratify the hierarchy of needs are both conscious and unconscious, but more often unconscious.
- Any one action may be directed at several needs simultaneously.
- Most people's needs are never more than partially satisfied, but their lower needs have to be relatively satisfied before they can move on to the higher ones.
- We sometimes undervalue a lower need after it has been met for a while, but we typically can do so only temporarily. Maslow gave the example of a person who quits a job rather than lose self-respect and yet after 6 months of starving is willing to take the job back even if it means losing self-respect.
- Those who gain the opportunity to work on the higher needs tend to engage in more socially beneficial behavior. As Maslow put it, "The higher the need the less selfish it must be. Hunger is highly egocentric . . . but the search for love and respect necessarily involves other people."[9]

The hierarchy of needs is an intuitively compelling theory. Think how hard it is to study on an empty stomach. If you are not in good shape, it isn't sensible to try to climb a mountain to enjoy the view. Place a book and a piece of bread in front of a starving person and there is little doubt which the person will reach for. The intuitive appeal of Maslow's theory suggests that it speaks to a widely shared understanding of human motivation, which probably accounts for much of the theory's popularity: It feels right to many of us.

The theory is not without problems, though. First, a case can be made that we do not experience our needs as a hierarchy. Rather, we tend to act on whatever need is currently least well met or most under threat and that we are in a position to do something about.[10] Threatened with failure, students may study so hard that they forget to eat. Eager for the pleasure of a good view, people in poor shape sometimes climb mountains anyway. There are starving people—for example, those fasting for a political cause—who will refuse the bread and take the book. Similarly, we may find that the higher needs, like the lower, can be only temporarily ignored and undervalued. That person who took back a demeaning job after 6 months of starving may well quit once again to regain self-respect, even if it means more starving.

Second, the theory lacks a sense of dialogical interplay between the more material and the more ideal needs. If, because of my aesthetic judgment, I do not like the meal before me, I will not eat very much, even if I was initially hungry. I may "lose my appetite," as we sometimes say. Similarly, there have been cases where starving people have refused the food sent by relief agencies because the food was unappetizing to them. Thus my aesthetic, ideal need can lessen the strength of my physiological, material need. Material needs also shape our aesthetic ideals, however. If I am very hungry, I am more likely to decide that unappealing food really does not taste so bad after all. In other words, there is a dialogic interaction between my state of hunger and my aesthetic sensibilities concerning what is good food.

Third, Maslow's theory could be seen as condescending to non-Westerners. The higher needs—self-actualization, the pursuit of knowledge, aesthetics—are also the achievements we stereotypically associate with the degree of "civilization" and "development" of a country or a people. Poor people in "developing" countries who must concern themselves more with the lower needs lead a lower form of existence, or so the theory could imply. The hierarchy of needs is therefore flattering to Westerners, who typically see themselves as being more developed and more civilized than non-Westerners. Part of the appeal of Maslow's theory, then, may be Western hubris.

And fourth, perhaps most important for this chapter, Maslow's theory cannot account for why we consume more material stuff than we need. According to the hierarchy of needs, no one should overconsume. Because their "lower" needs are satisfied, all wealthy and well-fed people should be composing symphonies, writing poetry, and volunteering for Oxfam. Sometimes, of course, wealthy and well-fed people do these "higher" things. But very often they buy more shoes, more clothes, another TV, and sometimes a mirror-tiled Rolls Royce instead.

The Original Affluent Society

In fact, we moderns are the real materialists, perennially concerned with the "lower" needs, argued the anthropologist Marshall Sahlins in his classic 1972 essay, "The Original Affluent Society."[11] We who are so rich are far more preoccupied with material things than any previous society. Thus, in a way, maybe we're not particularly rich, suggests Sahlins, even in comparison to hunter-gatherers, who are usually regarded as the poorest of the poor. In his words, "By common understanding, an affluent society is one in which all the people's material needs are easily satisfied."[12] Sahlins argues that hunter-gatherers eat well, work little, and have lots of leisure time, despite living on far less than modern peoples. And not only are the material *needs* of hunter-gatherers easily satisfied by their manner of living, their material *wants* are as well—because they don't want much. Hunter-gatherers are thus the world's original rich, for they are rich in terms of meeting their "lower" needs and their "higher" ones too.

Time-allocation studies conducted by anthropologists with the few remaining (and fast disappearing) hunter-gatherer societies show that it does not take long to gather and hunt. Typical adult hunter-gatherers work 2 to 5 hours a day. In that time they secure a diet that compares very well with our own in calories, protein, and other nutrients. The rest of the day, the typical hunter-gatherer has lots of time open for hanging around the campfire chatting and visiting, singing songs, exchanging information, telling stories, making art objects—thus satisfying the "higher" needs for belongingness, love, esteem, self-actualization, knowledge, and aesthetics. Nearly everyone in hunter-gatherer societies is some kind of artist. Anthropologists have long been impressed by the incredible richness of "primitive" sculpture, costumes, music, folktales, and religion and have filled many a museum and library shelf with evidence of these. But we moderns are mostly much too busy to develop our artistic sides, and work away our lives. As Sahlins put it, the biblical "sentence of 'life at hard labor' was passed uniquely on us."[13]

Another distinctive feature of hunter-gatherers' lives is that they have to keep moving house, usually several times a year, when the local hunting and gathering gets thin. Many early observers, particularly missionaries, took this constant movement as a sign of shiftiness, as well as taking the hunter-gatherers' great amount of leisure time as a sign of laziness. They thought hunter-gatherers should settle down and do something productive, like raising crops. But here's what one hunter-gatherer told a visiting anthropologist: "Why should we plant when there are so many mongomongo nuts in the world?"[14]

Perhaps most confounding to modern observers is the apparent disregard in which hunter-gatherers hold material goods, despite their seeming poverty. Here's how one anthropologist described the attitude toward possessions of the Yahgan Indians of South America:

Actually, no one clings to his few goods and chattels which, as it is, are often and easily lost, but just as easily replaced. . . . A European is likely to shake his head at the boundless indifference of these people who drag brand-new objects, precious clothing, fresh provisions, and valuable items through thick mud, or abandon them to their swift destruction by children and dogs. . . . Expensive things that are given them are treasured for a few hours out of curiosity; after that they thoughtlessly let everything deteriorate in the mud and wet.[15]

Why don't the Yahgan bother to put things away in clean and dry places? Not because they have no clean and dry places or have no time to construct them. Rather, hunter-gatherers have their own version of the law of diminishing returns, says Sahlins. The returns from hunting and gathering dwindle after a while as nearby game, roots, and berries are gradually harvested. So the group has to up and move. They have to carry with them what they want to keep, though. But if you can remake what you need wherever you go, and if the pace of your work life is gentle enough that you have plenty of time to do this remaking, and if you enjoy this remaking as a communal and artistic activity anyway, why trouble yourself to haul it? And why care much about what happens to things after they are used?

Consequently, hunter-gatherers do not bother with an institution like private property. Individuals do not amass goods and commodities, and what goods and commodities there are in the community are equitably distributed and communally held. If you make a particularly nice bow and your neighbor breaks it hunting or your neighbor's child breaks it playing, there's no need to fuss. Now you have an excuse to sit around the fire and make another one, even nicer. We who worry ceaselessly about goods and commodities live by the great economic motto of "Waste not, want not." The great economic motto of the hunter-gatherer is, as Sahlins wrote, "Want not, lack not."[16]

But the hunter-gatherer life is not an Eden that the rest of us have been thrown out of. It has its struggles. Hunter-gatherers do have to move often, and they also have to keep their population

low. Excess infants and those too old or too sick to make it to the next place must be killed or must go off alone into the bush to die so as not to harm the group. It's their "cost of living well," as Sahlins says. This trade-off may sound grim, but compare it to the many tragedies of our own lifestyle: stress, repetitive and meaningless work, far less leisure, individualistic isolation bred by economic competitiveness, and other tragedies that we each might list.

The hunter-gatherer's cost of living well may still sound grim. But Sahlins's point remains: You do not have to have a lot of money or goods to live well—to lead a life that affords a focus on the needs Maslow termed "higher"—and thus to be rich. As Sahlins says, "The world's most primitive people have few possessions, but they are not poor. . . . Poverty is a social status. As such it is the invention of civilization."[17]

Using Maslow's hierarchy as a measure, it is we moderns who may be the poorer, for we must spend so much more of our time in work, securing our physiological and safety needs. Wealth, that most basic measure of material well-being, depends on how you look at it. Being rich isn't having a lot of stuff. It's having everything you want. If you don't want much, you won't want much.

Consumption, Modern Style

One of the great modern sins is being late. Reputations are sullied, grades sunk, and jobs and friends lost through lateness. Consequently, lateness is something that modern people are perpetually anxious about. Most of us wear watches, constantly check them throughout the day, and regularly synchronize our readings with the community standard that is broadcast on TV and radio and displayed on the clock on the wall and on the computer. And we often inquire of others what their watches read. "What time do you have?" we ask, meaning the reading on the person's watch. Being moderns, we can easily guess at another meaning—how *much* time the person has: very little.

But if timekeeping devices can be found on the wall, the computer, the television, and the wrists of so many of our associates, why bother to wear one ourselves? (I don't, in fact.) If you are in any social setting where precise timing needs to be adhered to, chances are a timepiece of some sort is there already.

About 20 years ago I learned why people wear watches nevertheless. I was working as a geologist in the Talamanca Mountains of Costa Rica in the middle of a dense rainforest some 3 days' walk from the nearest road. (I was mapping the rock formations for an American mining company, a job I later came to regret because of the environmental and social implications of what I was doing—but that's a story for another time.) Our supply helicopter had suffered a minor crash that decommissioned it for awhile, and we had to trade for food with the local Bribri Indians. The Bribri in that area, and at that time, maintained a mixed economy of hunting, gathering, and limited agriculture. The missionaries had been through, so local people owned radios and wore modern-style clothes, and a few times a year they mounted trading and shopping expeditions to town. They knew what money was and much of what it does.

One local man who traded with us even sported a watch. He would often ask me what time it was and, upon receiving the answer I gave from my watch, check down at his own. (I wore a watch in those days.) After a few days of these exchanges, thinking to make a little small talk, I asked to have a look at his watch, mentioning that it appeared to me to be quite a nice one. I was shocked to discover that in fact it was broken, missing a hand. It clearly had been inoperable for some time.

"How ignorant these people are!" a coworker exclaimed when I told him the story later. But rather than being a sign of his ignorance, this man's broken watch was a sign of his sophistication. He understood perfectly well what a watch was really for: status. He could tell time just fine without one—that is, he was completely competent to temporally coordinate his activities as well

as his local community required. Living in a latitude where the day length and path of the sun hardly change throughout the year, he had only to check the sky. Although he had no need for a functioning watch, his sophistication had given him another need, however. It had given him an awareness of something he never knew before: that he was "poor" and that others might consider him even poorer unless he took some conspicuous measures to give a different impression.[18]

The Leisure Class

A century ago, Thorstein Veblen argued that this form of sophistication is what lies behind modern materialism. In his 1899 book, *The Theory of the Leisure Class,* Veblen argued that most of modern culture revolves around attempts to signal our comparative degree of social power through what he famously termed *conspicuous consumption,* as well as through *conspicuous leisure* and *conspicuous waste.*[19] It is not enough merely to be socially powerful. We have to display it. Power in itself is not easy to see. We consume, we engage in leisure, and we waste in conspicuous ways to demonstrate to others our comparative power. In other words, we demonstrate our power by demonstrating our material wealth, because wealth is the surest indicator of power in modern life.

There is an important environmental connection here. Veblen argued that conspicuous consumption, leisure, and waste are convincing statements of power because they show that someone is above being constrained by the brute necessities of material life and the environment. Because of your wealth and position, you do not have to engage in productive activities yourself. You can command the environment through your command of other people, a command made possible by wealth and social position. Environmental power thus indicates social power, and vice versa.

Let me give a few examples of each form of consumption. By *conspicuous consumption,*

Veblen had in mind visible displays of wealth, such as expensive homes, cars, clothes, computers, boats, and the like, as well as sheer volume of consumption. The material visibility of these displays shows one's social ability to command a steady flow of material goods from the environment. Such display is, I think, well known to all of us.

Conspicuous leisure is often more subtle. By this term, Veblen meant the nonproductive consumption of time, an indication of distance from environmental needs—from productive needs—and thus a sign of wealth. The most obvious example is a long vacation to a faraway and expensive place, two weeks at a Club Med hotel, say. But Veblen also had in mind social refinements, like good table manners, which require sufficient time free from productive activities to master. Maintaining a pristinely clean home is a similar demonstration of time free from productive necessities. Wearing the clothing of leisured pursuits—sports shirts, jeans, running shoes, backpacks—as daily wear is another form of conspicuous leisure, for such clothes suggest that a person regularly engages in nonproductive activities. Choosing forms of employment that are far removed from environmental production, such as being a lawyer or a corporate manager, is a particularly important form of conspicuous leisure, Veblen suggested. He noted that most high-status and well-paid jobs are far removed from environmental production, which is why he referred to the wealthy as the "leisure class"—not just because the wealthy have more leisure time.

By *conspicuous waste* Veblen meant using excessive amounts of goods or discarding something rather than reusing it or repairing it. Examples might be buying the latest model of a consumer item and throwing out the old, running a gas-guzzling power boat at top speed, or routinely leaving food on your plate. Those who can afford to waste in these (and countless other) ways thus demonstrate their elevation above material concerns.

Veblen also pointed out that the leisure class engages in *vicarious consumption, vicarious leisure,* and *vicarious waste*—that is, consumption, leisure, and waste that others engage in because of your wealth. The vicarious can be a highly effective statement of social and environmental power. Veblen had in mind here everything from parents who dress their children in expensive clothes and send them to college with a new car and credit card to male business executives who insist that their wives refrain from productive employment.

Veblen's terms overlap (as do probably all categorical distinctions about social life). For example, wearing leisure clothes can be simultaneously a form of conspicuous leisure and conspicuous consumption; leisure clothes like designer jeans and name-brand running shoes are far from cheap, and everyone knows that. The occasional fashion for ripped jeans, which emerged for a while in the late 1960s, reemerged for a while in the early 1990s, and seems to be coming back again now, is a form of conspicuous waste: Who but the wealthy could afford to deliberately rip their clothes and be so confident about their social status as to wear them in public? Thus, the same pair of designer jeans could be a form of conspicuous consumption, conspicuous leisure, and conspicuous waste.

In a way, all modern materialism can be reduced to just one of these: conspicuous waste. Conspicuous consumption is wasteful, and leisure is a waste of time. As Veblen put it, modern society is guided by "the great economic law of wasted effort"—a theoretical, and satirical, dig at utilitarian economics and its idea that modern life is guided by ever-increasing efficiency.[20]

I'd like to highlight two important ecological implications of Veblen's analysis. The first stems from the relative subtlety of conspicuous leisure. Consumption and waste are generally much more conspicuous than leisure. It is hard to put a price tag on good table manners, a clean home, or time spent watching television. Nor can friends and associates see you when you are away on your winter holiday. Perhaps that is part of the reason why tourists are so fond of bringing back gifts, knickknacks, and a tan. These visible symbols of a vacation trip allow you to turn inconspicuous leisure into conspicuous consumption and conspicuous waste.

The greater visibility of consumption and waste is ecologically significant because leisure is potentially less environmentally damaging. Spending time with family and friends, reading books (particularly books borrowed from family, friends, or the library), taking a walk, riding a bike—leisure activities like these consume fewer resources than spending your salary on the latest bit of loud and colorful plastic. Leisure is not always less environmentally damaging, however. It depends on how you engage in it. For example, travel—particularly travel by air and automobile—consumes energy and creates pollution. But in general, consuming or wasting time is less environmentally damaging than consuming or wasting things.

The second and more important environmental implication of Veblen's work is the competitive and comparative character of conspicuous consumption, leisure, and waste. To be conspicuous, you have to exceed the prevailing community norm. As long as others are also attempting to signal their social power through conspicuous consumption, leisure, and waste, the levels required to make a conspicuous statement of power continually rise. Therefore, the environmental impacts from conspicuous consumption, leisure, and waste also continually rise.

To summarize Veblen, through wealth we signal our power over the environment and thus over society. When we can engage in conspicuous consumption, leisure, and waste, we feel socially powerful. But as this is a comparative and competitive matter, we must continually up the ante of conspicuous signals of wealth and power. As a result, we moderns are motivated in our environmental relations not by a hierarchy of needs but by a hierarchy of society.

Positional Goods

Although Veblen's theories do have their limitations, as I'll come to, let us first explore the ideas of a contemporary scholar whose work bears a close affinity with Veblen's: the economist Fred Hirsch.

Why do we experience so much scarcity in the world? Hirsch argues that scarcity is due not only to physical limits in the supply of goods but also to social limits. Conventional economics tells us that when many people want something of which there is not very much, shortages are likely when demand exceeds supply. Hirsch, on the other hand, argues that people often want something precisely *because* it is in short supply. The supply and demand of a good are not independent phenomena, with the price set at the point where they meet. Rather, there can be important interactions between supply and demand. Hirsch avers that, for some goods, demand will go up as supply goes down and demand will go down as supply goes up. As Hirsch puts it, "An increase in physical availability of these goods . . . changes their characteristics in such a way that a given amount of use yields less satisfaction."[21]

The point is, scarce goods create an opportunity for conferring status and prestige upon those who gain access to or possession of them. As Mark Twain wrote, describing the famous whitewashing scene in *The Adventures of Tom Sawyer,* "[Tom] had discovered a great law of human action, without knowing it—namely, that in order to make a man or boy covet a thing, it is only necessary to make that thing difficult to attain:"[22] Hirsch calls such difficult-to-attain things "positional goods," goods whose desirability is predicated at least in part on short supplies, limited access, higher prices, and consequent social honor or position.

The notion of positional goods helps us understand why some goods and not others become the objects of conspicuous consumption. Goods that are in short supply, or can be made to be in short supply, are most likely to take on positional importance. One example of such a good is lakefront property. The amount of shoreline on lakes is limited by the physical landscape and the expense of reengineering that landscape. Hirsch suggests that, although we rarely admit it to ourselves, part of the desirability of such property is the fact that there is so little of it—particularly in places that have a good climate and are relatively close to cities. (There are plenty of lakes up north in the tundra.) The same is true of having a place in the country. If everyone lived in the countryside, it would it be so desirable (nor would it be the countryside).

Moreover, says Hirsch, the owners of positional goods may deliberately attempt to limit access to these goods, increasing their own positional advantage. An illustration of what Hirsch has in mind are some political movements to preserve the countryside, such as the 2-acre-minimum lot sizes that many American exurban communities instituted in the 1970s and 1980s. Local proponents argued that 2-acre lots would limit development and thereby protect wildlife habitat and preserve rural character. Hirsch would say that such zoning provisions provided a means for exurban residents to pull up the drawbridge behind them, even though they might not admit such a motivation to others or even to themselves. I might add that, in fact, 2-acre zoning accelerates the deterioration of habitat and rural character by increasing the amount of land consumed by any new development. It is environmentally far more effective to concentrate development in a few areas and leave the bulk of it open.[23] Two-acre zoning does, however, ensure that only those wealthy enough to afford a lot of that size will move in, protecting the social honor of the exurban landscape.

The concept of positional goods also helps us understand the social pressures that sometimes result in the extinction of valued species of plants and animals. If a species is particularly valued, one might expect that those who appreciate it would do everything possible to protect it. The reverse is very often the case.

For example, on August 7, 2003, the Australian customs ship *Southern Supporter* spotted the Uruguayan fishing boat *Viarsa* in the territorial waters of Australia, just above the Antarctic circle. The *Viarsa* was fishing for the rare and sought-after Patagonian toothfish—also known as the Chilean sea bass—whose oil-rich flesh is much prized in sushi restaurants in Japan and the United States. A single fish can fetch $1,000. Consequently toothfish stocks are, at this writing, virtually in collapse. Since 1988,

the toothfish has been protected under an international conservation agreement, something called the Convention for the Conservation of Antarctic Marine Living Resources, which most nations have signed. Australia is among those, and the *Southern Supporter* gave chase to the *Viarsa*—a 7,000-kilometer chase, in fact, across the southern oceans. Three weeks later, with the help of ships from Britain and South Africa, the *Southern Supporter* caught up with the *Viarsa*, and in 20-foot seas arrested its crew and took control of the 150 tons of toothfish on board, worth $1.5 million.[24]

Why do people prize toothfish so much? In part for its taste, no doubt, but also for the positional value of eating such rare fish. Indeed, when one considers the wide variability in what peoples of the world consider good-tasting food, one has to wonder if part of the very taste of toothfish is its status value. As the supply of toothfish goes down, the enjoyment some find in this taste will only go up. The price will go up too, making the poaching of toothfish all the more attractive an endeavor for boats like the *Viarsa*.

The same can be said of the trade in rhino horn, which is a favored ingredient in some Chinese traditional medicines, particularly as an aphrodisiac, and is also a traditional accoutrement of masculine pride in Yemen, where rhino horn is used to make the handles of *jambiyya* daggers. The world population of rhinos as of 2001 was approximately 17,000 in the wild for all 5 surviving species, but the positional value of them for aphrodisiacs and *jambiyya* daggers is such that each full-grown horn is worth around $40,000. The result is continued rhino poaching and break-ins at hunting lodges, where the horns are sawed off the stuffed heads on the walls.[25]

It can only be seen as a sad irony that the establishment of conventions and reserves to protect rare and endangered species contribute to their positional value by decreasing their supply on world markets. The more we protect them, the more they become sought after. Which doesn't mean protecting them doesn't work. For example, rhino numbers are up 50 percent since the mid-1990s because of conservation efforts.[26] But the positional consequences of protecting rare and endangered species greatly complicates conservation work.

Hirsch's analysis of positional goods can also be extended to our concepts of beauty. If scarcity makes something desirable, then, in a way, scarcity makes something beautiful. The most beautiful countryside is rarely the most ordinary. The most admired forms of wildlife are rarely the most common. This suggests to me a tragic point. Destroying some of the environment can sometimes make the rest of it seem more beautiful.

Goods and Sentiments

A Veblenesque portrait of social motivation is a familiar form of social critique in modern life, and it can have a certain intuitive appeal, particularly when one is in a cynical frame of mind. Most of us have, I imagine, leveled Veblenesque charges at those around us—at least in our minds—reducing the behavior of others to greedy, competitive, self-serving display. We can easily imagine others having these motivations because, I believe, we have often sensed them in ourselves.

But there is more to people than a will to gain power and to show off. Many sociologists have long contended that ascribing all human motivation to *interest,* the desire to achieve self-regarding ends, is too narrow a view. As humans, we are equally motivated by *sentiment,* the desire to achieve other-regarding ends revolving around our norms and social ties.[27] It is wise, though, to maintain a critical outlook on the sentimental side of human motivation, lest we be seduced by the potential flattery of such an interpretation of social behavior. I try to maintain such a critical outlook in the pages that follow.

The Reality of Sentiments

We can get a handle on the sentimental side of motivation for acquiring goods by looking at the way we "cultivate" meaning in objects, to use the language suggested by Eugene Rochberg-Halton.[28] One of the principal sources of the meanings we cultivate is the network of our social ties. The goods we surround ourselves with show not only how we set ourselves apart from others—Veblen's point—but also how we connect ourselves to others. They are talismans of community.

We all can give many personal examples. Here is one of mine. For many years, until it wore out completely, one of my favorite T-shirts was from a softball team I used to play on, the Slough Creek Toughs. We were all geology students—my undergraduate major—and the team name came from the name of a rock formation, the Slough Creek Tuff. It was neither a particularly clever name nor a particularly nicely designed shirt, but the shirt brought back pleasant memories of good times with friends from long ago. This shirt was not an emblem of the "old boy" network of my student days, for I have since changed professions from geology to sociology, and it has been years since I saw any of the team's former members. Perhaps there is some social advantage in the conspicuous leisure of wearing a T-shirt, but it is hard for me to see what social advantage I gained in wearing that particular—rather plain and obscure—T-shirt. I think what I gained was simply a chance to express a sentimental connection to others, and mainly to express it to myself.

Not all social scientists would agree that such an interpretation is justified, though. An important theoretical tradition, long established in economics but also in other social sciences, argues that all we ever do is act on our interests, as best we understand our interests and the possibilities of achieving the desires that stem from them. This is often called the theory of *rational choice.* Veblen's theory of the leisure class is an important forerunner of this tradition. A close parallel is the theory of the selfish gene in evolutionary biology. Rational choice theory would argue that I had lots of self-serving reasons to keep wearing that old T-shirt. For example, I might wear it because one of my interests is to have a good opinion of myself, and one route to such a good opinion is the self-flattery of believing myself to be motivated by more than self-interests. In this view, sentiments are thus a self-serving fiction.

The rational choice perspective yields many fruitful insights. But it is also extraordinarily materialist in approach. As I argue throughout this book, theories of social life that emphasize either the material or the ideal generally turn out, on closer inspection, to be unbalanced. Although we cannot discount the accuracy of a purely materialist or purely idealist perspective out of hand, a case can usually be made for the equal importance of the other side of the dialogue.

Let me try to make such a case here.[29] Consider the rational choice view that sentiments are a self-serving fiction. Now it may be true that sentiments always have self-interest behind them. But that is not how you and I experience sentiments, at least not always. We experience our sentiments as sentiments—as feelings of concern, affection, empathy, and affection for others; as commitments to common values and norms; and frequently as the lack of these feelings and commitments (such lacks being equally manifestations of our sentiments). Thus we may at times give up or refuse material gain because we experience concern for, and commitment to, the interests of others. We may also hold dislikes for others and their values that run contrary to our potential for material gain—refusing a high-paying job with an unpleasant boss in an environmentally damaging industry, for example.

Now perhaps there is always some hidden agenda of self-interest behind such refusals of personal material gain. But if we do not consciously experience interests behind our sentiments, we must then be basing our conscious decision making at least in part on other criteria. In other words, as long as the agenda of self-interest really is truly hidden—hidden even from the self—sentiments will be important sources on their own of what it pleases us to do.

In any event, as I have elsewhere written, there is simply "no way of knowing that that hidden agenda always exists, for, after all, if it does exist, it is often hidden."[30] But what we can know is what experience tells us does exist: that we have

conscious orientations toward material goods that are both self-regarding and other-regarding, both materialist and idealist, both interested and sentimental.

Hau: The Spirit of Goods

One aspect of the sentimental experience of material goods is what the Maori people of New Zealand traditionally called the *hau,* the social spirit that attaches to gifts.[31] A Maori wise man, Tamati Ranaipiri, once explained the *hau* to a visiting anthropologist this way:

> Let me speak to you about the *hau.* . . . Let us suppose that you possess a certain article and that you give me this article. You give it to me without setting a price on it. We strike no bargain about it. Now, I give this article to a third person who, after a certain lapse of time, decides to give me some things as a payment in return. . . . It would not be fair on my part to keep these gifts for myself, whether they were desirable or undesirable. I must give them to you because they are a *hau* of the gifts that you gave me. If I kept these other gifts for myself, serious harm might befall me, even death. This is the nature of the *hau,* the *hau* of personal property, the *hau* of the gift, the *hau* of the forest. But enough on this subject.[32]

Hau is the Maori word for both "wind" and "spirit," much as the Latin word *spiritus* means both "wind" and "spirit," and it is probably not accidental that two such widely separated cultures should have such a parallel. All peoples recognize that there can be a kind of palpable, yet intangible, presence in things. For Tamati Ranaipiri that presence was the interconnected *hau* of personal property, gifts, and the life-giving forest. This interconnected *hau* watched over the movement of goods through the community to make sure each gift was reciprocated. In a way, the soul of the person who gave the gift—that soul being connected to the wider soul of the forest—lingered on within the gift, even after it had been subsequently given to someone else. As the anthropologist Marcell Mauss observed, "This represents an intermingling. Souls are mixed with things; things are mixed with Souls."[33] Through this mixing, as Mauss also noted, the tangibility of gifts brought a Maori group together, causing them to recognize and to celebrate something intangible: their sentimental connections.

Think about it. Articles we receive as gifts have a very different influence on our behavior than articles we buy for ourselves. The same is true for any good that we come to appreciate not just for its material purpose (if it even has one) but for the association we make between that good and a person or persons. We moderns still mix souls with things.

The wedding ring I wear on the fourth finger of my left hand is an example. It has no material purpose, and only modest material value. And yet if some experimentally inclined social scientist were to offer me an absolutely identical ring, plus $100, I would refuse the trade. I would refuse it for $1,000 and probably for $10,000—though at this level I am less sure! But even if I weaken at such a figure, my ring, I believe, remains more than a cold, material object to me.

What makes my wedding ring more than a material object to me is my sentimental sense that it has a *hau,* in this case the *hau* of two souls joined in marriage. Similarly, my old Slough Creek Toughs T-shirt contains the *hau* of that softball team. Although I could go to the store and buy an end table for my living room that is not as stained and wobbly as the one my grandfather made, no store sells end tables that embody the *hau* of my grandfather. All of us, I imagine, could point to similar spirited articles of social sentiment among our own possessions.

Goods are thus not merely objects of social competitiveness and social interest. They are also the means by which we remind ourselves, and indeed even create, the web of sentimental ties that help support our feelings of social communion. In the words of Mary Douglas and Baron Isherwood, material possessions serve our interests,

"but at the same time it is apparent that the goods have another important use: they also make and maintain social relationships."[34]

Sentiments and Advertising

Most goods today, however, do not have a *hau.* In this age of the global economy and the shopping mall, most of the goods that surround us were made by people we will never meet, bought from people we do not know, and chosen primarily because of price and convenience. We care about these purchased goods because of how they serve our interests. They are socially empty, or nearly so.

Companies routinely try to persuade us that their wares are not socially empty, however. Advertisers routinely appeal to sentiments to pitch products, and it is instructive to examine the techniques they use. The agenda behind sentimental appeals is very often not so hidden.

The principal form of advertising is price advertising. With so many purchasing options available, it is not easy to persuade consumers to spend their cash on a particular product. Moreover, most people do have considerable resistance to ads. They know that ads are manipulative propaganda.[35] From the extravagant "blow-out clearance sale with unbelievable values" to the simple statement of object and cost that is the norm in classified ads, advertisers have long found that price is the single most effective means of generating sales.[36]

But price advertising does have limits to its effectiveness, particularly when a rival is advertising a similarly low price. In addition, emphasizing the monetary aspect of a transaction reminds the potential purchaser that the principal interest of the seller is similarly financial, undermining consumer trust in the quality of the good. So, in order to divert attention from the fact that in reality the seller is out for our money, advertisements routinely try to appeal to our sentiments.

One popular technique is to claim that a product is being offered for sale out of concern for you. Here's a sample newspaper ad in this *you* genre:

Truly Exceptional
Service Starts
with Careful Listening

It is why your Republic Account Officer makes sure to obtain a precise picture of your financial goals, time frame, risk acceptance, and other key factors. He keeps these constantly in mind as he looks after your interests.

So year after year, you can count on us for the exceptionally complete, timely and personalized service that makes Republic truly unique.[37]

A rather dull ad. Yet note how, after the banner, the words *you* or *yours* appear in every sentence. But whose interests does a Republic Account Officer really look after?

In addition to service, advertisements attempt to bestow a feeling of concern for *you* through claims to offer choice and individualized products. "Double the size and even more choice," reads an ad for a new branch of Marks and Spencer, Britain's largest retailer. "Have it your way at Burger King," went a popular slogan of a few years ago—a remarkable claim for a company that sells food made on an assembly line. Specialty shops make a related pitch by seeking the business of only a select group of customers with particular needs. "The Choice for Big or Tall Men" runs the slogan for High and Mighty, a men's clothing store in a large shopping mall in Newcastle, England. Ads like these evade the mass-produced, machine-made, *hau*-less origin of modern goods by saying, See, we care enough about you to provide just your size and color and taste. Mom herself couldn't have done it better at her sewing machine at home.

You advertising may exhibit supposed sentiments on the part of merchants, but of course it also appeals directly to the buyer's status and power interests. Statements about the merchant's commitment to every wish of *you* entice the buyer with a romance of the customer's high status and power over the merchant. Indeed, after price, status is likely the principal theme of advertisements. "The finest watch in the world

will only be worn by exceptional people," runs an ad for Audemars Piguet. "Compromise shouldn't enter your vocabulary, let alone your garage," puffs an ad for Volvo. A store name like High and Mighty is another effort to cash in on status. Status advertising is particularly characteristic of ads for clothing and luxury goods. Similarly, companies often boast of their own reputations as the "best in the business," not only to proclaim the quality of their products but also to establish a status enticement to "shop with the best."

Few of us like to feel that we are mainly motivated by a desire for social status, however. Whether or not we are only fooling ourselves about our sentimental concerns, thinking purely in terms of status and interest does leave one feeling a bit hollow, and probably thinking as much of the advertiser. So ads very often try to convince us that the product on offer is not just for status display, but for displaying love too.

Christmas advertising is notorious for this. Dad (it is usually Dad) hands his college-age child the keys to the gleaming car in the background, as the music swells. Happy children play with this year's rage toy while Mom (it is usually Mom) looks on contentedly. Similar "hooks" appear in other seasonal ads, particularly those for the Hallmark holidays invented by the advertisers, and most popular in the United States: Mother's Day, Father's Day, Secretary's Day, and the like. Veblen would argue that the real motive behind buying your child the latest piece of expensive plastic junk is vicarious consumption, and I believe it would be hard to deny the common existence of such a desire. Yet vicarious consumption is far more likely to be psychologically palatable if we experience it as, at least in part, an expression of sentiment. The dialogical converse also applies: We are more likely to consume vicariously through those for whom we have strong sentimental ties.

Ads often portray a more generalized sentimentalism too, placing a kind of good-for-the-world, friendly, family values frame around the item on offer. "Get Together" proclaims an ad for Nokia cellular phones opposite a photograph of a seven-hands handshake. "It's nice to meet you" runs an ad for LG Semicon, along with a photograph of some of the company's chip designers. "It took you a long time before you could walk. Air France will save you some when you want to fly," reads the caption of a photo of a father's hand helpfully reaching down to a toddler. Here as well, *you* is a prominent theme in the advertising copy.

Green Advertising

A new form of sentimental hook is green consumerism. Companies like The Body Shop (cosmetics), Ben and Jerry's (ice cream), and Whole Foods (an American organic supermarket chain) seek to demonstrate through the environmental and social good works they support that they are concerned about more than profit. They also make a sentimental appeal to the guilt we feel over our own consumptive habits.

The catalog of Gaiam—an American mail order and Internet "multi-channel lifestyle company" whose mission is "to provide choices that allow people to live a more natural and healthy life"—is an example. It is full of expensive *you* products, personal care items that could hardly be deemed essential but are made with organic cotton, recycled rubber, and the like. Environmentalists might be pleased to see that Gaiam promotes the use of organic and recycled products. But there must be some disappointment in seeing them pitch items like $200 rattan "basket shelves" for towel storage (one of the "healthy basics for the bathroom," according to the company Web site), $360 indoor water fountains ("providing water's healing ambiance for any environment," reads the caption), and $3,339 king-sized mattresses made from organic cotton (the twin-sized are just $1,899).[38] The message is that you can consume conspicuously and still be an environmentalist. Indeed, you can be conspicuous *about* your environmental consumerism, when friends and family visit your home. Sentiment itself becomes display.

The environment is also a common theme in the ad campaigns of major corporations, particularly oil companies, automobile manufacturers, pesticide firms, and other industries with spotty environmental records. "Green-washing" is what critics call it, and perhaps with some justice.[39] "It's nice to know the environment also impacts the auto industry," comforts the headline of an ad for Saturn cars. Opposite the headline is a photo of "the Saturn plant, as seen from just inside our white picket fence," which surrounds the company's Spring Hill, Tennessee, facility. And instead of the looming, metal-sided building one expects, the photo shows a pasture, a lake, and three children playing, one with a cute little scrape on his nose—another sentimental hook. The ad copy describes how much Saturn recycles, how the company has kept in farming most of the land it acquired for the facility, and how it has landscaped the site so that the automobile plant is hidden from view. Other companies' ads boast about how they make large contributions to environmental campaigns, sign their managers up for 2-day short courses in environmental protection run by Greenpeace, and support campaigns such as Britain's "Young Ethical Entrepreneur of the Year," which runs slogans like "You don't have to harm the environment to make money."

In this age of widespread support for environmental concerns, a green halo is good for a corporation's image. To be sure, some of the things that corporations do to acquire that halo truly may help to resolve environmental problems. It is a good thing that Exxon contributes money to the coffers of the Nature Conservancy, that The Body Shop allows customers to recycle their bottles, that Ben and Jerry's supports the local dairy farms of Vermont, and that corporations in general are learning that, in fact, it is possible to make money in more benign ways. We should not lose sight of the environmental significance of green business practices. But we should also recognize that good environmental citizenship makes a corporation's sentimental appeal to consume all the more potent.

Goods and Community

Why are appeals to our sentiments so potent? Social scientists have long observed the way the individualism of modern life has weakened the ties of community. We feel the lack of these ties, even though we may not consciously recognize it. So we try to buy community, the psychologist Paul Wachtel has argued. We try to buy a feeling of community in the goods we purchase for ourselves and the goods we buy for others, and we try to gain status within our community through the goods we display. Goods, then, are a substitute for social needs. In Wachtel's words,

> Faced with the loneliness and vulnerability that come with the deprivation of a securely encompassing community, we have sought to quell the vulnerability through our possessions. When we can buy nice things, and we can look around and see our homes well stocked and well equipped, we feel strong and expansive rather than small and endangered.[40]

Moreover, suggests Wachtel, a vicious circle is in operation: The more we lose community, the more we seek to find it through goods—and the more we seek the wealth to attain these goods, the more we immerse ourselves in the competitive individualism of the modern economy, thus undermining community. Meanwhile, the environment is undermined as well.

The Time Crunch

Part of the problem is simply a lack of time. The hunter-gatherer life of leisure is lost to us (perhaps to our overall benefit), and with it went the abundant opportunity for interaction with our families and communities.

Loss of time got really out of hand in the early years of the Industrial Revolution. In 1840, the average worker in the United Kingdom (the first country to experience widespread industrialization) put in 69 hours a week.[41] By the 1960s, in response to widespread protest over these conditions, the average workweek had fallen to half that throughout the industrialized world. Many observers foresaw the coming of a society that had hardly any need for work as improved machines replaced the drudgery of early industrialism and as a new sense of a social contract between workers and employers ensured that time demands remained reasonable.

Yet in the United States the length of the workweek is now back on the upswing, and the trend seems to be spreading throughout Europe.[42] Rising competitiveness in a globalizing economy, low job security, declining government controls, and weak (or even nonexistent) unions together encourage workers to acquiesce to employers' demands for long hours. The economist Juliet Schor estimates that the average American worker in 1987 was putting in 163 more hours of work a year than in 1967, the equivalent of a month of 40-hour workweeks.[43] Simultaneously, paid time off—vacation, holidays, sick leave—had slipped back by several days, despite already being at levels far below those of most European countries, where paid vacation alone is commonly 4 to 6 weeks, by law, even for low-paid workers with just a year of service in a company.[44] In the United States, the norm is now just 10 days of vacation after a year's service, and there is no legal mandate for even this much. (See Figure 2.2.) The percentage of large and medium-sized U.S. companies that offer any paid vacation time at all dropped from 96 percent in 1988 to 89 percent in 1997.[45]

Schor suggests that this time crunch may be much of the reason that consumerism is so pronounced in the United States. Americans are trapped in what Schor calls the cycle of "work-and-spend": They must maintain a highly consumptive lifestyle in order to be able to put in all those hours at work. The clothes to wear to work, the several cars most households need to get there, the time-saving home conveniences and prepared food—these are the unavoidable costs of holding down a job, or the two or three jobs many Americans now work. This work-related consumption in turn increases the amount of time spent shopping. Second to Internet use, shopping is the fastest growing use of time in the United States—and much Internet use is itself spent on shopping.[46] The result is even less time for other pursuits—like spending

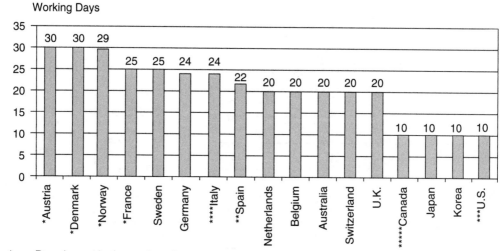

Working Days

*   Based on a six-day workweek
**   Thirty total calendar days
***   No statutory minimum—96% of employers offer at least two weeks (10 days) (2002 data)
****   May vary according to industry agreement
*****   15 days in Saskatchewan

Figure 2.2   Variations in legally mandated minimum vacation time across the world, for employees with one year of service. Note that the United States is the only country in this group for which there is no mandated minimum. However, 96 percent of U.S. employers offer 10 days.

time with family, eating meals together, visiting with friends and neighbors, joining clubs, and participating in local voluntary organizations, all activities that surveys show have fallen off in the United States since the 1950s.[47] (See Figure 2.3.) With everyone doing so much consuming, the pace of competitive display ratchets up, leading to yet more need for work. More than the people in other wealthy countries, Americans find themselves working and spending, spending and working, rather than enjoying the vacation time they don't have anyway. Indeed, very often American workers don't even take the limited vacation time they do have, so caught up are they into the culture of work-and-spend.

The time crunch propels environmental damage along with consumerism. The raw materials to support this high level of consumerism have to come from somewhere. Moreover, with so little vacation time, Americans have less opportunity to use leisure as a status symbol, generally a less

environmentally damaging form of conspicuous display than consumption and waste.

Similar trends are underway elsewhere—for example in Britain, where work hours and shopping hours are up, and participation in voluntary organizations is down.[48] Although consumerism is most pronounced in the United States, other wealthy countries are not far behind. Indeed, as several social critics have commented, it appears that shopping is now the industrialized world's leading recreational activity—especially when we consider that television watching and Internet use are themselves increasingly shopping activities, in view of the volume of ads and the growth of credit card purchases through Web sites and shoppers' television networks.

Increases in productivity per worker have been such that people in all the wealthy countries could be working far, far less. For example, Schor has calculated that in the United States everyone could work a 4-hour day, or only 6 months a years, and still have the same standard of living that prevailed

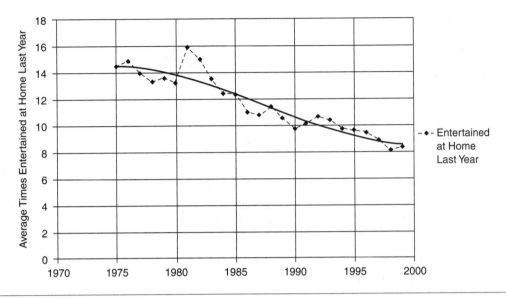

Figure 2.3 Social effects of the time crunch in the United States: The decline in entertaining at home, 1975–1998.

in 1948.[49] But the people of no country have chosen such a course. Perhaps we have not been allowed to choose such a course, and perhaps we have not allowed ourselves to choose it. Probably, and dialogically, both are true. Nevertheless, we work and we spend, and we simultaneously drift further away from one another as we increase our rate of environmental consumption.

Consumption and the Building of Community

The rhetoric on consumerism and its relationship to the loss of community can easily get overheated, though. To begin with, although we are frequently critical of grabs for social status and social power, few would deny the central importance of status and power to one's social-psychological health. All of us need some status and power within our communities. Indeed, we are critical of unequal distributions of status and power because these needs are important to everyone. The granting of a degree of status and the power with which it is closely associated is something we expect from our communities. Moreover, that expectation helps build our commitment to our communities.

Consumption can also enhance community, despite all the competitive individualism it can promote. Consumption can have a kind of festive air about it. Christmas gatherings, wedding ceremonies, and birthday parties have some of the hallmarks of potlatch—festivals of community in which we strengthen social ties through gift exchange—as anthropologists have argued.[50] Some *hau* exists even in the consumer society. And in addition to circulating *hau* through gifts, we make community through the goods we consume in common. Reciprocal exchanges and what Douglas and Isherwood called "consumption matching" can bring us together.

But Douglas and Isherwood carried this argument too far when they wrote that "consuming at the same level as one's friends should not carry derogatory meaning. How else should one relate to the Joneses if not by keeping up with them?"[51]

Must we really keep up materially with someone to relate to him or her socially? This is, no doubt, quite a common approach to fellowship.[52] But such an attitude quickly divides a society into class-bounded patterns of community. Note that Douglas and Isherwood did not suggest that one should lower one's consumption level to that of, say, the Collinses as a way to find community.

When we engage in consumption matching, we nearly always attempt to match those above us in status. In other words, consumption matching is rarely only about building community.

Just as it would not be accurate to ascribe all consumption to competitive display, it is not accurate to ascribe it all to reciprocity and fellowship, as Douglas and Isherwood do. Both motivations can exist together. The consumption of goods generally represents a double message, a complex mix of competition and community, interest and sentiment. This complexity leads to considerable ambiguity in the meaning one person can read from another person's consumptive act. This ambiguity, to be frank, is often socially useful when we engage in a little *you* advertising of our own.

The Treadmill of Consumption

Meanwhile, the cycle of competitive and communal consumption accelerates. As one tries to keep up with the Joneses, the Joneses are trying to keep up with the neighbor on the other side, and up the line to Liberace, the Rockefellers, the Walton family, Queen Elizabeth, the Sultan of Brunei, and Bill Gates. And Bill Gates, the sultan, and the queen are constantly looking back over their shoulders.

Although the desire for more—more money, more stuff—is pervasive, one's level of wealth has little to do with a sense of happiness, at least beyond a certain minimum. A 1982 study in Britain found that unskilled and partly skilled workers, the bottom of the pay scale, were indeed less happy than others (measured by asking if a respondent was "very pleased with things yesterday"). But skilled manual workers from the lower middle of the pay scale were actually slightly happier than better-paid, non-manual, professional workers.[53] Several American studies have found that the poor are least happy but the wealthy are only slightly more satisfied with their standard of living than are others.[54]

A cross-national comparison from 2002 shows the same weak relationship between wealth and happiness. Ghana was one of the three poorest among the 68 countries surveyed, yet had one of the highest levels of reported happiness. Only eight countries reported greater happiness than Ghana. Colombia was tied for happiest, yet was the 25th poorest. The wealthiest countries do tend to be among the happiest. But among the wealthy nations, greater riches does not lead to surer satisfaction with life. Austria, France, and Japan are some of the world's richest countries, yet they reported happiness lower than about half the countries in the survey. The United States, the second richest country in the survey (and the world, after Luxembourg), registered the same happiness levels as El Salvador, the 51st richest (or 18th poorest) country in the survey and one of the poorest in North America. However, taken as a whole, the poorer countries in the survey showed a far wider range of happiness, and the least happy countries were all poor ones. (See Figure 2.4.)

There is also no certain link between economic growth and increasing happiness. For example, the percentage of Americans who report themselves as "very happy" peaked in 1957 at 53 percent and has not recovered, despite continuous national economic growth since that time.[55] Even in happy, wealthy America, the link of increased wealth to life satisfaction is not clear—except for the poor.

The lack of this link is something of a paradox, given all the effort put into wealth accumulation and economic growth. It is the paradox of a positional economy. Levels of consumption are constantly devalued as, through general economic growth, more people attain them. Because this constant devaluing affects everyone on the economic ladder equally, no one is made happier than anyone else by moving up a rung, aside perhaps from the very poor. Consequently, economic advancement in an expanding economy has little to do with differences in overall happiness. You only gain in this comparative game when you are fortunate enough to advance in comparison to others, and by definition that advance must be limited to a few. We cannot all

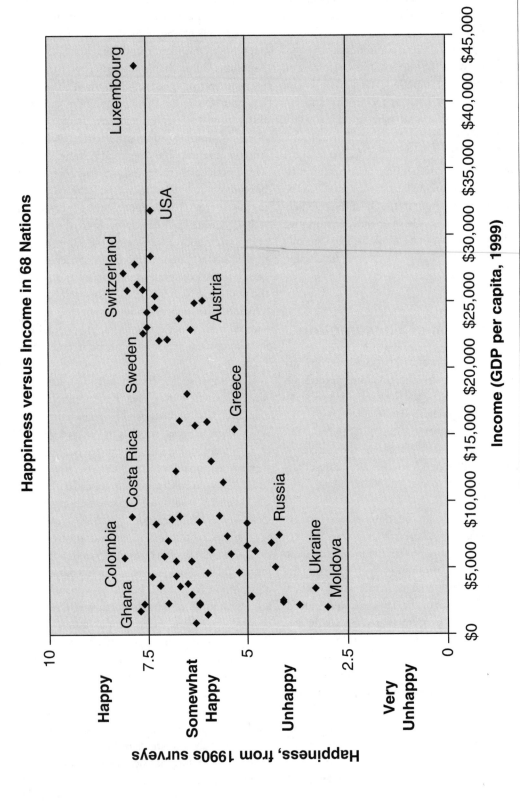

Happiness versus Income in 68 Nations

Figure 2.4 Average reported happiness in 54 countries.

Figure 2.5   The treadmill of consumption: Even as consumption increases, satisfaction often remains elusive.

be like Bill Gates. Perhaps he is a supremely happy person. I don't know. But by definition, only one person can be the world's richest.

Yet still we try. We could all be like the Collinses, but although consumption may be an act of community, there is more to it than that. So we try to be like Bill Gates instead. Meanwhile, Bill Gates has gotten even richer, relative to everyone else. The result is no end to our wants and little improvement, if any, in our satisfaction—despite increased consumption of goods. This whole process of moving materially ahead without making any real gain in satisfaction can be termed the *treadmill of consumption*.[56] (See Figure 2.5. I discuss a parallel treadmill, the treadmill of production, in the next chapter.)

Moreover, at one level or another, most of us are aware that money and goods are not happiness—even in the United States, that paragon of consumerism. A 1989 Gallup Poll asked Americans to rank what was most important to them, and "having a nice home, car, and other belongings" came out last among nine options.[57]

A 1995 survey I helped conduct among Iowa farmers (who, as a group, are sometimes accused of being concerned more about having a big new tractor than about the social and environmental implications of their farming practices) showed a similar result.[58] These kinds of responses, which are common throughout the world, have been shaped by cultural values every bit as deep as consumerism. Virtually all the world's major philosophical traditions counsel that money is neither the route to happiness nor saintliness, as Figure 2.6 shows.

Sometimes, however, it takes a shock to put things, pun intended, in proper perspective. On a late flight across the country a few years ago, I got to talking with a flight attendant about a recent tragedy in her life: Six months previously her home had burned to the ground. Although no one was hurt, the house was a total loss. "How awful!" I exclaimed.

"No, not really," she replied. "Friends and family immediately came to my husband and me, giving us a place to stay, helping us clean up and

Religion or Culture	Teaching and Source
American Indian	"Miserable as we seem in thy eyes, we consider ourselves . . . much happier than thou, in this that we are very content with the little that we have." (Micmac chief)
Buddhist	"Whoever in this world overcomes his selfish cravings, his sorrows fall away from him, like drops of water from a lotus flower." (Dhammapada, 336)
Christian	"It is easier for a camel to go through the eye of a needle than for a rich man to enter into the kingdom of God." (Matthew 19:24)
Confucian	"Excess and deficiency are equally at fault." (Confucius, XI.15)
Ancient Greek	"Nothing in Excess." (Inscribed at Oracle of Delphi)
Hindu	"That person who lives completely free from desires, without longing . . . attains peace." (Bhagavad-Gita, II.71)
Islamic	"Poverty is my pride." (Muhammad)
Jewish	"Give me neither poverty nor riches." (Proverbs 30:8)
Taoist	"He who knows he has enough is rich." (Tao Te Ching)

Figure 2.6   The teachings of world religions and major cultures on consumption and materialism.

salvage what we could, loaning us money, getting us back going again."

She paused, and reflected. "It taught me what is really important, and that's people. It's not your things."

Similar reactions are well known to social scientists who study the social consequences of disasters.[59] Major disasters in which many of one's friends and family suffer or even die are deeply troubling to the survivors, but disasters that take property and not lives—as can happen, for example, in floods that rise slowly enough for residents to evacuate—can actually leave people feeling better some months after the event.[60] The cleanup efforts bring people from behind the doors that usually separate them and join everyone together in a common endeavor. Unburdened of their possessions, they rediscover their community, without the ambiguity of the double message of goods.

Which suggests something significant, I think: Not only do we consume more than we need, we also consume more than we want.

CHAPTER 3

Money and Machines

We are becoming the servants in thought, as in action, of the machine we have created to serve us.

—John Kenneth Galbraith, 1958

An ordinary day, nothing special. You get up, glare at the clock, flick on the radio for a weather forecast. A fatuously excited announcer is exclaiming about the fabulous once-in-a-lifetime sale this weekend at Loony Lucy's, a local computer discount store. Hit the switch. Maybe the weather channel on cable would be better. Where's the remote? The screen comes to life just as the forecaster finishes with the segment on world weather, and the picture fades to a shot of a lush tropical beach, empty except for a lone sun umbrella emblazoned with a commercial logo you don't recognize. "Have you ever . . . ," the voice-over begins. Who cares? Click. You look out the window to gauge for yourself if it's going to rain today, and you notice the company van from your neighbor's carpet cleaning business in her driveway. Her car must still be in the shop. "Our machines mean clean," the van's side panel promises. Jeans are fine for today, you decide. You reach for the unfolded pair from the pile of clean clothes you

haven't put away yet. "Levi's" reads the label on the right rear pocket. (Nice jeans.) Four ads already, and you haven't even made it out of the bedroom.

The previous chapter described how the materialism of modern life is propelled by social-psychological desires for status and social connection. But these desires are not fixed, and they can be manifested in many different ways. The organization of social life shapes the desires we experience in daily living and their manifestations. This chapter explores the economic and technologic basis of social organization and how, through interaction with culture and social-psychology, economic and technologic factors help create the material motivations of modern life.

The inescapable presence of advertising, even in our bedrooms, is an obvious example of how technology and economics shape our motivations. Yet there is a need here for dialogical caution. Economics and technology are often construed as imperatives. As Stephen Hill has written, "The *experience* of technology is the experience of apparent inevitability," a statement that applies equally well to the experience of the economy.[1] Contrary to that experience, a constant theme of this chapter is that technology and the economy are not imperatives. We do have control over them, even as they have control over us. We can resist their influence and frequently do. We can resist the technologies of advertising.[2] We can switch off the radio and the TV; we can lobby for social controls on the amount and form of advertising on them. But simply by being present as something to resist or to succumb to, ads—and technology and the economy more generally—nevertheless unavoidably shape the conditions in which we form our desires and motivations.

The shaping of motivation by economics and technology is of particular importance in understanding why we consume so much more than we need. The current arrangement of the economy and the current use to which we put our technologies tend to encourage not only consumption but growth in consumption and thus in the economy. Economic growth, as many have observed, has become the most widely considered thermometer not only of economic health but of the social and political health of nations. As David Korten has written, "Perhaps no single idea is more deeply embedded in modern political culture than the belief that economic growth is the key to meeting most important human needs."[3] A rise or fall in economic growth is always headline news, and politicians constantly gear their efforts toward encouraging growth—in part because growth serves many powerful economic and technologic interests and in part because growth has become a central cultural value. Economic growth is a dialogical matter of both material interests and cultural ideals.

It is important to recognize that economic growth (and consumption too, for that matter) does not in itself lead to environmental damage. As the environmental economist Michael Jacobs notes, certain forms of economic growth, such as investment in companies that promote the use of green technologies, may in fact be beneficial to the environment.[4] However, the structure of economic interests does tend to overwhelm efforts to direct economic growth in ways that do not damage the environment. The pressure for economic growth tends to shift environmental considerations off our collective and individual agendas. Economic growth can take such a hold over our lives that issues of sustainability, environmental justice, and the rights and beauty of nature fade from concern.

A further theme of this chapter is the relationship of economic growth to economic inequality. Without economic inequality, motivations for keeping up with the Joneses through conspicuous consumption disappear, because we are all equal to the Joneses. Understanding the origins of economic inequality is thus another central problem of social organization for environmental sociology to consider.

The Needs of Money

In most of the world, money is now the principal means of arranging for one's material needs and wants, and in much of the world it is virtually the only means. Thus the prudent person maintains a good supply of money, if possible. Money is useful stuff. Money is power. Because money is so powerfully useful, most of us wish for more of it rather than less.

In order to have money, though, you have to keep it moving—to keep it mobile through the economy. Stuffing it in a mattress, even a very secure one, is a rather shortsighted practice. Because of inflation, money left by itself decreases in value. Also, the uncertainties of the market lead us to nurture our money so that we are not left short. For instance, the possibility that employers may decide to downsize keeps nearly everyone at some degree of economic risk. Another source of risk is the business cycle, the seemingly inevitable tendency of any nation's economy to take a periodic downturn, increasing unemployment and other forms of economic stress. Consequently, almost everyone with any accumulation of money seeks to build with it a cushion that will at the very least retain, if not increase, its size and comfort. For these reasons alone—putting aside for the moment the common desire for simply having more—those with money invest it, preferably in a way that offers high returns.

The inclination to seek high returns resonates throughout the economy. A bank can offer good interest rates only because of its own success in investing its depositors' money in loans, stocks, bonds, and other monetary instruments with strong returns. If the bank fails to offer competitive interest rates, it will lose depositors and possibly be forced to close. We often choose to improve on the rate of return banks offer us by investing (if we have the time and sufficient capital) in stocks, bonds, and other financial markets. Managers of mutual funds and individual investors, like banks, seek a high rate of return for these investments. Mutual fund managers want to keep customers, and individual investors want to make it worth their time to play the market themselves. Even if an individual invests in socially and environmentally responsible stocks, bonds, and mutual funds, the tendency is to seek the highest rate of return possible from those opportunities.

Those of us with no savings—perhaps most especially those of us—also usually look to increase our stock of money. We sell our labor power, auctioning it to the highest bidder. We seek to purchase goods—even positional goods—at low prices. And sometimes we trade work and goods informally to avoid depleting our scarce cash stocks.

In other words, nearly all of us find ourselves continually seeking more money—even to hold our economic place—which almost unavoidably leads us to assume the motives of the market: Seek the highest returns for labor and capital, and minimize costs. Sell high, buy low. The needs of money become our needs too.

This *generalization of the market* has the important consequence of promoting political interest in economic growth. If everyone is to have more wealth at the end of the year than at the beginning of the year, the economy must grow. This is simple math. Most politicians therefore see economic growth as a potential way to maximize the number of people who have been made wealthier—and

thus, they hope, to maximize votes. Consequently, virtually all modern governments try to promote economic growth.

But there are no guarantees that growth will increase everyone's wealth, let alone that it will increase everyone's wealth equally. Growth in overall wealth may well be accompanied by growth in inequality. Indeed, without mechanisms for continually releveling the playing field, an increase in inequality is probably an unavoidable consequence of growth. Even if everyone gains at least some wealth, the trend toward inequality will persist, since the wealthy can almost always take better advantage of investments, labor auctions, and other economic opportunities—an economic version of what the sociologist Robert Merton once called the "accumulation of advantage."[5] Thus, although in the short term economic growth may help resolve political conflict, as many politicians hope, in the long term economic growth may only exacerbate it.

Nevertheless, country after country continues to seek political salvation in economic growth. Environmental concern usually remains on the political sidelines, bumped aside by the political momentum for economic growth, and economic inequality compounds as countries increasingly bump releveling mechanisms to the sidelines as well.

The Treadmill of Production

The momentum toward economic growth, economic inequality, and environmental sidelining is greatly heightened by the competitive pressure for production faced by firms and by the disadvantaged position of workers in this competition.

To maximize profits—a common desire and, because investors have to be repaid and retained, a common need of business—each firm tries to produce more goods more cheaply than the others. Merely making a profit isn't good enough. A firm continually needs to maximize its profits or investors will withdraw their support and put their resources in a firm that does. (Employee-owned and employee-financed firms can often shelter themselves from the maximizing pressure of investors, however.) As the environmental economist Richard Douthwaite has written, "It is not just that firms like growth because it makes them more profitable: they positively need it if they are to survive."[6] Repaying and retaining investors requires economic success on a scale of months, quarters, and years, diverting attention from longer-run issues like the environment.

Firms are interested in more than just repaying and holding on to their investors, however. They are also interested in profit for themselves. Owners and management usually decide to put as much profit as they can in their own pockets, after paying their debts, paying for needed reinvestment in the business, and paying employees enough to keep them coming to work. Thus it is a virtually universal pattern, although by no means economically necessary, that employers get paid more than employees. (Indeed, it is a virtually universal pattern in both nonprofit and for-profit institutions that those who have the most control over budgets are generally the highest paid.)

In sum, the tendency of unfettered market forces is for increased production, increased environmental consequences, and increased inequality.

A Widget Treadmill

Say I'm a widget maker. To set myself up in widget making, I probably had to borrow quite a bit of money. Machinery, land, buildings, labor—all these have to be paid for, often before the business is generating sufficient returns to cover these costs. Over time, the loans have to be repaid, which requires paying back more than the value of the loan. (Creditors want their profit too.) If I raised capital through selling stock, those investors have to be repaid as well, and at a level of return that attracts their investment in the first place. In short, I'm under a lot of pressure to make a profit.

Let's say I am a good widget maker, though, and I have managed to figure out a way to keep my production high enough, my costs low enough, and my market big enough that the books are balanced. And let's say that I am doing well enough to take home a good profit for myself, not just for my creditors and investors.

But I am not the only widget maker. You make widgets too. Like me, you are also interested in profit, perhaps even a bit more interested in it. Maybe your house is not as big as mine, and your car is not as fancy. Maybe your workers have asked for a raise, and you do not want to take it out of your own paycheck, however large it may be. Maybe your suppliers have just raised their prices. Maybe your shareholders are putting pressure on you, threatening to dump your stock in favor of a more profitable enterprise. Maybe all of these things. So you try a bold move. You agree to pay your workers a bit more, but only if they agree to a new kind of widget-making machine that increases your factory's output considerably but requires fewer workers to run it. You work out a deal whereby the workforce shrinks over time through retirement. No current employees lose their jobs, you are paying higher wages, and yet your labor bills fall over time. Prices drop as your new widgets flood the market, but because your output is now so high, your profits go up nevertheless. Sounds great for your company.

Meanwhile, I've got to find a way to deal with these lower prices. My investors are increasingly dissatisfied, but I'm stuck with my old widget-making machine and my old rate of output. Your new widget-making machine is patented, and you've put a very high price on the rights to the technology. So I call up some local government officials and politicians and ask to have some labor and environmental laws relaxed. Otherwise, I tell them, I will have to close my plant or move it elsewhere. I have always been a good contributor to the political party in power. Besides, the region needs jobs. The politicians agree and relax the laws. Meanwhile, I pressure my workers into accepting a pay cut in order to keep the plant open. Because the new labor laws have undermined their bargaining position, they accept.

This solution works fine until the government in your area also relaxes the labor and environmental laws affecting your company. (You are a good campaign contributor as well.) Now I have to try something else. I have already pinched my workers as far as they will go, and they are ready to strike. The government is cracking down on illegal foreign workers, and I can't find cheaper labor anywhere else. I have also pinched my creditors as far they are willing to go before they call in their loans and shut me down. My mood is grim.

Then one of my engineers calls to say that she thinks she has a way to increase production even more, if I can just acquire the capital to put into place the even better widget-making machine that she has just dreamed up. Although the new machine will use a toxic chemical, that should be okay under the newly loosened environmental laws. The idea is intriguing, but I fear that this plan will so flood the market with cheap widgets that prices will drop even further. I still will not climb out on top.

Then I hear that the national government is mounting a summit on free trade with a formerly hostile power, and I sign on as an industry representative. The deal concludes favorably, and I suddenly have a new market for widgets. I install my engineer's new widget makers in all the production lines, having used the promise of a new market to attract the necessary capital, and things are looking great. Pollution has increased quite a bit, and the workers are still upset about their low pay, but I am turning a profit once again.

Then the widget makers in that formerly hostile country start feeling pinched, and they pass the pinch on to their own national government and their own engineers and their own laborers. They also send industrial spies into my plant to figure out what I am doing. Since free trade works both ways, pretty soon their widgets are coming over here. My profit drops, but I am still alright because I was able to pay off some loans before the foreign widgets started coming in. I consider reinvesting in a still-faster version of my new widget-making machine, but I decide to sit tight to see what you do.

You are desperate. You threaten your workers with a pay cut, and they counter-threaten with a strike. You try boosting prices and mounting an ad campaign that promotes the supposedly higher quality of your widgets. But the campaign is a bust, orders drop, and some of the backlog of widgets in your warehouse develops rust. Your reputation for quality, in fact, goes down.

So you are faced with two general choices. One is to cut your losses and shut down your factory. This move would lower the overall output of widgets and raise prices, to the benefit of your competitors—like me—who are still making widgets. This would be emotionally hard for you to take, though. The other choice is to try to attract new creditors, to come up with a new invention, to win more concessions from your workers, to discover another new market, to talk to your local government about loosening more laws or about giving you a tax break, or to find some other means of keeping the money coming in and the products going out. But if you choose the latter course, the foreign competitors and I will probably try to respond in kind, which will increase overall production, lower prices, and raise economic pressures once again—all the while diverting attention from environmental considerations.

In broad outline, this is a familiar and endlessly repeated story in industry after industry. Through competition and increased production, returns to capital—profit—decline over time, creating what the environmental sociologist Alan Schnaiberg and others have termed the "treadmill of production."[7] (See Figure 3.1.) It's a process of mutual economic pinching that gets everyone running faster but advancing only a little, if at all, and always tending to increase production and to sideline the environment.

The Struggle to Stay on the Treadmill

But there are limits to how fast people—and competing companies—can run. You can only work so hard. The common adjustment mechanism is

Figure 3.1 The treadmill of production: Mutual economic pinching keeps us always struggling to increase production, often with little regard for social and environmental consequences.

for someone to be forced off the treadmill—to choose the first option—lowering production to some kind of equilibrium with costs and prices. This is an outcome that everyone on the treadmill resists, however. The second option, making competitive adjustments, tends to be favored—at least initially. Eventually someone does get forced off the treadmill, though. But the struggle to find new customers that goes on before someone gets forced off usually means that the market expands in the process. The common result is fewer, bigger businesses—monopolization—and a higher level of overall production, often much higher. Meanwhile, those who are forced out of the market often switch to making different products or delivering different services, increasing the overall level of production of the economy by creating new treadmills.

As firms struggle to stay on the treadmill, they cut back where they can. The results are usually job losses and increased economic inequality as well as further disregard for environmental consequences. The social conditions of industrialism have generally given workers less control than management, owners, and shareholders over cutbacks. The worldwide democratic revolution of the past couple of centuries still pretty much stops at the boardroom door. By constantly pointing to the threats posed by the treadmill of production, and by pointing to the hungry pool of unemployed people, management is able to win the consent of workers to take home less than an equal division of a company's profits.

Not only do firms struggle to stay on the treadmill, people do too. Those who lose their jobs may one day find new employment, but they are often forced to accept positions lower on the economic ladder than they previously enjoyed, if they are to have a position at all. The unemployment caused by the treadmill of production may be temporary (or may not be), but it also provides another opportunity for maintaining unequal distribution of income across a corporation, and thus across society at large.

In recent years, the ability of workers to bargain for more of the treadmill's proceeds has slipped even further, leading to declining incomes, despite overall economic growth.[8] Consequently, rates of corporate profit have regularly exceeded the economic growth rate. Typical rates of corporate profit are currently in the range of 2 to 12 percent, while typical rates of economic growth are in the range of 1 to 3 percent.[9] This differential is possible only if some are getting less than others. It is thus a measure of the extent to which the pressures of the production treadmill have been turned into an opportunity for the rich to get richer.

Meanwhile, the environment continues to be largely ignored.

Development and the Growth Machine

The dynamics of the treadmill also have an important spatial dimension, which leads to the constant conflicts over development that are familiar to local communities everywhere.

As the sociologists Harvey Molotch and John Logan have observed, local businesses have an interest in local economic growth: Investment is often relatively fixed in space. Buildings, land, machines, and a well-trained workforce are hard to move around, and firms try to create as much economic activity as possible for these fixed investments. Consequently, business leaders almost universally advocate pro-growth policies that increase the circulation of capital through their local area. Although local business leaders are often in competition with one another, one thing they can usually agree on is increasing the size of the local economic pie. They band together into a variety of alliances that Molotch and Logan call "local growth coalitions." And to the extent that these coalitions can persuade local government of the importance of increasing local economic activity, growth becomes a leading cause of political leaders as well, making them a part of coalitions for growth.[10]

The result is that a city or a town acts as what Logan and Molotch termed a "growth machine," dedicated to encouraging almost any kind of economic development—frequently with little regard for environmental consequences or the wishes of affected neighborhoods. Local people have spatially fixed investments of a different sort, and because of them conflict with growth coalitions often arises. Logan and Molotch call these local investments the "use values" of a place: homes, strong neighborhoods, supportive networks of friends and family, feelings of identification with the local landscape, aesthetic appeal, a clean and secure environment. Business, on the other hand, is interested in the "exchange values" of places, the ways that places can be used to make money. The use values that local people gain from a place are often incompatible with the exchange values business can gain. Maintaining open land for a park versus using that land for a housing development is a common example.[11]

And when there is conflict, the pro-growth business interests typically win. Neighborhood groups tend to be far less organized than local growth coalitions and are usually less able to influence the political process. Moreover, neighborhoods may feel divided allegiances between what is happening in some other neighborhood and their own economic interests, sometimes leading to not-in-my-backyard politics as opposed to not-in-anybody's-backyard politics. In the face of such divided interests, local governments tend to follow the pro-growth policies of the more united, better-organized business community.

A further result of the politics of the growth machine is an environmental conflict in the tasks we set for local government. On the one hand, government is expected to promote economic growth; on the other hand, it is expected to monitor and regulate environmental impacts.[12] Sometimes this dual role results in well-thought-out development projects that promote economic growth without compromising the local environment. But, depending on the outcome of the political process, it can also turn government into an economic fox that guards the environmental chicken coop.

The "Invisible Elbow"

Adam Smith, the eighteenth-century founder of modern economic theory, envisioned that individual competitive decisions would guide us all toward prosperity by increasing production and efficiency. He suggested the famous image of the "invisible hand" to describe this process. The treadmill of production, however, makes the economy act like what Michael Jacobs has described as the "invisible elbow." Even if the goal is merely to hold one's place on the treadmill, economic actors are involved in a constant jostle. Although this jostling is often unintentional—Jacobs says it is usually unintentional—both people and the environment get compromised in the process. "Elbows are sometimes used to push people aside in the desire to get ahead," Jacob writes.

> But more often elbows are not used deliberately at all; they knock things over inadvertently. Market forces cause environmental degradation by both methods. Sometimes there is deliberate and intended destruction, the foreseen cost of ruthless consumption. But more usually degradation occurs by mistake, the unwitting result of other, smaller decisions.[13]

The elbowing effect that Jacobs describes is more technically described by economists as "externalities," economic effects not taken into account in the decision making in a market. Externalities may be divided into two broad types. Increased inequality and pollution are examples of *negative externalities*, costs not included in economic decision making and generally borne by those who did not make the decision. There may also be *positive externalities*, benefits that were not taken into account in an economic decision, and which may have wide utility, such as more efficient production or, conceivably, an economic arrangement in which individual economic choices promote greater equality and less pollution. The problem with Smith's image of the invisible hand is its rosy suggestion that the treadmill's market competition leads only to positive externalities. Jacobs's invisible elbow points out that negative externalities are also common consequences of the treadmill.

Externalities are not necessarily invisible, though, as Jacobs also points out. As we rush along the treadmill, we may be well aware of some of the consequences of flying elbows. The *visibility of externalities* is enormously significant for our social decision making. The ability to see and appreciate an externality, whether positive or negative, is the first step toward creating the social conditions that promote the former over the latter. If we are unaware of something, we are certainly unlikely to direct our actions with that something in mind. Creating this visibility is a political act of considerable social and environmental importance.

Factory Farms for Iowa Hogs

The controversial expansion of "factory farms" for hogs in Iowa illustrates well the politics of treadmills, the spatial conflicts of a growth machine, and the visibility of externalities.

Iowa is regularly the United States' leading producer of corn and soybeans. But unless you have a huge farm, it is hard to make a living raising only corn and soybeans. Decades on the treadmill of production have cut profit margins to the breaking point for many Iowa farms. Consequently, many of them have long been converting their cheap grain into something more valuable: pork. For years this worked quite well, as wholesale pork prices routinely ran some 20 to 30 percent above farmers' costs. Iowa became the country's leading pork producer, accounting for some 26 percent of the nation's total production.[14]

Figure 3.2   A large-scale hog confinement facility in Hamilton County, Iowa. Such "factory farms" for livestock are becoming increasingly common throughout the industrialized world, despite concerns about their implications for human health, animal health, economic justice, and the environment. Note this facility's attempt to ward off criticism through use of patriotic symbolism.

Eventually, though, large investors learned of this windfall. Since about 1992, several large corporations—Premium Standard, Murphy Family Farms (now owned by Smithfield Foods), Heartland Pork, and Iowa Select, among others—have been erecting huge hog production facilities in Iowa or contracting with local farmers to do it for them. "Hog lots" or "large-scale hog confinements," as they are often called, raise hogs indoors in vast metal buildings. Commonly 3,000 to 5,000 hogs are raised at a single site, divided among several buildings. The biggest facility in Iowa can handle 30,000 animals.[15] Feeding, watering, and waste removal are handled by machine, and sprinkler systems keep the hogs cool in the hot Iowa summers. Grain is trucked in from surrounding farms. The hogs never see the light of day. (See Figure 3.2.)

Aside from size, factory farms for hogs actually represent little in the way of technological innovation. Iowa farmers have been using hog confinement systems since the mid-1970s, albeit on a much smaller scale. Thousands of Iowa

farms have small "confinement units," largely built by the farmers themselves; each of these farms raise up to a few thousand animals a year using techniques similar to those of the larger corporate confinements. Even the scale is not all that new. Large-scale hog confinements have been in use in Europe since the 1970s, particularly in Denmark and the Netherlands. Some "contract growers" even established a few large-scale hog confinements in Iowa in the 1970s and 1980s, although these were still considerably smaller than the massive units that are currently sprouting in rural Iowa.

The massive scale of the new confinements has touched off a heated debate in Iowa about their social and environmental consequences. The environmental problems mostly relate to the vast quantities of manure the big hog factories produce. Hogs are large animals, and they do little but eat in these facilities. A confinement with 10,000 hogs produces the equivalent effluent of a city of about 40,000 humans. The new large-scale hog confinements, however, have not erected the equivalent sewage treatment systems. Instead, the manure flows into artificial lagoons where it is stored until it can be applied as fertilizer to surrounding fields.

Using manure as fertilizer is generally a good thing. Properly handled, it turns a waste product into a resource. But when so much manure is concentrated on a single site, proper handling becomes very difficult. Manure lagoons often leak into groundwater and streams, causing fish kills and water pollution. Sometimes the lagoon walls collapse, resulting in massive manure spills. Between 1996 and 2002, Iowa suffered 152 spills from hog and cattle manure lagoons. Some 5.7 million fish are estimated to have died when the spills hit the state's waterways.[16] Also, for convenience, the manure is generally applied to the fields closest to the lagoons, often at rates far above what the crop and the soil can absorb— again resulting in water pollution.

Another side effect is a terrific smell, sometimes strong enough to drive neighbors from their homes when the wind is wrong. Hog manure is pungent stuff, but the manure in storage lagoons is particularly strong because of the anaerobic bacterial activity promoted by the airless conditions in a big lagoon. The anaerobic smell of hog manure now pervades the Iowa countryside and even wafts into town, especially when the large-scale confinement operations pump out their lagoons and apply the manure to the fields. Property values are down so far in some affected areas that owners who want to move find they can't sell their homes. Houses have been simply abandoned in some cases, and have been given up to vandalism and to methamphetamine labs.[17]

The social controversy centers around the threat that the big operations pose to Iowa's smaller hog farmers. The market for Iowa pork is not endless, and farmers, rural communities, and their advocates protest that the large-scale operations are forcing prices down and driving a lot of Iowa farmers out of business. Indeed, during the winter of 1998–1999, the price farmers got for hogs dropped to around 9 cents a pound—far

below the 40 to 43 cents a pound considered the average break-even point for Iowa hog farmers. Prices later recovered, but thousands of small farms were driven out of hog production during the market crash. In the early 1990s, Iowa had some 35,000 hog farms. As of 2001, there were only 10,500.[18]

The corporate hog producers argue that the big operations create new jobs for those who work in them. Small farm advocates counter that big operations destroy more livelihoods than they create, that the new jobs are lower paid, that independent farmers are being converted into non-unionized workers, and that communities will ultimately suffer. Moreover, there have been a number of charges of exclusionary links between meat packers and the large-scale hog producers, shutting out small farms from sales and forcing them to accept lower prices.[19]

Still other issues are the humaneness of the production method for the animals themselves and the human health effects of the meat. Is it right, critics ask, to raise animals completely inside, where they are given almost no room and where they know no world other than concrete and metal? Moreover, to raise animals in such close confinement, the big operations must mix feed with a "maintenance dose" of antibiotics that helps prevent the rapid spread of disease among the animals in the confinement barns. Outbreaks are still frequent, however, and so the animals often receive larger doses. Plus industrial farms like these often feed hogs (as well as chickens and steers) antibiotics as a growth promoter. Many of these antibiotics are the same ones used in human medicine. There is now widespread concern among health professionals that agricultural antibiotic use is an important factor in the well-documented declining ability of antibiotics to fight human diseases, as the constant presence of antibiotics selects for drug-resistant strains of bacteria. One study found that 70 percent of all antibiotic use in the United States is for livestock production, mostly for uses other than the treatment of sick animals.[20] (Another 14 percent is used as a pesticide in fruit and vegetable production.)[21] In light of this, the American Public Health Association has called on the U.S. government to eliminate the nonmedical use of antibiotics in agriculture, and the American Medical Association has issued a similar policy statement.[22] The European Union has already banned the practice.[23] But it still goes on in hog confinements in the United States and Canada, big time.

The social and environmental consequences of large-scale hog confinements are classic examples of the negative externalities of a production treadmill. Through political debate, these externalities have become socially visible, generating considerable controversy and conflict. Often people have found their allegiances divided, particularly when they, relatives, or friends are receiving some economic benefit from a big hog lot. Rural communities have been split. In one small Iowa town that I am familiar with, some people stopped speaking to each other in church and took to shaking their fists at the passing pickup trucks of locals who supported large-scale hog confinements. There was even a protest on the town green. These are not actions undertaken lightly in small towns.

The acrimony over these issues eventually prodded the state government to take some action. The Iowa governor established a commission, Iowa State University began hosting an annual conference on livestock odor, and the state legislature pondered new laws. The lobbying was intense. David Yepson, a prominent Iowa political commentator, called it "the hottest issue in Iowa."[24]

As of 2003, it would be safe to say that large-scale hog confinement interests have pretty much won the debate, at least for the time being. In 1995, the Iowa legislature passed a law imposing some mild environmental regulations on lagoon building and manure spreading as well as requiring that new hog lots be at least 1,000 feet from any homes. The legislature also required hog lot owners to pay into a special fund for cleaning up the sites of abandoned hog lots, should they later move on. But the legislature also banned what it described as "nuisance lawsuits" against the facilities and reaffirmed that localities do not have a right to regulate hog lots on their own, thus taking away the main legal tools that communities might use to stop the construction of hog lots.[25]

Basically, the hog lot operators got what they wanted. The protection against nuisance suits and local regulation gave the industry great latitude in building large-scale confinements. The environmental legislation introduced some constraints, but in exchange these rules gave the industry a way to demonstrate that it was being a "good neighbor" by following the standards set by government. And the main externalities remain external. Currently under state law, hog lot operators do not have to pay for the smell and the social inequality they create, nor for any water pollution they cause. (There have been a few fines leveled for fish kills caused by major spills, however.) These costs are passed along to local water users, the neighbors who must deal with the smell, and the government agencies that provide the social services—unemployment compensation, job training and job placement, welfare, and possibly substance abuse prevention—that may be needed for people who have lost their jobs and farms.

Part of the reason the large-scale confinement operators have thus far won the debate is because of their success in making a couple of political arguments. First, the large operators pointed to the rapid development of large-scale hog confinements in North Carolina, America's second largest pork production region, since the late 1980s. While North Carolina has been gaining market share in pork production, Iowa, although still number one, has been losing ground in most years. Second, the Iowa hog lot companies argued that their production would be essential for holding on to meat packing, another important Iowa industry that is under threat from elsewhere. Although they didn't call it this, the confinement industry argued that the imperatives of the treadmill of production require big hog lots for Iowa, and preferential treatment to bring them there.

Small farm and environmental advocates disagree. Small Iowa farms kept the meat-packing business going for years, and could do so in the future, they argue. Also, they point to different production techniques that would be competitive with confinements if they didn't get such preferential treatment, and which are far friendlier to the environment and far more manageable for small farms. There has been much interest in one technology in particular, something called "hoop houses," in which about 150 hogs are reared in simple, open-ended, fabric-covered buildings about 75 feet long, 30 feet across, and 20 feet high, with the floor piled with deep beds of straw. The animals get fresh air and get to root in the straw. The straw traps their manure and its smell, while helping control disease through the sterilizing heat of the composting straw and manure mixture. They're cheap to build. Hogs seem to like them. Antibiotics are usually not necessary. And they don't stink. But because the big meat-packing plants would prefer to deal with a few big customers, and because many of the costs of confinements have been externalized, hoop houses have gained only a small (but steadily increasing) share of the Iowa hog market.

Meanwhile, the search for new markets is on. Trade missions have been shuttling off to Southeast Asia, trying to find new markets for Iowa pork among the burgeoning economies of that part of the world. The Iowa governor has even gone along, another example of government picking up the tab for the treadmill of production. Some small producers have been experimenting with marketing the meat from hoop houses and other non-confinement systems as a "natural" product among consumers concerned about health, animal welfare, the environment, and the condition of farmers and rural communities. A substantial market for such meat has already developed in Europe and shows signs of developing in the United States and Canada.[26] At the time of this writing, however, the governor has yet to mount any trade missions on behalf of such a product.

The Social Creation of Treadmills

Despite the air of inevitability that often pervades economic discussions, it is human actors who direct the course of economic development. As the controversy over large-scale hog confinements in Iowa demonstrates, the treadmill of production is fundamentally a social process—the outcome of the interests of various social actors, the power that those actors have, and the level of their concern for the interests of others.

The Treadmills Inside

The treadmill of production also depends upon how we understand our interests—that is, upon the ideas and sentiments we bring to bear on our lives. In other words, there is an important ideal dimension to the treadmill of production.

For example, our productivist mentality depends in part on our sense that hard work is a moral virtue—a historically recent notion of virtue, in fact. (Chapter 6 considers the origin of this notion of virtue in some detail when we explore the theories of the sociologist Max Weber.) We usually regard laziness as somehow immoral, even when working harder will only secure far more wealth than we physically need. In other words, we work hard not only to maintain our footing on the treadmill of production but also because we have internalized the notion that hard work is virtuous.

The idea that hard work is virtuous is particularly pronounced in the United States and Japan, as many have commented. (See Figure 2.2.) The prevalence of this attitude is likely part of the reason vacation time is typically about 2 weeks a year in these two countries. Japanese and American workers have not fought harder for longer vacations in part because doing so would seem culturally inappropriate, which in turn perpetuates the cultural inappropriateness of long vacations. Meanwhile, both countries fall ever deeper into the cycle of work-and-spend discussed in Chapter 2.

In other words, the treadmill of production is not just an external pressure that we must conform to; it is also a pressure that comes from within. At some level, most of us actually want to work hard—we think reflects well on us—although

Figure 3.3   Interconnected treadmills.

probably not as hard as the treadmill of production often requires.

Given the speed increasingly required to stay on the production treadmill, it is probably materially advantageous that most of us are committed to the idea that hard work is a virtue. This advantage does not mean, however, that external forces determine internal ones. The relationship between external forces and internal forces is a dialogical one. True, hard work helps one stay on the treadmill, but hard work also leads to an acceleration of the treadmill—thereby creating conditions that encourage people to work even harder. Internal social factors such as a person's values thus support and are supported by external social factors like the economic speed of a production treadmill. The treadmill within and the treadmill outside create each other.

The interplay between the pressures of the external and the internal is equally characteristic of the treadmill of consumption. Like the virtue of hard work, the desire for *more* is something that nearly all of us from time to time feel inside. And yet these wants of consumption are based on material standards that, because of competition, are continually going up. The desire for *more* is thus both an internal source and an external product of the treadmill of consumption—another dialogue between the ideal and the material dimensions of social life.

The Dialogue of Production and Consumption

The treadmill of production and the treadmill of consumption are also dialogically interconnected. (See Figure 3.3.) Increasing the pace of one treadmill increases the pace of the other. But also, the desire to increase the pace of one treadmill depends in part upon the social conditions created by the other.

For example, the desire for *more* is propelled by both the treadmill of consumption and the treadmill of production through the relationship between *more* and profit. Because you need profit to survive on the production treadmill, the treadmill of production encourages people to regard profit as a virtue. But in order to demonstrate your success in attaining the virtue of profit, you need to consume *more*. You need to buy a BMW or its equally conspicuous equivalent. Of course, consuming *more* is a desire that, because of the consumption treadmill, you likely already had. We want profit to consume just as we consume to demonstrate profit. It's a dialogue—although perhaps not one well calculated to support sustainability, environmental justice, or the rights and beauty of nature.

Hard work is another internal treadmill that is propelled by both production and consumption. Hard work keeps us going on the production treadmill, as the previous section describes. But it also keeps us going on the consumption treadmill by helping us to rationalize inequalities in consumption. "God helps those who help themselves," we often hear. Perhaps the real theological help is moral: relieving guilty consciences through the message that it's alright to consume *more* as long as you worked hard for it.

The internal treadmills of *more* and of hard work, then, dialogically connect the treadmills of production and consumption. Of course, you cannot have production without consumption and vice versa—at least not for long—as classical economics readily recognizes. But classical economics typically treats production and consumption as if they were separately generated phenomena, balanced by price. That balancing is often the only acknowledgment of dialogical interconnections. But what a fully dialogical approach suggests is that production and consumption do not merely balance each other; they create each other.

Moreover, the treadmills of production and consumption do not just mutually condition internal values like hard work and the desire for more. They also dialogically organize the external circumstances in which we have these values.

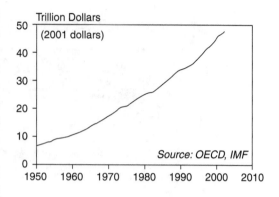

Figure 3.4   Accelerating treadmills: Rising gross world product, 1950–2002.

Here is where economic inequality plays its most important dialogical role. The inequality created by the treadmill of production helps create the conditions under which the Joneses are constantly rising above us, fueling the treadmill of consumption. That fueling in turn creates the opportunity for further acceleration of the production treadmill, and its frequently unequal economic outcomes. It's a vicious dialogical circle: The production treadmill creates inequality, which creates the consumption treadmill, which creates more inequality and a further speeding of the production treadmill, thus keeping the whole cycle whirling ever faster. (See Figure 3.4.)

The Dialogue of State and Market

Another central dialogic relationship is between the state and the market. Markets function best when the state intervenes least, we are often told. The glory of the West is its "free market" economy, as opposed to the failed centrally planned economies of the old Soviet bloc. Here's the classic definition of that glory, from an introductory economics textbook of a few years ago: "Markets in which governments do not intervene are called *free markets*."[27]

But recall the way government is hooked on the treadmill too. Western politicians know that their political future hangs from the thread of economic growth, as this chapter has discussed. And recall the way that businesses encourage politicians to keep their focus here through lobbying and political contributions. That's because both politicians and businesses recognize that state intervention is in fact as central to capitalist "free market" economies as it is to a "centrally planned" economy. A heck of a lot of central planning, and central control, goes on in both. Where would a market economy be without a police force and a court system to enforce contracts, limit fraud, regulate trade, and establish product standards? Where would it be without a trustworthy money supply? Or without trade agreements with other nations and the political muscle, including military muscle, to back them up? Or without an independent body to enforce property rights? Otherwise you might try to steal from me, and I from you, without fear of retribution from anyone but each other. And no market society could last long today if it ran so roughshod over workers and the environment that its political legitimacy was undermined. Plus, there are all the other "free" services that government provides the market—like roads, an educated workforce, and a healthy and productive ecosystem. Moreover, in terms of sheer dollars spent, government is about half to a third of the total economy in most Western nations—including the United States, that paragon of the free market. In other words, the treadmill is hooked on government as much as the other way around.

But isn't this heavy role of government the main problem facing Western economies today? Sure, maybe we can't get rid of government entirely, but can't we get rid of all the red tape and regulations, or at least most of it? Can't we at least have a *freer* market?

The answer to this question is to ask another question: Freer for whom?[28] Let's take a typical case of government intervention to enhance a "free market," like the banning of nuisance law suits against hog lots in Iowa and the prevention of local control over where hog lots can be placed. Is there any less regulation in Iowa as a result? It is true that hog lot owners are freer to do what they want, without fear of retribution, but those who object to hog lots are now a lot less free. It's much harder to sue hog lots now. If you meet an unsympathetic judge who deems your suit a "nuisance," you'll have to pay the legal fees of the other side— a strong restraint on advancing any suit at all, no matter how strong you think your case is. And local people can't use local zoning ordinances to control hog lots either. Or take the "clear skies" initiative recently advanced by the U.S. government. Under it, industrial facilities would not have to upgrade pollution equipment when they upgrade plants, unless the upgrade is more than 20 percent of the cost of that aspect of the facility. Factories would be freer to do what they want to do, but everyone else would be a lot less free to pressure factories to clean up their pollution.

Freedom is like that. Freedom for one person entails constraint for someone else. As an old English proverb put it, "Freedom for the pike is death for the minnow." This is why the philosopher Isaiah Berlin, from whom I learned of that proverb, used to speak of two kinds of freedom: *freedom-from* and *freedom-to*, the freedom from others stopping you from doing what you want and the freedom to take agency over the conditions of your life, which is to say other people. Berlin liked to call freedom-from "negative liberty" and freedom-to "positive liberty." The pike eating minnows experiences negative liberty from anyone stopping it from gorging at the minnows' expense. If minnows could stop the pike, perhaps by enlisting the help of some piscine police force, they would experience positive liberty to take action against being gorged on.[29]

Which makes it sound like free markets are about negative liberty and the absence of regulations while positive liberty is what we get through regulation. So if you want more freedom-from—more negative freedom—you need deregulation. Many have read the implications of Berlin's argument this way.[30]

But that is to see negative liberty in purely individualistic terms. For you to have freedom-from, someone else will probably have to be denied it.

For hog lots to have freedom *from* complaint, others must be denied freedom *to* complaint. In other words, freedom-from requires as much regulation as freedom-to. It's just a different kind of regulation. The "deregulation" that many call for in support of the negative freedom of the "free market" or a "freer market" is what we might call *negative regulation*, regulation-*from*—that is, regulation *from* interference. The kind of regulation we are used to calling regulation is *positive regulation*, regulation-*to*—that is, regulation *to* interfere.[31]

And they both require copious lines of legal code in the statute books of every government. Take the U.S. Code of Federal Regulations. In 1980, it took 164 volumes to hold its 102,195 pages. By 2002, it had risen to 207 volumes and 145,099 pages—a 42 percent increase in pages—despite years of efforts at "deregulation" and "reinventing government."[32] But there was no deregulation here. Rather, it was mainly re-regulation of the negative sort. And given the increase in the lines of code required to contain it all, the implication we can draw is that a "freer market" actually requires *more* regulation and interference by government, not less.

The Social Creation of Economics

We can summarize the usual results of these dialogues as follows:

- Decline in rates of economic return
- Bargaining with labor
- Bargaining with the state
- Search for new markets
- Fewer workers and more investment per unit of production
- Monopolization
- Increased production
- Increased state intervention and regulation
- Social inequality
- Reinforcement of the desire for *more* and the virtue of hard work
- Reinforcement of the treadmill of consumption

- Conflicts over development
- Sidelining of environmental concerns

None of these outcomes is inevitable. As Alan Schnaiberg, John Logan, and Harvey Molotch have reminded us, treadmills are political. That is, treadmills result from the actions of human agents pursuing what they take to be their interests and sentiments. If we do not like the result, it must be because we have not fully understood what our interests and sentiments are, or because the current distribution of power has prevented us from attaining our true interests and sentiments.

To achieve the outcomes we desire, we must first recognize the *social creation of economics*. The pinching pressures of the treadmills of production and consumption encourage us to think of the economy as something outside of us, over which we have little control, as an external structure to which we must submit. And true, the economy has power over us. But we also have power over it. The economy is a result of countless individual decisions, as classical economics has long taught, with effects that present themselves as external structures. Yet it is precisely the fact that the economy begins with real human agents that makes it dialogically possible to direct the economy—by changing the circumstances in which we make our individual decisions.

Those economic circumstances are the result of bargaining among social actors such as the state, labor, and management. They are the result of legal precedents, of moral judgments, and of power relations within society. They are the result of the invisibility of externalities and the current limits to our imagination. They are the result of negative regulation and positive regulation, as well as negative liberty and positive liberty. Economies create societies, but societies create economies. Through bargaining between competing interests, through the selective involvement of the state, through the dynamics of the distribution of social power, through the moral visions of those involved, we shape the economic structures that shape us.

The Needs of Technology

"Not another call! I'll never get this lecture written!" I groaned as I reached for my ringing office phone. "Hello. This is Mike Bell," I said, hoping my impatience wouldn't show in the tone of my voice.

"I'm glad I reached you, Professor Bell," came a pleasant middle-aged male voice.

"Well, I hope I can be of some help," I replied, trying to sound interested.

"I hope so too," he quipped, and we both laughed. "You were recommended to me as a speaker for a conference I'm organizing on how local communities can adapt to technological change."

I was warming up to him. Still, he said *"can* adapt," I noted to myself. I wonder if what he really means is *should* adapt.

"That sounds interesting," I cautiously replied. "Who is sponsoring the conference and whom do you expect to attend?"

"I'm the development coordinator for several towns in the northern part of the state, and we're trying to put together an evening program for local people about hog lots. Are you familiar with the issue?"

"Oh sure," I said. "Of course." I lived in Iowa at the time, and you'd have to have been a complete recluse to avoid hearing about the controversy.

"Then you'll appreciate the importance of the conference," my caller continued. "The problem is, people don't like change. But hog lots are coming, and coming fast. So we'd like you to talk about how communities can adapt to them."

I thought for a moment. It did sound like he meant *should*, not *can*. Finally, I replied, "This sounds like an important conference. I'd be happy to speak. But I'd like to speak not just about how communities can adapt to technological change. I'd also want to discuss how technologies can adapt to people. After all, it is people that invent technology."

Now it was his turn to say, "That sounds interesting." Then he added, "I'll have to discuss it with our planning board, though. I'll get back to you."

A week later he called again, a bit more curt. "The board decided that it would like to keep the focus on how communities should adapt," he said. "Thanks very much for your willingness to participate, but . . ."

Can adapt had indeed become *should* adapt. He said it himself.

Technology as a Dialogue

I tell this story to introduce another of the central dialogues of environmental sociology, the *dialogue of technology.*[33] People often point to technology as one of the great motors of social change. One of the truisms of modern life is how much we have been changed by our technologies. The automobile, the tractor, the airplane, electronic media, birth control, the computer, the atomic bomb—these are all frequently cited examples of the role of technology as a social actor, as an independent agent of social change. Technology is also often seen as central to the pinching demands of the production treadmill. Indeed, we are often asked to accept the fact that more change will be coming in our lives because of technology. As my caller suggested, we had better be prepared for it, like it or not.

Our cultural training as Western modernists may make it particularly hard to see technology as an ecological dialogue, as an interplay between the material and the ideal, the external and the internal—as something that conditions our lives at the same time that we condition it. The metaphor of the machine, with its vision of sequential and linear causality, has become our master metaphor of technology. The word *technology* itself immediately conjures up images of machines. But a dialogical conception more accurately describes what technology is and does. A dialogical conception helps us to see that, like the economy, technology is not a mechanical imperative—unless we allow it to become one. Technology, too, is a social creation as well as a force that shapes the forms our social creativity takes.

For critics and supporters alike, there is great rhetorical attractiveness in a deterministic view of technology. In an attempt to energize us into action against a form of technology, critics sometimes portray it as a grim juggernaut that is rolling over our lives.[34] On the other hand, supporters like my phone caller often claim that there is little we can do once the Pandora's box of technology has been opened, and that we had better make way for the changes that are bound to result. "Get big or get out" was the dictum of U.S. Secretary of Agriculture Earl Butz in the 1970s, explaining why American farmers had no choice but to buy bigger tractors and bigger farms.

Thus, fear mongering is used by both sides. The logic of neither argument holds up, however. If technology is an uncontrollable juggernaut, then there is no point in asking us to try to resist it: We can't. If technology is an unclosable Pandora's box, then there is no need to ask us to make way for it: It is coming anyhow. Both arguments, in fact, logically depend on our having at least some control over technology.

As sociologists Keith Warner and Lynn England argue, technology is more than mere machines: Technology is all the techniques we have for gaining our desired ends. The knowledge of how to work a computer is just as much technology as the computer itself. Technology is the "how-to" of life, Warner and England write.[35] As such it is not the sole product of external forces: of juggernauts and Pandora's boxes. Technology is something that human agents create. Plenty of human choice is involved.

But once we have made those choices, we will find that our future options have gained not only new possibilities but new limits. In other words, technology is not only a *how-to,* it is also a *have-to.* Humans make technology, and technology makes humans. Technology shapes the conditions of our lives and thereby helps direct the kind of choices we will feel compelled or inclined to make in the future. Technology does indeed structure our lives, but it is we who make that structure and pattern our lives accordingly. *Technology is political.*

Technology is thus not a mechanical structure but a *social structure,* a form of social organization that we control as it controls us.

Technology as a Social Structure

The automobile is an increasingly prevalent example of technology as a social structure. The automobile industry produces 41 million cars every year, and the world fleet now stands at some 531 million.[36] Nearly every household in Canada, the United States, and Australia has at least one, and the average for the United States is almost two (1.9, to be precise).[37] The United States now has more vehicles for personal use than it has drivers (204 million vehicles for 191 million drivers, as of 2001).[38] Vehicle-to-people ratios are lower in other countries, but rising rapidly. Only 20 percent of Japanese households had cars in 1970, but 72 percent did in 1988. Comparable figures apply to most of Europe. In France, 20 percent of households now have two or more cars.[39] Many poorer countries are also seeing big increases. In 1979, the roughly 1 billion people of China had only 150,000 private cars; by 1996, they had 2.7 million; by 2003, more than 10 million.[40] Car sales in India increased by 40 percent in 1994 alone, and annual sales are now more than 700,000 per year.[41]

The consequences are truly catastrophic. (See Figure 3.5.) More than 40,000 people die in traffic accidents each year in the United States, nearly as many Americans as died during the entire Vietnam War and far more than die of AIDS each year. For those over the age of 1 and under the age of 35, traffic accidents are the leading cause of death in the United States.[42] The 6 million annual car crashes in the United States injure almost 3 million people, meaning that more than 1 out of 100 people will be injured in any given year.[43] There is thus a very high likelihood that lifelong residents of the United States will be injured in an automobile accident at some point in their lives.

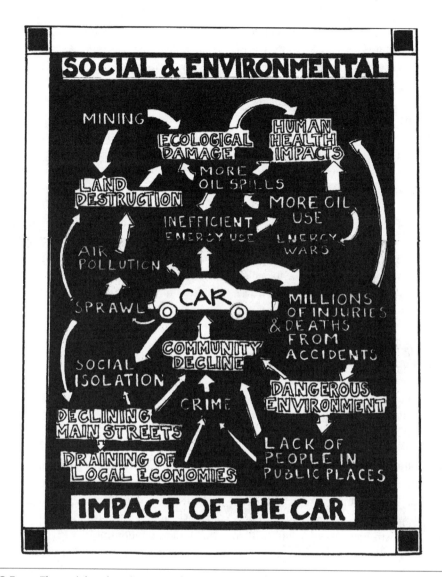

Figure 3.5   The social and environmental consequences of the car.

The death rate per capita from automobile accidents is even higher in Portugal, Greece, Estonia, and Latvia. But U.S. figures are among the highest in the developed world—mainly because Americans drive so much, as U.S. death rates per mile driven are relatively low.[44] Worldwide, about 1.2 million people die each year in traffic accidents, and many tens of millions more are injured.[45] Most of these are in the less developed nations, where road conditions are often very poor, despite fewer cars.

And the trend is up. The World Health Organization reports that in 1998 road accidents were the ninth leading cause of death injury worldwide, and projects that if current trends hold it will be the third leading cause by 2020.[46]

Millions of other animals also die each year because of traffic. In Britain, one study found that roads claim the lives of tens of millions of birds a year.[47] Comparable losses no doubt occur in all automobile-dominated countries.

Cars and trucks remain serious polluters, despite efforts to clean up emissions. Growth in the use of cars and trucks has wiped out much of the gain from emission controls, and most large cities remain enveloped in smog and fine particulates. In Britain, according to a government study, automobile exhaust kills 10,000 people a year.[48] A 2000 study published in the leading British medical journal, *Lancet*, found that in France, Switzerland, and Austria 40,000 people die every year from causes that can be linked back to air pollution, about half of it from cars.[49] The figure for the United States is 70,000 per year. The figure for the world, according to the World Health Organization, is 3 million per year—again with about half of that due to vehicle exhaust.[50] So the worst damage that cars and trucks do may be effects that we rarely think about and connect to them.

Cars and trucks are also important contributors to global warming and acid rain; according to one estimate, some 15 percent of greenhouse gas emissions come from automobile tailpipes.[51] Motor vehicles also have substantial indirect environmental impacts through the mining required to supply vehicle manufacturers with raw materials, the oil spills and other toxic waste disasters associated with keeping the fuel coming, and the consumptive patterns of land use with which cars and trucks are associated. Road noise can also affect the reproductive success of many wildlife species.[52]

Traffic has a huge impact on the quality of places. Traffic is noisy and dirty and turns even quiet streets into potential sources of death for us and our children. Cars bring out the worst emotions in drivers. Inside their wheeled cocoons, drivers commonly experience fury over slight infringements on the social decorum of traffic. "Road rage" is what the media call it. Drivers cut each other off, zoom close past bicycles, and accelerate right up to jaywalking pedestrians, threatening all with death and maiming. Streets are a major means by which we encounter the wider community. Through their danger, noise, and dirt, automobiles have made our daily encounters with one another hazardous and unpleasant.

By terrorizing public life in these ways, cars contribute to the erosion of social commitment.

Why, then, are cars so popular? The standard answer is because cars are so convenient. Cars vastly increase our personal mobility, it is often said. They are an incredibly flexible and relatively inexpensive form of transportation. They protect travelers from inclement weather. They reduce physical labor. Cars, it is claimed, are simply a better way of getting around. To be sure, traffic is sometimes a problem, and so too is parking; but, goes the standard answer, bigger roads and parking lots can take care of these annoyances. And of course, we also gain a certain amount of personal pride and romance from owning an automobile, leading to what Americans term their "love affair" with the "dream machine." The pride and romance are understandable when one considers the superiority of automotive transport. Right?

The Social Organization of Convenience

At the center of this familiar argument about the benefits of cars is the image of technological choice, of opportunity, of convenience, of cars as a better how-to. Taking a bus or a train is so inconvenient. It is no wonder that people across the world are adopting the car as soon as they have opportunity, we are often told.

But the convenience of cars is not a mere matter of a machine that makes our lives easier. A dialogical understanding of technology points to the *social organization of convenience*—the way that we often set up our lives around a particular technology so that it becomes difficult to do things any other way. (See Figure 3.6.) A dialogical understanding of technology thus points to the common transformation of a how-to into a have-to. If we allow the alternatives to disappear, it indeed becomes hard to do things any other way—which is precisely what has happened with cars.

Yet the transformation of a how-to into a have-to is by no means inevitable, as cars also show. It depends on how we spend our money and allocate

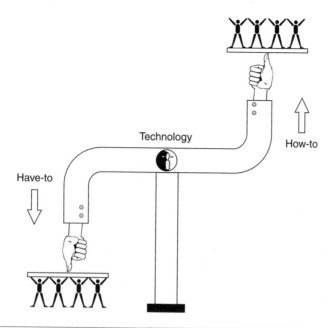

Have-to

Technology

How-to

Figure 3.6   The social organization of convenience.

our resources. Supporters of the car often point to the substantial government subsidies given to public transportation. Private transportation, the argument goes, pays its own way through gasoline taxes and highway tolls. But many studies have challenged this view by pointing to the hidden subsidies that cars receive—costs that are paid out of general revenues, not automobile-specific taxes.[53] In the United States alone, according to a study by the World Resources Institute, such subsidies total $300 billion every year.[54]

Some $68 billion of the hidden subsidies for cars goes to road and highway services. Highway patrols; parking enforcement; police work in tracking down stolen vehicles and responding to accidents; and street maintenance—these are very expensive car-related services. Another $13 billion goes to road and bridge construction and repair not covered by gas taxes and other user fees. Road maintenance—snow removal, patching, pavement marking, litter removal, grass cutting on the sides of highways—adds another $12 billion not covered by user fees.

One of the largest hidden subsidies is for parking. Approximately 87 percent of trips in the United States are by car, and 90 percent of these travelers find a free parking space when they get there.[55] The average annual cost to business of one free parking space is $1,000 per year, taking into account what it costs to build and maintain a parking lot and the lost opportunity of developing that land for something else. The same is true for the "free" parking spaces provided by shops. These costs are passed along to customers through higher prices. Of course, drivers help pay for those prices when they shop, and all of a company's employees who drive to work get the same subsidy for parking. But anyone who arrives at work or at a store by some other means is also paying for those spaces and is being denied what amounts to a salary bonus and a price discount for the car drivers—to the tune of $85 billion per year.

Motor vehicle accidents cost the United States $358 billion a year. Most of this cost is borne by drivers through their own insurance. But some $55 billion is not, largely because of the medical costs incurred by the pedestrians and bicyclists who are involved in accidents.

Additional hidden costs include the price of military intervention to keep oil flowing from places like the Middle East and the cost of air pollution on health, crops, and buildings. These figures are hard to pin down, but the World Resources Institute study estimated them at roughly $60 billion a year. Some other studies put these numbers far higher.[56]

The $300 billion in hidden subsidies for cars and trucks works out to 15 cents for each of the 2 trillion miles Americans drive each year. If a vehicle gets 25 miles to the gallon, the annual subsidy works out to $3.75 per gallon. Per vehicle, the subsidy is $1,579 a year.[57] Another study—which included higher figures for the health costs of air pollution, pollution cleanup, and a figure for the economic inefficiencies of automobile dependence—came up with a whopping nine bucks a gallon and $5,000 per car per year.[58] No wonder Americans drive so much.

The hidden subsidies for the automobile are classic examples of negative externalities, costs that the actor does not directly bear. Hidden subsidies are more than economic matters, though. They are also political matters. Powerful lobbies—such as the American Automobile Manufacturers Association, American Automobile Association, the American Petroleum Institute, and the various road-building associations—do what they can to keep these subsidies flowing in ways that benefit their industries.

During the 1930s and 1940s, General Motors went one step further. Using a company called National City Lines (NCL), a firm it set up for this purpose, General Motors went around the United States buying up the country's vast network of electric streetcar lines. GM then proceeded to convert these lines to buses, figuring that buses would not be as effective as streetcars at countering demand for automobiles, and that GM could sell buses in the meantime. Firestone Tire and Rubber, Phillips Petroleum, Standard Oil, and Mack Truck agreed with this strategy. These companies purchased much of the stock of NCL and helped finance its bus lines with sweetheart supplier contracts.[59]

In the 1970s, the U.S. government successfully brought suit against NCL for antitrust violations.

But the damage had been done. The streetcar rails had been ripped up, and roadways had been expanded in their place. As a lawyer representing NCL at the trial put it, "This was all part of a very reasonable corporate strategy to develop a market."[60] Economically reasonable—but illegal.

The history of cars thus shows how we often socially organize (and sometimes socially manipulate) the convenience of a technology so that it comes to seem the most appropriate way to do things. The pattern of our lives, from where we live and work and shop to how we arrange our family life, from the kinds of things we expect from government to the kinds of things we expect of our neighbors, all come to revolve around and thus reinforce the convenience of the car. In this way, the convenience of a car comes to be what Robert K. Merton termed a "self-fulfilling prophecy."[61] As Merton observed, if we decide a thing is true and plan accordingly, very often it turns out just that way.

The Constraints of Convenience

But convenience also constrains. To say something is convenient is to say that we find our lives constrained so that some other thing is not convenient.

Again consider the car. We drive because we have allowed the location of common destinations to become decentralized, on the assumption that most people own cars. We drive because the bus now comes only every 30 minutes and the train once an hour, and maybe not at all. We drive because even if the schedules for the bus or the train fit our own, they probably do not go where we need to go, given that land use has become decentralized. We drive because little provision for bicycles has been built into the streets, because sidewalks are nonexistent or unpleasantly close to a thundering stream of traffic, and because the places we now have to go are so far away. There is no freedom in a car. We drive because this how-to really has become a have-to.

My point is not that we would have more freedom with more buses and trains, trams and light rail, bicycle lanes and sidewalks. Freedom always exists in a dialogue with constraint. If we were to organize our lives so that these technologies were the most convenient ways to get places (as they in fact still are in parts of some cities, mainly in Europe), we would still find our lives constrained. We would, for example, find it most inconvenient to use a car. Roads would be narrower, far less parking would be available, and land use would reflect the denser and more centralized patterns that make walking and public transport "convenient."

But although such a reorganization might not bring us any more freedom and convenience, it would not bring us any less either. And the pattern of convenience that public transportation, walking, and traditional town planning brings could in fact cost far, far less—less pollution, less land and energy consumption, less community alienation, and less loss of life.

Technological Somnambulism

Why, then, do we accept the increasing dominance of cars, despite their considerable social and environmental impacts, when more benign alternatives are readily at hand? The same question could be asked of other technologies and habits of doing things. "The interesting puzzle in our times," Langdon Winner has written, "is that we so willingly sleepwalk through the process of reconstituting the conditions of human existence"—a phenomenon Winner called "technological somnambulism."[62]

In this section I briefly take up three answers to this puzzle: the phenomenology of technology, the culture of technology, and the politics of technology.

Phenomenology

Phenomenology means the manner in which we experience everyday life, and one of the central experiences that phenomenologists have long emphasized is *routinization*. If you stop to think about it, even the simplest tasks of everyday life are extraordinarily complex. We need ways to simplify what we do, and making routines is a common way.

Alfred Schutz, the founding figure in this area of sociological research, liked to use the example of walking out to the street corner to place a letter in a mailbox. This simple task is filled with presumptions about how the world works: The postal service will pick up the letter. Postal workers know how to read in the language I have used. The person I am sending the letter to knows how to read this language. There is such a thing as letter writing, and the post office and the person to whom I am writing understand that. There is such a thing as a postal service. There is such a thing as a mailbox, and there is no hungry monster at the bottom of the mailbox, waiting to eat the letter. In order to get to the mailbox, I need to get up, put my feet forward, cross the room, open the door, walk down the hallway, get my coat, put it on, open the outer door, step outside before I close it, close it, walk to the street, and so on.

If one did stop to think about all the presumptions involved every step of the way, one would likely never reach the door. Instead, through accumulated experience, we establish a series of little routines—*recipes of understanding*—that we can call upon without having to think the whole thing through each time.

The metaphor of recipes is quite appropriate; routinization is exactly what a cook's recipe allows. Say I have just found out that a friend is having a birthday and I decide to bake a cake as a surprise. It is four in the afternoon and the cake needs to be ready by seven if the surprise is going to work out. But how do I bake a chocolate cake, and what kind of chocolate cake should I bake? I certainly do not have time to experiment much, so I reach for my family's favorite recipe for chocolate cake, a recipe I have followed many times before and I know is likely to please. I bake the cake in time, and it is a big hit—because, through my use of a recipe of understanding, I had routinized the process of baking a chocolate cake.

Making use of any form of technology—and mailing letters and baking cakes are both forms of technology—requires a similar process. I know a little bit about how my computer works, although far from everything. But if I stop to think about all that I know every time I urge my fingers to strike the keyboard, it would take me all day to write this sentence, if not longer. I know that my computer works and, given the time constraints I have, I must usually be content to proceed with no more than that tacit confidence— technological sleepwalking.

But suppose a lightning bolt were to strike the building I'm in and send a charge through the electric lines that melts some essential bit of my computer's innards? (In fact, that happened to me once.) How could I keep on writing? I'm quite good about backing up computer files, but many of my files are stored only electronically. Until I got my own machine working again, or bought a new one, I would have to borrow a computer from someone else to read my backup files. If one were available, I might have to contend with software I'm not quite used to. Still, despite these annoyances and economic barriers, I would only reluctantly resort to pen and paper, because doing so would force a major reorganization of my work habits.

The point I'm trying to establish is that our technological routines tend to lock us into continuing those routines and into trying only new routines that mesh well with our older ones. If something disturbs our technological sleepwalking, we will likely do all we can to walk around the disturbance, re-close our eyes, and return to pleasant walking slumber. And if this tactic fails, we may suddenly awake in a startled panic, having lost our confidence in the secure ordering of our experience.

The threat of broken technological routine was widely experienced in the United States during the gasoline shortages of the 1970s. The Arab oil-producing states of the time instituted a cartel to limit production, resulting in much higher prices and widespread gasoline shortages. Local governments instituted various rationing strategies, such as alternating "odd" and "even" days for buying gas, depending on whether a car's license plate ended in an odd or even number. In the Washington, D.C., area, motorists were prohibited from buying less than 5 gallons of gas, to prevent hoarding through topping off tanks. In a car-dominated society, this rule produced near-hysteria. A neighbor of my mother-in-law, who lives near Washington, D.C., drove around the block for an hour one day, trying to empty her tank enough to be able to buy 5 gallons of gas.

The result of this panic attack in the middle of the technological night was not a United States with more public transportation and more centralized land use. Rather, the result was a United States that will go to war to keep the oil flowing and the cars rolling, as the two Gulf Wars later demonstrated. Routinization follows the patterns of technology we have socially organized as the convenient way to do things. And once these routines are in place, they reinforce the same patterns of social organization that gave rise to them in the first place.

Culture

The same kind of dialogical momentum underlies the relationship between technology and culture.

We perceive all technological knowledge through the cultural lenses we use to make sense of our world. These lenses provide our technological means with technological meaning. Without culture, without meaning, we would not know what to do with our technological means. Yet technological means help shape technological meaning. The means available to us mold our contours of choice and thus our sense of the possible. By structuring the character of experience, means affect and sometimes even justify our cultural ends. We love cars in part because cars are now the main way we have to get around. Means become meaning.

Not only does technology shape culture, however; culture also shapes technology. Should we come to believe that cars are ugly, dangerous, and environmentally and socially destructive (a change I think may be under way), we may decide to reorganize our lives so that cars are less necessary. We may invent new technology to fit our new cultural aims. Meaning becomes means. Should we maintain a cultural commitment to what we see as the beauty, freedom, and pleasure of cars, we will be unlikely to seek alternatives—an outcome that equally represents the cultural shaping of technology.

Technological progress is one widespread example of the dialogue of means and meaning. On the one hand is our cultural faith in progress: We have gained so much in organizing our lives around technological change, who could dispute its value? We therefore ask for more new and wondrous technological means. On the other hand is our continuing effort to discover such new and wondrous means: We have given up so much in organizing our lives around technological change, how could we go back now? We therefore find ourselves compelled to entrust our lives to the future benefits of further technological change. To do otherwise would take an enormous realignment of our cultural commitments, a rude awaking from our technological sleepwalk.

Signs of such a realignment of meaning are, however, increasingly apparent—in part because of problems with the means. Pollution, danger, increasing social inequality, and the loss of traditional forms of beauty were never mentioned in the technological promise, and yet they have all occurred. But as long as technology keeps delivering on its promise of ever more wonders . . .

Fears that technology might not even do that may have been behind the quasi-religious reactions to the infamous "Y2 bug." Remember that night? Hardly anyone mentions it now, perhaps out of embarrassment. But the predictions of what would happen when computers cashed in their chips at midnight on New Year's Eve, 2000, are just astonishing to recall. In case you don't remember what all the fuss was about, computer engineers had designed the calendars inside most computers, particularly big mainframe ones, to count only the last two digits in the number of a year and to assume the 1 and the 9. Consequently, when the year 2000 (2K in computer-speak) came around, all these computers were expected to reset their clocks to 1900, tangling the subtle dynamics of programming. Normally sober publications like the *New York Times* and *Scientific American* published astoundingly dire predictions of what might happen. Phone lines and electric transmission lines would go dead. Computer-controlled factory production lines wouldn't function. Air traffic control computers would have to be shut down. Automobiles with computerized Engine Management Systems wouldn't start. Some fire engines wouldn't start. Automotive air bags would be spontaneously activated. Land mines would explode. Digital watches would go blank. Medical equipment would lose calibration and give faulty readings. Pharmacies wouldn't dole out refills because prescriptions would show up on the screen as expired for a century. Elevators would stop. Pacemakers would stop. Fire sprinklers would turn on and wouldn't turn off. Nuclear power plants would explode. Nuclear weapons would be automatically launched. Stores would run out of food as refrigeration equipment switched off, processed food production lines shut down, oil refineries stopped producing fuel for transporting produce, crops failed because of fertilizer shortages, and people everywhere stripped store shelves bare in a massive spree of panic buying. Lawless looting would take over our cities as desperate people struggled to survive. Vigilantism would become the only form of law and order as police forces and the military became incapacitated by the collapse of communication and transportation systems.

Talk about waking up the sleepwalkers. Millions of people took this very seriously. The Web was full of sites advising people how best to stock up for the collapse of commerce and how to defend their homes from looters. Probably most people in the computer-dependent countries at least had a look in their kitchen cupboard to make sure there was plenty of canned food and pasta on hand, as well as making sure their wallets were full in case ATM machines really did stop working, as many predicted would be the case for at least a few days. A friend of a friend of mine even flew down to Fiji for the coming of Y2K, in case of Armageddon in the United States—"bugging out," as it was called at the time.

Government and industry took it all very seriously too. "Y2K readiness" and "Y2K disclosure" became significant factors in investors' evaluation of stock values. In October 1998, President Clinton signed into law the Year 2000 Information and Readiness Disclosure Act during the midst of National Y2K Action Week, and told government agencies to spend whatever was necessary to set their computers right. Other wealthy nations followed suit, and the World Bank set up the Year 2000 Initiative to help poorer nations debug their computers. According to some estimates, hundreds of billions of dollars were spent worldwide.[63]

And then virtually nothing happened, even in places like Russia, where computers were old and more likely to have the bug, and where almost nothing was spent on "Y2K readiness," due to the post-Soviet disarray of its government and economy. Y2K quickly became "Yawn2K," and the Y2K bug became the "Y2K bust," as the media smugly put it afterward. But as smug as some tried to be, it was but a thin mask over a red-faced industrial world.

How could we have gotten it so wrong? Probably because of the threat Y2K presented to the quasi-religious character of what is rightly called our "technological faith." As Lewis Mumford, probably the greatest critical scholar of technology, put it, "If anything was unconditionally believed in and worshipped during the last two centuries, at least by the leaders and masters of society, it was the machine."[64] The computer is undoubtedly the central contemporary icon in the religion of the machine. And to have this religious machine proclaim that the end is nigh, precisely on the date that some Christian traditions had long said the end was to be expected, was to touch deeply into our most ancient fears.

Yet after that moment of worldwide collective doubt, faith was restored, and the computer took up once again its continual advance into the network of our dependencies.

Sure, computers really are amazing. Amazement is the essence of the miracle. But my point is that cultural faith in technological progress dialogically propels us to reorganize ourselves around the computer as much as the existence of the computer alerts us to the possibility of such reorganization. And who speaks of Y2K now?

Politics

Technology is also political, as I earlier noted. The political character of technology is made plain both by instances of active manipulation of the market through lobbying for subsidies and by instances of popular resistance to technological structures such as the environmental justice movement. Technological politics can also be passive and tacit, though. Technology is political even when we are sleepwalking. Because of routinization and romance—because of the phenomenology and culture of technology—we tend uncritically to promote particular technological structures and their social interests, sleepwalking a political order into place.

A decision to organize your life around a certain technology draws you into becoming one of its political supporters. Once you have bought your house in the car-dependent and car-worshipping suburbs, you have organized your life in such a way that you are likely to promote continued car use. If gas prices rise or your car becomes old and unreliable, you cannot easily switch to another means of transport. You will likely find yourself paying the higher gas prices and buying a new car—as well as clamoring for better parking and new highways to bypass the traffic caused by all your neighbors' cars. (Your own car never causes traffic and parking problems.) You will likely find yourself maintaining a place in the line of social interests that leads to the subsidies for the automobile, as well as the automobile's social and environmental consequences, a line that stretches from you to the local garage to the automobile manufacturers to the road builders to the oil companies.

Technological somnambulism is technological politics. Because of it, we may ironically find ourselves in the frequent position of promoting technological interests we wish we did not have.

The Needs of Neither

People have a common tendency to externalize the economy and technology—to treat them both almost as forces of nature. We speak of economic and technical changes as being driven by efficiency, subtly implying that these changes follow the thermodynamic laws of physics regarding the conservation of energy. It would be unnatural to reject them, we seem to be telling ourselves. In a parallel way, we speak of these changes as being driven by convenience, suggesting again a kind of external objectivity to the course of technical and economic development. We must therefore adapt to these imperatives, we probably all find ourselves thinking at least occasionally, and live as best we can with their social and environmental consequences.

But neither the economy nor technology is an imperative. Neither has needs. They often appear to us as external structures, as forces over which we have little control, as ends to which we must give way. But for all their objective status as facts of the market and of science, money and machines are our own creations, a part of human culture. It is we who have the needs. What Lewis Mumford said of technology applies equally to the economy: "The machine itself makes no demands and keeps no promises: it is the human spirit that makes demands and keeps promises."[65] Technology and the economy take the shape that they do only in response to human demands, promises, and broken promises. There are no imperatives but our own.

Once set into motion, however, the mills of technology and the treadmills of production and consumption become social structures that shape our needs and interests, just as those needs and interests dialogically shape the mills and treadmills to begin with. We are quickly lulled into the routines and cultural desires organized by these structures. We find ourselves dropping off into both technological and economic somnambulism.

Yet the dialogical influence that the economy and technology have over us should not be a cause for despair. In fact, in that influence lies hope. By changing the conditions under which we find ourselves making the decisions that we do, we can reinforce our movement toward the ends we truly desire. All we need to do is wake up and decide where we really want to go.

CHAPTER 4

Population and Development

God forbid that India should ever take to industrialization after the manner of the West. The economic imperialism of a single tiny island kingdom [England] is today keeping the world in chains. If an entire nation of 300 million [India] took to similar economic exploitation, it would strip the world bare like locusts.

—Mahatma Gandhi, 1928

Thomas Malthus's *Essay on the Principle of Population,* originally published in 1798, is assuredly one of the most controversial works of all time. The book's basic argument is that, unless checked in some way, population growth tends to continue until it runs up against environmental limits, causing poverty, hunger, misery, and resource scarcity. The eventual result is a population crash.[1]

Although Malthus's ideas seem like common sense, you could etch glass with some of the critics' reactions. Friedrich Engels termed Malthus's theory a "vile and infamous doctrine," a "repulsive blasphemy against man and nature," for it implied that the poor, through their alleged

inability to control their reproduction, were to blame for their own poverty.[2] Others have called Malthus's theory "racist," for it seemingly places the bulk of blame for environmental problems on poor countries, and thus on people of color.[3] Still others, most notably economists confident about the ability of human ingenuity in a free market economy to overcome just about any problem, have labeled Malthus's views "nonsense."[4]

There truly is a lot to object to in Malthus's ideas as well as in many of the later applications of his argument. Yet his book continues to be the point of departure for discussions of the relationships among population, development, and the environment. Two hundred years later we are still arguing about Malthus because, despite the inadequacies of his book, it forcefully states a basic incontrovertible truth: The world is only so big. It offers only so much room for development and only so many resources for people to consume.

The idea that we might face limits does not mesh comfortably with the modern worship of constant growth. It represents a direct challenge to the treadmills of production and consumption around which we have organized so much of our lives. Much of the objection to Malthus can be understood as an ideological reaction to this challenge.

But Malthus also presented his theory of population and its environmental limits in a *deterministic* way—as something that is inevitable, beyond our control. In the previous chapter I argued against a deterministic view of the economy and of technology. Malthus's critics are right that we should not accept a deterministic view of population and the environment either.

Neither should we ignore the influence that the environment does have on society, however. The relationship between society and the environment is a dialogue. Each shapes, but does not determine, the other. We need to avoid both the deterministic outlook of crude Malthusian arguments and the anything-goes outlook of crude anti-Malthusian arguments. The goal of this chapter is to tread our way through the problems of Malthusianism and anti-Malthusianism and to come to a balanced understanding of the dialogic relationships of population, development, and the environment.

The Malthusian Argument

Many of the world's leading environmental thinkers argue that, despite his errors and overstatements, we still need to pay attention to the basic point of Malthus's thesis: the environmental and social threats posed by *exponential growth* in population, or growth that is constantly compounding.[5] Malthusians—those who agree with at least this much of Malthus—point out that, because of compounding, a constant rate of population growth leads to accelerating effects. Since the annual rate of growth also applies to the additional increments of previous years, not only will the number of people added each year go up, but the rate of the rise will constantly accelerate.

It's like a savings account. A deposit of $100 at a constant 10 percent annual interest rate will increase year by year, first $10 then $11, $12.10, $13.31, $14.64, and so on. Each annual increment is larger by a wider margin than the one before because the interest is applied to an ever-increasing

total. Because of compounding, the size of the increments can go up even if the growth rate falls somewhat, although the increments will eventually begin to drop if the growth rate falls sufficiently. Compounding is great news when you're trying to make money, but the situation is rather gloomier, say Malthusians, when we consider the appetite of a growing population in a finite world.

The rate of world population growth is in fact falling. The peak came in the mid-1960s, when the world population was growing at an annual rate of more than 2 percent.[6] By 2002, the rate had fallen to 1.18 percent.[7] We therefore have little cause for alarm, say some.

Not so, respond Malthusians. Because of compounding, the size of new increments to the world's population is still higher than it was in the mid-1960s, even though the growth rate has declined. Today's slower growth rate is applied to a bigger population, so the world's average annual population increase has nevertheless jumped from around 50 million a year in the 1950s to around 70 million in the 1960s to approximately 85 million a year in the late 1980s, although it has now fallen to about 74 million a year.[8] The time it took to add a billion people to the world therefore also sped up. It took 14 years—from 1960 to 1974—to go from 3 billion to 4 billion people. It took only 13 years to get to 5 billion in 1987, and 12 years to get to 6 billion in 1999.[9]

More than 90 percent of the world's current population growth is taking place in poor countries.[10] Growth in rich and middle-income countries is far slower. In Japan and 22 European countries, the projected growth rate for the 2001– 2015 period is close to zero or below, ranging from plus 0.3 to minus 0.9 percent a year.[11] In 45 countries, however, population growth is projected to be 2 percent or more a year, and 43 of these are what the UN Development Programme calls "medium" or "low" human development countries.[12] The United Nations reports that 20 of them will grow at 3 percent or faster between 2000 and 2005.[13] These may not seem substantially higher rates, but the power of compounding can be surprising. At a 2 percent growth rate, a country's population would double in 34 years. In

100 years, it would rise sevenfold. A country that maintained a 3 percent growth rate would double in size in 23 years, and after 100 years would see its population increase nineteenfold.[14]

Here are the numbers for a few individual countries. Afghanistan had just 23.9 million people in 2003 but is growing at 3.9 percent a year, which if unchecked would give it a population of 1.1 billion in 2103—larger than every country today except China. Nigeria had 124 million people in 2003 and a 2.4 percent growth rate, which if unchecked would lead to a population of nearly 1.5 billion in 2103—larger even than the China of today. Size of the base matters too. China is growing at just 0.7 percent, but if it continued at that rate, in 2103 its 1.3 billion people would be 2.6 billion.[15]

It is important to distinguish between a population's rate of growth and its level of *fertility,* the average number of children born to women in a population. Between 1970 and 2000, the world fertility rate dropped 60 percent, from 4.5 children to 2.7 children. In poor countries the rate dropped from 6.6 to 5.1, and in rich countries it dropped from 2.2 to just 1.7—less than what a couple would need to replace themselves.[16] And yet the number of people added to the world in 1970 was 78 million, only a small amount larger than the 75 million added in 2000. But a drop in fertility does not necessarily translate into fewer numbers of children born each year. Earlier high levels of growth often result in a population with a large proportion of young adults in the prime of their childbearing years. Lower fertility levels may thus result in just as many, or even more, births—an effect demographers term *population momentum.* Because of population momentum, it can be many years before a decline in fertility in a country leads to a slowdown in its population growth.

Nevertheless, fertility declines have finally begun to reverse the growth in annual additions to the world population. Some of the recent fall is attributable not to fertility declines but to increased warfare, to high rates of AIDS deaths in sub-Saharan Africa, and to sharp declines in life expectancy in the former Soviet Union due to economic dislocation. But the time it takes to add another billion people is increasing independently of these problems. The United Nations' demographers now predict that we will reach 7 billion in 2012, 13 years after, and a year slower than, the previous billion. They further predict that rates will slow considerably after that, as population momentum lessens, leading to a world population of about 8.9 billion in 2050, with the world growing at about 50 million people a year—about a new billion every 20 years.[17] (See Figure 4.1.)

Many Malthusians worry that we will still have too many people even if population growth levels out at that 8.9 billion figure, let alone continues to grow by a few billion more. Because of the treadmills of production and consumption, a constant population may still have an increasing appetite for material resources. Moreover, the same logic of compounding applies to consumption and production: A constant rate of growth means not only increasing effects but accelerating effects. Currently, population growth compounds this compounding. Increases in population come on top of accelerating per capita consumption and production. And even if world population eventually stabilizes, environmental impacts may continue to compound because of our growing appetite for resources.

The implications of compounding growth need to be considered carefully. On the one hand, growth in consumption, production, and population does not necessarily degrade the environment—at least theoretically. In fact, population growth itself has no environmental consequence at all. Any environmental impacts depend on what is being consumed and what is being produced by those increased numbers of people and on how they go about their consuming and producing.[18] Improved technology and social organization could possibly compensate for any potential impacts and even leave the environment in better shape than it was to begin with. We could, after all, decide to send a good bit of the human population to another planet someday, if we gain the necessary technological means.

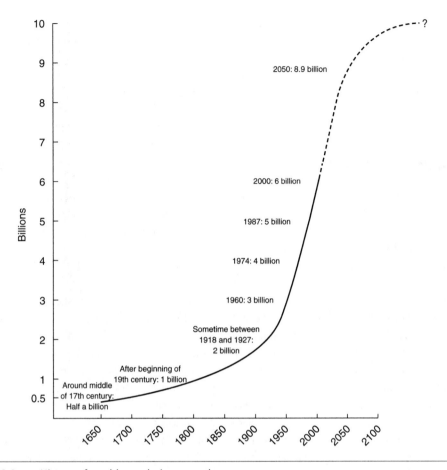

Figure 4.1   History of world population growth.

On the other hand, although there are no theoretically necessary environmental outcomes, there are some theoretically likely environmental outcomes of our current forms of consumption, production, and population growth. Consider climate change, air and water pollution, deforestation, loss of habitat and biodiversity, soil erosion, soil impoverishment, per capita declines in food availability, shrinking water supplies, and social differences in the distribution of environmental goods and bads. Challenges to the three central environmental issues—sustainability, environmental justice, and the rights and beauty of nature—are already well under way. Moving to another planet to escape the pollution of ours is not currently a realistic option (and in my judgment would be a sad reason for planetary pioneering even if it were). We need, therefore, to be "taking population seriously," according to Frances Moore Lappé, a longtime critic of Malthusian arguments, who might not be expected to hold such a view.[19]

In the remainder of this chapter, I review the three main categories of criticisms of Malthusian arguments: *inequality critiques, technologic critiques,* and *demographic critiques.* Along the way, I point out the environmental implications of these arguments in preparation for a final section on the dialogic role of the environment as a social actor. Because the relationships among population, development, and environment are dialogic and not deterministic, I argue that it is possible to change those relationships should we see problems in the current situation.

But before we wade into all that, we should consider the cultural factors that make population a perennially contentious and emotional issue.

Population as Culture

Population is more than just numbers. "Population means *people*," as the Independent Commission on Population and Quality of Life, which conducted a 5-year international study of population issues, observed in its 1996 final report. A South African witness in the hearings convened by the commission across the world put it this way: "Women have children; they do not have population."[20] Children are one of the most important sources of meaning and purpose in human life; they are central to our cultural values.

Population issues can fundamentally challenge these central values. Let's consider six ways.

First, many people sense a hint of misanthropy in Malthusian arguments. People have inherent value, inherent rights of existence, most of us believe. People are also the source of most of our central interests in life. To say that we should have fewer people sounds to some like people hating.

Second, population issues rapidly connect to issues of racial, ethnic, local, national, and religious pride. For some people, controlling population means diminishing the group. If our population shrinks, the feeling sometimes goes, our people will become less important in the world. And within a country, subgroups sometimes feel a sense of what the psychologist Dorothy Stein terms "demographic competition."[21]

Third, the techniques of population control confront some religious values. Conception and birth are processes that even in a scientific age still evoke awe and a feeling of mystery. Many people look to religion for a framework for understanding these mysteries. All the major world religions emphasize the sanctity of life, of course, but they interpret this sanctity in various ways. In some cases, their interpretations conflict with particular means of population control. Most notable is the contemporary Catholic Church's rejection of any method of contraception other than "natural" family planning—avoiding intercourse during the fertile period of a woman's menstrual cycle—as a means of population control. (The Catholic Church does not reject population control, just "artificial" contraception as a means of achieving it.) Moreover, population control threatens the sheer numbers of the faithful, a fact that many religious leaders have no doubt pondered.

Fourth, population issues are fundamentally related to sexual activity. To talk about population control is to talk about sex and sometimes to talk about controlling sex. You do not have to be a deep student of social life to recognize that issues relating to sexuality will likely be highly controversial. Moreover, because sex is a subject many find embarrassing or even immoral to talk about openly, even the mere discussion of contraception and other issues relating to population control can make some people anxious.

Fifth, population issues are necessarily gender issues. Reproduction lies at the center of conceptions of appropriate gender relations, with all the implications that these relations have for social power and social motivation. Population control can threaten social power dynamics built around gender by undermining the basis on which many people legitimize them, such as the still-common idea that because of child-rearing a woman's place is in the home.

Finally, family is a central source of social identity and feelings of transcendence. It is from family relations, in part, that we understand who we are. Most of us live through most of our adult years as parents, and we thereby gain a deep sense of who we are and who we should be. Without someone to fill the role of a child, you cannot be a "mom" or a "dad." Through children, we also gain a sense of transcendence over the confines of our own individual lives, a kind of immortality. Although we have other sources of transcendental values—such as religion, art, and the sense of having made a contribution to society through our work—children remain a particularly direct and accessible source. For many people, to suggest controlling population is to infringe on their principal solution to the problem of mortality: family.

These reactions are common, but they are not cultural necessities. Rather than misanthropy, population control could be seen as an enlightened form of being pro-people, for it may improve the quality of human life. Instead of diminishing the group, population control could be seen as a way to strengthen the group by making it more ecologically secure. As for religious values, our various traditions have a wide range of responses to population issues. For example, some accept contraception while others do not. Our level of comfort with sexuality is equally variable. Plenty of people feel little difficulty in openly discussing sexual matters. As for gender relations, changes in the balance of power between women and men can be seen as liberating rather than threatening. And instead of compromising family identity and transcendence, population control is seen by many as a more sure route to improving the life chances of all our families and children.

I raise these counterpoints to illustrate the diversity of possible cultural responses to the issues often raised by population control. Significantly, all these responses have moral implications. It therefore seems unlikely that any of us can evaluate population issues in a morally neutral way. Nor should we try to, for it is these implications that, in large part, make population issues so significant for us. But even though moral neutrality is not possible, we can still evaluate population issues in a reasoned way.

Being conscious of our own moral values seems a surer route to reason than falsely assuming that we have an unbiased perspective. With our moral passions in mind—including any opinions we may have concerning sustainability, environmental justice, and the rights and beauty of nature—let us now evaluate Malthusianism and the critiques of it.

The Inequality Critique of Malthusianism

Looking around the world, we can see an indisputable association between high levels of population growth, poverty, a wide range of environmental problems, and declines in per capita food production. For example, Africa has the highest overall rate of population growth of any continent and is simultaneously experiencing substantial declines in food production per capita as well as overgrazing, desertification, shortening fallow periods, and deforestation.

The question is why. Malthus would likely have seen diagnostic evidence in Africa for his view that population growth eventually overwhelms the productive capacity of the environment, leading to poverty and hunger. But the story is, at the very least, more complex.

A long tradition of scholars has even argued that the direction of causality should be reversed. It is not population growth that causes environmental decline and ultimately poverty and hunger. Rather it is poverty and hunger that cause environmental decline and population growth, as the poor struggle to gain their living. To understand the origins of poverty we should look not to population pressure, goes this counterargument, but rather to the history of international development and the social and economic inequality it has fostered between (and within) the countries of the world.

The Development of Underdevelopment

We sometimes forget, or at least overlook, that a scant century ago most of the poor countries of today were the colonial possessions of many of today's rich countries. As recently as 1950, only three countries in Africa—Egypt, Ethiopia, and Liberia—could claim full independence.[22] (See Figure 4.2.) A century ago, all of southern Asia, most of southeastern Asia and the Pacific Islands, and a substantial part of the Caribbean were also

Independent states

Area under colonial
control in 1950

Figure 4.2   Colonial control of Africa: As recently as 1950, only three African countries—Egypt, Ethiopia, and Liberia—enjoyed complete political independence from European colonial powers.

under the control of various empires. Much of the rest of the world was divided into spheres of influence that achieved a similar political result. Although colonization brought some benefits to the affected regions, Western Europe, Japan, the United States, and the former Soviet Union gained the most from these relationships, growing in wealth while their colonial possessions, for the most part, languished in poverty.

The period following World War II, however, saw a new global commitment to resolving these inequalities. The lessons of the war brought about a new global consciousness—a sense that we are all in this together, that the rich countries should help the poor, and that the right of self-determination applies to all countries. The United Nations

was one product of this consciousness. Partly in response to this new sense of global commitment, rich countries gave up their empires. New states sprang up everywhere as colonial powers pulled out. And in part, it must be said, the old empires folded up because the devastations of world war left few imperial countries with the financial or military means to maintain direct control over their former colonies.

But the commitment to helping poor countries was, at least in part, heartfelt.[23] Many believed that poor countries could modernize just as the West and Japan did once they were freed from colonial control. With education, industrial infrastructure, industrialization of agriculture, modern political institutions, and lots of exports and imports to connect these countries into the increasingly global economy, the poor countries could soon join the rich at the table of modern luxury and avoid the dismal prospect of Malthusian decline.

In a word, these poor countries lacked only one thing: *development.* Modernization would bring it. This is the basic tenet of an influential perspective known as *modernization theory,* an idea associated with many thinkers in many fields; within sociology, Talcott Parsons and Seymour Martin Lipset remain the best-known advocates.[24]

Perhaps President Harry S. Truman best stated the underlying spirit of modernization. As he proposed in his inaugural address on January 20, 1949,

We must embark on a bold new program for making the benefits of our scientific advances and industrial progress available for the improvement and growth of underdeveloped areas. The old imperialism—exploitation for foreign profit—has no place in our plans. What we envision is a program of development based on the concepts of democratic fair dealing.[25]

About this time (actually just a few years earlier, in July 1944), delegates from 44 countries got together at a quiet country resort in a place called Bretton Woods, New Hampshire, to chart the course of the world economy after the war. By that time, World War II seemed on its way to an inevitable close. Led by John Maynard Keynes, probably the most influential economist of the twentieth century, the Bretton Woods delegates sought to use the conclusion of World War II as an opportunity to fundamentally reshape global society and economy. Their stated intent was to make sure that such a calamity might never again occur. But as we shall see, grounds exist for a more cynical interpretation of the result, if not the intent.

Whatever the reasons were, the delegates set up two key institutions that have had an enormous influence on the subsequent course of economic development: the International Monetary Fund (IMF) and the International Bank for Reconstruction and Development, or, as it has come to be called, the World Bank. Both institutions make loans to countries for development purposes. The IMF gives mainly short-term loans to help countries balance their national budgets. The World Bank emphasizes loans for major infrastructure projects intended to have long-term effects: dams, roads, irrigation canals, schools—that kind of thing. Some of the money loaned by the "Bretton Woods institutions," as they are often called, comes from capital subscriptions from member countries, but most comes from the sale of bonds.

Since that time, several other international or "multilateral" banks have been founded, most with a regional focus, such as the Inter-American Development Bank and the Asian Development Bank. Most of the capital for international development loans comes from private foreign banks, generally in the range of 75–85 percent of the total, depending on the year.[26] But loans from multilateral banks are usually at least a part of most major development projects. Countries use the seal of approval of a multilateral loan to leverage development funds from private sources, both domestic and foreign. In addition to these sources, there has been an enormous proliferation of private international aid organizations and governmental aid agencies, which unlike the big development banks usually make gifts and not loans.

International development has become a major human activity, involving movements of capital equivalent to hundreds of billions of U.S. dollars annually. Currently, 12 percent of the GDP (gross domestic product) of the world's poorest nations is in the form of development monies from abroad.[27] The result of a half-century of international development and modernization, however, is continued disparities in wealth between countries. In fact, the gap between the rich and the poor has widened substantially.[28]

For example, between 1975 and 2001, per capita GDP in the wealthiest countries grew by 2.1 percent, but per capita GNP in what the UN Development Programme calls the "low human development" countries grew by just 0.1 percent. In some regions, GDP per capita actually fell during this period, such as sub-Saharan Africa and the former Eastern bloc countries.[29]

India and China are important exceptions, however. India's per capita GDP grew 3.2 percent between 1975 and 2001, and in China per capita GDP grew 8.2 percent.[30] Considering that these are by far the two largest poor nations (and by far the two largest of all nations), this is significant growth.

Nevertheless, a longer look shows an overall widening gap even with respect to India and China. For example, because of the United States' huge economic head start, the difference in per capita GDP between the United States and China increased by more than 30 percent between 1970 and 1992.[31] The accumulation of advantage, a process discussed in Chapter 3, also works at the level of nations.

Understanding Underdevelopment. The reason for the ever-widening gap between rich and poor lies in the structure of the world economy, say a number of social scientists. The treadmill-driven tendency to seek new markets and new places for investment has sent the capital of wealthy nations overseas. Poor nations have usually welcomed this investment, but most development funds have come in the form of loans, not gifts. Although aid and charity account for a significant portion of the capital flow, the rest has been sent with the expectation that it would be returned, with a comfortable margin for profit. The World Bank, for example, is a highly profitable institution, and its bonds are considered unusually secure investments. As of 1993, the World Bank had cleared $14 billion in profit for its investors.[32]

Meanwhile, poor nations have become mired in debt. Although the debt crisis faced by developing countries has received much international attention, debt continues to rise. As of 2001, the external debt of developing countries was over $2.44 trillion, and these countries were spending 6.1 percent of their GDP to pay it off.[33]

To put the level of international debt in perspective, economists often cite the ratio of a country's annual external debt service to the value of its annual exports, the source of the funds needed to pay off foreign creditors. In developing nations today, that ratio averages 13 percent—a considerable improvement from the 20 percent of 1990, yet still dire enough.[34] In several countries, it rises to more than 30 percent; in Sierra Leone it is a whopping 74 percent.[35] These countries therefore need to maintain at least a 13 percent profit margin on their exports (and return none of that 13 percent margin to investors within their own borders) in order to pay off their debt. This is a highly unlikely scenario. The typical rate of profit for a corporation ranges only from 2 to 12 percent, as Chapter 3 discussed. Moreover, in recent years the average economic growth rate in these countries has been running at only about 0.3 percent—something of an uptick from the 0.1 rates they've averaged since 1975, but still desperately difficult circumstances for digging out of a such a massive debt hole.[36] In short, these countries owe far more than they can comfortably pay back without impoverishing themselves still further. Despite these difficulties, the pressure to repay is such that only 30 out of the world's roughly 150 debtor nations failed to keep up with all their debt service obligations in 2000.[37]

Data like these support the *world systems theory* advanced by Andre Gundar Frank, Immanuel Wallerstein, and others.[38] World systems theory sees the process of development as inherently unequal, dividing the world into *core* regions and *periphery* regions. Because of differences in political and economic power, wealth tends to flow to the core regions from the peripheral ones, feeding the former and bleeding the latter. Thus, over time, development tends to exacerbate economic differences instead of leveling them. World systems theorists also sometimes point to regions that have some of the features of both core and periphery, what they term *semi-periphery* regions. Examples of core countries would be the United States, Japan, and the wealthier nations of Europe. Peripheral countries include Uganda, Zaire, Vietnam, Bangladesh, Ecuador, Panama, and many others. Countries like Costa Rica, the Slovak Republic, and Turkey would be semi-periphery. According to world systems theorists, core, periphery, and semi-periphery relations can emerge not only between countries but within them as well.

Figures on capital flows bear out the notion that, despite their commitment to international development, the core nations have received the most benefit. Between 1982 and 1987, for example, the net movement of capital from poor countries to rich ones was $155 billion. The figures vary from year to year, and in 1982 the net movement was more than $20 billion the other way—that is, to poor countries.[39] But the dominant trend over the half-century since the Bretton Woods conference has been much the same as it was during the period that President Truman termed the "old imperialism."

The Structural Adjustment Trap. The continued poverty of poor countries has been much exacerbated by a World Bank and IMF policy known as *structural adjustment,* a term coined by Robert McNamara, President of the World Bank from 1969 to 1981.[40] (McNamara was also U.S. Secretary of Defense during the beginning of the Vietnam War.) "Structural adjustment" refers to a comprehensive program of radical "free market" changes, such as reducing public services, liberalizing trade, emphasizing export crops, eliminating subsidies, and curbing inflation through high interest rates and reduced wages. The latter part of the program—expensive money and low pay—is what is euphemistically referred to as "demand management." Structural adjustment programs have been instituted in dozens of countries since the late 1970s, from Africa to Asia to the Americas to the former Soviet Union.

The idea of structural adjustment is to help—some say to force—countries to reshape their economy so that they can pay off their mounting debts. Private banks often reschedule and in some cases write off loans, but the World Bank and the IMF have been reluctant to do so out of fear of undermining their high bond ratings and thus being forced to raise the interest rates they offer investors.[41] So they encourage—again, some say force—debtor countries to adopt structural adjustment programs instead. Whether one calls it help, encouragement, or force, the two Bretton Woods institutions certainly give poor countries a compelling incentive to adopt structural adjustment: no more World Bank and IMF loans unless they do, which also means a greatly reduced ability to attract private foreign capital.

Free market policies may not seem like such a bad idea (leaving aside here the question of whether a free market can be said to exist, as discussed in Chapter 3). After all, these are the same policies most Western governments advocate for themselves these days. But the free market policies increasingly adopted by rich countries have been put into practice without anything like the severity and inflexibility the World Bank and IMF have imposed on poor countries throughout the world. "Shock therapy" is what World Bank and IMF officials informally call the regimen. The result has been devastating for the marginal peoples of nearly every country that has taken this stern medicine. Typically, under structural adjustment, basic social services such as education and health care have been sharply cut, and the price of formerly subsidized foodstuffs like bread has gone sky high, leaving the poor in often desperate circumstances.

Throughout the 1980s, the heyday of structural adjustment, "IMF food riots" plagued cities across Africa as starving people took to the streets, sometimes toppling governments.[42] And as investors have bought up farmland to produce export crops for the newly liberalized export trade, displaced peoples have moved into more marginal lands, promoting deforestation and land degradation. With less productive land growing food for local consumption, poor countries have found themselves more dependent than ever on imports to meet their basic food needs. Moreover, once displaced from their land, people in poor countries are less able to compensate for the newly increased food prices by growing their own. When you are poor, it is very risky to be dependent on money to get enough to eat.

Another result of structural adjustment is that many poor countries are in the unenviable position of exporting raw materials elsewhere, only to buy these materials back later as finished goods. Value is added elsewhere, and these poor countries must pay for that added value out of their scant stocks of foreign exchange funds, further crimping their ability to pay off foreign debts. The trade liberalization features of structural adjustment and a number of recent international treaties have also enabled companies from rich countries to come into poor countries and set up low-wage factories, later exporting the goods to places where people have enough money to buy them. The governments of poor countries, eager to attract the foreign investment needed to fulfill structural adjustment plans, often allow these companies to evade the environmental and labor laws they would have to contend with in their own countries. During the mid-1990s, for example, many lines of Nike sneakers were being assembled in Vietnam by women working 12-hour days at 20 cents an hour to make shoes they could never afford themselves—to the embarrassment of a number of celebrities who were paid millions to endorse Nike products.[43]

Under these conditions, poor countries get the short end of the economic stick of structural adjustment. Value is added in peripheral areas, but the peripheral areas do not get to keep much of that value. Local workers are paid almost nothing, and somebody else owns the products of their labor. By opening up poor nations for increased foreign investment under such unequal terms of trade, structural adjustment assists in draining value away from the periphery and toward the core.

Structural adjustment has been widely criticized, and the prestige of both Bretton Woods institutions has been severely undermined. The World Bank itself is now backing away from the policy. The World Bank's former chief economist, Joseph Stiglitz, has written widely on its inadequacies.[44] But the human and environmental damage has been done, reinforcing centuries of unequal exchanges between the rich and poor countries of the world.

The anti-Malthusian moral is this: The poverty experienced throughout the world is not just a population issue. (Some say it is not a population issue at all.) Poverty cannot be understood apart from the history of development, a history that has favored some regions over others. Any argument concerning the relationship between the environment and poverty needs to take this history into account.

Food for All

Malthusians point not only to poverty but also to the 900 million people who suffer from malnutrition as an indication of population pressures on the land. Anti-Malthusian critics of this position argue that, on the contrary, the world has plenty of food for everyone. The problem of food shortages, they contend, is really a problem of access to food and of overconsumption of food by those who do have access. The principal names associated with this counterargument are Frances Moore Lappé and the Nobel Prize-winning economist Amartya Sen.

One of the points that Lappé forcefully raises in a number of books is that there is little correlation, if any, between population density and hunger or between the amount of cropland per person in a country and hunger. The obvious example is Europe, which has some of the most densely populated countries in the world and yet very little hunger. Africa, which suffers from a far greater percentage of hunger, nevertheless has a far lower population density. Of course, much of Africa is desert and cannot be farmed. But even when considering the amount of cropland per person, Lappé finds no particular relationship with hunger. Japan has about 10 people for every acre of cropland and very little hunger. Tiny Singapore has 143 people for every acre of cropland and very little hunger. But Chad has 1.68 acres of cropland for every person—17 times as much as Japan and 240 times as much as Singapore—and experiences quite extensive hunger.[45]

Lappé also argues that, even at current population levels, the world has plenty of food. From 2000 to 2002, the world produced about 300 kilograms of grain per person per year, which is 1.81 pounds a day, or about 2,656 calories.[46] Except for an exceptionally active person, that would be an ample amount—let alone other calorie sources. (The recommended daily calorie intake for adult males in the United States is 2,000 to 2,200.) However, 37 to 40 percent of that grain, depending on the year, is fed to livestock. As many have pointed out, much of grain's food value to humans is lost because animals eat not only to put on mass but also for energy to stay alive. Various kinds of livestock take from 2 to 7 pounds of grain to produce a pound of meat.[47] With their high meat diet, Americans consume (directly and indirectly) approximately 800 kilograms of grain each year per person. In India, which has a diet low in meat, people consume (again, directly and indirectly) about 200 kilograms of grain per person per year.[48] Changes in the diet of the wealthy and a different distribution of food could raise the figure for India considerably.

In place of Malthusianism, Lappé (along with her colleague Rachel Schurman) advocates a *power-structures* perspective on food and population. Even though Japan and Singapore have little cropland per capita, they are wealthy countries; Chad and India have more cropland, but they are poor. And people who are wealthy have a lot more power, a lot more ability to gain the food they require, and a lot more "say in the decisions that shape their lives," as Lappé and Schurman point out.[49]

Lappé and Schurman argue that a power-structures perspective explains not only inequalities in access to food but also high rates of

population growth. A lack of control over their lives leads poor people to regard children as an economic resource. "Living at the economic margin," Lappé and Schurman observe, "many poor parents perceive their children's labor as necessary to augment meager family income. By working in the fields and around the home, children also free up adults and elder siblings to earn outside income."[50]

Given their lack of options, poor parents thus have a strong economic incentive to have lots of children, the inverse of Malthus's argument that population growth, through environmental decline, leads to poverty. Rather, Lappé and Schurman respond, poverty and environmental decline lead to population growth by decreasing the power people have over their lives, leading them out of desperation to seek economic security through having large families.

The Politics of Famine. Amartya Sen makes a similar argument concerning famine.[51] Famines, says Sen, are caused not by a lack of availability of food but rather by a lack of access to food. All societies have social systems for what Sen terms "entitlements" to food and other goods, such as the distribution of ownership of land to grow food and the ability to acquire food through trade, usually through the medium of money. Entitlements allow people to gain command of food and other goods. It is breakdowns in these systems that cause famines, Sen argues, not environmental decline.

Sen makes his case by analyzing four major famines in the twentieth century: the Great Bengal famine of 1943, the Sahel famine of the 1970s, the Ethiopian famine of 1973 and 1974, and the Bangladesh famine of 1974. He argues that in each instance sufficient food to feed everyone was on hand in the affected countries. The problem was that people could not get access to the food.

For example, in the 1974 Bangladesh famine, a series of summer floods on the Brahmaputra River largely wiped out one of the three annual rice crops and damaged a second one. But food imports and stocks of rice remaining from earlier harvests provided plenty of food throughout the crisis.[52] The real problem was that the flood threw a lot of farmers and agricultural laborers out of work. With nothing to harvest from one rice crop, and no chance to plant the next because of the continuing floods, laborers could find no paid work. Farmers didn't have much money either because they had nothing to sell. Consequently, these laborers and farmers couldn't afford to buy much rice. Also, the United States chose this moment to cut off its normal food aid, because Bangladesh was exporting jute to Cuba. In anticipation of shortages due to the flooding and the loss of U.S. food aid, the rice market went haywire. Prices for rice in Bangladesh jumped by 18 to 24 percent at a time when many people had little money on hand to make up the difference. Because of fluctuations in the labor market and the rice market, they had lost their entitlement to food. Somewhere between 26,000 and 100,000 people died of starvation and malnutrition within three months. The tragic irony was that in the country's warehouses there was more than enough unsold rice to feed everyone.

Similar kinds of arguments have been applied to other famines, such as the infamous Irish potato famine of the 1840s. While millions starved, Ireland continued to export large quantities of wheat to England (some 800 boatloads in all) because of earlier export contracts.[53] In the recent famines in war-torn Somalia, Rwanda, and Burundi, there may not have been sufficient food from local farms nor much exporting of food. But high population density relative to cropland was still not the cause of the starvation, some argue. Rather, because of the war, people were not given access to food, nor could they plant in order to feed themselves. War broke down their systems of entitlement to food.

Sen's argument has an important practical (and political) implication. If there is food available even in the midst of most famines, then the long-term solution to hunger in the world is not the importation of more food. In the short term,

in the midst of a crisis when people are dying, food imports are frequently necessary. But even if the long-term problem is the distribution of food, the long-term solution is not redistribution of food. Rather, it is redistribution of *access* to food, as Lappé and Schurman also argue. "What is needed is not ensuring food availability," says Sen, "but guaranteeing food entitlement."[54] In other words, don't give the poor food (except when they are starving). Rather, give them farms, give them jobs, and give them democracy.

Limits of the Inequality Perspective

The inequality perspective makes an important case for the significance of the social origins of poverty, population growth, and hunger. A purely Malthusian perspective, as nearly all scholars now agree, is clearly inadequate.[55]

Yet there is much that the inequality perspectives of Sen, Lappé, and Schurman cannot explain about hunger. Although Chad has a higher ratio of cropland per person than Japan and Singapore, and a ratio roughly equivalent to many European countries, not all cropland is equal in its productivity. The climate in Chad is quite dry, and production per acre is quite low. Much more significant than cropland per capita is annual grain production per capita, which runs at about 120 kilograms per person in Africa and nearly 500 kilograms per person in Europe.[56] The power-structures perspective of Lappé and Schurman needs to take into account the spatial distribution of environmental productivity, not merely wave it aside. Environmental productivity is itself a source of social power.

Nor does entitlement breakdown seem sufficient to explain all famines, as a number of Sen's critics have argued.[57] Six years of warfare in Europe between 1939 and 1945 severely disrupted systems of entitlement, as did the strife in Yugoslavia in the 1990s. But the disruptions of war in Europe did not result in the widespread starvation that Rwanda, Burundi, and Somalia suffered during their recent wars, nor the massive food imports that the war in Iraq necessitated. Europe has long had far more food production per capita. It is also striking to consider the relatively minor disruptions that led to the Bangladesh famine. At the peak of the famine, the price of rice rose only 18–24 percent. Bangladesh, however, is very poor. And with a population of some 141 million in a region the size of Greece (which has a population one-fifteenth the size), the country finds itself compelled to import much of its food, leaving its people dependent on something most of them have in short supply—money—in order to eat. Thus, most of the people of Bangladesh live very close to the margin they need to survive.

When you live close to the edge, both environmentally and economically, even a minor disruption can have a big impact. Bangladesh and all the countries that have experienced famine in the twentieth century are poor countries with unfavorable levels of grain production per capita. They have very marginal systems of both food entitlement *and* food production.[58] This is a dangerous combination. When a country is too poor to easily command food imports and when it doesn't have much local food production to begin with, it will have less food around for its people to be entitled to—even in good times.

The Technologic Critique of Malthusianism

In October 1990, the anti-Malthusian economist Julian Simon won a much-discussed bet with Paul Ehrlich, a biologist and a prominent figure in the Malthusian tradition. Ehrlich is the author of the 1968 bestseller *The Population Bomb,* which predicted widespread famine and starvation within 10 years, and Simon and Ehrlich published a series of counterattacks on each other from the early 1980s until Simon's death in 1998.[59] Simon bet that the price of five metals of Ehrlich's choosing—chrome, copper, nickel, tin, and tungsten—would fall during the next 10 years, as opposed to rising in the face of

Malthusian scarcity. Ten years later, the price of all five metals had actually dropped, after taking into account inflation. (They had agreed to pay each other the difference in value accrued by the market movement of $200 worth of each metal over the 10-year period. Simon would pay for all the metals that went up in price, and Ehrlich would pay for all the metals that went down. Ehrlich quite honorably sent Simon a check for the $576.07 difference.)[60]

It was a foolish bet for Ehrlich to make, even from a Malthusian point of view. Market forces are complex and reflect environmental conditions crudely at best. Many of the costs of natural resource production are externalized, disguising their true environmental (and social and economic) significance. Also, the prices of these metals have little to do with the resource scarcities—land, water, food—that would be significant to the poor and marginalized, those who are most likely to experience a Malthusian crisis, if anyone will. Even if the prices of the metals had gone up, the bet would have said little about Malthusian shortages.

A Cornucopian World?

Although the bet proved nothing, it did serve to highlight the debate between Malthusian arguments and a kind of anti-Malthusian argument often called *cornucopian,* of which Simon was the most prominent proponent. Simon controversially claimed that the solution to resource scarcity is actually to increase population. People, said Simon, are the "ultimate resource." A larger number of people means more brainpower and labor to work out technological solutions to scarcity, Simon argued. When confronted with scarcity, we apply our collective brainpower and find new sources of formerly scarce resources and new techniques for extracting them. In some cases, new technology will allow us to substitute different materials for ones that have become scarce, what Simon called the principle of "substitutability."[61]

Simon cited a variety of evidence to support his arguments. Population has successfully continued to increase, and increase rapidly, for the roughly 200 years since Malthus first published his book, Simon noted. As well, life expectancy has leapt to unprecedented levels, while infant mortality has declined considerably. Standards of living for many of us today are astonishing when compared with living standards of the past, which suggested to Simon that Malthusian limits are far from inescapable. The prices of most basic commodities have actually dropped over the decades, in line with the results of Simon's bet with Ehrlich. Simon also disputed the significance of acid rain, global warming, the ozone hole, and species loss, arguing either that these issues have been exaggerated by environmentalists or that they represent challenges that future technological innovation will overcome. He argued that, in fact, the state of the environment is now much improved, pointing to the drop in air pollution emissions in the United States and the many advances in public health.[62]

But Simon had—and has—many critics, and rightly so. One point that is often raised is Simon's neglect of social inequality. Although the lives of many have improved, since 1960 the percentage of the world's people who live in poverty, facing hunger and malnutrition throughout their lives, has remained much the same. The sheer number living in poverty has doubled.[63] It is true that even the desperately poor are generally living longer, in part because of medical and other technological improvements, but life expectancy is still very uneven across the world. Simon paints an overly rosy picture of the world. We can do better.

Simon's argument that more people means more brainpower to work out problems is also rather dubious. Sure, two people may come up with more ideas than one person (although they may also come up with the same ideas). But by Simon's argument, the Roman Empire should still be with us, continuing to expand, ever increasing the number of people enlisted into the task of solving the empire's problems. It is clearly not the sheer size of a society that makes it innovative. Innovativeness depends on social circumstances that encourage creative thinking, such as

democratic discussion and a good educational system, not mere numbers of people. In fact, greater numbers of people may only increase a society's stock of misguided ideas, if that society is set up in a way that stamps everyone in the same ill-conceived mold. Also, the kinds of improvements that Simon looked to are mainly high-tech. But the bulk of population growth currently is taking place among those who do not have the educational background to contribute to high-tech solutions.

Critics also doubt Simon's optimism about technology. With every advance in technological how-to, as Chapter 3 discusses, comes an equal measure of technological have-to. Technological freedom's relation to technological constraint is another of the dialogues of social life. Moreover, there are limits to what technology can do. Technology has indeed made possible substantial substitutions in the resources we depend on, often in the face of scarcity, such as the techniques for the use of fossil fuel that resolved the fuel wood and water power shortages of early industrialism. But will technology always come to the rescue in time to prevent serious problems? This question is particularly germane as we encounter limits in resources that seem less substitutable, such as land for agriculture, habitat for biodiversity, fresh water, and clean air. And even if we come up with an innovation, new technology can bring with it unfortunate unintended consequences, such as the substitution of HCFCs, a potent greenhouse gas, for ozone-depleting CFCs. Solving one problem often contributes to another. Besides, waiting for a shortage to stimulate innovation and substitution could put humanity on a path of crisis management in which we try to solve problems instead of avoiding them to begin with. This is a risky strategy, especially for the world's poor.[64]

The Boserup Effect

Ester Boserup offered a closely related but more temperate argument for how population growth can, in some circumstances, stimulate technological change. In a famous study of agricultural development, Boserup suggested that population pressure is a primary factor stimulating the adoption of more productive farming practices. Malthus held that population pressure reduces food availability, but Boserup's view was that population can increase food production by giving people an incentive to switch to more intensive farming methods.

Consider a low-population-density farming practice like shifting cultivation, in which farmers cultivate a particular parcel of land for a few years and then let it lie fallow for 20 or 30 years before cultivating it again. In the interim, the forest grows back, restoring the fertility of the soil and breaking the life cycle of crop pests. This is an effective and relatively low-labor method of farming. But it supports few people per acre. So as population grows, rural people shorten the fallow periods—already a technological change—until problems with fertility and crop pests increase and population pressures rise even more. At that point, and usually reluctantly, villagers begin cropping fields annually and using small plows, fertilizers, and pesticides to maintain fertility and control pests. Where possible, and if pressures remain high, they may eventually irrigate their fields and purchase high-yielding hybrids rather than saving their own seed. In most cases, these more intensive practices require more labor and higher cash outlays, making villagers reluctant to switch to them. But eventually people do switch, if they can, as demonstrated by the dramatic increases in food output in developing countries in recent decades.[65]

But Boserup was no starry-eyed optimist. She identified many qualifications to this process, which is now sometimes called the "Boserup effect." First, technological change is not the same as innovation. Population pressures provide the incentive to adopt technologies that have been invented elsewhere but that may not prove attractive until population pressures override labor and financial costs. Such pressures also encourage innovation, she suggested, but the principle at work is necessity, not Simonian collective brainpower. In

any case, "societies have most often advanced technologically by introducing technologies already in use in other societies," Boserup wrote.[66]

Issues of inequality can also limit the influence of a Boserup effect. The investments required to increase the intensity of production may not be available in developing areas. And if farmers do attain sufficient capital to intensify their operations through mechanization, they may also put farm workers out of work, increasing poverty and inequality.[67]

Boserup further noted that in conditions of *rapid population growth*, economic development may be severely limited.[68] Population density needs to be considered separately from population growth.[69] Whereas population density may provide the incentive to intensify production, rapid population growth may overwhelm the economic and social resources that are essential to intensification. Governments and local communities can be left constantly scrambling to provide a burgeoning population with education, health care, poverty relief, and infrastructure improvements like roads and irrigation. Rapid population growth also leads to a population with a high percentage of children requiring schooling and caregiving and thus competing for scarce funds and adult labor.

The problem of rapid population growth can be particularly pronounced in urban areas. When the population is generally poor, taxation does not yield sufficient funds to keep investing in new roads, public transportation, sewage lines, clean water supplies, school buildings, hospitals, phone lines, and power generation. Nor do people have enough money to attract much private investment to provide these services. Government officials and police receive low pay and turn to corruption to maintain their incomes, making it even harder to coordinate rapid growth. Kickbacks increase the cost of providing infrastructure, and polluters avoid regulations through payoffs to officials.

Even when the population is wealthier, rapid growth presents a serious organizational problem. Mexico City, capital of one of the world's largest upper-middle-income nations, is often pointed to as an example of the difficulty of planning in the midst of rapid expansion. Despite the horrendous traffic in the city, residents increasingly turn to cars as an alternative to inadequate public transportation, only making matters worse. Public transit services simply can't keep up with the rapidly increasing demand of the rapidly increasing population. Because of these planning difficulties, the likelihood of corruption increases. Thus, as industries and car owners bribe their way around regulations limiting polluting emissions, the 22 million people of Mexico City experience the worst air quality of any city in the world. In 1995, air pollution exceeded the World Health Organization's standard on 321 days. Joggers wear facemasks. Wealthy children play indoors or inside giant glass bubbles. During one particularly bad 5-day period in 1996, the city's health care services attributed an increase of 400,000 patients and 300 deaths to air pollution.[70] Los Angeles may be a similar, albeit less extreme, example from a high-income country.

We need to make another important qualification to the Boserup effect. Like Simon, Boserup did not allow a big role for the environment in her theories of technological change. But the environment can significantly limit the potential of a Boserup effect. The problem of the unintended environmental consequences of technological change, mentioned with regard to Simon's theory of technological substitution, also applies to Boserup's theory. New production strategies bring new consequences. Equally important, because of the pressure to increase environmental yields quickly, more intensive production often proceeds by increasing the overall level of resource use rather than by increasing the efficiency of resource use. Sometimes efficiency even declines, resulting in soil erosion, soil degradation, deforestation, and water shortages.

The Case of Miracle Rice

We hardly ever know ahead of time all the consequences of a technological change, and the story of the development of the high-yielding rice varieties known as "miracle rice" is a clear example.

During the 1960s and 1970s, intensification of agriculture swept through the developing countries, a transformation often called the "green revolution." Mechanization, irrigation, pesticides, a tenfold increase in fertilizer use, the introduction of high-yielding hybrids, rural road construction to open up new areas for clearing and cultivation—these practices allowed world grain production to increase 2.6-fold between 1950 and 1984.[71] The per capita world grain harvest rose by 40 percent.[72] Much of the gain was in rice, the centerpiece of the diet of billions. The success of "miracle rice" is a good way to assess the green revolution and our common feeling of technological optimism.[73]

The working lives of roughly a billion people are devoted to growing rice. Average worldwide consumption per capita is 145 pounds (dry weight) a year. In Bangladesh, the average person eats 330 pounds a year—almost a pound a day. The rice-dependent countries are also where much, if not most, of the world's population growth is taking place. However, these countries have little remaining land not already in paddies that could be brought into rice production. Increasing rice yields per acre and hectare is clearly an important challenge.

The success over the past 40 years or so in meeting this challenge can be largely attributed to the work of the International Rice Research Institute (IRRI), which was founded in the Philippines in 1959 with the goal of increasing rice production. The approach IRRI took was to develop new rice that could accept high rates of fertilizer application and would also be suitable for mechanical cultivation. Most of the local rice varieties in use around the developing world at that time were susceptible to a problem known as "lodging," or falling over from growing too tall. This problem is not particularly significant when rice is harvested by hand, so local farmers never felt a great need to select against lodging in maintaining their local rice varieties. But this characteristic of rice had to be dealt with before combines could be used. Also, lodging tends to get worse with fertilizer use, as the plants shoot upward in response to the easy flow of nutrients.

In rural Taiwan, some IRRI scientists found a wild variety of low-stature rice that they hybridized with conventional rice in 1966. The result was rice suitable for both heavy fertilization and mechanical harvesting. IRRI called this hybrid IR8, but it rapidly came to be called "miracle rice." Farmers across southern and southeastern Asia gave up their local varieties and bought IR8, and average yields of rice went up 30 percent between 1968 and 1981.

By the mid-1980s, though, the euphoria had pretty well worn off. A host of interrelated problems with miracle rice had emerged: increased pest damage, loss of genetic diversity, the killing of paddy fish, and increased social inequality.

Previously farmers had kept their own seed and selected it for suitability to local conditions. But with the coming of IR8, a huge percentage of rice land was soon planted with the same variety. A pest that could evolve to do well against IR8 now had acre after acre of the same variety to flourish in. Moreover, simultaneous increases in irrigation led farmers to crop two and three times a year in areas where they had previously cropped only once or twice a year. Multiple cropping did wonders for rice output, but the old pattern of drying out fields once a year used to interrupt the life cycles of pests and helped to keep them in check.

Farmers began applying the newly available pesticides, but all too soon the pests started evolving to resist the pesticides. IRRI went back to work to develop a new hybrid—and then another and another and another as new problems kept emerging. IR20 was resistant to a disease called *tungro* but was an easy mark for brown plant-hoppers. IR26 could handle the plant-hoppers, but it was easily flattened by wind.

IRRI researchers checked their records and found that a wind-resistant variety had been recorded in some areas of Taiwan, the same area from which the genetic material for IR8 had

come. But when the researchers went to Taiwan, they found that the wind-resistant variety had disappeared from use. All the local farmers were planting rice hybrids from IRRI, and no one had bothered to keep the seemingly outdated wind-resistant variety going. Eventually IRRI found a variety it could use, and came out with IR36. Four years later, though, the brown plant-hoppers had evolved and were again attacking the crops. In a few years IRRI was up to IR76, with more varieties to come—or so rice farmers must hope.

Unanticipated Consequences. IRRI's work has been widely praised for improving the diet and health of billions. Critics, though, point to the killing of paddy fish brought about by using the new hybrids. One of the major sources of protein in the diets of many rice farmers had been fish from their paddies. But the new pest problems associated with the use of hybrids forced farmers to apply pesticides at such high rates that the paddy fish were killed off in most areas. Consequently, some have argued, miracle rice has actually led to lower nutrition levels for local farmers at the same time that it has allowed more people to be fed.

Then there are the social and economic complications. The new rice farming requires more capital per acre. Fertilizer, pesticides, hybrid (and now biotech) seed, and combines cost money. Thus the new form of rice farming became accessible only to the wealthier members of rural villages. And soon they were producing rice so cheaply that other farmers could not stay in the game, starting a production treadmill that has thrown millions of farmers off the land.

Even wealthier farmers can manage the higher costs only if they have bigger farms. Formerly, tenant farming was very common in areas such as the Malay Peninsula. But now the landowners themselves need every piece of land to pay for tractors and other improvements, and tenants are finding it hard to keep their holdings. The political scientist James Scott has described the social implications of intensive rice production in Malaysia. He points out that the irrigation of paddies helped propel the move toward bigger rice farms. Without irrigation, landowners would never have been able to achieve the big harvests necessary to fund the switch to more intensive production.[74]

Intensification has been hardest on those who were too poor even to be tenant farmers. These villagers used to survive as field workers, but with the coming of combines to do the harvesting and pesticides to do the pest control, they are increasingly out of work. The village poor used to have a kind of unwritten contract with the wealthy. Poor villagers would work in the fields, but they expected *zakat*—the Muslim tradition of charity—especially when times were hard. But *zakat* is disappearing now as the wealthy find they no longer really need the poor, furthering the social inequalities brought about by the intensification of agriculture and fueling the migration of rural peoples to the urban shantytowns.[75]

Since 1984, the rise in world rice yields has slowed considerably. More and more farmers are reaching the 4-ton-per-hectare level that seems to be the practical maximum of current rice technology.[76] Yields in China and India have been stable since 1990 and have actually fallen somewhat in Japan.[77] Global yields are still increasing, but at a slower rate than population growth. Worldwide per capita yield of all grain dropped 14 percent between 1985 and 2002. (See Figure 4.3.)[78] Researchers at the Worldwatch Institute suggest that the declining responsiveness of crops to further fertilization, as well as "soil erosion, the conversion of grainland to nonfarm uses, and spreading water scarcity" is limiting the growth of grain production.[79]

Will this scarcity lead to another round of technological innovation? In 1995, IRRI announced another breakthrough: a new type of rice expected to increase yields by up to 25 percent, the first significant advance in rice production in a decade.[80] This "super rice" has, at this writing, yet to be made available to farmers, but there is great hope that it might one day push the

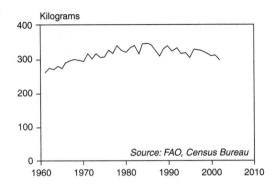

Figure 4.3 World grain production per person, 1961–2002: Despite a record harvest in 1998, the overall trend since the 1985 peak has been persistently down.

current plateau in rice yields higher. "Super rice" was developed using conventional hybridization techniques, but there is much work being done in genetically modified rice, now that the sequencing of the rice genome has been completed. IRRI has been promoting its new "golden rice," which increases the amount of vitamin A in rice and has a golden color, and which it developed using genetic modification techniques. It too has yet to be made available to farmers, though, as it in fact currently provides very little additional vitamin A and is something of a fertilizer hog. So IRRI is still at work on it. IRRI scientists have also succeeded in inserting some maize (corn) genes into rice, which they believe promises to boost yields substantially, and in inserting the genes of a widely used biological pesticide, a bacterium called *Bacillus thuringiensis*, into rice—what is called "Bt rice." But these too were not yet available to farmers at the time of this writing. (However, "Bt" versions of several other crops are now in use—"Bt corn," "Bt potatoes," and "Bt cotton.")

Critics worry about the environmental and moral consequences of bioengineering and other new agronomic techniques, as well as the likely continuance of patterns of social inequality. Even some bioengineers and financial analysts remain

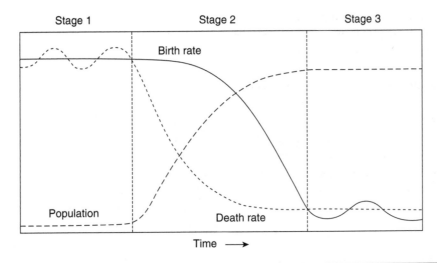

Figure 4.4   The demographic transition: In Stage 1, a stable birth rate and a fluctuating death rate roughly cancel each other out, and population remains low and stable. In Stage 2, the death rate drops while the birth rate remains initially high, and population rises rapidly. In Stage 3, the birth rate declines until it roughly matches the death rate, once again leading to a stable population—but at a much higher level. Scholars question the applicability of this model of population change to lower-income countries.

skeptical that technology can produce a "new green revolution."[81] Maybe it will. But we face the risk that it won't. And even if it does, will we be able to handle the social and environmental consequences?

The Demographic Critique of Malthusianism

Let's turn now to the third set of critiques of Malthusianism, beginning with the ideas of the demographer Frank W. Notestein. In 1945, Notestein offered a simple model of population that has since become central to the debate over population growth.[82] Looking over European history, Notestein suggested that development and modernization initially raise population growth rates but eventually lead to a return to a stable population, albeit at a higher level. Notestein distinguished three stages. (See Figure 4.4.)

Stage 1: In pre-modern times, countries experience high birth rates and mortality rates that roughly cancel each other out. Because of disease, malnutrition, and accidents, average life expectancy is about 35 years. Children and infants are particularly hard hit because of the diseases and fragility of childhood. Parents compensate by having a lot of children, a practice supported by pro-natal social norms and social institutions as well as the common use of children as a source of household and agricultural labor.

Stage 2: With the beginning of modernization, new scientific discoveries lead to improved health and an increased food supply, and industrialization increases wealth. Mortality levels fall, but pro-natal social norms continue to promote a high birth rate. Population growth rates climb, eventually to high levels.

Stage 3: Finally, social norms and social institutions catch up with the fact that children are quite likely to survive, leading to a fall in the birth rate. Increased urbanization promotes a lower birth rate because children are no longer seen as a labor supply for the farm. And with the coming of universal schooling, children become an economic burden rather than an economic resource. Changes in social structures associated with modernism lead parents to invest more in each child. Having fewer, better-educated, better-financed children becomes more attractive than spreading a family's investment over many children.[83] Also, as a country gains wealth through industrialization, it can more easily afford social security, pensions, health care, and other social benefits, reducing the tendency for parents to see their children as their future caregivers in old age.

Notestein called this sequence the "demographic transition," a theory that is closely related to modernization theory. Demographic transition theory is an implicit critique of Malthusianism. It suggests that, rather than expanding until environmental constraints cause it to collapse, population growth eventually levels off of its own accord. The same factors that lead to population growth—scientific advances, industrialism, and modernization—are also those that eventually lead to a return to population stability, once societies adjust to their newfound social and technological circumstances.

A New Demographic Transition?

Notestein based his model on the European experience. But scholars and development organizations seized on the idea that the less-developed countries might also eventually go through a demographic transition. If such an extension is correct, the solution to population problems would be for poor nations to continue down the path of modern development. Eventually, they theorized, the less-developed countries will grow out of rapid growth and the planning difficulties it causes. As a slogan that came out of the 1974 World Population Conference in Bucharest put it, "Development is the best contraceptive."[84]

The theory of demographic transition fits European history reasonably well (although there are plenty of exceptions, such as the drop in the birth rate experienced in many regions of France *before* mortality declined).[85] Yet there are substantial reasons to doubt the applicability of the demographic transition to the less-developed countries. A number of important conditions seem to set the contemporary less-developed countries apart from nineteenth-century Europe:

First, the rate of population growth currently experienced in most less-developed countries is considerably higher than the growth rate in nineteenth-century Europe. Since contemporary less-developed countries have been able to import already established medical technologies, mortality rates have declined much faster. At the same time, birth rates are far higher. Many European cultures of the nineteenth century practiced late marriage and frequent non-marriage, as opposed to the practice of early and nearly universal marriage in most contemporary less-developed countries. High fertility and low mortality has in turn led to a young age structure throughout the less-developed world, leading to population momentum as younger generations reach their reproductive years.[86]

Second, the poverty that leads children to be regarded as a labor supply may be intractable in the face of contemporary forces of global inequality. Economic structures that channel wealth toward core countries may limit the extent to which less-developed countries will ever in fact develop, or at least may very much retard the spread of development's benefits.

Third, an increasing chorus of critics doubt the very desirability of some of those benefits. The principal doubt centers on the homogenizing tendency of development and the charge that development proceeds from a West-knows-best point of view. Critics see development not only as economic imperialism but as cultural imperialism as well. In the words of Wolfgang Sachs, "From the start, development's hidden agenda was nothing else than the Westernization of the world."[87] Hidden in the idea of "development" is the presumption that those who are "underdeveloped" or "less developed" or "developing" are missing something—that there is something inadequate about them. Western education and Western values do not liberate traditional peoples, argues Helena Norberg-Hodge, another critic of West-knows-best development.[88] Rather, they deny traditional peoples the cultural tools to function in anything but a Western economy, trapping them instead. Given that unequal relationships of economic exchange may prevent poor countries from becoming developed, or may delay development for generations, the trap is particularly tight.

Fourth, there is the environmental critique. Levels and inefficiencies of consumption associated with the European demographic transition may simply be unsustainable, and as well may compromise environmental justice and nature's rights and beauty. Even though only the wealthy few currently enjoy them, such consumption levels already seem to be compromising the environment. The situation may become far worse when the whole world tries to keep up with the Joneses. Although we must avoid the simplicity of crude Malthusianism, we must also avoid crude anti-Malthusianism. If the rest of the world is to attain development, then the meaning and the techniques of development must change.

In light of these critiques, there is increasing agreement among population specialists that if the poor countries of the world are to achieve a demographic transition, they will have to do so by different paths than European countries took.[89]

Women and Development

One vision of those different paths sees women having a key role in development. Scholars and development organizations now see improving the status of women both as an end in itself and also as one of the most significant means of reducing rapid population growth and improving the life chances of poor children.

The first two decades of development efforts, 1950 to 1970, gave scarcely any consideration to the importance of gender. Women were largely invisible, both as actors in and potential beneficiaries (or victims) of the development process. In another pathbreaking book, her 1970 *Women's Role in Economic Development,* Ester Boserup was the first development scholar to highlight women, and it came as something of an academic bolt of lightning. Boserup pointed out that women in less-developed countries make vital contributions not only in the domestic sphere of reproduction but also in economic production.

In retrospect, Boserup's finding seems obvious, but at the time the official economic statistics of countries around the world consistently underestimated women's nondomestic work. For example, Egypt's national statistics for 1970 listed only 3.6 percent of the agricultural workforce as female. In-depth studies revealed quite a different picture. Half of women participated in plowing and leveling land, and three-quarters participated in dairy and poultry production.[90] A 1972 census in Peru registered only 2.6 percent of the agricultural workforce as female, whereas an interview study found 86 percent of women participating in field work.[91]

Boserup's survey found that, although there are substantial variations by region and by level of agricultural intensity, women do as much work in agriculture as men, if not more.[92] The kinds of agricultural work women and men perform do differ, however. Men tend to be more involved in the mechanized and animal-assisted aspects of production, such as plowing, and women tend to be more involved with hand operations, such as sowing seed and hoeing weeds, which are generally more laborious. Contrary to stereotypes about the greater physical capabilities of men, women in fact do the bulk of the world's physical work: sowing, weeding, washing, and carrying—lots and lots of carrying, of water, wood, and children, plus goods to and from the local market.

Indeed, women around the world, in country after country, rich and poor, work more than men do. Much more of women's work is outside of the market, but if we sum up all hours of work in and out of the market, women work more than men do. In the wealthy countries, it averages about 20 minutes a day, according to the UN Development Programme. In developing countries, women average almost an hour more work a day—57 minutes, to be exact.[93] These may not seem like big differences. But at the end of the day, those minutes of lost leisure are precious indeed. There is still truth to the old saw that men work from sun to sun but a woman's work is never done.

Development efforts, however, were ignoring the implications of development policies for the kind of work women do and for women's status. In many rural regions in less-developed countries, particularly in Africa, women collect the bulk of fuel wood essential for cooking food—another activity dominated by women. Development policies stressing exports encouraged poor countries to convert forest lands to timber and crop production, taking little notice of their importance as a source of fuel wood. Women soon found themselves walking miles and miles each day to gather fuel. In general, the kinds of economic activity stressed by development projects emphasized men's work, underestimated the agricultural contributions of women, and almost completely ignored domestic work, seeing what was outside the money economy as not really economic activity at all.

The status of women in households and communities, as well as in politics and the economy, was not seen as a development issue at the time Boserup wrote. In the years afterward, however, issues of women's status and gender relations came closer to the center of the development debate. Scholars came to recognize that women were disproportionately represented in the ranks of the poor. The United Nations proclaimed 1976 to 1985 the Decade for Women, and now few development projects go ahead without some explicit attention to women, albeit often cursory.

One reason why "women in development" (or WID, as it is often called by development specialists) has captured so much interest is the increasing recognition of the importance of women in population issues. Demographic studies find that the status of women, measured through their education and participation in the paid economy, is the most consistent factor in fertility reduction.[94] Women frequently want to reduce fertility rates, sometimes in contrast to their male sexual partners.[95] When men come to see women as economic equals, they tend to see them more as social equals as well, and women gain more say in family planning and other family decisions. Education gives women, as well as men, a broader understanding of possibilities, eroding fatalism and building a sense of empowerment. The greater economic standing of women in paid work in an increasingly monetarized world also means that childbirth and child care can become more of an economic burden than an economic opportunity for families. As opposed to general economic development of the structural adjustment and modernization variety, improving women's standing may be one of the principal paths to a demographic transition for less-developed countries.

Some feminist critics are suspicious of this approach to development, however, as it seems to view improving women's status as a means to the end of population stabilization, not as a moral end in itself. The emphasis should be on ending patriarchy, not on furthering women's economic development, argues Sylvia Walby.[96] Patriarchy is a system of social organization in which women consistently receive lower status and less social power than men—a system which, most scholars agree, still characterizes virtually all human societies. Emphasizing women's economic development may be misplaced priorities.

Part of the reason for this doubt about women's economic development is the tendency to relegate women to lower-paid work. As less-developed countries have tried to build their exports in order to reduce debt and comply with structural adjustment plans, they have promoted cheap factory work, generally performed by women. As Valentine Moghadam has put it, women are the "new proletariat worldwide."[97]

There is considerable controversy among scholars about this phenomenon, often termed the "feminization of labor."[98] Does it represent the continued subordination of women in a new form, or does it represent an opportunity for poor women to gain better lives for themselves and their families through one of the few means available to them? Is it empowerment or continued disempowerment?

I strongly suspect the answer is both. As other writers have argued, improving women's status is not simply a means to population stabilization and increased exports.[99] However it may be seen by the governments and development agencies involved, improved status is good for both women and their families. If nothing else, reproduction should be seen as a women's health issue. Half a million women die each year from pregnancy-related causes—some 200,000 through unsafe and illegal abortions and the others through childbirth, postbirth infections, and other illnesses. Ninety percent of these deaths occur in less-developed countries.[100] Better women's health also means better health for their children.

The persistence of patriarchy, despite improvements in women's health and economic and social status, seems undeniable. Eliminating patriarchal social relations is ultimately the only way to achieve equal status for women. But the fact that attention is finally being given to women in development (although perhaps not yet with sufficient sensitivity and commitment) should not be seen merely as a patriarchal ploy. Rather, it may be a sign that the world is beginning to acknowledge that improving the status of women is good not only for women. It is good for everyone.

Family Planning and Birth Control

Another controversial aspect of population is the use of birth control in family planning. The controversy stems partly from the coercive way that birth control has been applied in some instances, partly from moral judgments concerning some forms of birth control, and partly from questions about the significance of birth control technologies in reducing fertility.

The promotion of birth control has some serious black marks on its record. One of the worst instances was India's National Population Policy of 1976, initiated during the 18-month period between June 1975 and January 1977, when Prime Minister Indira Gandhi ruled as a dictator. Prime Minister Gandhi had been found guilty of election fraud, and in order to hold on to power she declared a national state of emergency. The press was censored, dissidents jailed, civil liberties curtailed. In this climate of extreme state control, the government put forth the National Population Policy under the direction of Mrs. Gandhi's son, Sanjay Gandhi. The policy emphasized sterilization—as well as health care, nutrition, and education for girls. Sterilization plans went quickly ahead, but the other aspects of the policy were more long-term and were for the most part ignored.

Most Indian states set bureaucratic quotas to monitor the "performance," as it was called, of the policy. Although people were paid for being sterilized, there was much coercive abuse as government officials in this strikingly undemocratic period in India's history struggled to meet their quotas. Near the capital, Delhi, the government set up vasectomy booths. People were harassed, threatened, and bribed. In about six months, some 8 million sterilizations were performed, mainly on the poor, who were vulnerable to the fees, harassment, and threats. They were probably more often targeted by the program as well. Hundreds died in the riots that broke out in protest, as well as through infections caused by the sterilization procedures. When Mrs. Gandhi finally lifted the national state of emergency, the program was quickly dropped.[101]

Instances such as this, or such as the sterilization of Native Americans that was carried out on some U.S. reservations, are intolerable. They can also lead people, in anger and suspicion, to associate all advocacy for population control with oppression. A number of critics have seen the concern about population as part of, to quote one author, a "racist eugenic and patriarchal tradition"—the fears of the rich and white about a rising darker-skinned horde, as well as an effort to control women's bodies.[102] Critics have had particular concern about the single-minded attention that some Malthusians have given to birth control as a means for reducing population growth, given that most contemporary population growth is outside the West.

Paul and Anne Ehrlich's 1990 book, *The Population Explosion,* may be a case in point. They predicted that "the population explosion will come to an end before very long. The only remaining question is whether it will be halted through the human method of birth control, or by nature wiping out the surplus."[103]

There is nothing explicitly, and perhaps not even implicitly, racist about such a statement. Nevertheless, critics have argued that placing all the emphasis on birth control as a solution to population growth leaves intact the social inequality that is the primary cause of population growth.[104] Whatever the explicit intent of the Ehrlichs' position (and I believe the Ehrlichs are in fact strongly committed to social equality), critics suggest that the implicit effect would be the continuance of social inequality of race, class, and gender.

But just because racism, classism, and sexism have been a dimension of some birth control policies, and possibly some theories, this does not mean that birth control is necessarily racist, classist, or sexist. Indeed, preventing people from controlling births can be just as racist, classist, and sexist as any ill-conceived birth control policy. Reproduction, I believe most people would agree, is a basic human right. But so too is the right not to reproduce. Most couples around the world voluntarily seek to control and regulate— to plan—their reproduction. Limiting their ability to do so can be coercive too.

One example of a policy of coerced reproduction took place in the late 1960s in Romania under the regime of Nicolae Ceauçescu, one of the most iron-fisted dictators of the twentieth century. In 1966, Ceauçescu suddenly declared any form of birth control, as well as abortion, illegal. Women had to undergo gynecological exams every 3 months to determine if they were complying with the new law. As a result, birth rates doubled, at least initially.

Maternal mortality doubled too, with about 85 percent of these deaths due to botched abortions, illegally performed. Women across Romania also began avoiding gynecologists as much as possible, skipping appointments and failing to sign up for them, even for routine gynecological checkups. The result is that Romania now suffers from Europe's highest rate of death due to cervical cancer. Infant mortality also went up considerably (by one-third) as parents neglected, abused, and even abandoned unwanted babies.[105]

Granting a right to control and plan births is not the same as approving of all forms of birth control and all national birth control policies. There is certainly extensive disagreement on the morality of some forms of birth control, particularly abortion. But one can disapprove of abortion and still support other means of controlling births.

The question remains, though, whether modern birth control technologies are effective means of reducing population growth. In detailed historical studies, scholars have noted that, at least in the European demographic transition, fertility decline generally began before modern birth control technologies were widely available. Indeed, in some places fertility declined even before industrialization began.

The point is, there is nothing new about family planning. People have been using, and continue to use, many family planning techniques other than the pill, the diaphragm, the condom, the sponge, and other modern birth control technologies. Practices such as late marriage, extended nursing, abstinence, rhythm, withdrawal, and polyandry, among others, can be and have been effective forms of family planning.

But no doubt modern methods can be even more effective, which is one of the main reasons why so many couples across the world choose them when they are available. The commitment to plan births is absolutely essential to the success of any family planning practice, however. If social conditions are such that people are unable or unwilling to make such a commitment, no technique can be effective. In other words, birth control and greater social equality can be complementary, rather than contradictory, social policies.

The Environment as a Social Actor

Malthus went too far. It is clearly incorrect to adopt a position of *environmental determinism*— the view that the environment controls our lives and that there is little we can do about it. Human population has certainly increased to unprecedented levels, despite environmental limits, and in many wealthy countries population levels have returned to stability for reasons other than environmental scarcity. Technological and social change have allowed societies across the world to increase the production of food and other resources. Although the numbers of the poor grew dramatically in the last half of the twentieth century, particularly in areas with rapid population growth, their poverty cannot be understood apart from the dynamics of the world economy.

But Malthus was not entirely wrong. Access to food depends not only on systems of entitlement; it also depends upon the environmental availability of food. Some resources seem hard to substitute with something else, even with the highest of technologies. And too often the risk inherent in some technologies puts the poor and marginal most in danger. Rapid population growth is also a problem in itself, apart from any environmental implications, both for organizing social benefits such as schools and a coordinated economy and for safeguarding health. In other words, rapid growth can cause poverty, just as it is itself a product of poverty.

Moreover, because of the compounding effects of population with consumption and production, the question of growth and development is not merely one of finding enough food to feed everyone. It is also a question of whether we will ultimately be able to sustain everyone—humans and other creatures alike—if the competitive consumption and production levels of the world's rich become the ever-escalating norm.

Accepting a degree of *environmental agency,* accepting the environment's causal role in social life, is not the same as accepting environmental determinism. The role that the environment plays in our lives depends upon our interactions with it. The environment is not a given. We shape the significance it has. The environment is, in effect, a different place depending upon how we wish to use it and how we envision what it is. An environmental resource is only a resource if, because of our technical and social relations and because of our ideas, we find it to be a resource. It is we who make resources as much as it is the environment that provides them to us. It is we who make the environment as much as it is the environment that makes us.

Perhaps the sociologist Fred Cottrel put it best: The environment limits what we can do and influences what we will do.[106] Take, for example, the process of technological change, which is often presented as constrained only by our imagination and not by the environment. Even the cornucopian vision of technological change presented by Julian Simon implicitly grants a considerable degree of agency to the environment. For Simon, environmental scarcity prompts technical innovation. Thus, the environment helps guide the directions in which we exercise our powers of imagination.

And we should not forget that the consumption and production in which the human population engages are aspects of the environment in their own right. They are not external forces that may or may not impact the environment. All human activities are part of the environmental dialogue of ecology.

One of the most important lessons to draw from that dialogue, I have tried to argue, is that population growth is a real issue in the conversation. But it is one that must always be understood within the context of consumption, production, and social inequality. Although birth rates among the wealthy are lower than rates among the poor, the consumption and production levels of the wealthy are far higher, and so are their per person environmental consequences, given current technological conditions. Social inequality—by region, class, race, ethnicity, and gender—is also in itself a principal factor in population growth, as well as growth in consumption and production. But population growth does have environmental implications. And since we are a part of the environment, those are necessarily implications for us and how we may live.

Yet perhaps the most important dialogical lesson is that we can change the ecological dialogue.

Changing the current dialogue of population growth seems to me to be a very good idea. Maybe we will be able to cope with the outcome of that dialogue in a way that provides general and sustainable well-being. Maybe. We're certainly not doing a great job of it now. But in order to do a better job, we need a dialogical understanding of the situation—an understanding that recognizes the complexity and interactiveness of social and ecologic life. For the problem of population is not just one of "too many people." Rather, it is also a problem of too many people with too much and too many people with not enough.

CHAPTER 5

Body and Health

There is a kinship between the being of the earth and that of my body. This kinship extends to others, who appear to me as other bodies, to animals whom I understand as variants of my embodiment, and finally even to terrestrial bodies.

—Maurice Merleau-Ponty, 1970

December 2, 1984, was the date. The people who lived in the shadow of Union Carbide's pesticide plant in Bhopal, the capital of the Indian state of Madhya Pradesh, knew it wasn't the best place to call home. The main product of the Bhopal plant was the insecticide Sevin. One stage of making Sevin requires the production of methyl isocyanate, or MIC, a highly toxic chemical related to the nerve gas phosgene, and which has the unfortunate property of reacting very strongly with a very common substance: water. So it has to be handled with unusual care. Even moisture in the air can be a problem. MIC is not the kind of thing that recommends itself to people looking for an area to settle down and raise a family in.

But the people of the Jaiprakash Nagar neighborhood 100 yards from the plant were poor and didn't have much choice in the matter. At least they had roofs over the heads of their families—if only tiny, ramshackle ones propped up by thin and shaky walls. As the residents drifted off to sleep that cool evening, the late-night voices of the neighborhood came filtering through those thin walls, as they did every night, a comforting music of place to those accustomed to it. Someone laughing in the distance. Someone comforting a crying baby. Someone rummaging around in the dark.[1]

On the other side of the chain-link fence separating the plant from the neighborhood, however, there was mounting panic. Production at the plant had been shut down for maintenance for a month. Workers were beginning the complex series of operations to get it up and running again. About 9:30, they started washing out a few lines with water, downstream in the production process from the MIC storage area, which should have been safe enough. But there followed a whole series of troubles, individually minor and collectively disastrous. A clogged valve. A line left open. A few standard safety procedures not followed. A dysfunctional safety mechanism—the burner that was supposed to scrub any gases venting from the system. A recent, poorly thought-out modification of the plant's initial

105

design that, in fact, connected the MIC storage area with the lines the workers were washing out. A recent reduction in the size of the work crew from 12 to 6. An inexperienced supervisor.

The last may have been the most crucial. Around 11:30, workers detected an MIC leak in the way they usually did: a burning in their eyes and throats. (This was far from the first MIC leak the plant had had. Although Union Carbide claimed that the Bhopal plant was the twin of a trouble-free one in West Virginia, it had been built without several of the safety features of its supposed twin.) The workers reported the problem to the supervisor, who shortly called a tea break, with plans to attend to the leak afterward, thus fortified with caffeine. By 12:30 A.M. (now on December 3), the reaction of MIC with water became too much for the system to contain. A major leak began as MIC from tank E610 started to rush past the dysfunctional burner and out into the atmosphere above the plant. At 12:40 A.M., burning eyes and throats ended the tea break. At 12:50 A.M., workers pulled a general alarm at the plant when they discovered they were unable to get the burner working. At 2:00 A.M., the leak petered out as tank E610 reached empty. At 2:15 workers pulled the public alarm siren and walked over to a nearby police control room to report that the "leak has been plugged" and to give the first public admission that there had been a leak at all.[2]

By then, thousands had already died. In the coming hours and days, thousands more would die. Some 5,000 to 10,000 in all would lose their lives, including a quarter of the residents of Jaiprakash Nagar and two other shantytown neighborhoods close to the plant. No one knows for sure how many.[3] The residents of the worst affected neighborhoods were not the sort of people whose troubles the local government pays much attention to, or who take their troubles (including their dead) to the government for help. Many died in their sleep, and there may have been some luck in that. Others awoke, breathless, coughing, with burning sensations, vomiting blood and frothing at the mouth, and rushed out of their homes in agony, right into the

depths of the chemical fog, before collapsing in the street. Tens of thousands of cattle died as well. The stench of death was everywhere. At least another 200,000 people were injured.[4]

Here are some reports from the local papers the next day:[5]

Jaiprakash Nagar, a sleepy locality of Old Bhopal, is today a ghost colony. Every second house in the locality has lost at least one family member in yesterday's night of horror.

This correspondent who went round the locality early morning found more than fifty dead bodies lying unattended and unnoticed. . . . The dead included mostly children below ten years of age.

The scene was so gruesome that it was difficult for survivors to identify their own dead family members. The neighbors were not willing to tell anything to anybody. They just sat glassy eyed, dumb-founded.

The tragedy continues today among the survivors. Numbness. Trembling. Polluted breast milk. Monstrous birth defects. Memory problems. Breathing problems. Immune system problems. Psychological problems. Plus it turned out that Union Carbide had been dumping large quantities of toxic waste on the site for years, polluting the land and the water below. Cleanup efforts are underway, but 20,000 people still live in the immediate vicinity of the plant, and had been drinking water from local wells for years before authorities started providing them with clean water in September 2000.[6] (See Figure 5.1.)

Survivors are still struggling for just compensation, and there was a worldwide hunger strike in their behalf in the summer of 2003. The Indian government has demanded the extradition of Warren Anderson, Union Carbide's CEO at the time, to face trial for culpable homicide. At this writing, the United States has not complied, and does not seem likely to.[7]

Figure 5.1   A protestor outside the fence at the former Union Carbide pesticide plant in Bhopal, India.

Enough. I know this is a grueling story to read about. I know because it was grueling to write about. But I tell it to remind us in a forceful way of a central implication of environmental questions: the health of our bodies. I also tell it to point out, in what I hope is an equally forceful way, that these questions of body, health, and environment are sociological ones as well. As Eric Klinenberg noted with regard to the hundreds of deaths in the Chicago heat wave of 1995, "We have collectively created the conditions that made it possible for so many . . . to die. . . ."[8] In other words, the tragedy of Bhopal was a social tragedy as much as anything else, patterned by factors by now familiar to a reader of this book. The patterns of our economy. The patterns of our technology. The patterns of our politics. The patterns of our distribution of environmental goods and environmental bads—of environmental justice. And, perhaps less obviously at first look, the patterns of our ideas and their mutually constituting interaction with our material conditions.

In this chapter, we explore these patterns with respect to the *environmental sociology of the body*. True, the Bhopal tragedy is one of the worst industrial accidents ever, with maybe only Chernobyl as a rival. It is hardly representative. But the cumulative impact of the countless ways, large and small, seen and unseen, that our bodies are affected by the technologies of our environmental interaction connects us all to these patterns.

Connects us all—the environmental sociology of the body is a way to explore ecological issues at the most personal of levels. Ecology, recall from Chapter 1, is the study of natural communities. But literally it is the study of *ecos*, which is ancient Greek for "home." Ecology is thus the study of natural home as community. Environmental sociology, recall as well, is the study of the biggest community of all—and thus the biggest *home* of all: the *abode* we share with everyone, human and nonhuman alike. A body is an abode too. As we will discover, perhaps surprisingly, for all its personal-ness, a body too is an abode we share with everyone.

Welcome to the Invironment

It may come as another surprise to learn that the body and health have not always had an easy and welcome place within environmental discussions. Indeed, the body and health have often been understood as diametrically opposed to the concerns of environmentalism.

Take health. Why do we alter the environment by draining swamps, dousing our crops with pesticides, and burning fossil fuels? To eliminate the habitat for insects that carry disease. To compete better with the creatures that would deny us a portion of that essential substance of health: food. To make our lives less grindingly arduous through heating, cooling, lighting, and mechanized transportation. Seen from this view, the environment seems a threat to health, not an aspect of it. Thus, concerns for public health, for eliminating hunger, and for human comfort have often promoted transformations of the environment, on behalf of our bodies, that run afoul of at least some conceptions of sustainability and the rights and beauty of nature, and even those of environmental justice. As a result, historically, the public health movement and efforts to end hunger have had surprisingly little to do with the environmental movement. While efforts to clean air, water, and land of pollution are certainly central environmental concerns, they have often taken a rhetorical backseat to efforts like wilderness and biodiversity protection. And many proponents of efforts to improve human comfort have long regarded the environment as something of an enemy.

Take the body. The very meaning of the word *environment* has a connotation of what is around us. The environment is our environs, not us. A body may have an environment, but it is something separate from it, the word seems to imply. Lurking inside this opposition may be something of a disgust for the body, at least in the minds of some. If you think through what it takes to maintain a body as a going entity, you are pretty much inevitably led to our links to the environment, and thus to the recognition that we are animals with animal needs. By keeping the body conceptually separate from the environment, perhaps we are unconsciously trying to ignore this embarrassing "low" reality of human life.[9]

But these oppositions in our thought are lessening. Increasingly, environmental concerns routinely embrace health and the body *as* environmental issues, and thus the body as intimately involved with the environment—a part of, not apart from: indeed its most intimate part.

In order to help that lessening along, I have a little term to offer, which I hope will be at least somewhat useful. We could continue using the terms *body* and *environment*, as traditionally has been done in the West, and try constantly to remind ourselves not to regard them oppositionally. But by establishing an initial separation, these terms force us to undertake an extra intellectual step to recognize their interconnections, their dialogue. So rather than speaking of the "body" and the "environment," I suggest we speak of the "invironment" and the "environment"—where the *invironment* refers to the zone of the body's perpetual dialogue *with* the environment.[10] *Invironmental issues*, then, would be issues that concern the dynamics of that dialogue, with health being perhaps the prime example.

In the usage I'm suggesting, then, *environment* is a more encompassing term than *invironment*. Some environmental issues—like, say, global warming or species loss—are not, in the first instance, invironmental issues. But as we consider more closely these, and probably all, environmental issues, we will likely discover that they have invironmental dimensions. Global warming has implications for food production, for water supplies, for the spread of disease, and more, including the sheer level of warmth with which bodies must contend in the summer. Species loss has implications for the loss of potential medicines and crop varieties that might help relieve concerns for health and hunger.

Species loss is also an invironmental issue of immediate concern for the nonhuman bodies involved—the bodies of the nonhuman animals who are losing habitat, being hunted, or facing competition from recent migrants to their ecological niche. In this chapter, I take an almost exclusively human-oriented stance because I have more than enough to say about the human invironment on its own. But the difference between the human and nonhuman invironments is another potential opposition we would do well to be wary of.

In sum, the environment is not only something "out there." It is also something "in here."

Living Downstream: Justice and Our Threatened Invironment

The ecologist and author Sandra Steingraber offers an apt metaphor for conceptualizing the connections between environment and invironment: "living downstream," she calls it in her book by that title.[11] Because of the body's perpetual dialogue with the environment, we are all always living downstream of what goes on around us. We may wish sometimes that we were separate. But we're not. We just aren't. Moreover, it turns out that, in matters of who gets what is coming downstream, we are neither separate nor equal.

Mercury and the People of Grassy Narrows

In 1970, a small band of Ojibwa Indians living in the Grassy Narrows reservation in remote northwest Ontario learned that they were literally living downstream. In that year, government authorities realized that some 20,000 pounds of mercury had been released over a 10-year period from a paper mill into the Wabigoon River, 80 miles upstream from Grassy Narrows. There, in

the river, ecological processes converted the mercury to methyl mercury, one of the most toxic substances to be found in any chemistry book. It steals a person's vision, hearing, agility, ability to feel, memory, emotional control, and eventually a person's life. The affected walk with a kind of stagger, a glazed and glassy expression on their faces.

Methyl mercury is a sly and crafty toxin. It has no taste and no smell. It can't be seen in the water or in the fish. It can't be felt either. As an Ojibwa elder described to a visiting journalist, "But you know it's there. You know it can hurt you, make your limbs go numb, make your spirit sick. But I don't understand it. I don't understand how the land can turn against us."[12]

This sense of everything, even the land, turning against you can be one of the worst effects of methyl mercury and other toxins that are largely invisible to our senses, as the sociologist Kai Erikson has observed.[13] As Erikson puts it, methyl mercury poisoned the minds of the Ojibwa of Grassy Narrows with "a pervasive fear that the world of nature and the world of human beings cannot be trusted in the old way."[14]

Not without reason. There is frequently much empirical justification for a feeling of persecution in invironmental issues. Although we all live downstream, there are definite patterns in the social characteristics of those who find themselves living closest to the outfall pipes of our industrial economy. The Ojibwa people of Grassy Narrows are poor and disenfranchised, and that is no sociological surprise. Study after study has documented a persistent finding: Those who get more of the bads are disproportionately those who receive less of the goods.[15]

The connection between violations of environmental justice and economic justice is often an interactive one, as the people of Grassy Narrow discovered. Once it became known that the river on which they had long relied for food and income was polluted with methyl mercury, the Canadian government banned fishing there. It had to be banned, of course, but that threw an already poor people out of much of the little work they had.

It also threw them, in a way, out of their culture. For the work we do is more than a source of income and sustenance. It is a source of pride and purpose, of self and the embedding of self in the lives of others. "We are now a people with a broken culture," is how Simon Fobister, chief of the Grassy Narrows band, put it.[16]

When your culture is broken, people often look for purpose in drink. At least so it was in Grassy Narrows, where after the closing of the river to fishing, alcohol abuse skyrocketed. Mortality rates skyrocketed, too, as alcohol abuse led to violence, accidents, and health troubles. As Erikson notes, out of roughly 400 members of the Grassy Narrows band, 35 persons—about 9 percent—died between 1974 and 1978. This is a huge mortality rate. Some 80 percent of these deaths were either directly or indirectly related to alcohol: suicides, murders, drownings, alcohol poisoning, heart failure from excessive drink.

Which is not to transfer the blame from methyl mercury to alcohol abuse. It is methyl mercury's poisoning of their minds, breaking their culture, that led to alcoholism problems among the Objiwa of Grassy Narrows. Plus there is a further cruel feature of methyl mercury's poisoning of the flesh: the way its effects mimic those of alcohol abuse. As Erikson observes, considering the physical symptoms of methyl mercury poisoning,

> Now if you were asked where one might find a group of persons with slurred speech and difficulty in focusing, with a lumbering gait and uncertain coordination, with a glazed and numbed look about them interrupted at times by violent outbursts of temper, what might you suggest?[17]

Thus, when alcohol abuse is also present, it can be a hard matter to ascertain with any surety that methyl mercury's effects are being directly manifested. It's a long, slow poison.

But either directly or indirectly, slow or fast, the result is the same. As another Grassy Narrows elder put it, "Now we have nothing. Not the old. Not the new."[18]

A Factory Explosion and the People of Toulouse

On September 21, 2001, at 10:15 on a Friday morning, a huge explosion ripped through the AZF (Azote de France) fertilizer factory on the outskirts of Toulouse, France. Something touched off a silo with 300 tons of ammonium nitrate, a chemical used in both fertilizer production and in explosives. It was like an earthquake. Some 27,000 nearby homes were damaged, and 11,000 seriously, with crumbled walls and missing roofs. Windows were shattered in stores two and a half miles away.[19] Eighty schools had to be closed for repairs. It left a crater 165 feet across and 33 feet deep. Miraculously, only 30 people died, mostly plant workers, although more than 2,000 people were injured.

Coming a scant 10 days after the September 11 tragedy, the AZF explosion hardly registered in the world's news. (I didn't hear of it at the time myself.) But it was one of the biggest stories of the year in France, in part because some worried that it might be connected with the events of September 11. There was much buzz in the French media about whether one of the workers who died, a Tunisian Muslim with reputed radical Islamist leanings, might have set off the explosion as an act of terrorism. But investigators eventually dismissed that theory as groundless. Although a definite cause has not been established as I write, investigators for the French judiciary believe that the cause was likely a spark from some of the other chemicals used at the plant, notably sulphuric acid, lime, and soda. In other words, sloppy procedures by the company were at fault, according to the investigators.

Much of the debate since then has been over corporate culpability in the explosion. In the now-common tangled chain of ownership that vertical integration and increasing scale have led to in industry after industry, the AZF brand is owned by Grande Paroisse, currently France's largest fertilizer company. Grande Paroisse is in turn owned by Autofina, the fifth largest chemical company in the world, and which is itself just a branch of an outfit called TotalFinaElf—whose awkward name is the result of a series of amalgamations that have made it the world's fourth largest oil company. The executives buying and selling chunks of business like so many deeds in a game of Monopoly often have little idea what is going on down the chain of ownership, which cannot be good for long-term investments in plant safety, critics argue.

Not that there should have been much doubt the AZF plant could be trouble some day. The European Union had some time ago given the plant a "Seveso" designation as a high-risk facility—a designation whose name derives from the Italian village of Seveso where, in 1976, an industrial accident at a pharmaceutical company released a toxic cloud of dioxin. A Seveso designation means a plant must be subjected to unusually strict safety procedures, including notification of nearby residents of the dangers of the facility. But Seveso guidelines were not being carefully followed at the AZF plant or in the surrounding neighborhoods. Nor were the guidelines being carefully followed at many of the other 371 Seveso-designated facilities in France—a point that had led the European Commission a few weeks before the blast to announce that it intended to take France to court to get it to comply with the Seveso directive.[20]

In fact, there wasn't much doubt locally about the dangers. It is no simple accident of blind planning that the residential area closest to the plant is one of the poorest districts in Toulouse, a section of the Le Mirail district of Toulouse. Across a highway from the plant, many Le Mirail residents live in a series of cheaply made apartment towers—*banlieues* is the French term for them, which sounds much nicer to the English speaker's ear than "housing projects"—a number of which were seriously damaged in the blast. The AZF plant was established in 1924 in what was then open countryside. Toulouse soon grew out that far, though, and when the suburban tide reached the factory zone, it was not the homes of the rich that were located there.[21]

In other words, the residents of the Le Mirail *banlieues* discovered for themselves the negative association between who gets the bads and who gets the goods of the environment. Why do people put up with this association? Because they often fear that what homes and jobs they do have depend on it. After all, living near a fertilizer plant is not exactly a sought-after situation for those with more choice in the market. Nor is working there.

As the mayor of Toulouse, Philippe Douste-Blazy, observed in the immediate aftermath of the explosion, "This kind of incident should date from another era. It's time to change. We must stop asking our citizens to chose between their work and their lives."[22]

Environmental Racism and the People of the United States

The findings of research on the environmental justice of the invironment—on what we might call *invironmental justice*—go beyond the association of lower income with greater bodily hazards. A person's social heritage can also influence her or his likelihood of facing greater invironmental threats. It is difficult to avoid the suspicion that the disenfranchisement of the people of Grassy Narrows had something to do with the political consequences of their social heritage. So too for the distribution of pollution in the United States, where there has been considerable research on this question. As with income, those from more advantaged social heritages are less likely to experience a threatened invironment. Within issues of environmental justice there are special challenges of *environmental racism*. (See Figure 5.2.) Or perhaps we might better term these challenges of *invironmental racism*—that is, social heritage differences in the distribution of environmental bads for the body, due to either intentional or institutional reasons. But I'll generally stick with the more conventional phrase, environmental racism, which is a broader and better known term.

Much of the early research in environmental racism focused on whether people of color were

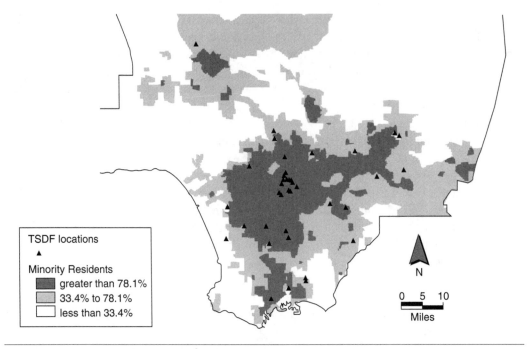

Figure 5.2   Evidence of environmental racism: Sites of toxic releases to the air and percentage minority in Los Angeles County, based on the Federal Toxic Release Inventory.

more likely or not to live in communities with hazardous waste problems. In 1987, the United Church of Christ's Commission for Racial Justice released the first of two controversial reports. Based on studies of zip codes, the reports concluded that African Americans and other people of color were two to three times as likely as other Americans to live in communities with commercial hazardous waste landfills.[23] A 1992 study found that 3 percent of all whites and 11 percent of all minorities in the Detroit region live within a mile of hazardous waste facilities—a difference of a factor of nearly four.[24]

Findings like these were central to the emergence in the early 1990s of the *environmental justice movement*. Originally a largely grassroots movement of local activists concerned about pollution in their neighborhoods, environmental justice now has a prominent place on the agenda of most national and international environmental organizations. Environmental justice has

become one of the central civil rights issues in the United States and elsewhere, helping create a political climate for change.[25] The U.S. government has taken these issues quite seriously and has undertaken several self-studies. As a result, in 1992 the U.S. Environmental Protection Agency admitted that it may sometimes have been discriminatory in its siting and regulatory decisions, and in 1994 President Clinton signed Executive Order 12898, which requires all federal agencies to work toward environmental justice.[26]

Some other studies of the siting of hazardous waste facilities, though, did not show similar results. In 1994 a team of University of Massachusetts sociologists—with funding from Waste Management, Inc. (WMI), North America's largest handler of wastes—published a report that contradicted earlier findings of pervasive environmental racism. This study showed no nationwide correspondence of toxic waste sites with race and no nationwide correspondence with poverty, although it did nonetheless find a relationship of toxic waste sites with blue-collar neighborhoods.[27] These results unleashed a storm of debate, in part because the study had been sponsored by the waste industry itself.

These studies on hazardous waste siting are difficult to compare, however, since they used different methods. Whereas the United Church of Christ study used zip codes for the analysis, the University of Massachusetts study used census tracts, a smaller unit. A case could be made that a smaller unit of analysis produces more precise results. But as well, a smaller unit of analysis can wipe out a statistical effect by subdividing to the point where its influence on any one unit becomes marginal. Also, the University of Massachusetts study excluded rural areas, and many toxic waste landfills are in poor rural regions with a high percentage of minority residents—such as Emelle, Alabama, a mainly African American community where WMI operates what was at the time the largest toxic waste landfill in the United States. The University of Massachusetts team later conducted a follow-up study (without funding from WMI) that did include rural areas. This time, they found a strong association of hazardous waste facilities with blue-collar working class communities, plus a slight association with African Americans living in rural areas.[28]

Researchers are starting to come around to the view that this kind of is-it-race-or-income debate is a bit beside the point, however.[29] For one thing, within the United States at least, race and income closely correspond and intertwine. To talk about one is largely to talk about the other. And when one is dealing with statistical categories that necessarily do a bit of jamming and cramming of the variety of the world to get it into the precise boxes needed for numerical calculation, some dimensions of things get compromised. Nevertheless, of 18 empirical studies of environmental justice in the United States published between 1998 and 2002, seven found race was significant,[30] five found social class was significant,[31] and six showed that both race and social class

were significant factors.[32] And every single one found evidence of environmental inequality.

They found that Los Angeles schools with high proportions of minority students tend to be located in areas with high levels of airborne toxics.[33] They found that in Florida people of color face much higher odds that their homes are located near a toxic chemical plant—up to five times higher, in some cases.[34] They found that in Michigan poor people and people of color are more likely to live in areas subjected to the toxic releases registered in the U.S. Environmental Protection Agency's Toxic Release Inventory.[35] They found that industrial-scale hog farms in Missouri are more likely to be located in counties with lower average income.[36] They found that poor people experience higher levels of ambient and indoor air pollution, worse drinking water quality, and more ambient noise (from streets and highways, for example) where they live.[37]

But whether by race or by class, such biases are a challenge to the environmental and invironmental justice we all have a right to enjoy.

Pesticides and the People of Everywhere

In 2003, nine people volunteered to let Mount Sinai Hospital researchers search their bodies for traces of industrial chemicals and pollutants—chemicals that their own bodies did not make. The researchers took blood and urine samples and ran test after test to see what else might be in there. What they found in the volunteers' bodies was an average of 91 different chemical pollutants. Among these chemicals, the volunteers averaged 53 that cause cancer, 62 neurotoxins, 53 immune system disrupters, 55 that cause birth defects or disrupt the body's normal development, and 34 that damage hearing. (Many of these chemicals have more than one effect.) Of course, these chemicals were present in only trace amounts, and the researchers used sophisticated equipment to detect them. But they were there.

Pesticides in World Use, 1997

WHO rating	number	percentage of all classified
extremely hazardous	33	5.5
highly hazardous	48	8.1
moderately hazardous	118	19.8
slightly hazardous	239	40.2
not hazardous	157	26.4
not classified	164	NA

Figure 5.3   WHO rating of pesticide hazards.

And although this was the most comprehensive assessment of individual "body burden," as toxicologists call it, there were many kinds of common chemical pollutants that the researchers were not able to study. So it is likely that 91 was a low estimate of the number of trace pollutants.

Can trace amounts sometimes amount to something? Many observers now think unfortunately yes. Increasingly, the leading medical journals are filling up with studies that link environmental chemicals with a host of diseases. Not all the studies show this link. But more and more do. It's an enormous topic, so I narrow our focus here to just one class of such potential threats: pesticides.

The Health Effects of Pesticides

Currently, the people of the world apply some 5.6 billion pounds of pesticides to the land every year, mostly for agricultural uses, including both chemical pesticides like atrazine and biological control agents like *Bacillus thuringiensis*.[38] In all, some 759 pesticides were in world use as of 1997.[39] And they're mostly toxic, some highly toxic. That's why we use them, after all: to kill things. Of that 759, the World Health Organization (WHO) classified 33 as "extremely hazardous," 48 as "highly hazardous," 118 as "moderately hazardous," and 239 as "slightly hazardous." Eliminating the 164 pesticides the WHO did not

include in its classification of hazard, that gives a figure of 74 percent of pesticides as being some degree of hazardous.[40] (See Figure 5.3.)

The WHO has some good reason to label three-quarters of pesticides as hazardous, according to toxicological and epidemiological studies. Take research linking pesticide use to birth defects, for example. A Finnish study found that women who worked during the first trimester of a pregnancy in agricultural occupations that used pesticides had double the normal rate of cleft lips and palates among their newborns. A similar study in Spain found that the rate was three times the normal. A study of 700 women in California found that those who lived nearest to crop areas where particular pesticides were in use had higher rates of fetal death due to developmental defects. In Iowa, a study found that rates of birth defects and congenital heart problems were elevated in communities whose water supplies were contaminated with atrazine, a common pesticide in the United States. The most dramatic study, perhaps, was a 1996 examination of birth defects in Minnesota, comparing western Minnesota—where most of the state's agriculture is—with the east side. This study found not only that farm families from western Minnesota had higher rates of birth defects, non-farming families in the western side did too. Plus the defects in the western side of the state followed the seasonality of pesticide application. Most pesticides are applied in the spring, and birth defects were highest for western Minnesota babies conceived in springtime.[41]

Or take the evidence linking pesticides to fertility problems for both men and women. There's the 2001 study of 225 men in Argentina who were experiencing fertility problems. Here researchers found an association between pesticide exposure, low sperm counts, and elevated levels of female sex hormones in their bodies.[42] Then there's a 2003 study from Missouri—similar findings.[43] And there's the 1994 study of 30 Danish organic farmers, published in the journal *Lancet*. This one found that the organic farmers (who use no pesticides on their farms) had a sperm count twice as high as Danish blue-collar workers.[44] As for women's infertility, a 2003 National Institute for Occupational Safety and Health study of 644 Wisconsin women found that those who had experienced fertility problems—defined as a year's unsuccessful effort to become pregnant—were 27 times more likely to have been involved in mixing and applying pesticides in the two previous years.[45]

Stick with me while I run through a few more facts and figures from studies of the health effects of pesticides. Here are a few on neurological and mental problems associated with pesticide use. A 2000 American study of 496 people with Parkinson's disease, and another 541 without, found that those with Parkinson's were twice as likely to have been active users of pesticides in their home gardens and lawns.[46] A 2000 Dutch study of 830 people found that those who had been regularly exposed to pesticides in their work were five times more likely to suffer "mild cognitive dysfunction"—which meant that they had trouble recognizing words, colors, and numbers, and had trouble speaking.[47] Earlier, a study from the mid-1990s of farm families in Colorado found that exposure to certain pesticides was associated with levels of depression six times the rate of the non-exposed.[48]

And here are some results from studies on breast cancer and prostate cancer, two of cancer's most pervasive forms. A 2003 Belgian study found that women with breast cancer were five times more likely to have pesticides in their blood.[49] This is in line with concerns that a number of pesticides are endocrine disrupters—that is, they mimic and interfere with hormonal activity. Endocrine disruption is in turn suspected to cause cancer in some cases. As for prostate cancer, a 2003 study of farmers and nursery workers in Iowa and North Carolina found elevated incidence rates.[50] A 2002 study found that workers at Sygenta Corporation's atrazine plant in St. Gabriel, Louisiana, are coming down with prostate cancer at three and a half times the expected rate for Louisiana.[51]

I could go on, and were this a book on environmental toxicology I would. But I think the point should be clear by now: There is a good deal of worrisome evidence about the invironmental effects of pesticides, effects that concern the health of all of us.

There is also evidence that disagrees with some of these findings. For example, a 1999 Yale University study of 1,000 women in Connecticut did not show a link between breast cancer and exposure to pesticides.[52] And the Environmental Protection Agency argues that the elevated prostate cancer rates at Syngenta's St. Gabriel plant are due to a sampling effect. Most prostate cancer is never detected, according to autopsy studies, so the research at St. Gabriel may just be showing the prostate cancer that would be expected for the general population, were a similarly comprehensive study of non-plant workers done.[53] Research is like that, which gives ground for much political debate as to whether particular pesticides should be banned. Atrazine, for instance, has now been banned in many European countries, while the Environmental Protection Agency in 2003 reaffirmed its continued use as the most widely applied herbicide in the United States.[54]

Many do not want to wait for all the pesticide studies to be done, however. That's in part because all the studies never will be done. This too is what research is like. So in the meantime,

New Zealand

France

United Kingdom

Sweden

United States

Germany

Japan

Figure 5.4   Many countries now have national organic certification labels.

many are turning to organic food, which in recent years has become one of the fastest growing sectors in food retailing. Growth in consumption of organics was running at about 20 percent a year in both Europe and the United States during the 1990s, despite its sometimes uncertain availability and generally high price, although it has recently declined to about a 10 percent growth rate.[55] In the United States, some 39 percent of consumers now use organic products at least occasionally.[56] In many cities, even conventional supermarkets have put in organic product lines. (See Figure 5.4.) Most of the major food corporations are busily buying up the smaller organic companies, in an effort to cash in on this booming market and citizens' increasing concerns with the health effects of pesticides.

Pesticides and Environmental Justice

But not everyone is buying organic food yet, including many who would like to. Lack of availability is indeed part of the problem. Price is the big barrier, though, due to market factors that go beyond the constraints of supply. "Yuppie chow" is what critics sometimes call organic food, and not unreasonably so in many circumstances. In an organic supermarket a mile from my house, part of a national chain of such supermarkets, tomatoes were selling for $5 a pound recently. True, these were specialty tomatoes—an heirloom variety raised by a local farm. But they don't have to sell them for so much, another local farmer told me at the farmer's market that is also near my home. She used to sell her own heirloom tomatoes to this store for a fraction of that $5 price. When she saw what the store was selling them for, she refused to supply the store any longer. (Now she sells them on her own at the farmer's market for $1.50 to $2 a pound, more than the wholesale price she had been getting, she informed me.) In other words, organic food often becomes vanity food—a positional good, as Chapter 2 termed such an item, limited in supply and thus a ready source for social display for those in a position to pay for it.

The use of organic food as a positional good raises issues of environmental and invironmental justice. While the still-uncertain (and perhaps inevitably uncertain) invironmental effects of pesticides have consequences for everyone, some people are better able than others to avoid these effects. It would be hard to escape all effects of pesticides. Even the wealthy have neighbors who douse their lawns with the latest chemical wonders, and even the wealthy sometimes find themselves in situations where it is difficult to eat as one might like. The wealthy have a considerable advantage in avoiding pesticides, though.

There are as well other social inequalities in pesticide exposure. Certain of us have increased vulnerabilities to pesticides and other toxins, especially at certain stages in the life of our bodies. Children and pregnant and nursing women have particular sensitivities that mean the same level of exposure can lead to outsized effects. When the body's cells are reproducing and growing rapidly, chances are particularly high that chemical pollutants can disrupt the body's development. Plus, children and many pregnant and nursing women eat more per body weight, increasing their level of exposure. They may also eat more of foods high in pesticide residues, such as many of the apples that go into apple juice, a staple of young children's diets in many countries.[57] And young children can increase their exposure through eating what they shouldn't and through playing with what they shouldn't—such as dirt from a lawn treated with pesticides, or pesticides stored at home. Even playing on the floor of a home with a lawn and garden treated with pesticides can increase children's exposure, because of chemicals tracked in on shoes, notes the U.S. Environmental Protection Agency.[58] The United States' 1996 Food Quality Protection Act tries to take children's sensitivities and exposure into account in the setting of pesticide residue guidelines, but few parents consider these matters in making food choices for their children.

Another source of children's exposure to pesticides and other toxins is from their own mothers. Breast milk turns out to be, unfortunately, remarkably sensitive to chemical pollutants. Some 200 different chemical pollutants have been detected in the breast milk of American mothers, according to a 1981 tabulation.[59] If a similar tabulation were done today, it would undoubtedly yield a substantially higher number. A particular problem are persistent organic pollutants, or POPs—chemicals like dioxin, PCBs, and the once-popular pesticide DDT (the latter usually in the form of DDE, a metabolic byproduct of DDT). As Sandra Steingraber observes, "Prevailing levels of chemical contaminants in human milk often exceed legally allowable limits in commercial foodstuffs."[60] Consequently, breastfed babies consume 50 times more dioxin and PCBs than do adults, according to recent studies, and a German study from 1998 found that breastfed babies have 10 to 15 times of the level of POPs in their bodies than formula-fed babies do.[61]

These are tragic findings. "On the one hand we have the chemical adulteration of human milk," notes Steingraber. "On the other is the bodily sacrament between mother and child. Can we speak of them both in the same breath? Can we look at one without turning away from the other?"[62]

That parents could be placed in such a quandary is also an issue of environmental justice and its invironmental reach into all our bodies.

The Sociology of Invironmental Justice

These are uncertain matters, though. I don't just mean the inescapable uncertainty of science, particularly when dealing with largely invisible matters like how much of a particular chemical has made it into our bodies, and the time it takes for any health consequences to be manifested. I mean also the uncertainty of whether those consequences will matter for a particular person like you or me, or for particular peoples like them or us. Chapter 9 on risk explores the sociological implications of these uncertainties in more detail, but here I want to raise an important issue of justice and how we think about it and act on it.

Let us say, for instance, that the risk of getting Parkinson's disease from pesticide exposure is on the order of 1,000,000 to 1. I don't know what the actual number is, and I'm not even sure that it could be known. But it is common enough to think of such an issue in such a way. Or let us say that the chances of being caught in the blast wave of a factory explosion are also 1,000,000 to 1. It might be. I don't know for sure, but certainly it is not a very regular occurrence. It's never happened to me or any of my friends, at any rate.

So maybe neither of these problems is something I should worry about. Besides, we need food if we are to solve the invironmental challenges of hunger. The pesticides produced at Bhopal and the fertilizer that Toulouse plant produced are very helpful in our battle with pests and with the Earth itself, it might be argued, and indeed often is argued. On the whole, pesticides and fertilizers are for the greater good of everyone, it is frequently said.

Of everyone? Really? Such might be the response to the view in the preceding paragraph. If a hazard has a 1 in 1,000,000 chance, that means in a country the current size of the United States 290 people will suffer from it, even die from it. You probably won't be affected, and so too for almost everyone else. But there are 290 people out there that hazard will indeed affect. So it would not be for the greater good of *everyone*. Likely most agree that it is not right for the majority to suffer for the benefit of a few. Yet is it right for a few to suffer for the benefit of the majority? Certainly, if you knew that you were going to be among that few, you would be unlikely to agree to such an arrangement.

The debate I have just sketched here is the essence of recent discussions among political philosophers about the meaning of justice and related ideas like human rights. This debate is not only an academic one, however. The social dynamics of environmental and invironmental justice to a large extent revolve around the way the debate plays out in contemporary society. If we are to understand the sociology of justice and its implications for invironmental health, we should inspect this philosophical question with some care.

What Is Justice?

The view that if something is for the greater good then it must be okay is technically referred to as *utilitarianism,* and it is an old and pervasive idea. The classic formulation of utilitarianism is that we should strive for actions whose tendency "to augment the happiness of the community is greater than any it has to diminish it," as the philosopher Jeremy Bentham put it in 1779.[63] Another standard phrase to describe the goals of utilitarianism is that we should promote "the greatest good for the greatest number."[64] It's called "utilitarianism" because the good is defined as "utility," or the degree to which an action promotes happiness.

Much contemporary thought is based on utilitarian ideals. We can see utilitarian ideals enshrined in, for example, the focus on growth in gross domestic product (GDP) as a mark of social improvement, what we might call *economic utilitarianism.* In this case, GDP is taken as a direct measure of the greatest source of utility in modern economies: money. If there is more of it around in the economy, people on the whole must be able to do more of what they want to do, which can only be for the greater good, the argument goes. Similarly, if the use of pesticides and other toxins helps feed the world and keep us in comfort, that must be for the greater good as well.

This deceptively simple and goodhearted notion has a few stingers, though. Most prominent is that utilitarianism (at least as conventionally understood) tolerates quite a bit of inequality in the distribution of the good. The greatest good for the *greatest number,* sure. But what if the greatest number's good comes at the expense of a smaller number of people? Moreover, there is nothing inherent in utilitarianism that requires the greatest number to be a majority of the population, or even any more than a small minority of it—or even any more than one person. All other things being equal, utilitarianism prefers to have the greatest good spread around a bit. But the greatest good comes first. So if GDP for the country goes up, then utility has gone up too, even if all the increase went to just a few, or even just to one. Besides, isn't a flourishing economy good for everyone in it?

And isn't an abundant food supply good for everyone too, even if many of us face greater cancer risks from the pesticides we use to get that abundance?

It may seem absurd to interpret the phrase "greatest good for the greatest number" in this way—as tolerating harm and as often amounting to great good for a rather small number.[65] But the logic of the primacy of economic growth as the be-all-end-all of the political good takes precisely this form. Economic growth is supposed to be a sign of great good for most of us, but is it always? Similarly for technology. New advances are supposed to enhance the lives of most people, but is that always so? Utilitarianism—and particularly economic utilitarianism—can easily lead to the perverse result of benefiting only a minority while professing to do the opposite. And even if there is benefit for the majority, should we be concerned about the minority who are disadvantaged?

John Rawls and Justice as Fairness

The philosopher John Rawls said that we should be concerned, and for a very selfish reason: we might ourselves wind up among the disadvantaged.[66] In his much discussed 1971 book, *A Theory of Justice*, Rawls asked that we stop for a moment and try to figure out what our principles of justice would be if none of us had any idea of where we will likely wind up in life. Put on an imaginary "veil of ignorance," as Rawls termed it, about your life chances and sit down with every else, similarly garbed. From this "original position," asked Rawls, what principles of justice would people come up with?

Rawls's answer is that we would all commit to two basic principles, and I'll quote him verbatim on this:

1) Each person is to have an equal right to the most extensive basic liberty compatible with a similar liberty for others.

2) Social and economic inequalities are to be arranged so that they are both (a) reasonably expected to be to everyone's advantage, and (b) attached to positions and offices open to all.[67]

In other words, Rawls says that if we didn't know where we would ourselves get to in life, we would want the greatest good for *everyone*, not just for the greatest number. We would also recognize that our own good must be realized within the context of others similarly, and justly, pursuing their own good. Liberty has constraints, most notably the liberty of other people. And we would recognize that we would not want others to seek advantage over us, and they would not want us to seek advantage over them.

We would also recognize that justice does not depend upon everyone being exactly equal. There are times when some forms of inequality are advantageous to everyone, if properly handled. Children gain some advantage from the authority their parents—who are more experienced in the dangers of the world—have over them. Students similarly, we must hope, gain some advantage from the greater experience of their teachers in the topic at hand. Citizens gain some advantage through the coordination of social organization afforded by having police officers, mayors of cities, licensed medical experts such as nurses and doctors, and the like. But these offices must be advantageous to everyone, Rawls argued, not just to a majority, and they must be open to everyone as well, in part to ensure that they are indeed advantageous to everyone.

Rawls distilled his entire 607 page book into the following sentence:

All social values—liberty and opportunity, income and wealth, and bases of self-respect—are to be distributed equally unless an unequal distribution of any, or all, of these values is to everyone's advantage.[68]

He got it down even more tightly when he offered a definition of the opposite of justice: "Injustice, then, is simply inequalities that are not to the benefit of all."[69]

Rawls called his approach "justice as fairness," and it is a form of *egalitarianism*.[70] Utilitarianism may often style itself as egalitarian, and it can have a democratic feel in its avowal of what adds to the "happiness" of the community as a whole. But in practice it can easily lead to outcomes that are clearly not to everyone's advantage, even if the total happiness of the community concerned has gone up. Utilitarianism might well accept a technology that increases the risk of cancer by 1 in 1,000,000, if more happiness was created than lost in the process. But justice as fairness would not accept such a technology. Maximizing happiness isn't its point. Maximizing fairness is.

The publication of Rawls's book touched off a huge discussion in political philosophy that continues today, even after Rawls's death in 2003. Most philosophers had long been troubled by utilitarianism, but hadn't quite put their finger on a more compelling way to think about what is just. Rawls certainly did that, in most readers' views, but his theory also presented new questions, in part through the issues it did not resolve. Most prominently, readers of Rawls found themselves pondering the *pluralism* of social life and how to incorporate social difference into political theory. Rawls's theory was a universalistic one. He thought it applied to everyone, everywhere. Many of his readers were not so sure.

Justice and the Problem of Pluralism

One such reader is the economist Amartya Sen, who while applauding much of what Rawls offered, has tried to build in a more pluralistic understanding of fairness.[71] Yes, says Sen, Rawls recognized that fairness didn't necessarily mean that everyone had to be equal in every regard, as long as that inequality was to everyone's advantage. But Rawls seemed to have in mind mostly unequal positions in social hierarchy that are helpful for social organization. What if not everyone wants the same "social values" that Rawls said should otherwise be distributed equally, or does not want them in the same degree and amounts?

For example, should the illiterate be given subscriptions to the *New York Times* and the Book of the Month Club? Not while they are still illiterate, Sen's arguments would suggest. Should Amazonian tribal people be air-dropped suitcases filled with $5,140 for each of them, that being the average GNP per capita in the world? Not if cash isn't something they need or is relevant to their lives. Should all men—and I mean this quite seriously—be given appointments at gynecologists' offices, or conversely should women be denied them? Not if men's bodies have little need for this medical specialty and women's bodies do.

If you read Rawls closely, his theory does not necessarily lead to any of these absurd outcomes. But Sen wants to make the pluralism of people's needs and wants more explicit. So he suggests that we think of people as having *functionings*—beings and doings they have reason to value, in the language of Sen—and *capabilities*—freedoms for attaining these beings and doings. Justice for Sen is maximizing people's capabilities to achieve their functionings. Lack of justice is when people do not have these capabilities. So too is poverty. Rather than seeing poverty as a lack of money, as conventional utilitarian conceptions do, Sen says poverty is *capability deprivation*, and our capabilities depend on a lot more than money. Ill health would also be a form of capability deprivation, a kind of poverty of the body that prevents one from attaining valued beings and doings.

Sen's work has been widely embraced, most especially by development agencies and scholars. The well-known Human Development Index (HDI) of the UN Development Programme is a direct application of Sen's ideas about poverty being more than a matter of money and a direct challenge to the standard GNP per capita approach. GNP per capita is a form of utilitarian thinking. It equates money with what we value, gives us no sense of inequality levels within a country, and it doesn't consider the variability in what people want. The HDI does not reject the significance of money in an increasingly monetarized world. But the HDI combines GNP per capita with measures of two other widely valued beings and doings: health (using longevity rates) and knowledge access (using literacy and school enrollment rates). It gives us a window (albeit an imperfect one) on the problem of within-country inequality by looking at a couple of measures of how people are doing aside from their average income. And the HDI gets a degree of pluralism into the mix by suggesting there is more than one route to increasing human well-being, rather than money alone. While a country's world rank in GNP per capita is typically similar to its world rank in HDI, often there are wide disparities. For example, the countries of Vietnam and Guinea have almost the same GNP per capita, but Vietnam has almost double the HDI figure—0.671 versus Guinea's 0.394.[72]

The philosopher Ronald Dworkin is another fan of Rawls, and of Sen's efforts to deal better with the pluralism of humanity. Dworkin argues that justice needs to be based on the recognition that we are all different, but that across that difference we need to extend an *equality of concern*. He worries that we might choose to pursue our differences in ways that compromise the pursuits of others, and thus compromise the first principle that Rawls said those wearing veils of ignorance about their life chances would agree to: that everyone's liberty needs to be compatible with every one else's liberty. And he worries that Sen's notion of functionings doesn't take that necessary balancing into account. Sen says we should give people the capabilities to achieve the functionings they have reason to value. But what if the functioning one person values conflicts with another's? For example, what if that one person values being a dictator? Dworkin also argues that if people do not apply themselves in the pursuit of what they individually value, equality of concern will be hard to sustain in the long term. (It's hard to maintain concern for someone who simply doesn't try.) Justice means the responsibility of concern for others and what they individually value, but it also means that we have responsibility for ourselves and what we individually value.[73]

Rawls came to have much sympathy for these and other efforts to combine fairness with difference,

and much of his later writing concerned this subject.[74] The details of his responses need not concern us here. But one thing that Rawls remained firm about—and something nearly all his critics also embraced—is that unless you have a pretty good idea that you're going to wind up in a privileged position you wouldn't choose to live in a society organized around utilitarianism. Rather, you'd want to live in a society organized around conceptions of justice that pay attention to everybody's needs and wants.

Power and Invironmental Justice

Every *body*'s needs and wants, that is, for everybody is a body, and that body is in constant dialogue with its environment and the other bodies, with their own needs and wants, that help constitute that environment. If we want a society organized around concern for every body, a society that strives for invironmental justice for all, then we would do well to consider why we so manifestly do not live in such a society today.

To answer this question, we need to begin with the following fundamental sociological observation: We do not wear veils of ignorance about our life chances. No one knows for sure where she or he will wind up. You could get hit by a car tomorrow and be in a wheelchair for the rest of your life. You could indeed get cancer or Parkinson's or any of a host of potential maladies and calamities. But based on the reasonable presumption that where I'm headed today is where I'll be headed tomorrow, we all have some confidence about our likely future lot in life, whether good or bad.

This knowledge makes utilitarianism an attractive philosophy for those confident that they will indeed be on the upside tomorrow, and for tomorrows to come. Moreover, those who are likely to end up on the upside of, say, the pollution that might accompany some broadly beneficial technological process with uneven downstream consequences are also typically the same people who are advantaged in society's decision making. Were it otherwise, those advantaged in decision making would be unlikely to promote that technological process. Consequently, we live in a society organized around utilitarianism far more than around justice as fairness, and the related notions of capabilities to function and equality of concern.

My point is not that those who are socially advantaged in decision making would reject justice as fairness out of hand. Rather, my point is that utilitarianism does not seem as personally threatening to the advantaged as to the disadvantaged. So the advantaged are less likely to easily envision its problems, and thus less likely to throw their social weight against the problems coming to pass. The origin of environmental injustices, then, may not lie in some widespread social rejection of justice as fairness as much as in the lack of rejection of utilitarianism by those in advantaged positions.

What I am describing are the invironmental consequences of inequalities in *social power*— people's abilities to exercise control over the social world.[75] Social power is not necessarily a bad thing, as Chapter 2 discusses. It would be neither an enjoyable nor a just world if people were not able to exercise some control over their life situation. This is precisely why Sen emphasizes the importance of people's capabilities to achieve the functionings they value. Given that this control has to be realized within the context of others similarly seeking to achieve the functionings they value for themselves, justice requires some means of balancing these capabilities in ways that do not disadvantage anyone. However, that balance does not now exist in many places, if any.

Which is not to say that those who exercise control over the social world in ways that do not advantage everyone are necessarily evil and cruel. The image of the exercise of social power as some kind of mad organist playing at will on the keyboard of social life is rarely apt. Utilitarianism retains much of its influence because it usually feels democratic, not demonic.

For example, an action that appears to benefit the community at large surely feels more democratic than one that doesn't. And if that action has the perverse consequence of benefiting only a minority, the majority can exercise its democratic control and prevent it from happening. We're not stuck with it, necessarily. We can vote it out.

But from an equal-concern perspective, there are still some problems here with utilitarianism. First, a democratic response like taking a vote on something may then disadvantage the minority who voted the other way. This is the problem Alexis de Tocqueville long ago pointed out with America's democratic experiment: the potential in a democracy for a "tyranny of the majority."[76]

Second, there's something in the very way we understand democracy that can also make it hard to prevent the perverse outcomes of utilitarianism. We generally understand democracy as a matter of ensuring that everyone has equal political standing—that everyone can vote, can organize meetings, can register their views with elected officials, and can run for office themselves. These are all important ideals. However, we are unlikely to attain these ideals without confronting an important material reality: Those with material advantages are likely to be a lot more advantaged by these ideals. What I mean is that, while everyone can potentially vote in a democracy, there are great inequalities in people's abilities to influence what is voted *on,* and what those who are voted *for* do with their offices. People with economic and other social advantages are far more likely to be able to organize effective social groups, to gain the ear of elected officials (as well as unelected officials), and to run successfully for office. The ideal of equality of political standing thus depends in part upon equality of material standing—and vice versa.

Take what happened in Bhopal, Toulouse, and Grassy Narrows. In each case, a large corporation was able to use its influence to establish industrial plants that horribly disadvantaged a minority, while contributing to GNP and to what could be argued to be environmental advantages for the majority—pesticides and fertilizer for food production and, in Grassy Narrows, wood pulp for paper, one of the great conveniences of this bodily life, even in a digital age, one could argue. At least in Bhopal and Toulouse, lots of people were well aware of the potential dangers to local people. In Grassy Narrows, too, there was reason to be worried. The 1950s discovery in Minimata, Japan, of methyl mercury poisoning from a plastics factory should have been a warning. Many say the warning signs are already loud and clear about toxic wastes, air pollution, and pesticides. Using utilitarian arguments both to themselves and to others, these consequences were and are ignored by corporate executives and by government officials. What's good for General Motors is good for the nation, it is sometimes said, and by extension what is good for any corporation is good for any nation. But from a justice-as-fairness point of view, the matter is far, far more complex.

Again, I want to emphasize that corporate executives and government officials are not necessarily being demonic when they violate fairness and equality of concern in favor of utilitarianism, through the exercise of their greater political power using the normal and legal channels. Under our current dominantly utilitarian understandings of justice and political process, there is no reason why they should do otherwise. These are their rights, in the current way we have organized our democracies.

Perhaps paradoxically, what we have in the world today is democracies of inequalities, in which we grant, so we think, equality of political standing without addressing material inequalities. Without the latter we cannot attain the former, however. What Rawls, Sen, Dworkin, and the millions who call for environmental and invironmental justice are asking for is not just democracies of inequalities but rather democracies of equalities. They are asking for not just democracy, but what we might term *isodemocracy*, democracy founded on equalities in both political and material standing—democracy in which the concerns of everybody and every body are the concerns of everybody and every body.[77]

Making Connections

Thus we continue to grapple with the central issue of the body in environmental matters: making connections. We moderns tend to regard our bodies, and our selves, atomistically. When considering matters of justice and the environment, however, we quickly encounter the connectedness of our bodies with the world. Our bodies live in context. The interactiveness of ecological dialogue impels us to consider our connectedness with care. Our health, among other things, depends upon that careful consideration.

Such consideration depends in part upon the conceptions that we bring to bear. Although this chapter has concerned some basic material fundamentals—body and health—it has equally concerned some basic fundamentals in the realm of our ideas. I did not highlight the importance of the ideal side of ecological dialogue as the chapter went along. But a moment's reflection should show it.

To begin with, the notion of an "invironment," that realm of the body's dialogue with the environment, represents the new conceptual place the body is gaining in environmental discussions. This is a recent change, as I noted. Earlier, issues of the body were often relegated to the sidelines of environmentalism, and environmental sociology as well. The body was always "there," of course, just as gravity was always there before the mythical apple conked Newton on the head. But the consequences of that *thereness*—and thus what that thereness actually is, for what something does is surely central to what it is—depends in part on how we understand it. The new connected understanding of the body's place in the environment is already leading to new environmental initiatives, such as the United States' 1996 Food Quality Protection Act. Health is now an environmental issue. Food is now an environmental issue. The body is now an environmental issue.

As well, our ideas of justice are changing. The efforts of Rawls, Sen, Dworkin, and others to shift us away from utilitarian thinking are already having some material effects. Again, the 1996

Food Quality Protection Act with the special attention it gives to the developmental differences of children's bodies is an example. Rather than using the utilitarian logic of greatest good for the greatest number, this portion of the act finds it fair to pay attention to the pluralism of our needs and to give equal concern for those different needs, even for the minority of the U.S. population who are children. Here again our ideas are having material consequences.

In this light, it is worth inspecting the debates over what are sometimes called "NIMBY" or Not-In-My-Back-Yard responses to environmental issues. Often the term NIMBY is used as a utilitarian weapon. Why should a small group of people concerned about the local environmental consequences of some development proposal stand in the way of the greater good? Conversely, people will often use NIMBY politics to in fact defend their narrow personal interests, by using whatever advantage they can gain through their social position. Similarly, with the new presence of the body in environmental issues, we are seeing the rise of what the environmental sociologist Melanie Dupuis has called "NIMB"—Not-In-My-Body responses.[78] These conflicts make NIMBY and NIMB politics highly contentious. Justice as fairness gets us beyond this utilitarian turmoil by saying not-in-*anybody's*-back-yard and not-in-*anybody's*-body unless it is to *everybody's* and *every body's* advantage. Justice as fairness says that justice is not a "zero-sum" game. There really are ways to arrange our lives to the advantage of everyone, if we appropriately apply our minds to the task.

Ideas may not be matter, but they do matter. And matter matters for our ideas. It's a dialogue, the most basic one of environmental sociology. It's a dialogue of connection and interconnection, of the unity of difference. This dialogue is no more evident than in that home, that abode, that we never leave, as long as we live: Our own bodies.

PART II

The Ideal

CHAPTER 6

The Ideology of Environmental Domination

No one seems to know how useful it is to be useless.

—Chuang Tzu, third century B.C.E.

The view from Glacier Point in Yosemite National Park is one of the world's most famous. From this overlook you can see a sweeping panorama of Yosemite, which many have called the most beautiful valley in America. A number of years ago, my brother and sister-in-law, Jon and Steph, were visiting her relatives in California, and they decided to take Steph's grandmother to see Yosemite, where she had never been. An elderly woman, she did not walk well, so they took her only to sites you can get to by car. You can drive right up to Glacier Point, and they did. As Jon later recounted the story to me, they helped Steph's grandmother up to the edge and stood there for a few minutes taking it all in. Then Jon turned and asked her, somewhat hopefully, "Well, what do you think?"

She considered the question carefully, and replied, "All that forest. What a waste. There should be people and houses down there."

When two people look out on a scene, a scene of any kind, they are unlikely to appreciate it in just the same way. Faced with the same material circumstances, we each see something different. Where my brother Jon saw the beauty of wild nature in that view from Glacier Point, Steph's grandmother saw wasted resources. Such differences are a part of our individuality. They also reflect social differences in the apparatus of understanding that we use to organize our experience. There are larger social and historical patterns in the distinctive mental apparatuses we each bring to bear on the world around us. In a word, there is *ideology* at work.

In this second part of the book, we take ideal factors as the point of entry into the ecological dialogue. As we saw in Part I, the other side of the dialogue is always close at hand, and we will find that here too. Investigation of ideal factors inevitably leads back to material questions. But the emphasis in Chapters 6 through 9 will be on the form the environment takes in our minds.

The independent power of ideas in our lives is well illustrated by the history of environmental ideas. The material conditions we now regard as

Figure 6.1   Night falls on New Haven harbor in Connecticut. The human domination of the environment is particularly characteristic of the waterfronts of industrial port cities.

environmental problems have long historical precedents, yet few people in the first half of the twentieth century questioned the increasing per capita appetite for resources, the spread of the automobile and its sprawling land use, the invention of yet another chemical or mechanical weapon for every instance of the environment's resistance to our desires. Early articles in *National Geographic*, for example, extolled the industrial might that spawned marvel after marvel, as their titles implied: "Synthetic Products: Chemists Make a New World," "Coal: Prodigious Worker for Man," "The Fire of Heaven: Electricity Revolutionizes the Modern World," "The Automobile Industry: An American Art That Has Revolutionized Methods in Manufacturing and Transformed Transportation." (See Figure 6.1.)

In the decades from 1960 on, though, the ideological situation changed dramatically in country after country, as Chapter 7 discusses.[1] *National Geographic*, to continue with that barometer of Western cultural values, began running articles with titles like these: "Our Ecological Crisis;" "African Wildlife: Man's Threatened Legacy," "Nature's Dwindling Treasures," "Pollution: Threat to Man's Only Home," "The Tallgrass Prairie: Can It Be Saved?" A different ideology had taken more general hold, at least among the writers and editors (and, we can presume, many of the readers) of this perennially popular magazine.

Scholars have studied the role of ideology in the ecological dialogue in two broad ways, largely drawing on historical evidence. First, they have considered the ideological circumstances that make domination of the environment thinkable and tolerable, focusing on understanding Western cultural attitudes that support such a relationship to the environment. Second, scholars have considered the ideological circumstances that make such conditions and such domination increasingly unthinkable and intolerable, focusing on the social origins of the environmental movement.

This chapter considers that first role of ideology; Chapter 7 the second. In this chapter, then, I examine the ideological origins of the view that human beings can and should transform the environment for their own purposes. Scholars argue that three Western intellectual traditions—Christianity, individualism, and patriarchy—have in large part provided the ideological rationale for environmental domination. These ideologies of environmental domination are by no means exclusively Western, but they are certainly heavily present in the West, which may help account for the central role of Western institutions in the industrial transformation of the Earth. As well, all three of these ideologies of environmental domination have close links with ideas about hierarchy and inequality, suggesting an ideological connection between environmental domination and social domination, as we shall see.

Christianity and Environmental Domination

A common explanation for the modern urge to transform the Earth is the rise of the industrial economy. But the next question to ask is, *Where did the industrial economy come from?* As I suggested at various points in Part I of this book, the development of economics should not be seen in purely materialist terms. Ideas of consumption, work, leisure, social status, and community infuse the economy as much as the economy infuses those ideas.

A major source of those ideas in the West is Christianity. As Max Weber argued in a famous 1905 book, *The Protestant Ethic and the Spirit of Capitalism,* Christian ideas—and, more specifically, Protestant ideas—form one of the great wellsprings of capitalist thought. It is more than accidental, said Weber, that the Protestant Reformation of the late sixteenth century immediately preceded the development of modern capitalism and the expansion of European economies all over the globe in the seventeenth, eighteenth, and nineteenth centuries. Capitalism is, in a way, a secular version of Protestantism.

The Moral Parallels of Protestantism and Capitalism

"A man does not 'by nature' wish to earn more and more money," Weber wrote, in the gendered phrasing of an earlier time, "but simply to live as he is accustomed to live and to earn as much as is necessary for that purpose."[2] So why do we work so hard to make more money than we need? A desire to maintain a place on the treadmills of consumption and production is part of it. But to leave the matter there does not answer the question of why we are on these treadmills to begin with.

The answer, suggested Weber, lies in the moral anxiety that early Protestantism inculcated in its followers. Medieval Catholicism was more forgiving, encouraging repentance and allowing last-minute, deathbed declarations of faith. If you were rich enough, you could literally buy your way into heaven by funding priests to say prayers for you and by purchasing "indulgences" from the church. But early Protestantism emphasized a kind of final weighing up of all the good and bad that a person had done in life, which made it harder to overcome one's misdeeds and made entrance into heaven less ideologically certain.

Figure 6.2   John Calvin, 1509–1564. Some scholars argue that Calvin's ascetic vision of Protestantism was one of the principal wellsprings of the capitalist spirit and its tendencies toward environmental domination.

A lot of the anxiety stemmed from the idea of predestination—the idea that one is preordained either to go to hell or to be one of the "elect" who goes on to heaven. Predestination was a common doctrine of early Protestants, particularly early Calvinists, and it ratcheted up moral anxiety by several notches. On the face of it, predestination seems a lousy way to motivate people, for it suggests that how you act in life doesn't matter. You are still going to go where it has been preordained that you will go. So why not lead a carefree life of sin, laziness, and gluttony? But the trick about predestination was that no one knew for sure who had grace—who was one of the elect and who was not—except through a person's worldly deeds. Those who were good,

moral, upright, and successful in this life must be the elect of the next life, early Protestant creeds such as Calvinism taught.

Thus, in order to convince themselves and the community that they were among the elect, early Calvinists became ascetics, denying themselves bodily pleasures like laziness and working incredibly hard to achieve the signs of success in this life. And they began to rationalize the work process, making work more orderly and efficient, in order to maximize their worldly signs of moral worth. Basically, said Weber, early Calvinism was a competitive cult of work, denial, and rationalization.

These same ideas still infuse capitalist economic life today, albeit without the religious framework (at least not explicitly). What has happened, Weber argued, is that we have secularized the idea that hard work and denial, rationally applied, are outward signs of how good and deserving one is. It remains one of the most basic assumptions of modern life that those who work hard are the most deserving, the most morally worthy of our admiration and of high salaries. Hard workers are the elect of the heaven of social esteem. It is they who have grace.

And now we have little choice but to be hard-working rational ascetics ourselves, even if (as is likely the case) we do not follow the religious tenets of early Calvinism. The anxiety of early Protestants produced huge accumulations of wealth. (If you work really hard and deny yourself, you are indeed more likely to be able to fill your wallet fuller. More likely: There is no firm correlation between hard work and wealth, as any coal miner or factory worker knows.) They reinvested this wealth, which led to even more wealth. And as each dedicated Protestant sought to increase his or her comparative success, the trend toward work, rationalization, and production accelerated. The treadmills of capitalism began turning ever faster. Soon one had to work hard, deny oneself, and rationalize one's life in order to attain any kind of economic foothold, for that was what everyone else was doing. Increasingly, people came to accept the idea that those who worked hard deserved to get more and to gain everyone's respect. Likewise they came to accept its corollary: that those who had less must not have worked so hard, and therefore deserved their fate. The Protestant ethic had become the spirit of capitalism.

The history of capitalist development provides some support for Weber's thesis. Modern capitalism arose first in the dominantly Protestant countries: England, Scotland, the United States, and Germany. Within Europe even today, the least wealthy and least industrialized countries remain the least Protestant: the dominantly Catholic countries of Portugal and Spain, and the dominantly Christian Orthodox countries of Greece and much of Eastern Europe. France and Italy fit less well into this pattern; both are dominantly Catholic but are heavily industrialized and infused with an ascetic work ethic. However, they both industrialized comparatively recently, and are still not among Western Europe's wealthiest countries.[3] Ireland, another dominantly Catholic country, is now one of the wealthiest in the world, but again this is a recent change.

Now modern capitalism is spreading well beyond the confines of dominantly Protestant countries, and even beyond the dominantly Christian countries. Religion is no longer the driving force. The capitalist spirit steadily enfolds country after country into its secularized ethic of ascetic rationalism. Economic structures have taken over from Martin Luther and John Calvin in spreading this spirit, even as this spirit dialogically propels the structures, as in the way hard work speeds the treadmill faster and faster. Ascetic rationalism has become what Weber termed "an iron cage."[4] As Weber put it,

This order is now bound to the technical and economic conditions of machine production which today determine the lives of all the individuals who are born into this mechanism, not only those directly concerned with economic acquisition, with irresistible force. Perhaps it will so determine them until the last ton of fossilized coal is burnt.[5]

In a way, we're all Calvinists now.

The Moral Parallels of Christianity, Science, and Technology

Weber is not the only scholar who has traced a connection between Western religion and social developments that greatly impact the environment. In 1967, the historian Lynn White published a short essay that remains one of the most influential and widely read analyses of the environmental predicament: "The Historical Roots of Our Ecologic Crisis." White's basic argument was that environmental problems cannot be understood apart from the Western origins of modern science and technology, which in turn derive from "distinctive attitudes toward nature that are deeply grounded in Christian dogma."[6] Not only does the economy of the West have religious origins, then, but Western science and technology do as well.

Many ancient cultures participated in laying the foundation stones of science—notably China and the Islamic world. Yet, White argued, "by the late thirteenth century Europe had seized global scientific leadership."[7] The achievements of Newton, Galileo, Copernicus, and other medieval scientists were accompanied by rapid advances in Western technology. White placed particular emphasis on the development of powered machines: the weight-driven clock, windmills, water-powered sawmills, and blast furnaces.

Even more significant, though, was the development of the moldboard plow in northern Europe during the latter part of the seventh century (see Figure 6.3). The moldboard plow dramatically changed human attitudes toward the environment, said White. Previous plows had allowed farmers only to scratch at the ground. These shallow plows were adequate for the light soils of the Near East and the Mediterranean, although they restricted agriculture to being pretty much a subsistence affair, with little surplus for trade. The generally heavy soils of the North, on the other hand, required a stronger plow. The moldboard was invented to cut more deeply into the ground, loosening up the heavy northern soils. The difficult work of the moldboard plow normally took the pull of eight oxen, as opposed to the one or two used by earlier plows.

Thus the moldboard plow was essentially a powered machine. In White's words, "Man's relation to the soil was profoundly changed. Formerly man had been part of nature; now he was the exploiter of nature."[8] Formerly we had seen ourselves on a par with the natural world. Now we saw ourselves as standing above it, at least potentially.

Why this change? This exploitative and domineering attitude toward the environment,

encompassing both unlettered farmers and scientific intellectuals, was so specific to one region that its origins must lie in a broad intellectual trend, White argued. The likely trend was one of the great intellectual revolutions of the Western tradition: the Christian ethic. For at roughly the same time that northern farmers were developing the moldboard plow to handle their heavy soils, White noted, they were also giving up paganism for Christianity.

For the pagan, the world is full of spirits. Every rock and tree is potentially animated by something. Nature is alive, organic, and magical. It is cyclical, and we are part of it. Early Christianity, on the other hand, building on Judaic philosophy, saw time as linear and nonrepeating, and it saw the environment as dead and inanimate, as separate from people. For early Christianity, the spirit w rld of God and the saints was not *immanent* in nature—that is, suffused throughout nature, making nature a direct embodiment of spirits—but rather *transcendent* above nature.

Moreover, early Christian doctrine taught that God gave the world to human beings to exploit, to change and recreate, much as God himself could do (which is why only human beings are made in God's image, many Christians believe). Changing nature was no longer a sacrilege. Indeed, all the Mosaic religions—Judaism, Islam, and Christianity—counseled that it was God's will that we do so. In the words of Genesis,

> And God said: Let us make man in our image, after our likeness; and let them have dominion over the fish of the sea, and over the fowl of the air, and over the cattle, and over all the earth, over every creeping thing that creepeth upon the earth. (Genesis 1:26)

Mosaic teachings thus gave us moral license to change the world as we see fit, White argued, a license gladly accepted and spread far and wide in Europe by Christianity. As White put it, "Christianity is the most anthropocentric religion the world has ever seen."[9]

Figure 6.3   A medieval illustration of an ox-drawn moldboard plow. According to historian Lynn White, the invention of the moldboard plow in about the seventh century radically altered European sensibilities toward environmental transformation.

The Greener Side of Christianity

The coincidence of the development of medieval technology and science alongside the spread of Christianity is intriguing and suggestive. The biblical license to dominate the Earth likely at least facilitated the development of technology and science. The association of the Protestant Reformation with the subsequent rise of modern capitalism and the striking parallels between contemporary secular morals and the ascetic rationalism of early Protestantism also suggest an important influence of religious ideas on our material conditions.

But we cannot conclude that Christianity unambiguously promotes science, technological progress, and capitalism at the expense of the environment. For one thing, Christianity has often been at odds with science. Consider the conflict between medieval scientists and the established church. The inquisition of Galileo for heresy is only the most well-known example. Far from welcoming science as a way of proving that, yes, God is indeed transcendent and that nature is an inanimate machine driven forward through linear time, the church found its authority threatened by the development of scientific thought. Even though almost all early scientists, including Galileo, presented their work as theological efforts to understand the true meaning of God, church authorities only grudgingly accepted the argument that science was about faith. And today, many Christian religious leaders object to a range of scientific techniques, such as genetic engineering. "Dolly," the sheep that Scottish scientists announced in 1997 had been successfully cloned, was greeted by many Christians as a blasphemy.

Another sign of Christianity's ambivalent views about environmental transformation is certain biblical passages. For example, right before the famous line in the Bible in which God tells Noah and his family to leave the ark and says, "Be ye fruitful, and multiply," which sounds rather domineering, there is a more ecological passage:

> And God spoke unto Noah, saying, Go forth from the ark, thou, and thy wife, and thy sons, and thy sons' wives with thee. Bring forth with thee every living thing that is with thee of all flesh, both fowl, and cattle, and every creeping thing that creepeth upon the earth; that they may swarm in the earth, and be fruitful and multiply upon the earth. (Genesis 8:15–17)

Note that in this passage, the animals too are given the right to "be fruitful and multiply"—in fact, even before people are given that right—and Noah is ordered to help make it happen. There is an even more ecological passage later on when God promises to establish a covenant both with Noah and with "every living creature," promising not to bring on another flood:

> And God said: This is the token of the covenant which I make between Me and you and every living creature that is with you, for perpetual generations: I have set my bow in the cloud, and it shall be a token of a covenant between Me and the earth. (Genesis 9:12–13)

This passage could be read as suggesting that humans are not the only beneficiaries in the rainbow covenant. The covenant includes "every living creature that is with you." And when the covenant is restated half a sentence later, human beings are not even specifically mentioned. The covenant is "between Me and the earth." (And indeed, many contemporary readers of the Bible take these lines in this more ecologically inclusive way.)[10]

Another problem with viewing Christianity as the unambiguous source of our faith in science, technology, and progress is that Christians are not the only readers of the Bible, nor the first. The connection that White saw between Christianity and technology is based on the Old Testament, a work that is revered by Jews and Muslims too. Thus White should have been able to find a similar connection between technological advance and the spread of the Old Testament among the peoples of those faiths. Yet he made no such argument, and it is not immediately apparent that he could have. Moreover, Christianity is itself a geographically and ideologically diverse tradition. The Eastern Christianity of Constantinople, for example, was not linked to the development of science and technology to the degree that the Latin Christianity of Western Europe was. Why not? Surely Eastern Christians had environmental constraints of their own to contend with and therefore had equal incentive to develop science, technology, and a domineering attitude toward the environment.

Thus White's focus on Christianity may have been somewhat misplaced. The environmental ideas he discusses—linear time, an inanimate world, the dichotomy between people and nature, anthropocentrism—are certainly not explicit aspects of the Bible. They do not appear in the Ten Commandments, nor the Sermon on the Mount, for example. And the Mosaic faiths, as we have seen, are neither exclusively Western nor unified in their teachings.

We might more accurately describe these ideas that support the domination and transformation of the environment as an underlying philosophy of the West, rather than of Christianity alone. This does not mean that religion has no role here, though. As the principal religious tradition of the West, Christianity must be amenable to such ideas if they are to remain widespread. Indeed, any religious tradition capable of gathering such a wide range of cultures under its tent must be amenable to a similarly wide range of interpretations. The origin of modern ideas about the relationship between humans and the environment is therefore likely more than merely religious.

Non-Western Philosophies and the Environment

Non-Western philosophic and religious traditions, however, do generally give recommendations for how humans ought to act toward the environment that are strikingly different from much Western thought. These traditions often promote a more egalitarian relationship with the Earth as well as an acceptance of the environment as it is.

Taoism, for example, advises *wu-wei,* or "nonaction," as the route to contentment. Nonaction does not mean non-doing. It is working with nature, instead of against it, by attempting to act without deliberate effort. (Translating Taoist ideas into Western terms is difficult, but "nature" is certainly close to what is meant here.)[11] Here is an explanation of *wu-wei* from one of the great Taoist classics, *The Way of Chuang Tzu,* which dates from the third century B.C.E.:

> Fishes are born in water
> Man is born in Tao.
> If fishes, born in water,
> Seek the deep shadow
> Of pond and pool,
> All their needs
> Are satisfied.
> If man, born in Tao,
> Sinks into the deep shadow
> Of *non-action*
> To forget aggression and concern,
> He lacks nothing
> His life is secure.
> Moral: "All the fish needs

> Is to get lost in water.
> All man needs is to get lost
> In Tao."[12]

Such a moral certainly does not appear to provide much license for transforming the Earth to suit human concerns. Rather, Taoism counsels us to forget human concerns so as to avoid the inevitable sorrow of materialism. When one "tries to extend his power over objects, those objects gain control of him," observes the *Chuang Tzu.*[13]

Yet as the geographer Yi-Fu Tuan observed, China has long been one of the regions of the world most transformed by human action, despite the influence of Taoism and Buddhism. The ancient Chinese canal system, the extensive clearing of the land for cultivation, the formal gardening style of Chinese park land—all these represent considerable alteration of the environment. Such transformations continue today in huge projects such as the Seven Gorges Dam, accelerating urbanization, the mechanization of Chinese agriculture, and the ready adoption of a consumer lifestyle by many of China's 1.3 billion inhabitants.

Nor are asceticism and rationalism new to non-Western cultures. Rationalism built ancient China's canals, agricultural system, formal gardens, cities, centralized government, and complex philosophical systems. Ascetic denial has long been a part of the training of Japanese samurai warriors as well as an important moral ideal in Japanese life.[14] The asceticism and rationalism of early Protestantism was not unique to the West.

None of this proves Weber and White fundamentally wrong. It just reins them in a bit. Medieval Christianity likely did play an important role in promoting our contemporary acceptance of environmental transformation and exploitation, at least in the West. Early Protestantism similarly helped promote the train of reasoning that led to the rise of modern capitalism and the secular ideas of hard work and rationality now common throughout the West. But religion was not the only path that led to these increasingly global sensibilities.

Individualism and Environmental Domination

Another path that has also led to environmental transformation is *individualism,* the emphasis on the self over the wider community that has long been a central dimension of the Western tradition. Individualism does not mentally prepare us to recognize how interconnected we all are with our wider surroundings, both social and environmental. With an individualistic frame of mind, we tend to ignore the consequences of our actions for those wider surroundings and therefore, because of our interconnections, sometimes for ourselves as well. Moreover, we in the West have understood that emphasis on the self in competitive and hierarchical ways. Thus we pursue our individualistic ambitions not just with "invisible elbows" that jostle others accidentally but with elbows deliberately braced for bumping and shoving aside whomever, and whatever, stands in our way.

Individualism, the Body, and Ecology

One of the many scholars who has connected our Western sense of hierarchical individualism with environmental domination is Mikhail Bakhtin, a Russian social theorist. Bakhtin pointed out that individualism deeply influences the way we regard the main medium by which we are connected to the environment: our bodies. Individualism encourages us to see our bodies as sealed off from others and from the natural world, with a host of consequences for what we regard as dirty, as repulsive, as polite, as scary, and as humorous. All of these cultural responses to how our bodies interact with the world have important environmental implications, as we shall see.[15]

Bakhtin based his argument on an unusual source: the quality of humor in the writings of the early French Renaissance writer, François Rabelais.[16] The novels of Rabelais are infamous for their scatological satire of French politics of the sixteenth century. They recount, in graphic detail, the outlandish and vulgar careers of Gargantua and his son Pantagruel, both fabulously obese giants. (The English word *gargantuan* derives from Rabelais's novels.) The two giants lead an outrageous life centered on feasting, drinking, excreting, copulating, giving birth, and other earthy acts. Woven through the stories are references to the political figures of the day, who usually appear in unseemly and ridiculous situations.

Rabelais's novels, published together nowadays under the title *Gargantua and Pantagruel,* caused quite a stir when they first appeared. Rabelais was often in political trouble because of them. But he also found widespread favor, even among many of the political figures he lampooned, because even the king and his courtiers found the novels downright funny. Still, it was controversial stuff.

The political references in Rabelais's novels no longer mean much to readers. His writings remain controversial, though—but for a different reason than caused Rabelais so much personal trouble: the style of the books, a style that many modern readers find distasteful and obscene.[17] Bakhtin sought to understand why it is the style of Rabelais's humor, rather than the subject of his humor, that is now so offensive.

Like Rabelais's novels, Bakhtin's answer caused quite a stir. His book on the subject, *Rabelais and His World,* could not be published until 1965, 25 years after it was written.[18] Writing during the height of Stalinist repression, Bakhtin too was often in trouble with the authorities. He was denied employment and eventually forced into exile in Kazakhstan during the 1930s. After World War II, he was able to regain the teaching job he had briefly held earlier at an obscure Russian university. Most other scholars thought him dead, though. Then in the 1960s, some graduate students at Moscow's Gorky Institute rediscovered him. Now that Stalin was gone, *Rabelais and His World* was finally published, and Bakhtin's earlier works were reread and brought back into print. By the time Bakhtin died in 1975, his works were being read all over the world.

I tell the story of Bakhtin's career because it highlights the strong reactions that people often have to reminders that our own bodies perform the same basic functions as any other animal's body. Why should it be that references to the body and all its everyday—and biologically essential—activities should be considered dirty and indecent? What could be more common-place than the body and its needs? So why is it usually considered a rude topic? Bakhtin argued that people did not always react in this way. We moderns are offended because of a historical shift in our conceptions of the body, from what Bakhtin termed the "carnivalesque body" to the "classical body."

The *carnivalesque body* is a body of intercon-nections and exchanges with the social and nat-ural environment. It is a body of openings and protrusions that connect us with other bodies and with the world around us: the mouth, the nose, the anus, the genitals, the stomach. Through these organs of connection, we exchange sub-stances, some made by the body and some brought into the body from other bodies and from the surrounding world: air, smells, food, saliva, nasal mucus, urine, excrement, the various genital fluids, sweat, tears, mother's milk. It is also a body that relishes bodily acts and desires: eating, drinking, laziness, sleeping, snoring, sneezing, excreting, copulating, giving birth, nursing, kissing, hugging. The emphasis of the carnivalesque body is on what Bakhtin described as the body's "lower stratum." The carnivalesque body is also an eco-logical body, a body that is forever interacting and exchanging with natural systems.

The *classical body*, on the other hand, is a body of separation from society and nature. Most of its orifices are hidden from view. Those that are not hidden are carefully controlled through rituals that de-emphasize their openness. Food is carefully introduced into the mouth with a fork, and the mouth is quickly closed again. The nose is blown into a Kleenex or handkerchief, and the mucus is carefully kept out of sight. The classical body does not belch, pass wind, cough or sneeze on others, eat with an open mouth, sweat, cry, or experience sexual desire. Excretory acts are kept strictly private. Openly discussing any of these activities is considered rude and immature,

unless carried out under the strict linguistic supervision of "polite" language, such as I am using here. Emphasis is on the body's upper stratum. And the body's means of ecological connection become shameful.

The Carnivalesque Body. Bakhtin drew the term *carnivalesque* from the annual pre-Lenten festival of *carnival*, once one of the most important dates on the medieval calendar but which survives today in only a few places. Carnival traditionally was the people's holiday, often lasting for days. It was a time of merriment, feasting, parades, danc-ing, music, and general indulgence. It was a time for the outrageous.

But most important, carnival was a time of connection. In carnival, the community became all one flesh. (The *carn* in *carnival* means "flesh.") Everyone, high status and low, joined together in celebration. It was a time of social "uncrowning," as Bakhtin termed it, a time when the high and mighty were brought back down to earth, the people's earth. By dancing together, by celebrat-ing the Earth's abundance with feasting and indulgence, and by joking together, often through references to the lower stratum of the body and to the substances that pass from and move through that lower stratum, people cele-brated their connections with each other and the world. Through these constant references to the bodily connections we all share—the joy of food, the pleasures of leisure, the desires of the flesh, the necessity of excretion—even the famous and highly esteemed were brought down to a common level. (See Figure 6.4.)

These carnivalesque pleasures are what we find described in Rabelais's novels, said Bakhtin.

Bakhtin makes a crucial distinction between the carnivalesque and bodily references that are merely gross and degrading, however. In carnivalesque humor, the subject of the joke is not brought beneath the tellers of the joke. Rather, it is egalitar-ian humor that seeks to unite everyone on the same earthy, bodily, social plane. We laugh not just at the subject of the joke but at ourselves too. Carnival-esque humor is not mere mocking. It is, as Bakhtin put it, "also directed at those who laugh."[19] It is

Figure 6.4 This painting from 1498—Piero di Cosimo's *The Discovery of Honey*—celebrates the festive and open-mouthed character of what theorist Mikhail Bakhtin called the "carnivalesque body." As in di Cosimo's painting, such a body relishes exchanges and interactions with society and the natural world, rather then presenting itself as a sealed-off monad.

laughter that joins us all together in the joke, renewing community. Degrading jokes, on the other hand, create hierarchy and separation. They seek to lower others without bringing them into the same common earthy community of bodily life.

Bakhtin wrote in defense of the carnivalesque. But he worried that bodily humor had become "nothing but senseless abuse. . . . Laughter [has been] cut down to cold humor, irony, sarcasm. It [has] ceased to be a joyful and triumphant hilarity."[20]

He also wrote to make a historical point. Why do we moderns have such trouble distinguishing between the carnivalesque and the merely gross? Why do we so often find any references to the body to be offensive and shameful? Because, Bakhtin argues, social mores have changed from medieval and early Renaissance times, in tandem with the modern rise of hierarchical individualism.

The Classical Body. Thus, a work like *Gargantua and Pantagruel* is generally offensive today not because of its politics (what offended some early Renaissance readers) but because of its affront to bodily individualism (what virtually all early Renaissance readers found deliciously funny). Today we find individualism a lot harder to laugh at. We are ashamed at references to our bodily connections with the world. Nature itself has become offensive.

This change is evident not only in humor but in modern codes of politeness, cleanliness, and privacy. Today we eat with cutlery, particularly in formal situations. Medieval people ate with their fingers. Today we find it impolite to eat with an open mouth or with slurping noises. Medieval people were not so troubled. We have historically astonishing standards of cleanliness for our homes and bodies. We confine most bodily acts to the privacy of the bedroom and bathroom. In fact, the bathroom has become a kind of modern shrine to the individual, and expensive modern homes often include one for every member of the family, plus one for any guests—four- and five-bathroom homes have become standard in exclusive housing developments. And we medicalize birth, death, and all the stages in between of the body's growth and interactions with life. We keep the environment as much at a distance from our bodies as we can. Again, medieval people were not so troubled.

Why do we do all these things? Because, Bakhtin argues, they are symbols of social hierarchy. In order to be elite, you need to separate yourself from the common people. Separation from nature and bodily functioning is a particularly convincing way to make that distinction. As Thorstein Veblen noted, elites try to remove themselves from environmental concerns in part because doing so indicates social power. Bakhtin would add that such environmental separation also entails showing oneself to be above bodily concerns. It requires what Weber would recognize as a kind of asceticism, a denial of bodily existence.

Having servants and machines to handle dirt, trash, and bodily excretions; being able to get through the day wearing the most impractical of clothes; traveling by means other than one's own bodily locomotion; maintaining impeccable standards of cleanliness for one's home and body; having a house and workplace big enough for separate rooms for private acts, and separate kinds of rooms for each kind of act—to acquire these forms of ecological and social separation requires power. It requires money and status. Such separation is far harder for those without money and power, thus clearly establishing who is on top and who is on the bottom.

Our desires for social distinction are thus intimately connected with our desire to distance ourselves from the body, from the Earth, and from ecological reality. We cannot admit that we are connected to the Earth, for doing so would undermine the very feeling of separation and distinction that modern life seeks. Seeking to live the life of the high-status individual, we model ourselves after the classical image of the body and find references to carnivalesque connection dirty and threatening. We pretend that we have no need to heed nature's call.

Balancing the Ecological Self and the Ecological Community

As often happens when someone hits upon a new idea, Bakhtin probably overstated his case. His portrayal of medieval and early Renaissance life seems filtered through a romantic mist.[21] This period was not a golden age of unending feasting, merrymaking, and communalism. There was much hierarchy then too, as well as grinding poverty, poor sanitation, and disease. Bodily connections with society and with the environment can be fatal, a point that surely was significant to medieval people. (But so too can be attempts to deny such connections.) Thus we cannot pass off the modern interest in sanitation and medical intervention as merely the product of raging individualism. (But overcleanliness can also be hazardous, and indeed is suspected by some researchers as being a factor in the dramatic rise in the incidence of allergies and asthma in the wealthy countries.)

We also need to be cautious about seeing the rise of a classical conception of the body and its implication of ecological separation as a purely Western phenomenon. Rather, it is characteristic of elites the world over. Nearly all elites adopt refined lifestyles that insulate them from the dirty, sweaty, smelly consequences of being a human animal. Bakhtin would have readily accepted this point, in fact. And he would have added that common people have long responded to the pretensions of the world's elites with carnivalesque humor. In Bakhtin's words, "Every act of world history was accompanied by a laughing chorus."[22]

Finally, we need to keep a sense of balance with respect to the carnivalesque and the classical. I for one am not prepared to lead a life of the purely carnivalesque. Besides, even during medieval times carnival was not an everyday occurrence, although the spirit of carnival was no doubt a more regular presence in the lives of medieval people. Probably it ought to be in ours. But neither should we give up all forms of bodily individuality. A sense of our own difference is, after all, essential to a feeling of connection, for there must be something to connect. It's another dialogue.

Yet we also need to balance a classical conception of our selves and our bodies with a carnivalesque understanding that we are part of nature. Evidence suggests that we may be coming around to this point of view. The West has substantially changed its attitudes about the body in the 50 years since Bakhtin wrote *Rabelais and His World*. Thanks in large measure to the social changes and social movements of the 1960s, we are no longer so ashamed to speak of the body (although there are signs that such shame may be on the rise again). Hippie culture and the women's movement both emphasized the importance of being open about the body, its needs, its functions, and its realities. Hippies emphasized a more natural body style, breaking the taboos of long hair for men and leg hair and underarm hair for women, for example. Feminists helped break down the misconceptions and sense of shame long associated with women's bodies, perhaps most notably through the publication of the revolutionary book *Our Bodies Ourselves*.

These social changes suggest a connection between environmental awareness and bodily awareness. It may be no accident that the 1960s saw both an environmental movement and a body awareness movement. In other words, accepting the importance of environmental interactions may depend in part upon accepting a more ecological—and thus less hierarchical and more democratic—conception of the body.

Gender and Environmental Domination

Another source of our domineering attitudes toward the environment is gender relations. Consider, for example, the common metaphors we in the West use to describe the environment and our interactions with it, metaphors that are strikingly sexual and militaristic. The pioneers in North America "broke virgin land" and cleared "virgin forest." Farmers have long spoken of the "fertility" of the soil, and surveyors and military commanders assess the "lay of the land." Mariners sail on the "bosom of the deep." The environment in general is "Mother Nature." We speak of abuse of the environment as "raping the land," and we speak of civilization as the "conquest of nature." The sex of the environment in these examples, sometimes implied, sometimes overtly stated, is female.

In light of the violence of some of the imagery—the "breaking," "clearing," "rape," and "conquest" of female nature—these are disturbing metaphors. They suggest, along with a range of other evidence, that there is an ideological link between the domination of nature and the domination of women. If patriarchal ideas pervade our thinking about society, then they likely influence our thinking about the environment as well, for we use the same mind, the same culture, to understand both.

The Ecology of Patriarchy

Note the common Western tendency to consider women as being closer to nature than men. Not only is nature female, but females are more natural, our traditions often suggest. We tend to associate women with reproduction, broadly understood—with the natural necessities of giving birth, raising children, preparing food, healing the sick, cleaning, attending to emotional needs—as well as with the domestic sphere, the realm of the reproductive and the private. In contrast, we have conventionally associated men with production—with transforming nature so that it does what we want it to—and with the public sphere, the realm of rationality, civilization, government, and business.

These gendered associations imply a clear hierarchy, with men on top. Western thinkers have often considered women inferior because of their alleged animalistic closeness to nature and men as superior because of their allegedly greater skills in the allegedly higher aspects of human life. Edmund Burke, the late eighteenth-century English philosopher, wrote that "a woman is but an animal and an animal not of the highest order." Hegel felt that "women are certainly capable of learning, but they are not made for the higher forms of science, such as philosophy and certain types of creative activities." Sigmund Freud mused that "women represent the interests of the family and sexual life; the work of civilization has become more and more men's business."[23] And here is Henry James, Sr.—father of the philosopher William James and novelist Henry James, and himself a prolific author—writing in 1853 on the subject of "Woman and the 'Woman's Movement'": Woman is "by nature inferior to man. She is inferior in passion, his inferior in intellect, and his inferior in physical strength." As he put it another essay, discussing "The Marriage Question," a wife is her husband's "patient and unrepining drudge, his beast of burden, his toilsome ox, his dejected ass, his cook, his tailor, his own cheerful nurse and the sleepless guardian of his children."[24] These characteristics of women and their lives were not social inventions open to interrogation and change. For these men, and many others of their time, these were the writ of nature.

The social implications of such patriarchal presumptions are quite troubling, most would today agree. Many writers also argue so too are the environmental implications. By demeaning women for their stereotypical association with reproduction and with nature, we encourage both the domination of women and the domination of the environment.

Ecofeminism. The work of these writers comes out of a relatively new tradition of scholarly and philosophical inquiry, *ecofeminism,* which explores the links between the domination of women and the domination of the environment and argues that the domination of the environment originates together with social domination of all kinds— across not only gender but also race, ethnicity, class, age, and other forms of social difference treated as hierarchies.[25] It is common for socially dominated groups to be linked with nature, ecofeminists observe. People of color have often been associated with savagery. Lower classes have often been seen as primitive and as having inadequate control over their emotions, leading to a greater tendency toward violence and sexual licentiousness. And women have often been relegated to the realm of nature and its reproductive requirements, as opposed to reason and civilization.

It seems that when we think social hierarchy, we think natural hierarchy—and probably vice versa, too. As the prominent ecofeminist Val Plumwood has written, the "human domination of nature wears a garment cut from the same cloth as intra-human domination, but one which, like each of the others, has a specific form and shape of its own."[26]

Environmental activists themselves have sometimes promoted the association of women with nature, for example by using the image of "Mother Earth." An ever-popular environmental slogan is "Love your mother," referring to the Earth. In this case, nature is positively valued, and the activists who use the expression probably feel that it therefore positively values women as well, reversing the traditionally negative connotation of being associated with nature.

This is an ideologically dangerous strategy, say some ecofeminists. Listen to this statement from Charles Sitter, senior vice president of Exxon, who used the image of Mother Earth to minimize the significance of the infamous 1989 *Exxon Valdez* oil spill in Alaska's Prince William Sound: "I want to point out that water in the Sound replaces itself every twenty days. The Sound flushes itself out every twenty days. Mother Nature cleans up and does *quite* a cleaning job."[27]

This "Mom will pick up after us" vision of the environment, as Joni Seager and Linda Weltner have termed it, is both ecologically problematic and sexist. As Weltner writes,

> Men are the ones who imagine that clean laundry gets into their drawers as if by magic, that muddy footprints evaporate into thin air, that toilet bowls are self-cleaning. It's these overindulged and over-aged boys who operate on the assumptions that disorder— spilled oil, radioactive wastes, plastic debris— is someone else's worry, whether that someone else is their mother, their wife, or Mother Earth herself.[28]

The point of ecofeminism is not to blame men for environmental problems. Nor are all ecofeminists women.[29] Ecofeminists, like other feminist scholars, are concerned about our patriarchal system of social organization, which is enacted by both men and women but results in the domination of women. What domination of women, you might say? Aren't we past all that, at least in the rich countries? Not yet, agree virtually all sociologists. Even in the rich countries, women are still paid some 25 percent less than men, both because they are more likely to be consigned to lower-wage jobs and to receive less even when they hold the same job as men. Many jobs and academic fields remain highly gender segregated. Women are far less likely to hold political office, especially at the highest levels. Women still do the bulk of reproductive labor. Women still do the majority of all labor, paid and unpaid. But these persistent patterns of inequality are not men's fault alone. They are everyone's fault. We all enact them.

Ecofeminists add to feminist scholarship the notion that the domination of nature is linked to patriarchy and other forms of social domination, and vice versa. But ecofeminists observe that women too have been active agents in the domination of nature. Plumwood points out that

> Western women may not have been in the forefront of the attack on nature, driving the bulldozers and operating the chainsaws, but many of them have been the support troops, or have been participants, often unwitting but still enthusiastic, in a modern consumer culture of which they are the main symbols, and which assaults nature in myriad direct and indirect ways daily.[30]

Patriarchal Dualisms. A key tenet of ecofeminism is that our cultural climate of domination has been built on dualisms—morally charged, oppositional categories with little gray area in between—that deny the dependency of each upon the other. Thus, man is man and woman is woman. Nature is nature and culture is culture. Our dualisms interlock into a larger cultural

system of domination, ecofeminists such as Plumwood argue: culture versus nature, reason versus nature, male versus female, mind versus body, machine versus body, master versus slave, reason versus emotion, public versus private, self versus other.[31] In each dichotomy, the first member of each pair dominates over the second. The core dichotomy, Plumwood writes, "is the ideology of the control of reason over nature."[32] The dominating side in each pair is culturally linked to reason, and the dominated side is culturally linked to nature.

This tendency to separate the world into antagonistic pairs, Plumwood suggests, is a legacy of a Western us-versus-them *logic of domination.* Ecofeminists like Plumwood advocate a different form of logic, one that recognizes gray areas and interdependence, and one that recognizes difference without making hierarchies. They want us to be able to make categorical distinctions that respect the diversity and interactiveness of the world and that do not rely on absolutist, mechanical, and hierarchical boundaries.

The Western logic of domination is not just an intellectual problem, argue ecofeminists. It has all-too-real material outcomes. Under Western rationality, the dominated and naturalized "other" does not receive fair environmental treatment. Women, people of color, people in lower socioeconomic groups, nonhuman animals, the land itself—all these groups tend to experience a lack of environmental justice because our cultural orientation is to regard them as generally less important and less deserving. Women, for example, are less likely than men to receive an even share of environmental goods. Worldwide, poverty rates are significantly higher for women—making women more susceptible to environmental bads as well.

But patriarchy also leads to the environmental oppression of men, even those from favored social groups. The patriarchal vision of masculinity leads men to take foolish risks with machines, chemicals, weather, and the land. Men often die as a result, or become maimed and diseased, which is some of the reason why men on the whole do not live as long as women. Thus, all of us have an interest in changing the current social order.

Gender Differences in the Experience of Nature

The dualisms of patriarchal reasoning also affect the way women and men experience the environment. Although, on the whole Western women and men experience the environment quite similarly, some significant differences suggest that we have indeed internalized some of the patriarchal stereotypes. In the late 1980s I conducted an ethnographic study of the experience of nature in an English exurban village. Although similarities far outweighed differences, village men described their natural experiences to me using significantly more aggressive, militaristic, and violent imagery. Village women emphasized a more domestic environmental vision based on their experience of nurturing in nature.[33] For example, men spoke of the pleasures of releasing their pent-up aggressive feelings through clearing brush and engaging in visceral rural sports such as "skirmish," a mock war game played in the woods with guns that shoot paint balls. As one village man described the game,

> I think when we were made, we were made with instincts to defend our tribe. . . . These instincts never get an airing. We sit in our office desks [isolated] from that danger, save-the-family type situation. . . . But when you go out there playing this game . . . it's like a dog that's been cooped up forever and then one day it's taken for a walk in the woods and it sees a rabbit. It sniffs it and all its primitive instincts come alive. . . . It's quite exciting when a ton of people are coming at you with a gun.[34]

No village woman described such pleasures. Nor did any village man relate stories of nurturing in nature such as those told to me by several village women. One village woman, for example, told a story about a family cat that helped raise two ducklings, extending nurturing feelings even across the divide of predator and prey. She tells the story best, so here it is in her words:

> We had a cat [Suzy]. We always had lots of cats. And this particular time I went to Harchester, and there were two little ducklings in a pet shop window. And like a fool I thought, well, the kids will like them. And I brought them home, didn't I? And Suzy became a mother and she got kittens, at this particular time. And of course she took the two little ducklings over, didn't she? So wherever she went with the kittens, the ducklings followed. And they used to sleep together in this cardboard box. The cat and the ducklings! . . . It's completely true. She would wash and cuddle the ducklings, just like they were her own. It's the mothering instinct, I suppose. . . .[35]

This is an incredible story, one that even got the family's picture in the paper, along with the cat and the ducklings. But significantly, this was a story that a woman told me. Her husband, whom I knew well, never mentioned it. This was her story, not his. Rather, he told me stories about rough weather and other hard environmental conditions and his feats of physical prowess and mental toughness in the face of these conditions. Perhaps village men and women told these different types of stories to conform to their expectations of what a male researcher should be told, and not to express their true feelings. Even so, it is significant that their expectations ran along such gendered lines.

I must emphasize once again, however, that the similarities between men's and women's stories far outweighed the differences. I must also emphasize that it is not helpful to blame men for experiencing nature in ways that I suspect most readers—both male and female—would regard as less laudable. The point of an ecofeminist perspective, as Joni Seager explains, "is not [to] reduc[e] environmental understanding to simplistic categories of 'wonderful women' and 'evil men.'"[36] Rather, the point is to highlight the environmental consequences for both women and men of patriarchal social structures and patterns of thinking, which both women and men bring into being.

The Controversy over Ecofeminism

Ecofeminism remains a controversial viewpoint. Much of the debate has surrounded the attempt by some ecofeminist writers, mainly in ecofeminism's early days, to subvert Western patriarchy by reversing its moral polarity. These writers propose that women and their associations with nature should be celebrated. Reproduction, nurturing, sensitivity to emotions, closeness to nature and the body—all these things are inherently good, the argument goes. Women should embrace these qualities that one ecofeminist praised as the "feminine principle," not reject them.[37] It's the other side of patriarchy's dualisms—reason, civilization, machines—that has made such a mess of things.[38]

Critics both inside and outside of ecofeminism object that such a position reifies the very social order that needs to be changed. It perpetuates the dichotomy between men and women as well as the negative stereotypes of women as irrational, as controlled by their bodies, and as best suited for the domestic realm.[39] Critics also argue that this reification is alienating and fatalistic because it implies that biological differences between men and women are at the root of patriarchy. Such a position, suggests Deborah Slicer, is best termed "ecofeminine" and not "ecofeminist."[40]

There is also a spiritual and religious dimension to some ecofeminism, associated with "goddess spirituality," Wicca, and Neopaganism. Spirituality and religiosity are, of course, important dimensions of human experience, and are not in themselves problematic. Nor is their any reason in pluralistic societies to complain about the beliefs and practices of religions and spiritual perspectives that may differ from one's own. However, spirituality and religiosity are matters of faith, not social science, and should not be confused as such. So it is important that the spiritual strands of some ecofeminism be kept carefully separate from its social scientific claims. Many observers object that this separation has not always been maintained.

Another criticism is that a perspective like Plumwood's implies that the "logic of domination" is mainly a feature of Western thought. Are Eastern cultures less patriarchal than Western ones? The evidence suggests not. Also, Eastern cultures have shown themselves to be quite capable of dominating nature. Either the "logic of domination" that infuses both our social and our environmental actions must not be exclusively Western, or the East must have its own logic of domination.

Also, in their effort to make clear the sexism that underlies some of our outlooks on the environment, ecofeminists have sometimes offered oversimplified arguments. For example, the patriarchal character of dualisms is not always so clear-cut. Consider the cultural association of women with nature and men with culture. In fact, the dualism often goes the other way, aligning women with culture and men with nature. Since Victorian times, one common stereotype of women has been that they are the bearers of culture and refinement and that they have responsibility for inculcating "civilization" in the next generation—and in men. One common current stereotype of men is that they are wild beasts driven by lust and violent passion, which women must tame for their own sake and for the sake of their children. Also, many of the spirits that various Western (and non-Western) traditions have sensed in the physical environment are characterized as male: Father Sky, the Greek sun god Apollo and ocean god Poseidon, the notion of a "fatherland."

Indeed, it is an important feature of ecofeminist thought that we must recognize the gray areas and the interactiveness and interdependence of our categories. Unless we continually remind ourselves of the dialogics of categories, of the dialogue of difference and sameness, we easily slip into one-sided, deterministic, and hierarchical arguments. And as ecofeminism also stresses, when you survey the world with a one-sided, deterministic, and hierarchical frame of mind to begin with, you are even more likely to slip in this way.[41] But ecofeminism has not always followed its own advice here as well as it might have.

In light of these controversial features of the ecofeminist debate, some social scientists have sought to find a different term to refer to explorations of the role of gender and patriarchy in social and environmental interrelations. "Environmental feminism" is what Michael Goldman and Rachel Schurman have suggested.[42] "Ecological feminism" is a similar phrase one increasingly encounters in social scientific literature. "Ecogender studies" is the term Damayanti Banerjee has offered.[43] Time will tell if these terms prove analytically helpful.

In any event, our environmental complaint with patriarchy should not be that it is wrong to create categories and draw distinctions. We need categories to recognize difference and thereby to build our theoretical and moral understanding of the world. (After all, ecofeminism itself represents a category—a category of thought.) But we also need better categories than the hierarchical, socially unjust, and environmentally destructive ones of patriarchy.

The Difference That Ideology Makes

These various theories of the environmental significance of religion, individualism, and patriarchy all have a common theme: the central roles of inequality and hierarchy in the way we think about the environment. Whether we are talking about the competitive desire to achieve grace through work, the notion that people and their God are above nature, the achievement of individual distinction through bodily distance from the world, or the dualistic thinking of patriarchy, social inequality influences our environmental relations.

I hope this chapter also makes it clear that social inequality has not only material but also ideological roots. This is another dialogue. Material factors structure our lives in unequal ways, leading to hierarchical visions of the world, just as ideological factors allow the material structures of inequality to develop and to persist.

Another common theme of this chapter is that, thus far, scholars have relied too much on the Western experience in formulating theories of the human transformation of the environment. Some of this neglect of the East has likely been due to a romantic view of the environmental sensitivity of that part of the world. But large-scale transformation of the environment in the East goes back thousands of years, just as it does in the West. Although this romantic view is flattering in some ways, it is also a back-handed insult, for it implies that the scientific and technological mind was beyond the ideological capabilities of the East. The view that the East was ecologically sensitive (until corrupted by the West) may thus perpetuate negative stereotypes of irrationality and backwardness.

Placing more emphasis on economic factors may help us understand how the ideology of transformation arose (recalling, with Weber, that any economic pattern is as much an ideological matter as a material one). The global spread of capitalism has been propelled by the accelerating treadmills of production and consumption, bringing with it social structures and ways of thinking that increase our orientation toward transforming the Earth.

But still the explanation is not complete. Environmental transformation was going on before capitalism arrived in both the East and West. Also, and perhaps even more important, we need to remember that the socialist economies of the former Soviet bloc and East Asia showed just as much tendency as capitalist economies to transform and dominate the Earth. We cannot point our analytic finger at capitalism alone.

In short, we do not yet fully understand the ideological origins of the transformation and domination of the Earth. And it may be that even after we take into account both material and ideal factors, we still will not fully understand these origins. One implication of a dialogical view of causality is that complete explanations are rarely, if ever, possible. The spontaneous creativity that comes out of social interaction has effects that can never be completely predicted.

Nevertheless, we should still pursue the analysis of social and environmental change. It is vitally important that we try to understand the material and ideal factors that dialogically shape, if not completely predict, our actions regarding the environment—particularly if we hope to guide those actions in a different direction.

CHAPTER 7

The Ideology of Environmental Concern

Rather than love, than money, than fame, give me truth.

—Henry David Thoreau, 1854

"It is our alarming misfortune," wrote Rachel Carson in 1962, describing the indiscriminate use of chemical pesticides, "that so primitive a science has armed itself with the most modern and terrible weapons, and that in turning them against the insects it has also turned them against the earth."[1] With these words, Carson concluded *Silent Spring*, a book that came like a thunderclap in a seemingly cloudless technological sky. (See Figure 7.1.) Because of chemical poisoning, argued Carson, it was a very real possibility—and indeed it had already happened in some areas—that a time could come when spring would arrive "unheralded by the return of the birds, and the early mornings are strangely silent where once they were filled with the beauty of bird song."[2] Carson carefully documented her claims with the results of hundreds of scientific studies, challenging science with science. Suddenly, the technological

utopianism of the postwar period no longer seemed so utopian.

Of course, we cannot assign an absolute beginning to any historical trend; history always has precursors. But so dramatic were the subsequent shifts in public opinion that it has become conventional, with some justice, to date the start of the modern environmental movement from the publication of *Silent Spring*.[3] My own mother, who read extracts from the book in a popular magazine, recalled to me the heated discussions it touched off among her friends. "It really shocked a lot of people," she explained. "We didn't have any idea that pesticides could be so dangerous. Nobody used to question these things."

Today, however, millions—even billions—do. The domination of the Earth has become increasingly unthinkable to increasing numbers of people in the years since 1962. In the International Millennium Survey of 60 nations from rich to poor conducted in 1999, 65 percent said that their governments had "done too little" to protect the environment, and 57 percent found the state of their environment "mainly

Figure 7.1   Rachel Carson, 1907–1964. A biologist for the U.S. Fish and Wildlife Service and a brilliant writer, Carson is widely credited with helping precipitate a great change in public attitudes toward the environment, particularly with her final book, *Silent Spring*.

history of environmental concern and a review of the theories advanced by social scientists to explain the recent flowering of this concern into the modern environmental movement. I argue that, in the face of environmental domination, counter-ideas have always been around. These ideas became much more widely held in the latter half of the twentieth century for three primary reasons: the rediscovery of the moral attractiveness of nature, the increased scale of material alterations of the environment, and the spread of democratic attitudes and institutions. It is, yet again, a matter of both the material and the ideal.

Ancient Beginnings

Environmental concern has a long history—perhaps every bit as long as the history of conscious environmental transformation. Like other creatures, humans unavoidably influence their surroundings. But the first decisions to consciously tinker with the environment likely prompted some heated debate. Is this safe? Is it moral? Perhaps even, is it beautiful? And will the gods approve? At the very least, these kinds of debates have been with us since the time of the ancient Romans, Greeks, and Chinese.

unsatisfactory" or "very unsatisfactory."[4] In the 1990–1993 World Values poll of 43 nations, 96 percent of the respondents said that they "approved" or "strongly approved" of the environmental movement. Most said they strongly approved.[5] There can be little else that so much of the world apparently agrees on.

Why this strong shift? Humans had been dramatically altering their environment for centuries without evoking a popular environmental movement. Yet even the most influential book can only crystallize concerns that must already have been held in dissolved suspension in the roiling sea of public opinion. How can we understand this ideological reorientation?

This chapter seeks sociological answers to this question. It does so through a sketch of the

Rome

The poet Horace loved his country villa in the Sabine hills above Rome. One day in about 20 B.C.E., he took up his wax tablet and his reed stylus and scratched out the following lines to his friend Fuscus:

> Fuscus, who lives in town and loves it,
>   greetings from one who loves
> The country . . .
>
> You stay in your nest, I sing my lovely rural
> Rivers, and trees, and moss-grown rocks.
>   Why drag out

Our differences? I live here, I rule here, as
soon as I leave

Those city pleasures celebrated with such
noisy gabble:

Like a professional cake-taster I run looking for good plain bread,

Just crusty bread, no honeyed confections,
dripping sweet!

If life in harmony with Nature is a primal
law,

And we go looking for the land where we'll
build our house, is anything

Better than the blissful country? Can you
think of anything?

Where can we sleep, safer from biting envy?

Is grass less fragrant, less lovely, than your
African tile?

Is your water as clear and sweet, there in its
leaden pipes,

As here, tumbling, singing along hilly slopes?

Lord! You try to grow trees, there in your
marble courtyards,

And you praise a house for its view of
distant fields.

Push out Nature with a pitchfork, she'll
always come back,

And our stupid contempt somehow falls
on its face before her.

Live happy with what you have, Fuscus,
and live well,

And never let me be busy gathering in
more than I need,

Restlessly, endlessly: rap me on the knuck-
les, tell me the truth.

Piled-up gold can be master or slave,
depending on its owner;

Never let it pull you along, like a goat on a
rope.[6]

Astoundingly modern-sounding sentiments
all. Like countless nature writers of the current
day, Horace "sings" the beauty of the countryside,
of rivers and trees and moss-grown rocks. And

like many in recent decades who left the city for
the country, Horace praises the simple life, close
to nature. He has no need for the urban con-
trivances of "honeyed confections, dripping
sweet." Just give Horace the plain crusty bread of
country living. Since "life in harmony with
Nature is a primal law," the country is the best
place to live, he proclaims. After all, grass can be
as beautiful to walk on as Fuscus's imported
African tile. The water in the country is pure and
sweet, Horace says, instead of the stale piped-in
stuff that Fuscus gets in town. (Although he mentions the lead in the pipes—Romans used lead
extensively in their plumbing—Horace couldn't
know about the added danger of lead poisoning,
as this danger was unknown at the time.)

Horace praises not only the naturalness of rural
living but also the social consequences. A country
life frees one from the "biting envy" of the city.
Horace doesn't want to live a life devoted to "gathering in more than I need," being pulled along "like
a goat on a rope" by the pursuit of money and
material possessions, and he warns Fuscus of these
dangers. In the poem's most famous lines, Horace
chastises those who contemptuously attempt to
avoid these social and environmental truths by trying to "push out Nature with a pitchfork." Nature
will "always come back," he warns.

That contempt was very evident in the Rome of
20 B.C.E. At that time, Rome was probably the
largest city ever known, with close to 1,000,000
inhabitants, the product of spectacular feats of
technology and engineering. A vast system of
aqueducts and pipes carried more than 200 million gallons (about a billion liters) of water a day
in from the surrounding countryside. The resulting urban effluent poured into the Cloaca
Maxima, an underground sewer large enough to
accommodate a small sailboat, and thence into
the badly abused River Tiber.[7] Wealthy Romans
enjoyed running water in their homes, even showers, as well as central heating. Common people
lived in *insulae*, apartment buildings the size of a
full city block and sometimes as much as seven
stories tall. Roman legionnaires had hot baths and
flush toilets in their military camps. (Flush toilets

Figure 7.2   Roman aqueduct, Segovia, Spain. Among the most elegant engineering structures of all time, these double-arched stone aqueducts are a demonstration of the remarkable power of Roman technology to transform the environment. Horace wrote his poetry about the importance of nature and rural life in reaction to this transformative power.

are in fact even older; the Minoans had them at the Palace of Knossos a millennium earlier.) Showers, baths, flush toilets, and seven-story apartment buildings—and a technology, economy, and empire capable of supporting it all: mighty pitchforks against Nature. (See Figure 7.2.)

The sentiments that Horace expressed were, we cannot doubt, in some measure formed in reaction to these new environmental transformations—transformations that also had social meaning for him. It was a culture of money and power that produced the technological pitchforks. The urban, commercial life of empire brought with it a widespread feeling that everything was becoming political—that social life was moved not by virtue but by self-serving desires for power, influence, and material possessions. Greed was overwhelming the Roman landscape and lifescape. And if all social motivations derived from the pursuit of interests, of materialist desire, where might one encounter an alternative?

For Horace, in nature. And what made nature so attractive to Horace still makes nature attractive today. Concern about nature cannot be separated from concern about social interests and how these shape our moral understandings.[8] Part of the attraction of nature stems from our struggles with the oldest of moral problems: the balance of power between us. And part of nature's attraction is its use in our struggles with the oldest of moral critiques: that interests underlie what we say, do, and believe. We look to nature for a moral base that lies outside ourselves, outside human power structures, and therefore outside the potential that we may have manipulated morality for our own ends. To experience nature is to experience an interest-free foundation upon which to build our motivations. To experience nature is to experience a point of rest from the constant charges that we act as we do because we seek power. To experience nature is thus to experience social innocence—or so we hope.

Horace felt that innocence in a country life. By living in harmony with nature, Horace believed, he could remain free of city dwellers' relentless pursuit of personal gain and their biting envy over others' piled-up gold. In nature Horace felt he had discovered a moral realm that lies beyond the reach of the pollution of human interests and materialist desire. The search for this interest-free realm of innocence is a kind of conscience, what I term a *natural conscience,* and it is fundamental to our moral thought.[9]

Yet was Horace truly above the pursuit of self-interest himself? Had he really put "biting envy" behind him through his celebration of a natural life? One way to read his famous epistle to Fuscus is that Horace was trying his best to build a bit of biting envy in his friend—envy for Horace's lifestyle in his country villa. Wealthy Romans loved country living and established country villas for themselves across the empire. The country house was already a positional good 2,000 years ago. Which is perhaps why, despite his opening avowal, Horace's epistle goes on very forcefully to in fact "drag out our differences."

In other words, the discovery of a natural conscience does not necessarily mean that one has truly escaped the moral problem of interests. (Indeed, much philosophical and sociological work suggests such an escape is not possible.)[10] But it does mean that one is grappling with the issue.

Horace was not the first to grapple with this problem, though. The search for a natural realm of moral innocence has frequently accompanied the rise of a complex, urban-dominated political life, and the growing wealth and social inequality that have so often been associated with such a life. For that we must begin even earlier, with the ancient Greeks, and, in a few pages, with the ancient Chinese.

Greece

Nature is an old and powerful idea. Words are not the same as ideas, of course; the same boat can carry many different loads. But it is illuminating to trace the origin of the word *nature* and the historical sequence of conceptual loads it has been asked to carry.

The boat of nature was first loaded up in Greece. The English word *nature* is a rendering of the Latin *natura,* which first appeared in the third century B.C.E. But *natura* was itself a Roman translation of the older Greek word *physis.*[11] (*Physis* also makes its way into English, serving as the root for *physics, physician, physical, metaphysical,* and so on.) *Physis*'s own roots are in the Greek *phy,* meaning simply "to be," and *phyein,* "to give birth." Although we can't be certain when *physis* was coined from *phy* and *phyein,* the word was nevertheless in use by the eighth century B.C.E. to connote the permanent, essential aspects of an object by which it might be forever known—a meaning that was apparently derived from an earlier use of *physis* to mean "birthmark."[12]

By the end of the fifth century B.C.E., however, *physis* had come to take on a wider and more significant meaning. The fifth century was a period of enormous change in Greek society, a period of fantastic growth in the power, size, and wealth of the city-states. After 480 B.C.E., when the Greeks defeated the Persians, to whom they had previously paid tribute, their economy began to expand mightily. The economic expansion brought wealth and urban growth. Athens grew to a size never seen before. Perhaps as many as 275,000 people lived there in 431 B.C.E.[13]

In such a place, and in such a time, it was hard not to be impressed with an urban truth: Money and politics, not the gods and other lofty concerns, moved the world of everyday life. At least that was the message of the Sophists, a group of itinerate philosophers known for their cynical and relativistic teachings about the reach of self-interest into all human affairs and beliefs. "It is for themselves and their own advantage," declared the Sophist Callicles, "that they make their laws and distribute their praises and censures."[14] Not the gods, but "man is the measure of all things," claimed Protagoras. Human laws are "designed to serve the interest of the ruling class,"

Thrasymachus observed. In his view, "the actual ruler or governor thinks of his subjects as sheep [and] his chief occupation, day and night, is how he can best fleece them to his own benefit."[15]

What the Sophists were saying is that the moral order, including religion, is based upon mere convention—*nomos,* to use the Greek word—not some principle external to human interests, such as God, justice, or what we have come to call science. Many Sophists were famous for their rhetorical skills, which they used as proof of their view that morality is just a kind of con game. Indeed, their practice of lecturing only for a fee (which Plato complained about in *The Republic)* was itself a kind of demonstration of the ultimate Sophist point: Even truth has a price on it.

The Sophists are often considered the bad guys of ancient Greek philosophy because of their apparent anything-goes vision of morality. If morality is human-derived, it follows that morality is whatever any human wants it to be, justice and inequality be damned. But most Sophists in fact were very concerned about social inequality and sought to expose hypocrisy. Their teachings fit well with the ambitions of the students who came to hear the latest Sophist to come to town. These were mainly young or disadvantaged citizens and free noncitizens eager to acquire the rhetorical skills essential for getting ahead in the city.[16] For them, the Sophist message was comforting and hopeful: The social order is not preordained.

The Sophist argument was ultimately circular, however, for if all morality is mere rhetoric and *nomos,* so too must be Sophism itself. There had to be somewhere else to stand. *Physis* suddenly sprang into widespread use as a word that might provide that foundation, a word that could root truth in something outside of human manipulation, rhetoric, bias, materialist desire, and self-interest— a word that could be a source of moral guidance in a jealous world of wealth and power. Hippocrates advised doctors that *physis* was the only true calling of medicine (and thus the term *physician).*[17] In the middle of the fourth century, Aristotle wrote several books on *physis,* most notably the *Physics,*

and went on to use it as his proposed foundation for a just society in the *Politics.*

Plato was a bit cautious about the word, though, perhaps because the Sophist opponents in his dialogues often based their arguments on *physis.* For example, Plato reports that the Sophist Callicles believed might-makes-right was a truth "nature herself reveals."[18] Such a view really would make Sophists philosophical bad guys, but we only have Plato's word on this. Whether or not this was truly a common Sophist position, Plato had recognized that *physis* was a bendable enough concept that might-makes-right could be justified with it. So he sought a different solution than *physis*—but one that was equally an effort to discover a moral realm beyond interest. He agreed that the Greek pantheon of gods had become a philosophical shambles. So he proposed a new kind of god, a great ideal or "form" that he claimed governed the order of things: the Good.

Plato argued that the Good was the divine agent of the world, what he called the Demiurge. As pure goodness, the Demiurge could not suffer from a materialist sin like envy. And herein lies the origin of the world, as Plato explained in *Timaeus:*

> Let us therefore state the reason why the framer of this universe of change framed it at all. He was good, and what is good has no particle of envy in it; being therefore without envy he wished all things to be as like himself as possible.[19]

So the Demiurge created the material world, using as a blueprint "his" own ideal goodness. In other words, the primal act of the universe was the denial of envy, of materialist desire. As a consequence, the whole world is good, and goodness is the whole world.

Thus was born a new manner of god. Not the quarreling, querulous gods that populated the old Greek pantheon. Not the jealous God of the Old Testament. But a god who cannot sin and whose very power stems from being separated from the backstabbing ways and moral sleight of hand of human society.

Aristotle apparently thought the Demiurge story was a bit silly, and he did not repeat it. Aristotle's distinctive moral contribution was his effort to get around the might-makes-right problem and to return to *physis* as a solution to the problem of justice. But he kept a bit of Plato in his argument, and agreed that the ultimate motor of the world, the "final cause" and "unmoved mover" of *physis,* was "the Good."[20] Nature was not, as some Sophists had apparently concluded, a source of anything-goes morality. It was, in effect, itself the Demiurge, and thus following nature was following the Good. Now nature was cured of materialist desire and could become a source of moral guidance in a world of envy and greed. The Greeks had discovered the natural conscience.

China

The classical Greeks were not the first ancient people to critique materialist desire. *The Song of the Harper,* an Egyptian text of c. 2600 B.C.E., had this to say: "Remember it is not given to man to take his goods with him. No one goes away and then comes back."[21] Similarly, the Egyptian sage Ptahhotep admonished, "Beware an act of avarice; it is a bad and incurable disease."[22]

But few pursued this line of thinking with the philosophical vigor of the classical Greeks and another group of ancient thinkers: the Taoists. By the fifth century B.C.E., about the same time as the Greeks, Taoist philosophers began to take a rather skeptical view of the human world. In China, as in Greece, this was an age of commerce and empire in which power and self-interest seemed greater truths about the way the world worked than earlier religious views. Taoist writings of the time abound in criticisms of the self-centered money interests overtaking ancient Chinese society. This critical impression grew into full-fledged doubt about the materialistic underpinnings of social life in general.

Lao Tzu (or rather the writer of the *Lao Tzu,* who is not known for certain) is famously direct

on the topic: "There may be gold and jade to fill a hall, but there is none who can keep them." You can't take it with you—clearly a reminder that many through the ages have seen fit to give. "To be overbearing when one has wealth and position," the *Lao Tzu* goes on, "is to bring calamity upon oneself."[23] Lao Tzu taught that "the sage desires not to desire and does not value goods which are hard to come by."[24] "Is this not because," Lao Tzu asks in a different passage, "[the sage] does not wish to be considered a better man than others?"[25] The *Lao Tzu* makes the point most plainly in the allegory of the "uncarved block," the simple, unadorned state it counsels people to emulate: "The nameless uncarved block is but freedom from desire." The secret to contentment is to "have little thought of self and as few desires as possible."[26]

Similarly, the *Lieh-Tzu,* another early Taoist work, taught the uselessness of the fancy art objects made for the aristocracy. One story in this book is of a certain prince of Sung who commissioned an artisan to carve a morphologically correct leaf out of jade. When the artisan returned with the jade leaf after three years' labor, it was so perfect that no one could tell it from a real leaf, and the prince was overjoyed. But when Lieh Tzu heard about it, he replied, "If nature took three years to produce one leaf, there would be few trees with leaves on them!"[27]

These critiques had a deep resonance, and we find them in many later ancient Chinese writings. The *Lii-shih Ch'un Ch'iu,* a compendium of useful knowledge put together for a third-century B.C.E. prime minister, portrayed commerce as a potentially corruptible tangent from the simple ways of agrarian society.[28] Writing about the same time, Chuang Tzu counseled against giving in to "desire," materialism, and ambition. As he wrote in "The Empty Boat," whoever "can free himself from achievement and from fame…will flow like Tao." He who has no power and no reputation "is the perfect man: His boat is empty."[29]

Chuang Tzu also extolled the virtues of simplicity in the story of a Taoist sage, Hsu Yu, who, when offered the rulership of a kingdom, exclaimed,

When the tailor-bird builds her nest in the deep wood, she uses no more than one branch. When the mole drinks at the river, he takes no more than a bellyful. . . . I have no use for the rulership of the world![30]

Materialist skepticism in ancient China, like Sophism in Greece, proceeded so far that many Taoists, particularly Lao Tzu, came to be deeply suspicious of all knowledge. The sage "learns to be without knowledge," wrote Lao Tzu.[31] "One who knows does not speak; one who speaks does not know."[32] Like the Sophists, the Taoists sharply criticized the deceptiveness of language. Here is Lao Tzu again: "Truthful words are not beautiful; beautiful words are not truthful. Good words are not persuasive; persuasive words are not good." The passage goes on to return to the problem of knowledge more generally: "He who knows has no wide learning; he who has wide learning does not know."[33]

But unlike the Greek Sophists, the Taoists had an alternative to self-interest, an alternative that provided a natural conscience they believed to be free from materialist ambition. The Taoists found their natural conscience in the *Tao,* or "the way," the principle that underlies things we in the West would term "natural"—in agrarian society, in the nests of tailor-birds, in moles and rivers, and in the leaves of trees. As the historian Fung Yu-Lan put it, Tao is "the unitary first 'that' from which all things in the universe come to be." It is "the all-embracing first principle of things," what Aristotle would have recognized as the "unmoved mover" of the world.[34] Tao is unaffected by human doings, but people do best when they allow themselves to be guided by it, and not by human desire.

Through the Tao, each thing obtains its *te,* its individual essential quality. Tao is within humans as well, and each human therefore has a *te.* We can allow *te* to express itself through *wu wei,* acting without deliberate effort.[35] Acting deliberately, what Taoists call *yu wei,* would inevitably lead one away from the Tao. Empty your boat, advise the Taoists, and drift along with the natural conscience of the Tao.

The Moral Basis of Contemporary Environmental Concern

In the centuries that followed, nature remained a central pillar of the natural conscience. But nature was often tied in with other concepts— religion, science, conceptions of bodily difference such as race and gender, and many other ideas and institutions that similarly claimed at least a partial foundation in "nature." Such ideas and institutions have been strongly criticized in recent years. Critics have argued, like the Sophists once did, that human interests do indeed motivate these sources of moral judgment. In an era of unprecedented growth in wealth, inequality, environmental domination, and political conflict, it seems to many that, rather than resting above power, our basic moral ideas—including those rooted in nature—are the products of power.

Consider race, once widely seen as a "natural," and therefore perfectly moral, basis on which to allocate social rewards and social position. Increasingly—and quite correctly, I think— people see the idea of "race" as a way those in power have sought to stay that way. Race is rapidly losing its former status as an interest-free fact of "nature." (Chapter 8 explores this criticism in more detail.)

It is a common fate of every widely accepted formulation of a natural conscience that it is subsequently subjected to careful critical scrutiny to see if it really does rise above the problems of human interest and the balance of power. We should welcome such scrutiny, I believe, although we often do not. The scrutiny of various visions of the natural conscience have been unusually intense in recent decades, though, and it is the defining feature of a cultural trend often called *postmodernism.* Although skepticism about human motivations is certainly not wholly new, as we have seen, the moral dilemma is particularly strong today: If all that motivates us is power and self-interest, is there then no truly moral place to stand?

These questions had already begun to occur with some force to Henry David Thoreau in the middle of the nineteenth century, as he walked through the woods near Walden Pond. He was by no means the only one to whom such questions occurred at this time. Many people worried about the direction and motivations behind the social and environmental transformations brought about by the burgeoning Industrial Revolution. And the moral solution that many found was the same: a return to a purer vision of nature—nature as the wild; as woods and winds, farms and fields, grazing sheep and flitting butterflies; as the nonsocial world. A few decades earlier, Beethoven had penned the *Pastoral Symphony.* A few decades later, Bierdstadt would paint *The Last of the Buffalo.* Cities were establishing parks, zoos, and botanical gardens, and the rich were taking up second homes in the countryside. Natural historians were reveling in the wonders of a nature beyond society, and the theory of natural selection was slowly accumulating evidence on Darwin's desk, even as the coming of industrialism was radically transforming those wonders. But Thoreau was a leading exemplar of this broad cultural change. (See Figure 7.3.)

Thoreau in particular loved walking. Thoreau walked "four hours a day at least," he tells us in the essay "Walking."[36] And when he walked, he found himself inevitably drawn to the west. "Eastward I go only by force," he explained, "but westward I go free."[37]

From his cabin on Walden Pond, the west led Thoreau away from Boston and into the open countryside. The freedom he felt in this direction was a social freedom—that is, a freedom from the social. Thoreau exalted,

Man and his affairs, church and state and school, trade and commerce, and manufactures and agriculture, even politics, most alarming of them all,—I am pleased to see how little space they occupy on the landscape. In one half-hour I can walk off to some portion of the earth's surface where a

Figure 7.3   Henry David Thoreau, 1817–1862. Nearly a century and a half after his death, millions still find inspiration in this quiet man's eloquent writings about the moral value of wild nature. His concerns remain our concerns.

man does not stand from one year's end to another, and there, consequently, politics are not, for they are but as the cigar-smoke of a man.[38]

Instead of the cigar smoke of politics, to the west Thoreau found the Wild. As he put it in the most famous line he ever wrote,

The west of which I speak is but another name for the Wild; and what I have been preparing to say is, that in Wildness is the preservation of the World.[39]

We can hear in Thoreau both a critique of power and interests and an alternative place to stand (or, rather, walk). What alarms Thoreau about society and the east is the play of human politics—the interest-laden "affairs" of church, state, school, trade, commerce, manufactures, and agriculture. But to the west Thoreau found release from power and self-interests. The vital serenity of the wild was, for Thoreau, the serenity of a realm without social conflict, for in the wild was no society with which to conflict. It was the serenity of what I have called in some of my research the *natural other*—a vision of an interest-free realm upon which to base a natural conscience.[40]

Like the Taoists and the Sophists, Thoreau carried his critique of material desire and self-interest into a suspicion of knowledge itself, especially the useful and arrogant knowledge of the technological ethos. Like the Taoists (and some Sophists, including the most famous Sophist of all: Socrates)[41], he praised ignorance and the recognition of how little we know:

> We have heard of a Society for the Diffusion of Useful Knowledge. It is said that knowledge is power; and the like. Methinks there is equal need of a Society for the Diffusion of Useful Ignorance, what we will call Beautiful Knowledge, a knowledge useful in a higher sense: for what is most of our boasted so-called knowledge but a conceit that we know something, which robs us of the advantage of our actual ignorance? . . . Which is the best man to deal with, he who knows nothing about a subject, and, what is extremely rare, knows that he knows nothing, or he who really knows something about it, but thinks that he knows all?[42]

It is the power behind knowledge that worried Thoreau the most, I believe. He saw in knowledge no authentic route to truth and self. That route was to be found in going west and opening oneself up to the wild, but without deliberate effort, again echoing Taoism. In Thoreau's words, "I believe that there is a subtile [sic] magnetism in Nature, which, if we unconsciously yield to it, will direct us aright." This sounds to me like *wu wei*.

Through this unconscious yielding to the natural other of the wild, Thoreau counseled, we can find our real selves, and even our real names, as opposed to the "cheap and meaningless" names we receive from society. "It may be given to a savage who retains in secret his own wild title earned in the woods," thought Thoreau. "We have a wild savage in us, and a savage name is perchance somewhere recorded as ours."[43] In that wild savage within, and in that savage name, Thoreau found a *natural me*—the imagination of a truer, more authentic self that we believe the natural other sees in us, as opposed to the me that society sees.

The sense of a "natural me" is a social psychological invention, of course. Authenticity and truth are in the end matters of personal conviction, not eternal and external points of reference that we all agree upon. So too for the authenticity and truth of the natural me. It is something we formulate, not something we are given. But the human and social origin of the natural me does not make it any less significant for the human and the social. Indeed, the problem of the necessary invention of that which must be believed to be non-invented makes the achievement of a convincingly non-invented invention all the more compelling. Confusing? Contradictory? Paradoxical? Yes. But we must experience it otherwise for the natural conscience, with its natural other and natural me, to work morally and ideologically.

In any event, Thoreau's formulation of the natural conscience was very influential and is still a touchstone for environmental thought today. Thoreauvian *wu wei* can be found in the voluntary simplicity movement in all its many manifestations. His natural other can be found in the wilderness preservation movement and in the restful, yet exhilarating joy that so many find walking in their own Wild Wests, imagining freedom from social conflict, social constraint, and social power. His critique of materialist desire can be found in the environmentalist's condemnation of waste, pollution, corporate irresponsibility, state inaction, and the greed seen to underlie it all. Thoreau's natural me can be found in the environmentalists' self-conception that they are motivated by the interests of something outside themselves, and perhaps their self-conception that they are less artificial people.

If it is not Thoreau's own *wu wei,* natural other, natural me, and materialist critique that inform contemporary environmental concerns, then it is something of close resemblance, whether arrived at through direct moral descent from Thoreau or through moral convergence with Thoreau.

A number of years ago, while doing research in England for a book about attitudes toward nature and the countryside, I had a memorably Thoreauvian conversation with a thoughtful, committed young man, very concerned about the environment. Nigel, as I'll call him, was also very concerned about the situation in Northern Ireland, and one evening we discussed the complexities and contradictions of that bitterly contested land. We found that we agreed that fault lay on both sides. There was a pause in the conversation, as we both let that thought sink in. And then Nigel said, "That's why I think I'm interested in the environment. You *know* what's right. It's clear where one should be standing. It's never that way with politics."[44]

I have no idea if Nigel had read Thoreau. Most of the 96 percent of respondents from that 1990–1993 world poll who supported the environmental movement almost certainly had not read Thoreau. Nor had they likely read the many environmental ethicists who followed Thoreau—such as John Muir, Henry Salt, Rudolf Steiner, Lewis Mumford, Arne Naess, Mahatma Gandhi, and Aldo Leopold—let alone those who preceded him, like Horace, the Sophists, Aristotle, and Lao Tzu. They don't have to have read these classic works. The ideas they represent are part of the cultural waters in which we all swim.

Which doesn't mean, however, that we are all cultural clones of Thoreau. We reinvent the natural conscience as much as we borrow it from our cultural history. We do this because such an idea continues to help us contend with the ideological conditions of our lives. Thoreau is admired today because we see our ideas in him as much as (if not

more than) we experience his ideas in us. The modern natural conscience is thus as much a new invention as it is a reinvention—as much a new discovery as it is a rediscovery.

The Extent of Contemporary Environmental Concern

The natural conscience is not all there is to environmental concern and its expansion into a broad popular movement in the last half of the twentieth century, however. In this section and the next, I argue that perceived environmental decline is an important factor in its own right. That is, there is an important material basis to the ideology of environmental concern.

This point may seem self-evident. But a number of scholars and critics of environmentalism have raised two potential counterarguments: First, that environmentalism is a passing flavor-of-the-month kind of issue and that people will rapidly lose interest, and second, that environmentalism is mainly an elite issue. Either counterargument, if true, would lessen the significance of the material origins of environmental concern.

The Persistence of Environmental Concern

In support of the flavor-of-the-month argument, it is important to note that the intensity of environmental concern varies considerably from person to person. This is something we all know from our personal interactions with others, and it also expresses itself in survey results.

Recall again the 1990–1993 World Values poll of 43 countries, in which 96 percent of respondents expressed their approval of the environmental movement. That 96 percent figure needs to be interpreted with care. For example, in that same poll, only 65 percent indicated that they were willing to pay higher taxes to prevent environmental pollution. This still is a significant percentage, but

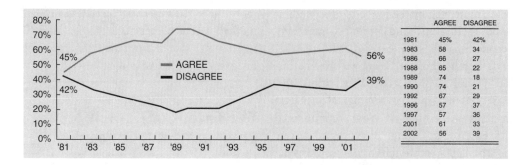

	AGREE	DISAGREE
1981	45%	42%
1983	58	34
1986	66	27
1988	65	22
1989	74	18
1990	74	21
1992	67	29
1996	57	37
1997	57	36
2001	61	33
2002	56	39

Figure 7.4   The persistence of environmental concern in the United States, 1981–2002. Although there have been ups and downs, responses to New York Times/CBS national polls have remained strong to the following statement: "Protecting the environment is so important that requirements and standards cannot be too high, and continuing environmental improvements must be made regardless of cost."

the idea of having to pay to prevent pollution did dampen the enthusiasm of many. And when presented with the statement "The government has to reduce pollution but it should not cost me any money," 55 percent of the sample agreed—meaning that only 45 percent were willing to pay to prevent pollution. Thus, the intensity of world support for environmental concerns dropped from 96 to 65 to 45 percent, depending upon how the pollsters phrased the question.[45]

Moreover, public concern for most issues follows a pattern that the political scientist Anthony Downs once called the "issue-attention cycle."[46] The vogue term for it these days is "compassion fatigue." Through the combined effects of boredom, the media's restless search for the new and novel, a realization that relieving the problem would entail significant costs, and maybe a sense that government must now be taking care of things, public interest in most issues tends to wane over time. Perhaps environmental concern too will drop.

And perhaps not. At least it was still high worldwide in that 1999 International Millennium Survey, although that poll asked substantially different questions than did the 1990–1993 World Values poll, making direct comparisons impossible. Nevertheless, we can at least conclude that public concern for the environment has shown considerable staying power. And in the United States at least, the general trend over the past 30 years is upward. In 1973, 34 percent of Americans felt that "environmental protection laws and regulations" haven't gone "far enough." In 2001, 44 percent felt that way. Similarly, in an even stronger test of environmental concern, in 1981, 45 percent agreed with the statement "Protecting the environment is so important that requirements and standards cannot be too high, and continuing environmental improvements must be made regardless of cost." In 2002, 56 percent said they agreed.[47] (See Figure 7.4.)

Environmentalism has had its ups and downs, though. After a dramatic upswing in the late 1960s, American environmental concern peaked shortly after the first Earth Day in 1970 and declined throughout the 1970s. As early as 1972, Anthony Downs was already predicting that interest in environmental problems would soon follow the issue-attention cycle into the shadows.[48] For a decade, it looked like he might be right. However, the 1980s brought a resurgence of concern, reaching the unprecedented levels recorded by surveys in the early 1990s. In 1992, 63 percent of Americans said environmental laws and regulation hadn't gone far enough, 7 percent higher than in 2002. And in 1990, 74 percent said that environmental improvements must be made regardless of cost, 18 percent higher than in 2002.[49]

Even if public concern is currently fading a bit, at least in some countries, environmentalism has shown itself over 30 years to be more than a passing fad. Concern will experience periodic downturns, to be sure, but environmentalism seems likely to remain a persistent topic of public discussion for the foreseeable future. Scholars now generally agree that environmental concern is widespread and long lasting, although variable in intensity over time and from person to person.

Social Status and Environmental Concern

Now let's inspect the common suggestion that environmentalism is an elite movement of the liberal, the white, and the comfortably well-off.

Early public opinion polls in the West found that, in fact, these social factors had relatively little influence on the level of environmental concern. A 1979 British survey found that supporters of the environmental movement did tend to be drawn from middle-class service professions: teachers, social workers, doctors, and the like. But the strongest opponents of environmental views—business leaders—had even higher incomes on the whole. And many lower-income people and trade unionists showed strong support for environmentalism.[50]

A more comprehensive 1992 American study, drawing on 18 years of national surveys conducted between 1973 and 1990, showed similar results.[51] Income had only a minor effect on a person's level of environmental concern, even during recessions. People who were younger, liberal, members of the Democratic Party, well educated, urban, and who did not work in primary industries like farming and forestry did tend to be more supportive of environmentalism. But again, these effects were slight; plenty of older, conservative, Republican, less educated, rural, and primary industry-employed people professed environmental support.

Finally, a comparative study across 18 wealthy nations, based on a 1990 survey, found little influence of social status on levels of environmental concern. Level of wealth had no effect, and being younger and being female had very slight effects.[52]

But in recent years, social status has emerged as an important predictor of environmental concern, at least in the United States—and in completely the reverse direction of the old charge that environmentalism is an elite concern. People from privileged social groups now tend to have significantly less support for environmentalism than others do. In general, support for environmentalism is somewhat higher among women and people of color, and quite a bit higher among people with lower incomes. For example, in a 2000 poll of voting intentions in the presidential race, lower-income groups were far more likely to call protecting the environment "very important" in their voting decisions. Among those making less than $30,000 a year, 67 percent called environmental protection "very important," and just 40 percent of those making more than $75,000 a year did.[53] Researchers have also recently noted what they term the "white male effect" in which white men tend to report considerably less concern with health risks, technological hazards, and environmental protection. In 1994 and 1996 national surveys, whites showed significantly lower levels of environmental concern than other groups. Among whites—and only among whites—gender was also a significant factor, with men registering lower levels of concern than women.[54]

Why? The evidence is at least coincident with the main conclusion of Chapter 6—that there is an ideological connection between social domination and environmental domination. As Linda Kalof and her colleagues note, "These anomalous attitudes of White men are likely the result of their historically privileged position regarding risk and power in society."[55] We may presume as much for the wealthy. Those with greater social power are less likely to suffer the consequences of environmental problems, and thus will be less concerned about them. Also, those with greater social power may tend to have less egalitarian attitudes, and thus less concern about the consequences of environmental problems for others—both other humans and nonhuman environmental others.

These are controversial findings and interpretations, and some may feel threatened or offended by them. So it is very important to remind ourselves that we are speaking here of tendencies and preponderances, not absolutes. Not all wealthy people, white people, and male people are among the less environmentally concerned, and not all poor people, people of color, and females are among the more environmentally concerned. These are statistical matters, and should not be allowed to become stereotypes.

But there may be some elitism in saying that environmentalism is an elite movement. It could be taken as implying that the poor are too ignorant or unsophisticated to comprehend the issues. It would also not be empirically accurate, and not only for the poor in a wealthy country like the United States. There is abundant evidence of considerable environmental concern among the poor elsewhere, as the Indian environmental sociologist Ramachandra Guha has forcefully pointed out. Consider the struggles of the Penan people of Malaysia fighting the logging of their forest home; the similar struggles of the Chipko ("hug the tree") movement of villagers in northern India; the hard-fought, and tragic, campaigns in Brazil and Nigeria that led to the murders of two of the world's most important environmental leaders, Chico Mendes and Ken Saro-Wiwa; the Amazonian native peoples of Ecuador protesting the despoiling of their forest home by oil companies. Environmentalism has become a significant feature of political debate in the world's poorest countries too.

The character of the "environmentalism of the poor," as Guha terms it, often differs significantly from the environmentalism of the rich. "First and foremost," Guha has written, "it combines a concern with the environment with an often more visible concern with social justice."[56] This heightened emphasis on environmental justice has also been central to the environmentalism of the poor in rich countries, as the thousands of community-level groups that have sprung up in the United States since the late 1980s demonstrate. These groups usually focus on the unequal distribution of environmental "bads," such as the location of toxic waste disposal sites and heavily polluting industrial facilities, blending environmental and social justice concerns, particularly over race and class, as Chapter 5 discussed.[57]

There is, then, little empirical support for the allegation of Lester Thurow and others over the years that, to quote Thurow, "poor countries and poor individuals simply aren't interested" in environmentalism.[58] In the early years of environmentalism, there may have been a grain of truth to this assertion, as access to education is of course higher for the wealthy. But the ideas of environmentalism have now spread well beyond the halls of the academy. It is no longer an elite concern, if it ever was. If anything, it is increasingly just the reverse.

Three Theories of Contemporary Environmental Concern

So how have these changes in environmental concern come about? Several theories suggest that the origin ultimately lies in changes in the material conditions of society—that increases in environmental concern began at a material moment in the ecological dialogue, moved to a ideal moment as understandings changed, and then has in turn led to attempts to change those material conditions. I'll compare three of these theories. First, I'll take up the political scientist Ronald Inglehart's theory of *postmaterialism*. Inglehart's analysis moves beyond the elitism critique of environmentalism, while at the same time returning to it in a way. Second, I'll consider the *paradigm shift* theory of Riley Dunlap, William Catton, and their colleagues. This theory traces the rise of broad concern with evidence of environmental decline that may, in time, lead to a fundamental shift in our ideologies. Third, I'll discuss the *ecological modernization* theory of many scholars, but in environmental sociology most especially Arthur Mol and Gert Spaargaren. Ecological modernization argues that we have recently begun to overcome the opposition of economy and ecology that has so long prevented us from embracing environmental concern.

Material changes, as we'll see, play a central role in all three of these theories. There is also a fourth major theory of environmental concern, the *risk society* thesis of Ulrich Beck, in which material issues figure prominently. In the first edition of this book, I discussed Beck's work at this point in my argument. But Beck's work is now most often applied in analyses of risk, and I accordingly moved my discussion to Chapter 9, a new chapter on risk. So I ask the reader to hold onto the threads of this chapter until we get there.

Postmaterialism

Since the early 1970s, Inglehart has been documenting a broad intergenerational cultural shift in wealthy countries across the world, what he terms a turn from "materialist" to "postmaterialist" values. The word *materialist* can be confusing. Inglehart does not have in mind here "materialist" in the philosophical sense of explanations that emphasize economy, technology, biology, and the physical, which is the way that I usually use the term in this book. Nor does he mean greediness. Along with his colleague Paul Abramson, Inglehart argues that younger generations are shifting away from "concerns about economic and physical security" (material values, in Inglehart's terms) and toward "a greater emphasis on freedom, self-expression, and the quality of life" (postmaterial values).[59]

Inglehart takes a leaf from Karl Mannheim, a Hungarian sociologist from the first half of the twentieth century, and his theory of generations, which suggests that people's basic values are formed in early adulthood and tend to persist thereafter.[60] Older generations were socialized in times when worries about money, health, and natural threats were much more of a concern, Inglehart suggests. Drawing as well on Maslow's theory of the hierarchy of needs (which I discussed in Chapter 2), Inglehart argues that economic improvements have allowed younger generations to focus instead on issues of aesthetics and self-actualization, such as freedom and quality of life.[61] Increased concern for the environment,

argues Inglehart, is one product of this "postmaterial" socialization among younger generations. Inglehart's basic point is that we're better off now—pretty much all of us, not just the elites—and can afford to worry about the environment.

Inglehart and his collaborators have assembled an impressive array of survey evidence to back up their claim that a shift to postmaterial values is under way in countries across the globe. As older generations die off, Inglehart argues, the overall proportion of postmaterialists will increase, with far-reaching implications for politics and lifestyle choices. Inglehart has been conducting periodic surveys over the past 25 years to determine whether the proportion of postmaterialists is actually on the rise. (The 1990–1993 survey of environmental values in 43 countries that I discussed previously was in fact only a small part of a larger survey led by Inglehart to test the postmaterialism hypothesis.)

In these surveys, Inglehart categorizes people as postmaterialist, materialist, or mixed by asking them which two of the following four choices should be their country's top goals:

1. Maintaining order in the nation

2. Giving people more say in important government decisions

3. Fighting rising prices

4. Protecting freedom of speech

Goals 1 and 3 are the materialist responses. Goals 2 and 4 are the postmaterialist ones. Any other combination is scored as mixed.[62]

Inglehart finds that a substantial shift is indeed underway. For example, in 1972 in the United States, 9 percent of those surveyed gave postmaterialist responses, and 35 percent registered as materialist. But by 1992, postmaterialists were up to 18 percent and the materialists were down to 16 percent. The proportion of mixed had also gone up, from 55 to 65 percent, also indicating a shift in a postmaterialist direction.[63] Inglehart has documented similar changes in Britain, France, West Germany, Italy, the Netherlands,

Denmark, and Ireland, as well as a slight postmaterialist shift in Belgium.[64]

Inglehart has also demonstrated a correlation in these surveys between postmaterialist values and support for environmentalism. For example, in one 1986 survey conducted in 12 European countries, 53 percent of postmaterialists strongly approved of the environmental movement, but only 37 percent of materialists did.[65] In that same survey, Inglehart notes, countries with more postmaterialists were also those that had taken more actions to protect the environment, indicating that postmaterialism also translates into environmental action. This is compelling evidence, and many researchers have applied this analysis to understanding the rise of the environmental movement in countries across North America and Europe.[66]

Questioning Postmaterialism. As compelling as this evidence for a change toward postmaterialist values may be, however, there is reason to doubt Inglehart's interpretation of its link to rising environmental concern.

To begin with, postmaterialism cannot account for the environmentalism of the poor, as Guha and other critics have pointed out.[67] The bulk of people in poor countries cannot be said to have postmaterialist values, and yet environmentalism is an increasingly central political issue in these countries—and for strong materialist reasons (among others): Threats to the environment threaten human well-being. Inglehart himself has recently noted the existence of environmentalism in poor countries and has suggested that its origin must lie in materialist concerns, rather than postmaterialist ones—a considerable concession.[68] (But we also need to be careful not to presume that the poor are incapable of anything other than materialist concerns. For example, some of the broadest visions of the environment are the holistic traditions of many native peoples.)

We also have grounds to doubt a postmaterialist explanation for environmentalism in the rich countries. First, there is Ingelhart's implication that greater wealth should correlate with declining concern for economic and security threats, and thus higher concern for the environment. And yet, as we have seen, increasingly the wealthy in the United States, at least, show lower levels of environmental concern than do people with lower incomes, in keeping with Guha's observations about the environmentalism of poor countries. Second, when you consider it carefully, it is evident that Inglehart's explanation rests on the idea that environmental issues are not real material concerns for the West. Environmentalism seems to represent for Inglehart the idyllic musings of a gilded society.

Many environmentalists, however, would no doubt respond that ecological threats are far from being issues of postmaterialism—of Maslovian aesthetic self-actualization. Ecological threats are material threats. Not that there isn't an important aesthetic (and moral, as I previously argued) dimension to environmentalism. But there are also important material considerations involved—considerations that concern both the rich and the poor. In other words, Inglehart may be falsely repeating, in more sophisticated terms, the old elitism charge against environmentalism.

Paradigm Shift

Other theorists agree that a broad, slow change is underway in the dominant outlook of the inhabitants of industrial countries, but reject the implicit charge of elitism in Inglehart. One such tradition is the *paradigm shift* thesis. Rather than seeing environmentalism as an affectation of the comfortable, this theory suggests that, in response to discrepancies between evidence of environmental threats and ideologies that do not consider environmental implications, people are slowly but steadily adopting a more environmentally aware view of the world. People are becoming more aware of the real material effects that industrial life has on the environment, and their ideologies are beginning to change to match this new understanding. The central feature of the emerging new paradigm is that we no longer see humans as exempt from environmental implications. We are coming to see ourselves as connected to the environment, not separate from it. It's a deceptively simple theory, originally proposed by the sociologists Riley Dunlap, William Catton, and Kent Van Liere in the late 1970s, and by Stephen Cotgrove and Lester Milbrath in the early 1980s.[69]

I say "deceptively simple" in part because measuring environmental awareness turns out to be quite difficult. Paradigm shift researchers have generally approached the question by distinguishing between two paradigms, one old and one new. Under the old paradigm, humans are exceptional creatures who are able to overcome environmental limits, and the basic goal of human society is technological mastery over nature for the purpose of wealth creation. Researchers have variously termed this view the "human exemptionalism paradigm," the "dominant social paradigm," and the "technological social paradigm." Under the new paradigm, humans are a part of nature and need to maintain a sense of balance and to live within limits in an interconnected world. Researchers have variously termed this latter view the "new environmental paradigm," the "alternative environmental paradigm," and the "ecological social paradigm."[70] The most common terms are the *human exemptionalism paradigm* and *new environmental paradigm,* usually referred to in shorthand as the HEP and the NEP. Based on this contrast, paradigm shift researchers have devised batteries of survey questions to assess how strongly a person adheres to one paradigm or the other.

The next measurement complexity is assessing why people's ideas might change from one paradigm to another. In a 1982 survey of the state of Washington, a research team from Washington State University approached this issue by distinguishing between *environmental beliefs* and *environmental values*—between how a person thinks the environment is and how she or he thinks the environment ought to be. For example, the researchers assessed environmental beliefs by asking people how much they agreed with a battery of statements such as "The earth is like a spaceship, with limited room and resources." They appraised environmental values with

statements like "People should adapt to the environment whenever possible."

It might be expected that beliefs and values would correspond fairly closely, but the Washington State survey found considerably stronger support for environmental beliefs than environmental values. Although 78 percent of Washington residents expressed some degree of an "ecological social paradigm," 57 percent of the respondents were what the researchers called "strong believers," and only 25 percent were "strong valuers."[71] The Washington State researchers argue that what is at work is the slow process of people's values catching up with their beliefs about external material realities—such as rising levels of pollution, the disappearing wild, and technological failures like Chernobyl and Bhopal.

Similar to Thomas Kuhn's theory of scientific revolutions, the Washington State team's conclusions suggest that we tend initially to hold on to our paradigms even in the face of contradictory evidence. But eventually we seek to bring the two—paradigms and evidence of the external world—into better correspondence, leading to paradigm change. As the Washington State team wrote, "Our analysis suggests that shifts in social paradigms are influenced primarily by external discrepancies."[72]

Questioning the Paradigm Shift. But we must be cautious in interpreting these survey results too. To begin with, there is the obvious problem of reducing such a complex matter as environmental ideology to only two categories. Such reduction may obscure ideological complexities more than it clarifies them.[73] A lot more may be going on. Dunlap and his colleagues have recently devised new version of the NEP scale, however, which is intended to help researchers tap into a wider range of facets of environmental concern.[74]

A closely related problem is deciding which ideology represents the environmental ideal. There are likely as many environmentalisms as there are people. Whose environmentalism, then, does one choose as the standard? Paradigm shift researchers have tried to draw this standard from the works of leading environmental writers.[75] But writers do not represent everyone (or there would be no need to conduct a survey), nor do they always agree (or they probably wouldn't bother to write). Inevitably, researchers have had to draw on their own understandings of environmental writers and environmentalism. There is thus a danger that paradigm shift researchers are only assessing the degree to which the rest of the world agrees with them about what environmentalism is.

Survey-based research also doesn't give respondents a chance to explain why they answered the survey questions in the ways that they did. Survey researchers have to presume ahead of time the kind of phrases and questions that might reflect the way people see things. But there is no opportunity on a survey to determine if a person interprets a question differently from the way the researchers intend. For example, I might reject the notion that "the earth is like a spaceship, with limited room and resources" because I don't like the mechanical and technological image of a "spaceship." I might see the Earth more as an organism. In other words, I might disagree with the statement even though I agree with the belief the statement is meant to assess.

Finally, there is the difficulty of assessing long-term ideological change with surveys of current public opinion. Paradigm shift researchers have on only a couple of occasions been able to resurvey the same population at a later date, and have found only modest and somewhat inconsistent shifts when they have done so.[76] The kind of ideological change that paradigm shift researchers hope to evaluate may be taking place over too long a time for surveys to document. The problem is, you can't go back and administer a questionnaire to the people of the past. Thus, survey research needs to be balanced with historical research.

These critiques do not invalidate paradigm shift research, however. Nor does it invalidate Inglehart's postmaterialism research, to which all of these critiques mentioned equally apply, except for the last about historical evidence. (Inglehart has amassed some impressive historical information by separating out age cohorts.) Measuring and understanding public opinion is

an inherently difficult task. All survey-based research faces these measurement problems. Without some simplifying assumptions, the question of ideological change probably could not be researched, particularly with the kind of large-scale public opinion polls that paradigm shift and postmaterialism researchers have emphasized. And even a grainy image of the overall state of the public mind is useful and important to have.

Moreover, it seems hard to deny that material factors must have ideological consequence. If our patterns of thought, our mental reflexes, had no bearing on our material conditions we would likely not last long. Or, to put it another way, if you keep stubbing your toe when you kick the environment, chances are you will eventually stop to reconsider why you were kicking it in the first place. And maybe that's what we're finally starting to do.

Ecological Modernization

Or so *ecological modernization* theorists would argue, but from a somewhat different standpoint. Based mainly on the earlier work of Ulrich Beck (of whom we will hear much more in Chapter 9) and Joseph Huber of Germany, among others, the Dutch environmental sociologists Arthur Mol and Gert Spaargaren contend that the recognition of environmental problems is starting to reshape the institutions and everyday social practices of modernity in fundamental ways. "The basic premise," writes Mol, "is the centripetal movement of ecological interests, ideas and considerations ... which results in the constant ecological restructuring of modern societies."[77] Material conditions (environmental problems) shape ideas (those interests, ideas, and considerations), which in turn reshape material conditions (the constant ecological restructuring). But this shaping and reshaping is not just a matter of individual ideologies of environmental concern, such as the theories of postmaterialism and paradigm shift discuss. This shaping and reshaping occurs as well at the level of our institutions and the social practices we find ourselves engaged in, whatever we may think about them individually.

Central to the process of ecological modernization is what Mol terms the "emancipation" of "ecological rationality."[78] What he has in mind here is that we increasingly consider more than economic, technological, political, and social reasons in making decisions about how to organize our lives. Ecological rationality has now come to have an independent force in social debates. We're on the road—maybe just the beginning of it, but on it nonetheless—to the huge, even radical, changes that we need to make to maintain what ecological modernization theorists call our "sustenance base." But the problem we faced was never modernization itself, say ecological modernization theorists. The problem was "simple modernization" driven by economy, technology, politics, and society that did not take into account ecological rationality. Put ecology in, in a serious and far-reaching way, and we can put our institutions and our daily lives on the ecological path. Put ecology in, and we can repair the "design fault," as Mol and Spaargaren term it, of an economic and technological order based on the presumption that ecology is a free service we need not pay much attention to.[79] Put ecology in, and we can overcome the long-standing conflict of business and the environment.

At first glance, ecological modernization can seem overly cheerful and hopeful. But many industries have made significant progress in retooling their businesses, embracing what has come to be called *industrial ecology,* and seeing environmental issues as opportunities and as indications of inefficiencies in their operations. Most wealthy nations now have developed environmental laws and regulations to encourage their economies in recognizing the services we gain from the environment and in becoming more eco-efficient, often with substantial savings to the economy. For example, in 2003 the Bush Administration of the United States released a report showing vast economic savings from environmental regulation. The study, by the Office of Management and Budget, found that the $23–$26 billion spent on retrofitting power plants to meet clean air standards saved the economy $120–$193 billion in money that didn't need to be spent on health problems and lost work days. For every dollar spent, $5–$7 was saved.[80] This recognition—particularly by an administration with a reputation for being unfriendly to environmental concerns—is an indication of the welcoming of ecological rationality into our basic social institutions.

Ecological modernization is also reshaping our daily practices. New standards are changing the machinery of our lives. Refrigerators, air conditioners, and plumbing systems are far more efficient on the whole than they used to be, using much less energy and water. Particularly in Europe, people are experimenting with new ways of living that reduce their personal consumption of the ecological services we were ignoring. Biking, car sharing, recycling, pre-cycling, composting, more efficient housing urban design, and more are all on the rise in some communities in Europe, and even in North America as well. Consumption and lifestyle choices matter a lot, say ecological modernists, and many citizens are working hard on this, with some success.

One of the ways that ecological modernizationists believe we are moving in a green direction is, controversially, through globalization. I say "controversially" because many environmentalists (and indeed many environmental sociologists) are quite critical of globalization, as they fear it can weaken environmental protection by giving priority to trade above all else. But as Mol argues in a recent book, many of our greatest environmental problems are global in scope, and many of our greatest environmental successes have been through global treaties that address them.[81] Take the Montreal Protocol, which has done so much to reduce the production of CFCs worldwide and to protect the upper atmosphere ozone layer. Or take ISO 14000, the environmental management guidelines of the International Organization for Standardization, guidelines which many businesses are increasingly trying to follow, particularly in Europe. Meeting ISO 14000 standards gives businesses confidence in the supplies and products they buy from each other, and thus greater confidence that consumers will trust the environmental practices behind their products. As of 2002, some 50,000 ISO certifications in 118 countries had been awarded to public and private sector organizations.[82]

Which doesn't mean that ecological modernization is a sure thing—that we can sit back and let it happen, now that ecological rationality has been emancipated and is starting to globalize. It would be serious misinterpretation of ecological modernization theory to assume that it will happen on its own, through some kind of automatic process. It will take, and is taking already, a lot of hard work by social movement organizations, by politicians, by government agencies, and by imaginative businesses, building collaborations between them. It will require *political modernization,* as ecological modernizationists call it—that is, forms of government that help bring diverse interests and ideas together in a cooperative, and yet at times critical, way. And it will take the active engagement of citizens making choices in their consumption that push the government and the economy along in their embrace of ecological rationality. No, ecological modernization is not an autonomous force. It is something we have to do, ecological modernizationists argue, in both senses of the phrase.

Questioning Ecological Modernization. Scholars have taken a great interest in ecological modernization theory in recent years, and have subjected it to rather vociferous criticism.[83] The volume of criticism, though, does not necessarily mean that a theory is a poor one. Rather, it can mean that a theory gets enough right that others pay attention to it, even if they disagree with much of it. Also, Mol and Spaargaren have been usually forthcoming in responding to the critics and in accepting many of their points, so as to improve ecological modernization theory.

Perhaps the main objection can be summed up in one word: modernization. The theory's embrace of that word and what it stands for—the value of science, technology, industry, capitalism, modern forms of government, and modern value systems—seems to some to ask that

environmentalists marry their enemies. Aren't science and technology's arrogance, industry's obliviousness, capitalism's treadmill and growth mania, government's globalization dreams, and modernism's universalistic values the roots of the environmental litany? Ecological modernization theory, say these critics, is at best accommodationist and at worst a rhetorical ruse to allow the current power structures in society to have their merry way, perhaps with a few minor reforms. It's a kind of Wonder Bread theory, some critics feel, that claims it builds stronger ecological societies 12 ways, step by step, day by day. Still creating pollution at your factory? Just tell everyone you're doing your ecologically modernist best.

Ecological modernizationists agree that they seek the solution to problems of science, technology, industry, and capitalism *in* science, technology, industry, and capitalism. But these institutions won't look the same anymore. "Ecological modernization theory puts forth a radical reform programme . . . ," writes Mol. "The institutions of modern society, such as the market, the state and science and technology, will be radically transformed in coping with the environmental crisis, although not beyond recognition."[84] Ecological modernization theory may be reformism, in other words, but it is radical reformism.

Or is it? Radical reformism seems to some a tremendously optimistic claim. As one critic put it, ecological modernization is "hobbled by an unflappable sense of technological optimism"—not to mention market optimism and governmental optimism. Ecological modernization theorists now accept this point, at least to a degree.[85] Early work on the theory was indeed hobbled by what the ecological modernization theorist Martin Hajer has called a "techno-corporatist" vision. Hajer advocates instead a "reflexive" vision—that is, one that emphasizes democratic institutions of discussion and debate that allow societies to "reflect" on where they are going, rather than being blindly led along through technological and corporate sleepwalking.[86] You could call the early vision "weak" ecological modernization and Hajer's "strong" ecological modernization, or perhaps "thin" and "thick."[87]

By embracing the necessity of democratic debate, ecological modernization theorists agree that we can't just wait for this stuff to happen. Building the institutions that enhance democratic debate is what ecological modernizationists mean by "political modernization."

Besides, ecological modernizationists ask, have you got a better idea—that is to say, a *realistic* better idea? If we have to wait for capitalism to fall before we get anywhere, we may have to wait a very long time. By then, the ecological mess could be insurmountable, as it indeed may already be. At least ecological modernization theory works from within the general situation we're likely to have for some time to come. And it claims that, while by no means certain, ecological modernization is at least possible.

Or is it? Some critics also argue that ecological modernization really only applies with any great success to a few countries in Europe, most especially Germany, the Netherlands, and the Scandinavian countries. It has little to say about the United States, for example, where environmentalists complain of virtually no progress in the past 25 years, since the great (and, at the time, revolutionary) acts of the 1960s and 1970s were passed: the Wilderness Act (1964), the National Environmental Policy Act (1969), the Clean Air Act (1970), the Endangered Species Act (1973), the Resource Conservation and Recovery Act (1976), and the Clean Water Act (1977). There has been little other than rear-guard action ever since, trying to hold on to some of the gains as mainly corporate interests systematically chip away at them, as the American environmental sociologist Fred Buttel has argued.[88] For example, at the same time the Bush Administration released the study praising regulation of power plant stacks, it was promoting its "clear skies" initiative, which many people object would remove most of the teeth of the Clean Air Act.

Ecological modernizationists respond that, yes, there's a long way to go, and yes ecological modernization is currently most developed in Western Europe. Yet with appropriate forms of globalization, it could spread much further, much more rapidly. The current configuration of the World Trade Organization is not a help, nor

is a growing trend toward unilateralism. But treaties like the Montreal Protocol, Agenda 21, and the Kyoto Accord can make a huge difference. As of 2003, there were 190 international environmental treaties, and the list is growing.[89] Moreover, many international development organizations like the World Bank are adopting greener policies.

Another criticism is that ecological modernization has little to say about issues of environmental justice. Nor does it have much to say about the rights and beauty of nature. Its focus is almost entirely on issues of sustainability. Ecological modernization theorists accept these points, though, and are working on ways to incorporate them into a revision of the theory.[90]

Finally, some critics worry that ecological modernization is normative—that it both describes a direction it thinks it is possible we could go, and says that is the way we should go. To which ecological modernizationists have a simple and direct answer: So? Don't you want to make the world a better place?

The Democratic Basis of Contemporary Environmental Concern

But why do people increasingly see that an important way to make the world a better place is through improving environmental conditions? If a mind is not already attuned to the implications of what paradigm shift theory calls "external discrepancies," and if information about the existence of these discrepancies is not heard by that mind, ideological change is likely to be slow—even in the face of substantial material threats to the environment. In the late nineteenth century, as the Industrial Revolution was still gathering steam, relatively few people thought much about the way the new industries were polluting, so strong was the faith in technological progress. But 100 years later, people are both much more attuned to environmental concerns and much more likely to hear about discrepancies between their values and reality. Both this attuning and this hearing have been given ears by the spread of democracy, its sensibilities, and its institutions. In other words, the origin of environmental concern lies not only in the material concerns explored by postmaterialism, paradigm shift, and ecological modernization theories. It lies equally in the other side of the ecological dialogue: in our ideas.

Democratic Sensibilities

"It is impossible," the historian Keith Thomas suggests, "to disentangle what the people of the past thought about plants and animals from what they thought about themselves."[91] A less hierarchical ordering of human relations is historically associated with a less hierarchical ordering of human environmental relations. I don't want to overstate the point; there are plenty of exceptions. But the rise of democratic sensibilities in the social realm does seem to be generally associated with the rise of parallel sensibilities in the environmental realm.

Consider the rise of environmental concern in the eighteenth and nineteenth centuries, what is often termed the "first wave" of environmentalism.[92] This is the period of the first national parks and the first environmental pressure groups; Henry David Thoreau and Ralph Waldo Emerson, Gilbert White and William Wordsworth; and so many more important figures in environmental thought and important "firsts" in environmental protection. Strikingly, this period also saw the rise of new ideas about how human society should be arranged. In 1690, John Locke published his *Two Treatises of Government*. In 1754, Jean-Jacques Rousseau published his *Discourse on the Origins of Inequality*. Inspired in part by the ideas in such books, the United States declared its revolutionary independence from Britain in 1776, and France had its own revolution in 1789. Country after country in the nineteenth century went on to make their own democratic reforms.

These new sensibilities concerning the rights of each human were accompanied by, or soon led to, similar concerns about what constituted decent treatment of the nonhuman aspects of creation. To a democratic mind, environmental exploitation just didn't feel right. Of course, the democratic mind had a long way to go (and still does). Slavery, colonization, racism, sexism, classism, and the rest had hardly disappeared, nor had the "environmental movement" as we understand it today begun. (Nor is the environmental movement always democratic, as the next chapter discusses.) But beginning in the eighteenth century and continuing throughout the nineteenth century, a broadening conception of human rights was accompanied by a broadening conception of natural rights and a greater valuation of both.[93] It is likely no accident that the great early writers for environmental reform were often important figures in social reform as well, such as John Ruskin, William Morris, and Henry Salt, not to mention Thoreau.

Steadily throughout this period, democratic concern grew not only for the rights (and beauty) of nature, but also for the equitable distribution of environmental goods and bads. This was also, of course, the beginning of the Industrial Age. But the material threats that industrialism posed to the environment were not by themselves enough to evince a concern for environmental justice. Democratic concern played a key role.

A voice of democratic concern for environmental justice is heard in this 1845 description of conditions in Manchester, England, the center of the young Industrial Revolution:

Looking down from Ducie Bridge, the passer-by sees several ruined walls and heaps of *debris* with some newer houses. The view from this bridge, mercifully concealed from mortals of small stature by a parapet as high as a man, is characteristic of the whole district. At the bottom flows, or rather stagnates, the Irk, a narrow, coal-black, foul-smelling stream, full of *debris* and refuse, which it deposits on the shallower right bank. In dry weather, a long string of the most disgusting, blackish-green, slime pools are left standing on this bank, from the depths of which bubbles of miasmatic gas constantly arise and give forth a stench unindurable even on the bridge forty or fifty feet above the surface of the stream. Above the bridge are tanneries, bonemills, and gasworks, from which all drains and refuse find their way into the Irk, which receives further the contents of all the neighbouring sewers and privies. . . . Here each house is packed close behind its neighbour. . . . The whole side of the Irk is built in this way, a planless, knotted chaos of houses, more or less on the verge of uninhabitableness, whose unclean interiors fully correspond with their filthy external surroundings. And how could the people be clean with no proper opportunity for satisfying the most natural and ordinary wants? Privies are so rare here that they are either filled up every day, or are too remote for most inhabitants to use. How can people wash when they have only the dirty Irk water at hand? . . . Everything which here arouses horror and indignation is of recent origin, [and] belongs to the *industrial epoch.*[94]

That voice of democratic concern was a young Friedrich Engels.

A short while later, George Perkins Marsh, a scholar and diplomat from Vermont, began questioning the long-term sustainability of industrialism's rapacious appetite for resources. In his 1864 book, *Man and Nature, or, Physical Geography Modified by Human Action,* Marsh argued that humans had unknowingly become a geological force in their own right—clearing forests, altering climate and the flow of rivers, shifting the pace of erosion—often to the detriment of human interests. Vast areas of Michigan's forest, for example, had disappeared in a few short decades of unrestrained cutting; Marsh's own Vermont had suffered the same fate. The result was soil erosion and more severe seasonal floods, since the forests were no longer there to absorb rainwater. Marsh's main goal was "to point out the dangers of imprudence and the necessity of caution in all operations which, on a large scale, interfere with the spontaneous arrangements of the organic or the inorganic world." We must now ask "the great

question;" concluded Marsh: "Whether man is of nature or above her."[95] This, perhaps, was the most difficult democratic question of all.

The same association between democratic and environmental sensibilities may be behind survey results showing an association between "postmaterialist" values and environmental concern. As I argued earlier, there is good reason to doubt that postmaterialism is closely linked with environmental concern, despite the association surveys have found. The reason for this association may be that Inglehart's four-item materialism/postmaterialism scale measures *democratization,* not a shift toward postmaterialism. In fact, Inglehart deliberately chose the two postmaterialist items on his scale—"giving people more say in important government decisions" and "protecting freedom of speech"—to reflect democratic attitudes, as he regarded such attitudes to be one feature of postmaterialism.[96] Furthermore, a low ranking of "maintaining order in the nation" (one of his two "material" items in the scale) may reflect democratic concern about authoritarianism—and not lack of material worries. And given that inflation is no longer a major economic issue in most wealthy countries, "fighting rising prices" (the other of his two "material" items) may not be an accurate gauge of material worries either.

In other words, we are left with three items in Inglehart's scale that potentially tap democratic sensibilities and one item that is probably irrelevant. Thus the correlation Inglehart found between what he called "postmaterialism" and environmental action may actually show instead that in the twentieth century democratic sensibilities continued to influence environmental ones.

Democratic Institutions

The institutions of democracy have been no less important to environmental concern than have democratic sensibilities. (See Figure 7.5.) For instance, the free press has played an absolutely central role in alerting the public to environmental problems, in creating environmental "hearing." And without democratic rights to assemble, to

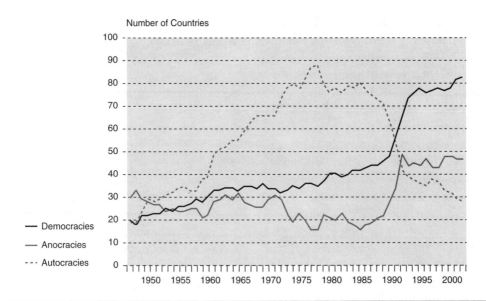

Figure 7.5   The spread of democracy, 1946–2001: Since the middle of the twentieth century, rising environmental concern has been paralleled by the development of more democratic political institutions in most countries around the world. A majority of the world's countries are now democracies. There has also been an increase in "anocracies," countries whose institutions lie in between democracy and autocracy, indicating a further spread of democracy but possibly also a "glass ceiling" in many countries.

protest, to vote, and to establish organizations and political parties that challenge the existing order, environmentalism would likely never have developed into a popular movement anywhere. No popular movement of any kind is likely without such abilities, as authoritarian governments have long recognized.

Consider how long it took for environmentalism to gain attention in the state socialist countries of the former Soviet bloc. Environmental problems went so long unattended that these countries now face some of the world's worst local environmental conditions.[97] When Mikhail Gorbachev came to power in the Soviet Union in 1985, bearing his policy of *glasnost,* which allowed a degree of political expression unprecedented in the Soviet bloc, its environmental movement suddenly came of age. Indeed, concern over environmental conditions was one of the major political forces behind the 1989 revolutions. The importance of this concern is reflected in the striking name of a Bulgarian environmental group that emerged in 1990:

Ecoglasnost. As Guha observes, this name "bears testimony to the inseparable link between democracy and environmentalism."[98]

Ecoglasnost has also been an important factor in the development of the environmentalism of the poor countries of the Southern Hemisphere. Poor countries are often—indeed are usually—authoritarian ones. If environmental concern in poor countries has sometimes been hard to discern, in part this has been because the absence of democracy's freedoms has prevented the expression of such concern. Those with the courage of a Ken Saro-Wiwa are rare. As Guha has also observed, "It is no accident that one of the more robust green movements in the South is to be found in India, a democracy for all but two of its fifty years as an independent republic."[99]

And perhaps democratization is the real source of the environmental movement, and not just a necessity for advancing it. The successes of the environmental movement may have more to do with new sensibilities about what "we have to do" than it

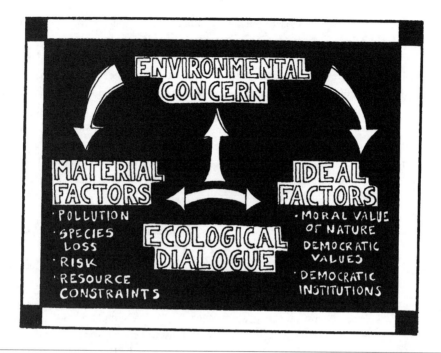

Figure 7.6   A model of the rise of environmental concern: Material and ideal factors shape each other, leading to change in environmental concern—which in turn reshapes the original material and ideal factors.

does the social recognition of the inefficiencies and hidden costs of taking ecological services for granted. The "design flaw" we are overcoming may be more our social exemptionalism—and its concomitant constraints on public debate, and on the accountability of governments and markets to the public—than it is our ecological exemptionalism.

But most likely of all, it is a good bit of both.

The Dialogue of Environmental Concern

Environmental concern is both new and old. Much of what makes this concern so constant are enduring moral issues: namely, social inequality and the challenges it poses to community. The desire to find a moral realm outside the reach of power and self-interest—the desire to find a natural conscience—represents another manifestation of the role social inequality plays in social-environmental relations, a role that has been one of the principal themes of this book. Democracy, both in its sensibilities and its institutions, is another way that we try to deal with the challenges inequality poses to us.

Another enduring source of environmental concern is the constancy of material environmental threats. Industrialization and urbanization have brought with them an enormous range of benefits, of environmental goods. But the costs, the environmental bads, have not been inconsequential. These material threats have continually confronted us with the moral threat of inequality—of the power of some to impose on others—and thus with the question of how we are to define and organize our communities, including that biggest community of all.

Not only has the material shaped the moral, though. Our moral sensibilities concerning the importance (or lack of importance) of democracy and a natural conscience have shaped our ability to conceptualize environmental problems as problems—yet another dialogue between the material and the ideal. (See Figure 7.6.) Material threats to the environment are closely inter-twined with ideological threats of environmental inequality.

The modern environmental movement can be described as a dialogue that connects the natural conscience, the condition of democracy, and the material state of the environment. Because of this dialogue, we have come to see the environment as morally attractive, morally compelling, and morally threatened. Raising our concerns in so many ways, the environment has become one of the leading issues of this or any day.

Postscript

My mother told me another story recently. (She's a great storyteller.) This one beautifully illustrates the dialogic connection between the material and the ideal, and the way that the untroubled mate-rial practices of one day can seem quite problem-atic under the ideological sun of a different day. I have to retell it.

My family is fortunate enough to have a sum-mer place in the Thousand Islands section of the St. Lawrence River, along the New York and Ontario border. I've been up there every summer of my life, and my mother has been up there every summer of hers. My grandmother was born there, and many of my great-grandmothers before that. (My grandmother's forebears were among the region's first white settlers.) The river is 4–5 miles wide in our area, more than 250 feet deep in places, sparklingly clear, and strewn with tree-green, gran-ite islands. The "garden of the Great Spirit," native people called it, and rightly so. It's one of the world's most beautiful places, at least to me.

But as much fun as the boating and swimming and hanging out with family and friends may be, island life is not without its hassles. One of the main ones is bringing groceries from the main-land, and disposing of any garbage afterward. Everything has to be loaded from car, to boat, to dock, to cottage on the inbound trip, and from cot-tage, to dock, to boat, to car on the outbound trip. It gets a bit old. These days we haul off whatever we don't consume and can't compost, but in my

mother's youth the approach was, shall we say, more environmentally casual. What wasn't con-sumed and couldn't be composted was taken out into the center of the river and sunk. A weekly task was loading up an old rowboat with empty bottles, cans, and other detritus, rowing out to the middle of the channel, and chucking it all in. Rather horri-fying to think about today—especially considering that at the time most cottages drew their water directly from the river, instead of from the wells that most families have now installed.

My mother reminded me of this old practice when, one morning, I found myself groaning over a garbage haul to the mainland. "Better than sinking it all out in the channel, like we used to do when I was a kid," she told me.

"Yeah, I guess so," I said, setting my last load into the boat. "Actually, definitely so," I continued as my mood improved with the loading done. A thought struck my mind. "But hey, Mom, didn't you ever think about the pollution you were causing, dump-ing straight into the river? I mean, the cottage water used to come straight from the river then, let alone the broader ecological effects of the dumping."

She thought a minute. "I do remember wondering about it," she replied. "Yes, in fact I remember asking my mother one time when she and I were out in the rowboat, sinking used cans and bottles. I must have been 10 or so. It must have been about the summer of 1940. And she said—I can remember this clear as a bell—'Don't worry about it. The river's bigger than all of us.'"

The river's bigger than all of us. I was astounded. "Do you think she really believed that," I asked, "or do you think she was making up a story to shut up an uncomfortable question from her own kid?"

"I think she really believed it. We all did back then. It was just part of the culture. We did lots of things you wouldn't dream of doing today. We just couldn't imagine that people could have such an effect on the environment—that things were so connected. That it just wasn't right. It was a different time."

Yes, it was. But not so different that a 10-year-old girl did not pause to wonder.

CHAPTER 8

The Human Nature of Nature

When I hear that nature is a ruthless competitive struggle I remember the butterfly, and when I hear that it is a system of ultimate mutual advantage I remember the cyclone.

—Raymond Williams, 1972

My family's favorite brand of ice cream claims to contain something it calls "natural vanilla" flavor. I never really thought about it much until, a few years ago, my son Sam asked me what was natural about it.

"Natural products are things people have done less to—you know, less manufacturing and processing," I told him. "Artificial vanilla flavor comes from a chemical made in a factory, and natural vanilla flavor comes from ground-up beans from vanilla plants," I said, pointing out the dark flecks in the ice cream. (I'm not even sure that's true, but that is what I said.)

Then I got to thinking that a heck of a lot of processing must go on in making "natural" vanilla flavor. Processors probably dry the beans in one machine, grind them up in another, and package them with yet a third. To grow the beans,

farmers likely use a crop variety that scientists have specially developed for the purpose. No doubt they grow them in a field cleared from a tropical forest with machines, kept clear of weeds and insects with machines, and harvested with machines—not to mention the generous use of farm chemicals at several points along the way. Suddenly those beans didn't seem so "natural" anymore.

I tried to explain all this to Sam, which was probably a mistake. Soon I found myself in a major philosophical wrangle with an 8-year old. "Everything's natural," Sam said, defending the ice cream we were both licking up.

There are a number of difficulties with such an all-encompassing view, and I tried to describe them.

"Then maybe nothing's natural," he suggested before I got very far. That's not exactly what I think either, but before I could explain why, a light bulb turned on somewhere in Sam's brain.

"Dad, I know. Everything that comes from the Earth is natural, and everything else isn't." He paused for a moment to work this thought through. "That means that solar power isn't natural because it comes from the sun and not the Earth."

Such are the hazards of having an environmental sociologist for a father.

But Sam was only trying to deal with some central philosophical issues that have beset environmentalism from its earliest beginnings in the ancient world through to the current day. They are central sociological issues too, for our philosophical resolutions have laid the moral foundations of environmental concern. In this chapter we explore the sociological origins and implications of the resolutions we have sought to Sam's dilemma: What is nature?

Whatever else it may be, nature is without a doubt one of the most powerful of human concepts. Some of the most noble and selfless things that people have ever done have been in the name of nature. Consider the Greenpeace activists who have gone out on the open seas in small rubber boats to put themselves between dolphins and a careless tuna industry. Or consider the anti-roads protesters in England who barricaded themselves in hand-dug tunnels underneath proposed highways in order to prevent the movement of heavy construction machinery. People have often put their lives on the line—and sometimes over the line, with fatal results—in defense of nature. They have sought to defend not only nature in the environmental sense but also nature as a democratic ideal. The notion of the "natural" rights of every person to a healthy, happy, fulfilling life in freedom has moved nations, governments, and their citizens to revolutionary acts of kindness and goodness.

But we also have to recognize that nature is one of the most dangerous of human concepts. The cultural history of nature is far from uniformly noble. For example, ideas of natural differences between humans—differences of sex, of race, of ethnicity, of talent and skill—have led to the enslavement of millions, the outright slaughter of further millions, and the oppression and mistreatment of millions more. We ignore this other side of nature at our peril.

Considering the difficult cultural history of nature, we would do well to exercise every critical caution in evaluating the uses to which we put the idea. To say that something is natural or to counsel that the appropriate course of action is to follow nature is to suggest something of immense significance for our moral values, for our identities, for our everyday lives, and thus for our politics. The previous chapter introduced the concept of the *natural conscience*, our common search for a realm that lies beyond the taint of social power and human interests and that might serve as an unbiased and external source of moral value and identity. But is such a realm possible? Can we truly escape the influence of our interests? This chapter takes a critical look at the relationship between ideas of nature and human interests, and at the implications of this relationship for the moral and political claims we make.

These are difficult issues that challenge us all. But since these issues are central to how we constitute our human community and our ecological community, it is crucial that we accept the challenge.

The Contradictions of Nature

"Can and ought we to follow nature?" the environmental philosopher Holmes Rolston once asked.[1] Answering this question depends upon resolving a basic contradiction in the idea of nature, the contradiction between what can be termed *moral separatism* and *moral holism*.[2]

Think of the contradiction this way. One of the truisms of the contemporary environmental movement is that people are part of nature and that environmental problems have emerged because we have tried to pretend otherwise. This is a holist moral point of view. But if we are a part of nature, there is no need to advise us to follow it, for we must already be doing so. How could we do anything but follow it? Under moral holism, "follow nature" is superfluous advice.

If people are separate from nature, the moral situation is no better. Since nature is different from us and is moved by different principles, it has no meaning for us. In fact, we probably can't follow nature, no matter how hard we try. Under moral separatism, then, "follow nature" is irrelevant advice.

As the sociologist Kai Erikson once observed, a moral value requires "a point of contrast which gives the norm some scope and dimension."[3] It has to give us a way to make moral distinctions. Otherwise, it will be a superfluous value. A moral value also requires a point of connection, however, if it is to be relevant to our actions. For nature to serve as a source of value that we can "follow," it has to be conceived in ways that provide points of both contrast and connection.

The contradiction between separatism and holism extends into the problem of power and interest, which is so central to the natural conscience. A natural conscience depends upon a person's subjective belief in a moral realm that lies beyond the reach of social power and the possibility of manipulation to suit the interests of some more than others. Such a realm requires separation from society if it is to be free from social influence, and it requires holist unity if it is to be relevant to social issues. But that unity immediately reintroduces the possibility that human interests may have been tinkering with what we conceive nature to be.

Any successful philosophy of nature must offer some kind of solution to these moral contradictions if it is to serve as a basis for a natural conscience.[4]

Ancient Problems, Ancient Solutions

The earliest philosophers of nature were well aware of the problems of holist superfluousness and separatist irrelevance. Aristotle, for example, worried about the "monism," as he termed it, in ideas like Plato's view that Goodness created the whole world and that, therefore, the whole world was good. Under such a philosophy, Aristotle wrote, "the being of the good and the being of the bad, of good and not good, will be the same, and the thesis under discussion will no longer be that all things are one, but that they are nothing at all."[5]

Aristotle suggested a way that we could distinguish the natural and the not-natural without falling into the problem of monist holism. That which comes into being "by nature," Aristotle argued, was that which had its "source of change" within itself.[6] Examples might be the movement of wind, the growth of plants and animals, the dynamics of fire. Since humans have an internal source of change—our body's processes of growth and development—much that humans do is also according to nature. But something whose source of change is outside of itself is not due to nature, said Aristotle. So anything that humans make is not due to nature, although the materials humans use may well be. Aristotle gave the example of a wooden bed. Wood grows according to natural principles of growth internal to the tree, but the shape it takes as a bed is the result of an external source of change: humans. So wood is natural, but a bed is not.

This is a clever solution to the contradictions of nature. Humans are a part of nature because they have a source of change inside themselves. But when humans use that source of change to alter something outside themselves, they are not acting in accordance to nature. Aristotle thereby provided points of both moral connection and contrast.

Aristotle also argued that nature is ultimately the result of the workings of "the Good" (an idea he retained from Plato, as Chapter 7 describes). Appealing to this godlike ideal allowed Aristotle to claim that nature was interest-free—that nature had been created by something that was removed from human influence—thus allowing him to establish a natural conscience.

This was not a perfect solution, however. Maybe we're acting in accordance with our internal source of change when we do something like construct a bed or build a particular form of society or foster certain societal-environmental relations. Who is to say? We may do unnatural things for natural reasons. Aristotle's approach also could not distinguish beds made by humans from dams made by beavers and hives made by bees. A beaver dam must be as unnatural as anything humans make, for it equally has its source of change outside itself: in beavers. In fact, every action of every creature induces changes in the world around it and must therefore be unnatural, collapsing the point of moral contrast Aristotle hoped to establish.

The ancient Taoists offered a solution of their own. Recall from Chapter 7 the Taoist distinction between *wu wei*, acting without deliberate effort, and *yu wei*, acting deliberately. *Wu wei* guides one along the lines of Tao, and *yu wei* leads away from it, a clear moral contrast. And because Tao is something larger and prior to humans, it lies beyond the taint of human interests and desires, thereby serving as a basis for a natural conscience. Taoists found a point of moral connection by suggesting that Tao is the underlying first principle of everything, including humans. Tao gives everything a *te*, its essential qualities. People can ignore their *te* and act *yu wei* or they can encourage *te* by acting *wu wei*—a separatism within a holism.

This solution, though, was not without problems either, and later Taoist philosophy tried to grapple with some of these dilemmas. One problem was that acting without deliberate effort seemed a contradiction in terms. Taoism seemed to be counseling people to make a deliberate choice to act without deliberation, to desire to be without desire. Thus, in order to adopt the Taoist solution you unavoidably introduce desire and interest, undermining its value as a source of a natural conscience.

Perhaps more problematic, though, is the issue of how one is to know when one is acting according to one's *te* and when one is not. Perhaps my *te* is to construct buildings and bridges. Perhaps my *te* is to be ruler of the world—not because I myself desire it but because my *te* just happens to flow along such lines. In fact, it would be going against Tao not to exercise such a *te* to the fullest, suggested Kuo Hsiang, a Taoist from the first century C.E. In his words,

> *Wu wei* does not mean folding one's hands and remaining silent. It simply means allowing everything to follow what is natural to it, and then its nature will be satisfied. . . . Hence, let everyone perform his own proper function, so that high and low both have their proper places. This is the perfection of the principle of *wu wei*.[7]

Of course, practically any human action can be justified on such grounds, and thus the Taoist point of moral contrast also collapses.

Later thinkers offered solutions to these problems. For example, a standard Taoist response to the problem of deliberately choosing to be undeliberate is that it's a matter of getting things going, like setting afloat down a river on a raft. You do have to make the choice to get on the raft, to be sure, but after that the river of Tao takes over.[8] But the fact that later thinkers found it necessary to offer solutions highlights the continuing centrality of the problem of nature's moral contradictions for Taoism.

The Contradictions of Contemporary Environmentalism

These contradictions continue to confront all of us, and contemporary environmentalism is constantly rethinking its solutions to them.

Take the very idea, so pervasive in environmentalism, that nature is good, and that it is best to do things the "natural" way—to use natural materials like cotton and wood and paper, instead of nylon and concrete and plastic, for example, or ground-up vanilla beans instead of "artificial" vanilla flavoring. The word *natural* here sets up a clear moral contrast between good and bad. But what law of nature does nylon, concrete, or plastic break? These substances are derived from the materials of nature and the Earth: petroleum for nylon and plastic; sand, water, limestone, and other crushed rock for concrete; and whatever it is they use to make artificial vanilla flavor.

Sometimes people say that the difference is that materials like nylon, concrete, and plastic have seen more processing and refining (the basis for distinguishing the natural that I initially suggested to my son). They are more the product of human actions than are cotton, wood, paper, and "natural" food. This is an empirically dubious claim, though, as anyone familiar with what goes on in the growing, harvesting, and processing of cotton, wood, paper, and "natural" food can attest to.

The moral claim being made is also dubious. Such an argument rests on a distinction similar to Aristotle's: Things that come about through their own internal source of change (or *more* through their own internal sources of change) are natural (or *more* natural) and not the product of human desires and interests. But are not humans a part of nature? Is that not also one of the great moral arguments of environmentalism? Anything humans do must therefore be natural, including making plastic—as well as cities, automobiles, toxic waste, and even atomic bombs. Indeed, what human has ever broken a law of nature? If it were a law of nature, how could a human have broken it? By this logic, nothing could be more—or less—natural than an atomic bomb.

Or take the idea of wilderness, which is often seen, particularly among North Americans, as the fullest expression of the true ends of nature and environmentalism. Thoreau sought in wilderness a restful release from the pollution of politics, and millions still do today. And what is wilderness? At least as the political process has defined it, wilderness is national parks and other areas of land set aside from deliberate human interference. But isn't the very setting aside of land a deliberate human action, thereby making wilderness the product of human intention rather than the result of its absence?

Perhaps the Taoist response applies here—that establishing a national park is like setting a raft afloat. But then a critic might ask, If humans are natural, why should we exclude houses, roads, open pit mines, and McDonald's from wilderness areas? And why should we see cities and farms as less wild and less in need of the attention of environmentalist concern?

The moral problem is that environmentalism needs to establish the relevance of nature to humans by arguing for our unity with it and, at the same time, to contrast humans and nature in order to set aside a realm that is free from the pollution of human interests. Upon this basic moral contradiction modern environmentalism uneasily rests.

Nature as a Social Construction

The point I've been leading up to is one that virtually all environmental sociologists recognize today: Whatever else nature might be, it is also a *social construction.*[9] Nature is something we make as much as it makes us. How we see nature depends upon our perspective on social life. And as this perspective changes across time and place, history and culture, nature changes with it.

The British sociologist Raymond Williams, in a classic 1972 essay, put it this way:

> The idea of nature contains an extraordinary amount of human history. What is often being argued, it seems to me, in the idea of nature is the idea of man; and this not only generally, or in ultimate ways, but the idea of man in society, indeed the ideas of kinds of societies.[10]

(Williams, writing in an earlier day, uses *man* to mean all people.)

Williams's point is that we look at nature through social categories formed by human interests. Our image of nature depends upon *social selection* and *social reflection*. We tend to select particular features of nature to focus upon, ignoring those that do not suit our interests and the worldview shaped by those interests. Moreover, the categories we use to comprehend nature closely reflect the categories we use to comprehend society; social life is so fundamental to our experience that all our categories reflect our social perspectives. Because of social selection and social reflection, "nature" is an inescapably social—and political—phenomenon.

I give several extended examples in a moment. But first let me point out that such a perspective on our perspectives of nature is itself a perspective on nature—one perhaps best labeled *postmodernist.* Since the 1960s, an increasing number of social theorists have been arguing against the objectivist notion of a world in which there is only one truth about any one thing, the truth that best represents "the way things really are." Such a simplistic view is characteristic of the technological and scientific faith of modern society, say postmodern theorists. Truth is socially relative. What you see depends on who you are and not just on the character of the world "out there," postmodernists argue. And so too for an idea long associated with our conceptions of truth: nature.

Nature and New England's Agricultural Decline

An example of a selective vision of nature, guided by social interests, is the oft-told story of a famous event in North American environmental history: the decline of agriculture in New England. (New England is the traditional name for the six most northeasterly of the United States—Maine, Vermont, New Hampshire, Massachusetts, Connecticut, and little old Rhode Island.) I draw this example from some of my own research.[11]

The Traditional Story. New England, it is widely acknowledged, is a lousy place to farm. It's too rocky and too hilly, and the soil is too acid and too infertile to raise decent crops. As soon as European settlers could, they loaded up their wagons for the better lands of the American breadbasket in the Midwest and West. That chance came with the opening of the Erie Canal in 1825, which provided the first cheap means of shipping grain back to the East. Now there was a way for farms west of the Appalachians to get their products to market. Most of New England's farmland was promptly abandoned. If you walk through the region's vast woods, you can still see the miles of stone walls—the field boundaries thrown up by farmers in their back-breaking

struggle to get enough rocks out of the ground to plant a few crops. No wonder the region has so little farmland today.[12]

This view of New England has been widely accepted by scholars. As two economic historians wrote,

> In an agricultural sense it is customary to speak of New England as "rock-ribbed," thin-soiled, hilly, unfriendly, hard-scrabbley, and other uncomplimentary terms. Yet, when one travels over the area with an eye to farming rather than history, culture, or industry, even a native of the region must admit that the unenthusiastic terms, for the most part, approach the truth.[13]

A series of dioramas at Harvard University's Fisher Museum of Forestry beautifully portray the "hard-scrabbley" view of New England. The dioramas show, in captivating detail, the changing landscape of New England through history, using a single portion of Harvard's own forest in Petersham, Massachusetts (where the museum is), as an example. The diorama for 1740 shows a settler clearing a homestead out of the virgin forest. (See Figure 8.1.) The one for 1830, labeled "The Height of Cultivation for Farm Crops," shows a land almost completely cleared for farming, with fields lined mainly by stone walls. (See Figure 8.2.) The diorama for 1850, though, shows an abrupt turnaround in New England's agricultural fortunes. It's labeled "Farm Abandonment" and displays a secondary growth of trees already starting to retake the land. (See Figure 8.3.)

Few have ever challenged this account.[14] In fact, the notion of "abandoned New England" has become a part of the region's identity and is nostalgically promoted in tourist books, popular histories, and scenic calendars of the area. New England's rock-ribbed, thin-soiled hills are also the butt of a number of common jokes often told in (and out) of the region, including some rather clever ones. One of my favorites (and I was born in New England) is the following description of the area's land:

Figure 8.1 Harvard Forest Diorama for 1740: "An Early Settler Clears a Homestead." This photo of the diorama, and the two that follow, illustrate the social construction of nature—the way our views of nature are shaped in part by our social perspectives.

Nature, out of her boundless store,
Threw rocks together, and did no more.

Then there's this one about Maine, one of the country's leading potato-producing states:

Maine's number two crop is potatoes. Its number one crop is stones.

But perhaps everyone's favorite is the following one-liner:

If the United States had been settled from the Pacific coast, New England would not yet have been discovered.[15]

This last one has many variants, and sometimes ends, "New England would be a national forest."

Setting the Record Straight. It's a great story, and most people love it. But it's plain wrong. Agricultural census records show that, rather than contracting after the opening of the Erie Canal, agricultural land in New England expanded until 1880. In fact, it experienced only a small decline until 1910, with agricultural land in the northern New England states continuing to expand up to that date. Only after 1910 did a sharp drop occur. The majority of the decline, some 58 percent, took place after World War II, more than 100 years after the Erie Canal (and later the railroads) began shipping cheap grain East. True, large-scale agricultural expansion did not occur in New England during the nineteenth century, as it did in the midwestern and western states. But neither was there widespread abandonment of farms in New England.[16]

Figure 8.2   Harvard Forest Diorama for 1830: "The Height of Cultivation for Farm Crops." This view shows an extensively cleared landscape just at the time of the opening of the Erie Canal in 1825.

Moreover, crop yields in New England are comparatively high, contrary to its infertile image. New England's per acre yields of corn, oats, wheat, barley, and buckwheat exceeded national averages in the late nineteenth century. It's harder to make national comparisons today because agriculture is so specialized. One of the few crops still grown in most states is corn silage, and New England's yields are 30 percent above the national average—even higher than yields in Iowa, the country's most famous corn-growing state. And New England farmers use only modest amounts of fertilizer, despite their higher yields.[17]

New England farms also make a lot of money. In the late nineteenth century, the southern New England states were among the country's leaders in value of farm products per acre of farmland. In 1889, Massachusetts, Rhode Island, and Connecticut ranked second, third, and fourth in the nation. A hundred years later they were doing just as well. In 1987, Connecticut, Massachusetts, and Rhode Island ranked first, third, and fifth in the nation in value of farm products per acre of farmland—ahead of even California, Florida, Iowa, and Illinois. (Total value of farm products is far higher in these bigger states, of course, but not the average per acre of farmland.) The northern New England states—Vermont, New Hampshire, and Maine—ranked considerably lower in both 1889 and 1987, because of their less intensive production and greater distance from markets. But they still ranked, and continue to rank, in the top half of the nation.[18] (See Figure 8.4.)

Figure 8.3   Harvard Forest Diorama for 1850: "Farm Abandonment." The diorama suggests that, by this time, the effects of the Erie Canal have led to widespread farm abandonment as western settlers began to ship cheap grain back East. Contrary to the history told by the dioramas, in most of New England, agriculture actually continued to expand for another 50 to 70 years. But because of the way it appeals to political interests, nostalgia, and the myth of technological progress, the dioramas' version of New England's history has seldom been challenged.

The figures I cite are in most cases from the national agricultural census, about as basic a source as there is. How could scholars have gotten it so wrong, then? Probably because, at some level, they wanted to—just as I, a New England native, want to set the record straight.

Social Selection and New England's Nature. The conventional view is not without evidence. It is true that rural population did decline precipitously in New England shortly after the opening of the Erie Canal. Many travel accounts written in the nineteenth century describe, usually with considerable anxiety, abandoned farmsteads all across the New England countryside. But as the historian Hal Barron has pointed out, increased mechanization allowed (and encouraged) fewer farmers to farm more land, depopulating the countryside while keeping production going.[19] The same process still goes on today in much of the West and Midwest. The Iowa countryside, for example, is strewn with abandoned farmsteads, even as Iowa remains the nation's most agricultural state in terms of the percentage of land—more than 90 percent—devoted to farming.

Some New England farmland was indeed abandoned as early as 1830, even as overall land in agriculture continued to climb in the region. One tract of early abandoned land is the area

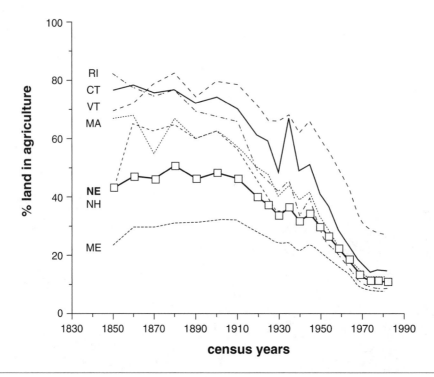

Figure 8.4 Land in agriculture in New England over time: The thick line represents the average for New England as a whole; the other lines are for individual states. Note that the peak of agriculture for New England is around 1880, and that most of the eventual decline occurred after 1950. Note also that these figures include both cleared land and some wood-land, as most New England farms have always included some forest. Thus, at the height of New England agriculture in 1880, the proportion of cleared land was about a third of the region.

where Harvard University now has its forest and on which the Harvard Forest dioramas are based. But these were isolated cases. Not surprisingly, this early abandoned land now has some of New England's best forest on it, which is why Harvard chose such a site for its forest in the first place. The Harvard Forest dioramas, then, are not wrong for the specific site they depict. It's just that the history of the Harvard Forest has to be placed in a wider context.

And finally, much of New England's land is undoubtedly poorly suited to row-crop agricul-ture. There are definitely lots of rocks in those hills. But nineteenth-century farmers were not foolish, and they never tried to grow crops on the hilly and rocky ground. Where possible, they used it for pasture, but most of it they never cleared for farming

at all. (They did cut practically all of it for timber and fuel wood, though, at least in southern New England.) At the 1880 peak of land in agriculture in New England, only a third of New England was cleared, according to the census; excluding Maine, the figure is 49 percent.[20] New England is not the Midwest. The proportion of farmable land is far lower. But the land that was farmable was, in fact, good land—at least as good as Midwestern land, and better according to some measures.

Thus, the conventional view of New England's agricultural history is not without evidence. But it depends on a selective reading of the historical record. This selection suits particular views of human society, particular social interests, as Raymond Williams would have readily recog-nized. I discuss three such views.

First, it is no accident that the conventional view of New England's hard-scrabble nature was promoted mainly by economic historians, who tend to relish anything that appears to show a victory of rational market forces. For them, New England has been the grudging bearer of the myth of technological progress and the economic glories of Western expansion.

Second, as a negative example of allegedly lower-quality farmland, the New England story has also suited some political interests. The "farm bloc," long a powerful lobby in Congress, is drawn mainly from western and midwestern states. Consequently, government subsidies have been structured to benefit most the crops dominated by western and midwestern farms. Between 1989 and 1991, for example, the proportion of economic returns to farming from direct government payments was just 0.9 percent in New England—well under the 6.5 percent figure for the whole nation for that period. In some western and midwestern states, such as Montana and North Dakota, it was more than 15 percent.[21]

And finally, the New England story felt right to urban and suburban New Englanders for whom it represents the loss of rural life, a loss about which they sometimes feel nostalgic and wistful. Meanwhile, the expansion of urban and suburban life—with its great demand for land and with the higher salaries that city jobs generally yield—was largely responsible for the great loss of New England farmland following World War II.[22]

But urban and suburban residents, farm bloc politicians, and economic mythmakers need not take the blame, according to the traditional story of New England agriculture. The decline was due to nature itself and to the hardscrabble legacy it left New England—not to us. And in that externalization of cause, these selective views of New England's nature can perhaps offer some stony comfort.

Nature and Biology

I turn now to an example of both the social selection and social reflection of nature: Charles Darwin's theory of natural selection—the idea that species change over time as the most successful individuals pass on their distinctive traits to following generations. (Let's not be confused by terms here. Darwin's theory of "natural selection" is not at all the same as the theory of "social selection" in nature, although, as we shall see, the former does exemplify the latter.)

When Darwin's book on natural selection, *On the Origin of Species,* appeared in 1859, it was an instant sensation, and intellectuals gave it close scrutiny and debated its implications. Among the earliest readers were, perhaps surprisingly, Karl Marx and Friedrich Engels. They immediately picked up on a correspondence in Darwin's theory that irritated them considerably: It very closely resembled the economic theories of free-market capitalism that were so fundamentally altering the character of English society and, increasingly, world society. As Marx noted to Engels in a private letter in 1862, "It is remarkable how Darwin recognizes among beasts and plants his English society with its division of labour, competition, opening of new markets, 'inventions,' and the Malthusian 'struggle for existence.'"[23]

Consider some of the key mechanisms and results of natural selection that Darwin identified:

- *The incredible diversity of life:* To Marx, that sounded like the division of labor advocated by capitalist economists.
- *The competition for reproductive success:* Marx heard here the echoes of capitalist competition.
- *The link between new species and the discovery of new ecological niches:* This sounded suspiciously like the opening of new markets.
- *The selection of the best features from the range of variation that any species exhibits:* Marx saw here the idea of technological progress through new inventions.
- *The struggle for survival caused by the tendency of populations to increase unless checked by external constraints:* That sounded like Thomas Malthus's theory of population.

Marx's argument was that the categories Darwin used to understand evolution were originally social categories—that natural selection was social reflection. Engels later extended the point to social selection (that's selection, not reflection, or not reflection alone), noting that Darwin placed selective emphasis on competition in nature as opposed to cooperation, a more socialist vision of nature. Thus, the theory of natural selection was actually a theory of natural capitalism.

Darwin, in fact, agreed to some extent. In later writings, he described how he hit upon the theory of natural selection when, in 1838, he "happened to read for amusement Malthus on *Population*," shortly after returning from his voyage around South America on board the HMS *Beagle*.[24] (During this famous voyage Darwin made many of the observations, such as the diversity of Galapagos finches, that served as key evidence in *On the Origin of Species*.) And Darwin drew additional ideas, as well as the phrase "survival of the fittest," from the writings of Herbert Spencer, a mid-nineteenth-century social theorist.[25]

Metaphors and general patterns of understanding easily flit back and forth between our theories of the realms we label "society" and "nature." Chemists talk about chemical "bonds," and sociologists talk about social ones. Physical scientists talk about natural "forces," and social scientists talk about the social kind. Ecologists talk about community, and so too do sociologists—a parallel I have repeatedly emphasized in this book. Thus, perhaps it should come as no surprise that the two scientists who first hit upon the theory of natural selection—Darwin and his lesser-known contemporary, Alfred Russel Wallace—were living in the midst of the world's first truly capitalist industrial society: 1840s and 1850s England.

Nevertheless, the flitting back and forth of concepts between science and social life deserves special scrutiny because of the way it sometimes allows science to be used as a source of political legitimization. It was this process of *naturalization* that most concerned Marx and Engels. As Engels put it,

> The whole Darwinist teaching of the struggle for existence is simply a transference from society to nature. . . . When this *conjurer's trick* has been performed . . . the same theories are transferred back again from organic nature into history and it is now claimed that their validity as eternal laws of human society has been proved.[26]

There is no evidence that Darwin himself had a conscious mission of proving the value of capitalism through discovering it in nature. But witness the way we routinely talk about the economic "forces" of capitalism, such as innovation and competition, as if they were pseudo-natural processes, implying that any other arrangement would be somehow unnatural. Consider the way we often hear the marketplace described as a "jungle" in which you have to "struggle to survive." Naturalization can subtly give us the sense that the current form of our economy is inevitable and that it is foolishly idealistic to think otherwise.

We should be wary of this subtle power. Whether or not we agree with capitalism, or with its current manifestations, we should expect that the argument for any economic arrangement would be made on more explicit grounds.

Nature and Scientific Racism

What may be even more worrisome, though, is the tragic history of naturalizing arguments by scientists attempting to prove inherent differences in the capabilities of human "races." The controversial 1994 book *The Bell Curve* was only one in a long series of such attempts.[27] But what is distinctive (and hopeful, in a way) about that book is that, unlike many earlier efforts in scientific racism, it was almost immediately widely discredited by the scientific community.[28]

Morton's Craniometry. By contrast, it was decades before scientists began to see the flaws in *craniometry,* a nineteenth-century scientific fad that compared the cranial capacities of different races. Samuel George Morton, a Philadelphia doctor of European descent, was the leading figure in craniometry. Morton spent years assembling a collection of more than 600 human skulls from all over the world—no easy feat in the 1830s and 1840s, when intercontinental travel was limited to sailing ships. He published three books on his detailed studies, which, not surprisingly, showed that Europeans had the biggest brains on the planet.

This work made Morton famous. When he died, his obituary in the *New York Tribune* read, "Probably no scientific man in America enjoyed a higher reputation among scholars throughout the world, than Dr. Morton." His obituary in a South Carolina medical journal read, "We of the South should consider him our true benefactor, for aiding most materially in giving to the negro his true position as an inferior race."[29]

Morton's method was first to assign skulls to a particular race. Then he would turn the skull upside down and fill it up with mustard seed poured in through the foramen magnum, the hole at the base of the skull where the spinal cord enters. He then poured the seed back out into a graduated cylinder to determine the volume. By this method, he determined that whites had an average cranial capacity of 87 cubic inches, Native Americans 82 cubic inches, and blacks 78 cubic inches.[30]

Morton later became discouraged with using mustard seed. He noticed that, because of their lightness, mustard seeds packed poorly and gave widely variable results when the measurements were repeated. So he switched to lead shot, which gave far more consistent results. He repeated his earlier measurements, and the average volumes for all the skulls went up. But the average for black skulls went up 5.4 inches, for Native Americans 2.2, and for whites 1.8. As biologist and historian of science Stephen Jay Gould points out,

Plausible scenarios are easy to construct. Morton, measuring by seed, picks up a threateningly large black skull, fills it lightly and gives it a few desultory shakes. Next, he takes a distressingly small Caucasian skull, shakes hard, and pushes mightily at the foramen magnum with his thumb. It is easily done, without conscious motivation; expectation is a powerful guide to action.[31]

Morton still could record a comforting hierarchy of races, though, even with the new method. But the use of mustard seed was only one of many problems with Morton's work. Gould reanalyzed all of Morton's data and found them littered with statistical errors. (As a dedicated scientist, Morton was committed to empirical accuracy and published all his raw data, allowing Gould to reanalyze them a century and a half later.) Averages for whites were rounded up and for blacks rounded down; usually large skulls from nonwhite races in his collection were often excluded, without explanation, from final tabulations; and the sample itself was highly selective.[32]

Two problems with the selectivity of the sample stand out in particular. First, Morton did not consider the effect of stature on cranial capacity. Taller people tend to have bigger brains, just as they tend to have bigger feet. People from different regions of the world vary in their average height. For example, a quarter of Morton's sample of Native Americans came from the graves of Peruvian Incas, a small-bodied people with correspondingly small brain sizes, but only 2 percent (three skulls) came from the Iroquois, a tall people with correspondingly large brains. Morton did note in his raw data the height of the skeletons most of the skulls came from, but he did not understand (or did not wish to understand) the influence stature had on his results.

Second, Morton did not consider the effect of gender in his sample. Women tend to be smaller then men and thus to have smaller brain sizes. Not surprisingly, Morton's sample of English skulls, the group that recorded the largest average cranial capacity, came entirely from males. His sample of black "Hottentot" skulls, which gave a very low figure, came entirely from females. Here again, Morton noted the gender of most of the skulls in his collection but did not understand (or did not wish to understand) the significance gender had for his sample.

Gould took these errors into account, recalculated Morton's averages, and found no significant differences between "races." But even if racially significant differences in cranial capacity remained, we have no basis for assuming this would indicate greater intelligence. As Gould points out, elephants have far larger brains than humans and yet we do not consider them more intelligent than us.[33] Also, given that all Morton measured in the end was differences in stature, his results would equally well demonstrate that people with the biggest feet have the biggest brains as it would that people of a particular skin color have the biggest brains. But as foot size does not have anything like the cultural significance of skin color, Morton did not pause to consider such an interpretation.

Huntington's Environmental Determinism. Another infamous example of scientific racism was the study by Yale University geographer Ellsworth Huntington of the relationship between climate and the degree of civilization of a people, written up in his 1915 book, *Climate and Civilization.*

Huntington attempted to determine this relationship by the supposedly objective method of sending out a questionnaire to "about fifty geographers and other widely informed men in a dozen countries of America, Europe, and Asia," and asking them to rate the level of civilization in their locale.[34] Huntington compared these results with the level of what he called "human energy on the basis of climate," by which he meant the effect of the local climate on people's ability to get up and do the things that need to be done (to borrow a line from *A Prairie Home Companion,* the popular U.S. radio show). Climates that are too warm, Huntington reasoned, encourage laziness; too cold, lethargy—and so on for factors such as rainfall, sunshine, and cloudiness. Huntington then drew up a global map of the level of human energy, another for the level of civilization, and compared them.

Lo and behold, he found just what he was likely looking for—that the climate of Europe and the northeastern United States was associated with the highest levels of civilization. Europe and the northeastern United States were, of course, predominantly white regions of the world, and Huntington himself was white. (It is perhaps also worth noting that Yale University is in the northeastern U.S. city of New Haven, Connecticut.) And on this basis, Huntington concluded, "The climate of many countries seems to be one of the great reasons why idleness, dishonesty, immorality, stupidity, and weakness of will prevail."[35] (See Figures 8.5 and b.)

This study was intended to be serious science, and Huntington was a famous man. Today, his method seems ludicrously biased. Huntington's "geographers and other widely informed men" almost certainly rated the level of civilization of a place on the basis of what their own experience told them was "civilization." Most likely, they saw lives similar to their own as civilized and ones dissimilar as uncivilized and filled out their questionnaires accordingly.

Of particular interest here is Huntington's environmental argument. Although extremes of cold and heat definitely create difficult circumstances for humans—which is why few people live in the Sahara Desert or at the Arctic Circle—the influence heat and cold have on matters like "idleness," "stupidity," and "weakness of will" is far from certain. In fact, one could easily reverse Huntington's line of reasoning and argue that difficult climates might actually produce peoples with the *greatest* strength of will, the least idleness, and highest intelligence, for otherwise they could not survive such extreme conditions. And indeed, the technological (not to mention the cultural) achievements of the Inuit in the Arctic tundra, the Tibetans in the high Himalayas, and the Bedouins in the deserts of the Middle East

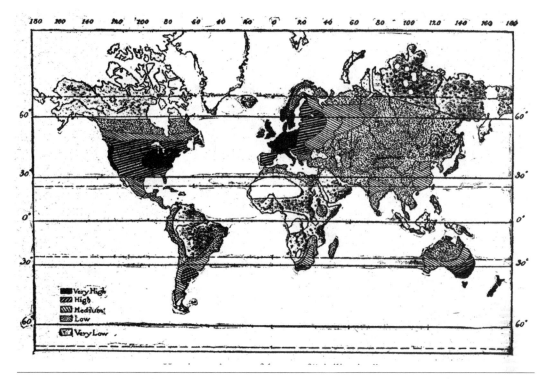

Figure 8.5a   Environmental determinism: Using a Eurocentric standard, the geographer Ellsworth Huntington argued that the amount of "civilization" across the world could be related to the amount of "human energy" created by different climatic regions. Above, Huntington's map of "civilization."

and North Africa rank, in my view, as some of the greatest in human history.

Why did Ellsworth Huntington and Samuel George Morton make these racist arguments, and why did they achieve high prominence and acceptability in their day? Probably because the socially powerful are not impervious to criticism about their dominant positions, and they seek some source of ideological comfort.[36] This is part of the power—and danger—of nature as a social idea: the way we so often attempt to use it to legitimate social inequality. If nature is a realm beyond social interest, then its truths must be beyond blame and responsibility. Anything nature may apparently demonstrate about human differences can be ascribed to something external to social power. Nature can then serve as an interest-free foundation for human interests,

the unmoved mover of power relations. But is it ever really that?

Environment as a Social Construction

Nature is closely interrelated with a number of other important ways that we conceptualize the environment, and a growing body of scholarship investigates the social power relations involved. In this section we sample some of these ways, beginning with the concept of wilderness.

The Wilderness Ideal

As I discussed earlier, wilderness is a contradictory idea. The highest exemplar of the

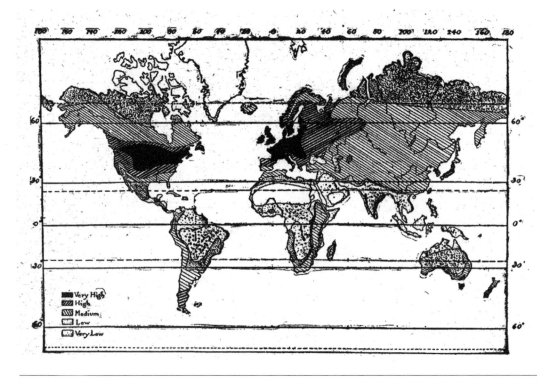

Figure 8.5b   Environmental determinism: Ellsworth Huntington's map of "human energy according to climate."

natural, it is also based on the often forcible absence of, and regulation of, one widespread aspect of the natural world: people. Most wilderness areas are routinely patrolled by rangers (frequently armed) who monitor boundaries and police human activities within. Often our wilderness parks have been created through the removal of the people who were living there previously.

As Ramachandra Guha has pointed out, such an approach to environmental protection is based on a culturally specific understanding of what the environment is and could be, one specific to North America in the main.[37] The idea of the national park originated in the United States, and the initial model was one of a wilderness region with few people. Because of its low population density and vast areas of rugged terrain, the United States had large

regions with few people during the great age of park establishment in the late nineteenth and early twentieth centuries. It was relatively easy to remove the few people who were there. The native peoples had already been removed, for the most part, and the settler populations in these rugged and remote zones were thin on the ground. Such is not the case in most of South and Southeast Asia. There, people live virtually everywhere, and setting aside any large area usually means setting substantial numbers of people aside too.

Also, people and wildlife in populated areas may coexist harmoniously, which is often why enough wildlife yet remains to attract interest in establishing a park. For example, when the Keoldeo Ghana bird sanctuary was established in Bharatpur, India, local villagers were told they would no longer be able to graze their livestock in the area. The villagers protested, and a battle broke out with the police in which several villagers were killed. After the grazing ban was enforced, scientists discovered that in fact bird populations declined. It turned out that grazing kept down the high grass, creating better habitat for the insects that many of the birds depended on. Nevertheless, the grazing ban remains in force.[38]

Although local villagers usually take the bulk of the blame for the loss of wildlife in their area, the more important culprits often are poaching by hunters supplying primarily urban clients, earlier hunting by tourists and local elites, and the general decline in suitable habitat because of the spread of plantation forestry and plantation agriculture.

Also, establishing a wilderness park may actually increase the number of humans in an area by promoting tourism. In the case of Indian tiger reserves, Guha notes, the effect has been to replace local people with urban and overseas tourists and a full complement of upscale hotels, restaurants, and stores. As it takes capital and knowledge of middle-class life to set up tourist accommodations, the remaining local people often do not get much economic benefit from the establishment of a tiger reserve, aside from a few low-paying jobs.

Nancy Peluso has described a similar history in southern Kenya.[39] There, the Masai tribe of migratory pastoralists has been confined to increasingly smaller reserves and "sedentarized" to make way for game and wildlife reserves, particularly for rhinos and elephants. The process began in the early 1900s, when, in response to the demands of big game hunters and conservation groups, the British colonial government established the Southern Game Reserve. At the time, however, officials did not see the Masai as a threat to wildlife, and the Southern Game Reserve was set up within the Masai reserve. But since the 1950s, a "wilderness" model of wildlife protection has taken hold. The old Southern Game Reserve has been replaced with four reserves that exclude the Masai completely and are surrounded by extensive buffer zones in which the Masai are required to adopt "group ranches" for their cattle, imposing yet another alteration of the Masai culture and economy.

There is little evidence, however, that the traditional Masai lifestyle was in conflict with the survival of rhinos and elephants. Peluso points out that, rather than being a threat to wildlife, with whom they had coexisted for thousands of years, the Masai helped maintain the savanna environment through their migratory cattle grazing. As long as it is managed properly, cattle grazing can actually increase the availability of grass for wildlife by stimulating regrowth. Grass grows most rapidly and nutritiously when it is kept short (although not so short that it has trouble providing energy to its root system). Also, cattle fertilize as they graze, providing the regrowing grass with helpful nutrients. Rather than the low-intensity cattle grazing of the traditional Masai, the main sources of rhino and elephant decline have been big game hunters and the ivory trade.

Excluding the Masai from the new reserves in fact had just the opposite effect of what was intended. The Masai got angry and began killing some elephants and rhinos. Also, some Masai collaborated with the ivory trade in protest. Alienated from their traditional lands and traditional ways for the supposed benefit of wildlife, the Masai suddenly found themselves competing, rather than coexisting, with the rhino and the elephant. Corrupt park rangers and government officials, however, have been the main culprits in the continuing loss of wildlife to what Peluso terms the "ivory wars."[40]

Wilderness is, in the end, a state of mind more than a state of nature. Habitat provision is certainly vital for protecting biodiversity. The question is, Are habitat and humanity natural opposites, or merely conceptual ones? As the environmental historian William Cronon has written, "It is not the things we label as wilderness that are the problem—for nonhuman nature and large tracts of the natural world do deserve protection—but

Figure 8.6   Lawren S. Harris's 1927–1928 painting *Lake and Mountains*. Harris's painting shows an ideal wilderness with no trace of human activity. Such a nonhuman conception of wilderness sometimes leads to ecological misunderstanding, as the text describes.

rather what we ourselves mean when we use that label."[41] (See Figure 8.6.)

Guha's, Peluso's, and Cronon's point, then, is not that the United States should give Yellowstone Park to housing developers, or that Canada should turn Banff into a ski resort. Theirs is a more practical suggestion: that we should not universalistically, and imperialistically, promote such a culturally specific notion as a no-people vision of wilderness in places where it may lead to social injustice and may even undermine biodiversity.

For all its moral attractions as a realm free of politics, wilderness is nevertheless deeply political. There are unavoidable human consequences to the provision of habitat for wildlife—which does not mean that wildlife habitat is wrong or unimportant. It does mean, though, that we need to think through the implications for both humans and nonhumans.

Tourism and the Social Construction of Landscape

Tourism, it is sometimes said, is the largest and fastest-growing industry in the world. Such a statement is hard to verify—the definition of the tourist economy can be as narrow as hotel bookings and plane fares or as broad as the cost of the rubber one wears off one's shoes walking in the neighborhood park. But tourism indisputably has become big business.

Much of what tourists travel for is the look of a place and the occasion (or excuse) that look provides for what we must see as the *culture of leisure*. Although the local culture may be part of the experience, most tourists spend the bulk of their time in the separate world of the hotel, the historical site, the beach, and the wilderness park—all places rarely frequented by local people, unless they happen to work there. In other words, tourists tend to objectify a landscape, using its visual qualities as a cultural opportunity for leisure.

To some extent, the tendency of tourists to concentrate on the look of a place is a matter of access. Local property boundaries limit physical access to those deemed to have rights to a particular area. But visual access is hard to limit in a similar way—people can't easily be confined to keeping their gaze trained only on those spots where they have been granted a specific legal right to look. The landscape can be veiled through the strategic placement of walls and roads, but these only create a different visual effect. A landscape would still exist for outsiders to "consume" through what the sociologist John Urry has aptly termed the "tourist gaze."[42]

Of course, local people experience landscape visually as well. Since their lives and work are tied up in the local land, though, their visual experience has many more levels to it. They see the land differently; it means something different to them. As Thomas Greider and Lorraine Garcovich have written, "Every river is more than one river. Every rock is more than one rock. . . . Every landscape is a symbolic environment. These landscapes reflect our self-definitions that are grounded in culture."[43] We see landscape differently, and for different purposes, depending upon who we are.

The social significance of a landscape depends as well on some things that we can never see: the social associations we experience in it. A landscape can be alive with a kind of spirit, connections and associations that we may have when we are in that place. These connections and associations may be general feelings, but they may also be of specific things, even specific people who somehow

seem to be there, though we well know they are not. We commonly invest a landscape with, well, ghosts—a sense of the presence of that which is not, and those who are not, physically there. Through these *ghosts of place*, we build a feeling of attachment to that place through our attachment to the ghosts we sense there.[44]

A person local to an area, for example, may recall vividly events that friends and family participated in at a particular place in the landscape. He or she will likely be able to conjure up the mental images of friends and family involved in those events and to sense a connection to those places through those social attachments. The field where childhood friends used to play. The tree planted by a parent. His or her own ghost at the playground of the old school. The particularly deep sense of personal presence that generally comes with legal ownership of a place.

Tourists, of course, do not have these local associations and generally do not "see" these local ghosts—except for those conjured up, often simplistically, at historic sites, in heritage museums, and in tourism literature.[45] But tourists, too, need to "see" the landscape in some way to give it significance. The purely visual has no meaning. There is a close interrelationship between what we see and what we "see," for locals and tourists alike.

Tourism promoters play to the tourist's need to "see" by giving access to some readily accessible ghosts. As the environmental sociologist Clare Hinrichs describes, the state of Vermont in the northeastern United States has been particularly effective at giving tourists something to see in their imaginations. "To speak of Vermont is to conjure up a broader vision of a balanced, beneficent rurality," Hinrichs writes.[46] This conjured ghost of rural life can then be attached to the state's mountains, ski slopes, ice cream, cheese, maple syrup, and pancake mix—even to its mail-order Christmas wreaths. "Send a bit of the Vermont woods home for Christmas," Hinrichs reports one ad as reading, allowing one to tour Vermont, to "see" it, without ever leaving home. The landscape itself becomes an exportable commodity.

Local people are often ambivalent about the consequences. Turned into postcards and advertising slogans, a landscape can bring in the tourist's dollars. But often the benefits of tourism are not widely spread. The jobs are generally low paid and seasonal. Tourist dollars may also give local people the feeling that they have lost control of their community, and in the case of indigenous peoples, their culture as well. Tourism can also be an environmental disaster. Accommodations for tourists frequently burden local water supplies, eliminate sensitive habitat, and increase pollution, as well as intruding clumsily on the spirit (and spirits) of a place. The wilderness and rural charm that brought the tourists to begin with may soon become no more than a postcard and a slogan, even for those who live there.

Thus, the experience of a landscape—both what we see and "see"—is political. The point Urry and Hinrichs are making, however, is not that tourism should be banned and that tourists have no right to see or "see" the land in places where they do not live. The visual and imaginative qualities of a place are a kind of commons, something we all share. Landscape provides an important point of social connection in a world that is increasingly divided into no-go zones to which access is granted only to those with money.

But tourists and the tourism businesses they support are usually at an advantage in conflicts over landscape. Tourists tend to be wealthier than local people, and tourism businesses are often backed by corporate interests and by national and regional governments eager to generate foreign exchange and tax revenues. In such a situation of inequality, it is particularly challenging to manage a commons democratically.

Environmentalism and Social Exclusion

The final example of the relationship between conceptions of the environment and social power that I consider is the use of environmental arguments for social exclusion.

This is an unfortunately common phenomenon. Suburban and exurban zoning controls, for example, are often instituted with the expressed intent of maintaining open space, wildlife habitat, and the "character" of an area, among other goals. Such controls, though, can have the not-so-hidden effect of raising the cost of acquiring a residence in these areas, excluding poorer people from moving in and sometimes forcing them to move out. Moreover, rural areas in most of Europe, Canada, and the United States, the principal exception being the American South, are almost entirely white, and most suburban areas remain primarily so. Restrictive zoning policies help perpetuate this historical segregation—a point not lost on at least some rural and suburban residents.

In a study of an exurban Canadian village on the far commuting fringe of Toronto, Stanley Barrett found that some residents had moved "out in the country" in part to escape the multiracial and multiethnic city. One white woman who had recently moved from the city spoke very directly on the issue: "That is one thing that I like about it here—none of those people," she said, referring to blacks and Asians.[47]

Environmental arguments are also sometimes used to argue for restrictions on immigration. As a member of several national environmental organizations, I used to get a lot of environmental junk mail (something that ought to be considered an oxymoron). I don't get as much now, since I starting trying a number of junk-busting techniques. Still, environmental organizations I've never contacted or never even heard of will sometimes send me urgent appeals, action alerts, fake surveys of my opinion on various topics, and other grabs for my cash. A number of years ago I must have gotten into some marketer's database of people concerned about population growth, something I do believe is an important environmental issue. At the time, the U.S. Congress was considering some important immigration bills, and organizations like Population-Environment Balance, Negative Population Growth, Zero Population Growth, and FAIR (the Federation for American Immigration Reform) used the occasion to flood my mail slot with appeals and surveys. Their literature's frequent use of xenophobic and other dubious arguments caught my eye (and raised my ire), and I saved some of it. Here's how the letter I received in 1990 from Population-Environment Balance, signed by their "Honorary Chairman" Garrett Hardin, began:[48]

Dear Friend:

Why do so many of America's environmental problems persist despite our efforts to solve them? We Americans work hard to improve our individual lives and our country as a whole. Yet, even though we continue to make these sacrifices, we continue to suffer from worsening problems such as *environmental degradation, traffic jams, deteriorating infrastructures, and homelessness.*

The pitch here is that "we Americans" are not to blame for environmental problems, traffic jams, infrastructure deterioration, and homelessness. We work hard and sacrifice everyday. The letter continued:

. . . THERE IS A SOLUTION! . . . But before we can discuss the solution, we must fully understand *the primary cause of these problems—overpopulation.* . . . You may ask, how did we become overpopulated? Natural increase—more births than deaths—is one factor. The reality is, however, that *illegal as well as legal immigration is a major cause of population growth in the already over-crowded United States.* . . . Unrestrained, the effects of this immigration-generated population growth on our environment and quality of life will continue to become more obvious and more serious.

In other words, the "SOLUTION" is getting rid of *them.* Although the letter points out in passing that "natural increase . . . is one factor" and elsewhere states Population-Environment Balance's

support of birth control and sex education, nowhere does it specifically recommend smaller family size in the United States. Nor does it mention reducing the consumption levels of "we Americans" as a solution to environmental problems. Instead the letter shifts the blame onto legal and illegal immigrants, who it implies are, among other things, clogging the streets with their cars.

The letter goes on to call for a limit of 200,000 legal immigrants a year, about a third of the then-current figure of 650,000, what it calls the "replacement level" that would balance annual emigration from the United States. The letter also links population growth to a host of other issues, including crime, stress, urban sprawl, taxes, living expenses, and unemployment (but without explaining what the links might be), pushing as many "hot buttons," as marketers say, as possible.

Garrett Hardin is a widely respected environmentalist, author of one of the most famous essays of all time on environmental issues, "The Tragedy of the Commons," which I discuss in the last chapter. He is also known for promoting "lifeboat ethics"—the dubious idea that there is room for only so many, and that rather than sink the whole boat we will simply have to deny some people a place on board.[49] Here in this letter we learn who those entitled to a place in the boat are: the current citizens of the world's wealthiest and most powerful country. The basis for that decision is evidently the social power of those who already have a seat.

The Dialogue of Nature and Ideology

Nature, for all the moral security we expect it to provide, is a contradictory and contested conceptual realm. Although we often see it as a source of conscience that is free of the pollution of social interests, nature is inescapably social. Nature is a social and political phenomenon as much as a physical one, as many environmental sociologists have recently argued. The French social theorist Bruno Latour even suggests that there is no such thing as nature, only "nature-culture."[50] The American environmental sociologist Bill Freudenburg and his colleagues make a similar point, arguing that we need "to resist the temptation to separate the social and the environmental, and to realize that the interpenetrating influences are often so extensive that the relevant factors can be considered 'socioenvironmental.'"[51]

Actors and Actants

It is important to recognize some limits here, though. What we have long thought of as nature is certainly a social construction. All human ideas are necessarily social constructions; we are social, and therefore so are our ideas. But is that all nature is? Is it only a social construction? Indeed, is that all *anything* is—including the very idea that ideas are social constructions?

Social constructionism is an important insight, yet it runs several theoretical dangers. To begin with, it can become a kind of universalism itself, as everything reduces to the social constructionist perspective. This is an internally contradictory result. The moral and theoretical foundation of social constructionism is the need to recognize the existence of "truths," not truth. Second, if one conceives social constructionism as advocating a subjective point of view, it runs the danger of becoming a kind of Sophist solipsism—helpful as a form of social critique about power and perspective but incapacitating for any effort to improve social and environmental conditions, lest we commit another social construction. A social constructionist might come to regard any advocacy of social and environmental reform as hopelessly intertwined with power interests and therefore might cynically retreat from any social involvement. Finally, untempered social constructionism can wallow in a purely ideal realm, unwilling to engage the material side of the ecological dialogue.

There are several responses to these potential theoretical dangers. First, we need to recognize that there is nothing wrong with committing a social construction. The value and appropriateness of a social construction depends, of course, on what the social construction is. But we also need to recognize that there is more to human experience than ideas—and more to human experience than social life. It is not only ideas, and not only society, that fill our days. There is a material side to life and to social life, and that material side interacts with our ideas and our patterns of social organization.

The point is, we are unlikely to make up whatever vision of nature we want, at least not for long. There is a certain *social inconvenience of "nature"* that will, in time, guide the kinds of social visions we take toward it. King Canute, ruler of England 1,000 years ago, thought rather well of himself and supposedly once commanded the tide not to come in—with predictable results. He never tried it again.[52] Social understandings of the environment that don't work don't last long. Material consequences matter.

Bruno Latour and his colleagues have argued that we should regard the elements of what we often call "nature" and the "environment" as actors in a common network with human actors. The word *actor* has a distinctively human sound to it, so Latour suggests that we call all these network elements, human and otherwise, *actants*, lest we fall into our old oppositions again. These actants mutually constitute one another, Latour says, through what he calls *actor networks*. What makes us human is our understanding of how the rest of the world interacts with us, how it responds to us in the ways we conceptualize as the ways humans are responded to. It's a tough concept to grasp at first, and you might want to read the preceding sentence one more time. But it's a very everyday act. How do I know I am human? Because the world responds to me in the ways I conceptualize it should respond to humans—as opposed to, say, a bird or a fish or a rock or the wind that blows. Of course, I did the conceptualizing (with a lot of help from my society) to begin with, and I respond to the world's responses in ways that stem from that conceptualization. I know the actants I interact with through their *performances*, as Latour calls them, in combination with my conceptualization of their performances. And my conceptualizations of myself and the performances I give in return are what constitute me as an actant in the network as well.

It's a very dialogic matter. Latour calls his approach *actor network theory*, and many environmental sociologists are finding it a useful way to think about the "inconvenience" of the world, while at the same time recognizing our own constructions of our experiences of that inconvenience. Latour likes to say that his approach gets us past a lot of unhelpful oppositions, especially nature versus society and fact versus belief. He sees our understandings of the world as what he calls *factishes*—hybrids between facts and beliefs. Factishes help us in the essential act of what Latour calls *fabrication*, the simultaneous creation of knowledge and actor networks. (Latour likes puns. He wants to point out here the human role in "fabricating" our knowledge, but also that there is a fabric of actants in a network who have an equal hand in fabricating knowledge.) Actor network theory thus helps us to see the interaction of—and the mutual constitution of—material and ideal factors in the dialogue of ecology, in "nature-culture."

The history of the theory of natural selection is a good example of the mutually constituting interaction of the material and the ideal. The correspondence between the rise of capitalism and the theory of natural selection may suggest that society was reflected in Darwin's vision of nature. But that doesn't mean Darwin just made it all up. Rather, it could be argued that before the rise of a form of social organization like capitalism people did not have the conceptual resources—the forms of understanding—needed to envision natural selection. Before this form of social "seeing" developed, people were not able to see natural selection. A certain cast of mind is prepared to see things that other casts of mind cannot—but there has to be something there to "see." Indeed, the fossil record provides abundant material evidence—abundant

performances, in Latour's terminology—that corresponds with Darwin's basic propositions.

But then, in turn, these correspondences help amplify the cast of mind that Darwin turned toward them. Darwin was thus changed by his interactions with fossils, Galapagos finches, and other actants in the network that was created by, and helped create, the theory of natural selection. Darwin was a different actant as a result, just as the theory of natural selection in time vastly changed human interactions with nonhumans, leading among other things to the discovery of genes, and thus changed the performances of those other actants. For just as an actor's performance is shaped by the audience's response to it, so are nonhuman actants' performances shaped by the response of humans to them, and vice versa. What something is, is what it does in the world. And what it does in the world is shaped by how the world responds to it.

Resonance

Nonetheless, however much we fabricate (in Latour's sense) the conditions of our lives through involvement in actor networks, a network of mainly human actants feels quite different to us then one with both human and nonhuman actants. We respond to such a network differently. We perform in it differently. And we think about it differently.

But not as differently as we often say is the case. Similarities in the categories we use to understand human networks and human/nonhuman networks are striking. Moreover, these categories experience parallel changes. Again, the theory of natural selection is a case in point.

In the twentieth century, there developed a more socialized version of capitalism than Darwin knew. Social services, worker protection, free education, and assistance to the poor became standard features of most democratic societies. At the same time, a more socialized understanding of evolution developed: ecology, which stresses holism and mutual interdependence in the nonhuman world. And as we have come to adopt a postmodern skepticism about "progress" in the human world, biologists have adopted similar views about "progress" in evolution. In place of the every-day-we're-getting-better-in-every-way implications of Darwin's ideas about competitive selection of the fittest, biologists now stress the importance of random events like the meteorite crash that doomed the dinosaurs. They also question the extent to which animals are perfectly adapted to their environments, another Darwinist idea that seemed to imply progress in evolution.

The evidence is out there—the performances are out there among nonhuman actants—for these new views of evolution. Geologists are pretty sure that on the Yucatan Peninsula of Mexico they've found the crater caused by that meteorite. Such a finding, though, has social effects. For example, it probably feeds our feeling that the direction we are going in is not certain to end well—that, to echo the title of an Elvis Costello song, "accidents can happen." It fits with, and therefore promotes, our current sense of anxiety. Thus, our ideas of the condition of our human networks reflect our ideas of our other networks, and vice versa. It's a two-way process, a search for a common language for understanding the conditions of our lives. It's another dialogue.

But the dynamics of these mutually supporting parallels is largely an unconscious process. I like to think of it as a kind of intellectual *resonance*. That is, we tend to favor patterns of understanding that work well across—that resonate with—the range of our experience. We feel an intuitive sense of ideological ease when a pattern we know from one conceptual realm seems to apply in another.[53] Darwin's theory of natural selection resonated with the Victorians' enthusiasm for the new capitalist way, just as the devastating crater that wiped out the dinosaurs resonates with our turn-of-the-twenty-first-century mood of doubt. It just somehow seems righter—the way a more resonant musical instrument just somehow seems to sound better—when we encounter such parallels.

The value of social constructionist arguments is that they alert us to the ideological implications of resonance and urge us to confront our intellectual ease. The results may be emotionally and politically challenging, but sometimes that's just what we need.

Maybe the best way to conclude is to go back to my philosophical wrangle with Sam. The answer to the question "What is nature?" is that everything is and that everything isn't. Both are true. Nature is an inescapably human conception, just as humans are inescapably a conception of nature. We construct nature and nature constructs us. It's a paradox, but it makes ecological dialogue possible—and necessary.

CHAPTER 9

The Rationality of Risk

"Safety," the wife of Pablo said. "There is no such thing as safety. There are so many seeking safety here now that they make a great danger. In seeking safety now you lose all."

—Ernest Hemingway, 1941

Click. It's April 15, 1996, again. Click. The pixels start glowing. Click, click, click. *The Oprah Winfrey Show.* There's Oprah with three guests. Gary Weber of the National Cattlemen's Beef Association. Dr. Will Hueston of the U.S. Department of Agriculture. Howard Lyman of the Humane Society. It's the controversial episode about Mad Cow Disease or BSE—Bovine Spongiform Encephalopathy—and the human manifestation that comes from eating the infected cows, new variant Creutzfeldt-Jakob Disease (nvCJD), which is terminal and incurable. Oprah is introducing Lyman to the studio audience.[1]

"Howard Lyman is a former cattle rancher, turned vegetarian," says Oprah. "You hear me? Former cattle rancher turned *vegetarian*—we want to know why—and executive director of the Humane Society's Eating With Conscience Campaign. You said this disease could make AIDS look like the common cold?"

"Absolutely," replies Lyman.

"That's an extreme statement, you know?" Oprah challenges.

"Absolutely," says Lyman again, taking the challenge in stride. "And what we're looking at right now is we're following exactly the same path that they followed in England. Ten years of dealing with it as public relations, rather than doing something substantial about it. One hundred thousand cows per year in the United States are fine at night, dead in the morning. The majority of those cows are rounded up, ground up, fed back to other cows. If only one of them has Mad Cow Disease, [that] has the potential to affect thousands. Remember today, [in] the United States, 14 percent of all cows by volume are ground up, turned into feed, and fed back to other animals."

Oprah seems a bit shocked. "But cows are herbivores. They shouldn't be eating other cows."

"That's exactly right," says Lyman. "And what we should be doing is exactly what nature says. We should have them eating grass, not other cows. We've not only turned them into carnivores, we've turned them into cannibals."

"Now see, wait a minute, wait a minute." Oprah goes back to the challenge mode. "Let me just ask you this right now, Howard. How do you know the cows are ground up and fed back to the other cows?"

"Oh, I've seen it. These are USDA statistics. They're not something we're making up."

Oprah addresses the audience. "Now doesn't that concern you all a little bit, right here, hearing that?"

The audience intones a collective "Yeah!"

"It has just stopped me cold from eating another burger!" adds Oprah.

The audience breaks out in applause.

Click. Talk of risk is still in the air today, perhaps even more so than in 1996. We are fast entering an "age of risk," say some observers.[2] Along with cloning, globalization, virtual reality, and other defining terms of our time, the twenty-first century appears to be culturally and politically saturated with the language of "risk." BSE, GMOs, pesticides. Hazardous waste, lead, VOCs. Radon, dioxin, smog. Cancer, heart disease, AIDS. Car accidents, plane crashes, train derailments. Global warming, the ozone hole, rising sea levels. Everywhere we turn it appears we are confronted with some new risk. A few years ago it was Alar-contaminated apples, today it is GMOs—genetically modified organisms. And tomorrow . . . ? In the words of one prominent sociologist, Ulrich Beck, we have become a "risk society."[3]

But what is risk? And why are we suddenly all talking about it? Do we really live in such a perilous time that risk defines the spirit of our age? Are we all seeking an unattainable safety like the characters in Hemingway's novel, or is there something else going on? As I write, there is a media storm surrounding the discovery in December 2003 of the first U.S. cow with Mad Cow Disease, and much finger pointing about who is responsible for it: Lax USDA rules. Industry pressure to keep the rules lax. Sloppy farm practices in Canada (the cow was born in

Canada). But no one is yet known to have come down with nvCJD from eating U.S. beef. As of January 2004, there have been worldwide only 155 documented cases of nvCJD, 145 in the United Kingdom, and only one each in the United States and Canada—both people who picked it up in the U.K.[4] At the time of Oprah's show on the subject, the worldwide figure was about 15—and none in the United States.[5] Yet Oprah swore off hamburgers, and her fans roared their approval.[6]

This chapter brings the perspective of environmental sociology to these fears, doubts, and uncertainties. In so doing, I offer a distinction that I believe can help us better understand our worries: a distinction between *risk* and *risky*.[7] When I refer to *risk* in this chapter, I mean our sense of what we should worry about, and how much—the ideal side of worries and fears. When I refer to *risky* in this chapter, I mean the organizational, technological, economic, and biophysical potential of our circumstances for disrupting our goals and intentions—the material side of worries and desires. I try to show that this distinction between risk and risky leads, once again, to an appreciation of the dynamics of ecological dialogue.

Many things in this world *can* go wrong precisely because there are many things in this world *to* go wrong.[8] For example, you could get hit by a car walking to work. A rare and expensive book you purchased online could get damaged or lost in the mail. A truck carrying toxic chemicals could run off the road and release noxious gases into your neighborhood. A thunderstorm in the middle of the night could cause a power outage, which causes the alarm on your digital clock not to go off, which causes you to miss the bus, which causes you to miss your final exam in your environmental sociology class, which causes your A to slip to a C+ because your instructor does not allow rescheduling for missed exams, which causes . . . [9] These are all examples of the risky quality of life, of the material worries that daily confront us. But is this to say, however, that there is more risk in life today? You are, after all, unlikely to experience any of these calamities, and you are highly likely to live a longer and healthier life than the people of the past. But you may worry less, or just as much, or even more, albeit about different things. You may, after reading this paragraph, rush out and buy a battery-operated backup alarm clock for the next time you have an exam to take or a plane to catch. You may have one already, because of your sense of the risk in your life—your sense of the worries involved in getting successfully through the day.

This chapter, like the previous three, enters the dialogue of ecology from an ideal "moment"— that is, from the moment of the ideal. And like in the previous three, the material side of things is never out of the room, excluded from the conversation. While the chapter focuses on the question of risk, the question of the risky is also continually in our minds. Unavoidably so, for the two—risk and the risky—help constitute and reconstitute each other. In this constitution and reconstitution, as we shall see, risk and the risky raise important questions about some of the most fundamental issues this book has traced: knowledge, democracy, and dialogue.

Rational Risk Assessment

Let's click this time to an *Oprah* episode that never happened. Oprah is just introducing her fictional guest. Maynard Haskins, we'll call him.[10]

"Maynard Haskins is a former race car driver turned anti-car activist," Oprah is saying as the pixels come to life. "You hear me? Former race car driver turned *anti-car activist*. We want to know why. He's the executive director of AutoBAN, the Automobile Banning Activists Network, and the author of a new book by that title—*Auto Ban: How We Can Save Millions of Lives and Rebuild a Humane Society*.[11] You said that automobiles make Mad Cow Disease look like the common cold."

"Absolutely," replies Haskins.

"That's an extreme statement, you know?" Oprah challenges.

"Absolutely," says Haskins again, taking the challenge in stride. "But it's a far bigger epidemic than Mad Cow Disease, or even than AIDS. Only 153 people have ever died from Mad Cow Disease, and just two in the United States. But in 2002 alone in the United States, 42,850 people were killed in automobile accidents and 2,914,000 were injured. The latest mortality figure for AIDS in the United States is for the year 2000—16,110 deaths. That's a lot, but it's about a third as many as died in automobile accidents. Plus, the rate of automobile deaths is up and the rate of AIDS deaths is down, way down."

Oprah seems a bit shocked. "But cars are supposed to be safer now. Seatbelts, airbags, better design, and better roads are supposed to be making driving less dangerous."

"That's exactly right," says Haskins. "But we're driving so much more. And what we should be doing is exactly what nature says. We should be feeding our cars hydrogen or running them some other nonpolluting way. Because cars actually kill almost as many people with air pollution as they do in accidents—another 35,000 a year in the United States. Worldwide, 1.2 million people die in automobile accidents every year, and another 1.5 million die from the air pollution cars cause, making 2.7 million deaths in all. Actually, to be strictly fair in our comparisons we should note that worldwide more people die from AIDS each year—3.2 million in 2002—mostly in poor countries. But we haven't included in these figures any of the millions that die each year from the effects of obesity—heart disease, diabetes, some cancers, and more. Lack of exercise from increased car use is a major part of the world obesity pandemic, although it is hard to calculate exactly how much. Taking that into account, cars almost certainly kill more worldwide than AIDS does."

"Now see, wait a minute, wait a minute." Oprah goes back to the challenge mode. "Let me just ask you this right now, Maynard. How do you know all this?"

"Oh, I've seen it. These are statistics from the United States government and the World Health Organization. They're not something we're making up."[12]

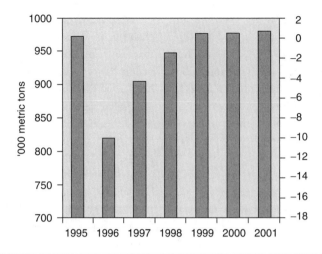

Figure 9.1   Effect of concern about Mad Cow Disease on beef consumption in Britain, 1995–2001.

Oprah addresses the audience. "Now doesn't that concern you all a little bit, right here, hearing that?"

The audience intones a collective "Yeah!"

"It has just stopped me cold from driving another car!" adds Oprah.

The audience breaks out in applause.

Possibly, such a talk show might take place some day. But it is very unlikely that Oprah, or anybody else, would respond by swearing off cars—to the cheers of the studio audience. And yet, comparison of death rates shows cars to be far, far more risky than the likelihood of catching nvCJD, the human manifestation of Mad Cow Disease, in the United States or even in Britain, where most Mad Cow deaths have occurred. Still, Oprah was not alone in swearing off beef, at least for a time. Millions in Britain did, sending the price of beef to the cellar, and thousands of British farms with it. (See Figure 9.1.) And some in the United States are doing it now, with the renewed attention to Mad Cow Disease started by that sick cow found in a Washington State herd in December 2003. How many people have sworn off cars?

The issue at hand here is *rational risk assessment*—the idea that we should compare our best knowledge about the rates and probabilities of hazards and choose the least dangerous alternative. Anyone who doesn't is being irrational, this theory states. Risks, according to this perspective, are calculable "facts" to be measured, recorded, and evaluated. Additionally, the rational assessment perspective believes not only that risks *can* be evaluated independent of political, social, or cultural context, but that they *should* be.

It's a version of what is more generally called *rational choice theory*, which Chapter 2 discusses. The basic premise of the rational choice perspective is that the individual is a purposeful, calculating actor, seeking to maximize her or his interests. As Jon Elster explains, the rational choice perspective views action as beginning with "the logically most simple type of motivation: rational, selfish, outcome oriented behavior."[13]

Rational risk assessment has had an extensive following among natural scientists, engineers, government officials, and corporate managers, and is usually closely associated with risk-benefit analysis. And while rational risk assessment has been less attractive to social scientists, as we shall see, its influence can still be seen among them.[14] The rational perspective was the earliest theoretical framework for understanding risk. Consequently, it found a place for itself at the forefront of the field that it still retains in many quarters.[15]

Much of what makes this theory so attractive is that it provides a simple understanding of human behavior that can be easily translated into public policy.[16] Other theoretical approaches to risk that try to take account of culture, norms, social structures, and power are difficult to reduce to the simple line graphs, pie charts, and percentage tables that policymakers and the public have become used to seeing. In short, in a fast-food, fast-analysis world, the rational risk assessment provides an easily understood and homogenized formula.

Questioning the Rational Risk Assessment Perspective

Theoretical perspectives, however, are like a house. No matter how sound and well built they may appear on the surface, if their foundations are weak or if they are built upon unstable ground, they can eventually topple. The reign of the rational risk assessment perspective in the field of risk is threatened for this very reason, argue a growing number of social scientists—including me.

Recall the observation in Chapter 2 that people do not always act in their own interests—that people often deliberately act in ways that are other-serving, as much as in ways that are self-serving. People are moved by their sentiments as much as by their interests. That is to say, risk assessments are based as much on norms and values as on calculation. For example, cars are highly valued in modern culture, however foolishly from the perspective of our interests in staying alive.

Of course, the point of rational risk assessment is that we should not be so foolish. As Maynard Haskins does not share the widely held cultural value of cars, he would no doubt quite agree. But most people, for better or worse, do appear to share this cultural value, at least to some degree, and continue to drive cars, even though rational risk assessment advises against it. Culture, in this case at least, trumps rationality.

Well, no, not really, a rational risk assessment advocate might respond. Culture is itself a kind of interest and a kind of rationality. Our norms and values and other-serving ends are as much a part of our interests as our self-serving ends. We can add all this into the calculation of the threat a risk poses to us. No trouble. In fact, a number of rational choice theorists make precisely this more sophisticated argument.[17]

There are two problems with such a response. The first is a philosophical one—that turning everything into interest makes a *tautology* of rational choice and rational risk assessment. If everything we do is motivated by an interest, then whatever people are doing must already be rational, within the context of the constraints with which they must contend. There can be no irrationality, and therefore no need ever to make a rational argument for doing something differently.

The second problem is that of *incommensurability.* Let us say that we may wave aside the problem of tautology. Let's call that critique a kind of unhelpful philosophical logic trick. If so, then rational risk assessment and rational choice are still left with the problem of how to compare the utility and interests of, say, death by car accidents, pollution, and obesity with the cultural value of the car as a "dream machine." Cultural values simply are not in the same units of measurement as death rates. Comparing the importance of cultural values with death rates becomes a hugely uncertain endeavor, not easily amenable—and perhaps not amenable at all—to calculation. What is the value of a life? What is the value of a value? Sometimes people will kill to defend a cultural value. Sometimes people will sacrifice their own lives to defend a cultural value. However much as others may regard such acts as abhorrent, we do need to recognize that some people sometimes regard their interests in this way. And who is to judge who is right? Which raises another problem of incommensurability: Not only may one person hold incommensurable values, the values of two or more people may also be incommensurable.

Rational risk assessments often try to get around the problem of incommensurability through risk-benefit analysis. The idea is to put every aspect of a problem in the same unit of analysis so that everything can be directly compared. The usual unit is money. The usual way to get something like cultural values, death rates, and the value of clean air into monetary units is to assess what people are willing to pay for them, through surveys—*contingent valuation* is the technical name for it—and other procedures. But contingent valuation presumes that people find it possible to put prices on matters like the value of a life, or that they tacitly put prices on such things through their spending behavior. In other words, it presumes the problem of incommensurability away.

As well, risk-benefit analysis tends to be riddled with accounting problems in following the full consequences of a risk through an economy. Much is often left externalized, and critics' standard responses to any risk-benefit analysis is to argue that something left out needs to be put it, and vice versa. Consequently, there are usually contentious conceptual issues about what counts as being an economic consequence and what does not. For example, many might reject the notion that deaths from weight problems can be considered a risk associated with cars, as there are ready ways to make up any calorie imbalance, such as choosing to eat less and exercise more.

Which leads to another conceptual problem with rational risk assessment and rational choice: the degree to which it really is about choice. Because when you think about it, "rational" and "choice" are something of a contradiction in terms.[18] At least in its purest form, rational choice sees us all as carbon-based calculators, constantly assessing our environments in the never-ending quest to maximize utility. If all you are doing is calculating the highest utility, there is no choosing to be done. You are just a computer spitting out answers into your consciousness. To say that individuals have "choice" as rational and calculating actors is no different from suggesting that your computer has a "choice" when you have it add 2 plus 2.

Now, perhaps these criticisms of rationalist perspectives are a bit over the top. After all, most contemporary rational risk assessment and rational choice theorists do not have such a narrow view of rationality. Among other things, they recognize that people's processing ability in making "choices" is limited by time, information, and understanding. Some of them are also working on incorporating norms and values into the theory.[19] But once you begin to deviate from a narrow understanding of rationality—by including norms, values, culture, emotions, and whatever else you care to incorporate into it—where do you stop? The slope is a slippery one. If you include culture in your understanding of rationality, why not trust. And if trust, why not love, and so on. And soon you are left with an understanding of rationality that tells us nothing (well, almost nothing). All it says is that individuals have reasons for doing what they do, which doesn't really add to our understanding.

Plus, we often do not choose the risks we bear in life. Rather, they are imposed upon us. Often we may not recognize that imposition. For example, most people regard using cars as a personal choice of the most convenient way to travel, and not a choice they make within the context of the social organization of convenience, described in Chapter 3. Powerful social forces, most notably real estate developers and the automobile and oil and gas industries and the influence they have gained in the halls of government, have over time created much of the historical impetus for our car-dominated lives. Consequently, it is often hard to choose to travel a different way. Even if you think trains are safer than cars (as a rational risk assessment would quickly show to be the case), you can't take one if there isn't one. Even if you realize you could get more exercise if you walked or took your bike, you'll find it hard to take the time if development has followed the sprawl model. It may also be quite dangerous, if there are no sidewalks or bike paths. Choice, then, is always socially constrained, and thus is not choice in the pure sense we usually associate with the word.

But people usually do not see their use of the car as an imposition. They typically see it truly as a choice, as something voluntary—which is much of the reason why few of us have sworn off cars. As I describe in more detail following, people are far more likely to accept a risk if they perceive it as voluntary. Furthermore, factors such as emotions, a sense of civic duty, and feelings of trust have also been shown to play a role in how we think about risks and what our responses should be toward them.[20] We are embedded within a social context. What we think and how we act are shaped by the social environment we find ourselves in.

Finally, rational risk assessment assumes that the "facts" relevant to an issue of risk can be known. However, the facts are not always so clear, and by extension, then, neither is risk. Risks are not something we can typically see "out there." You cannot see dioxin, radon, or radiation. But even these phenomena are not risks until we define them as such. Rational risk assessment is really rational assessment of the *risky,* not of risk. Or, better put, rational risk assessment assumes that risk and the risky are the same.

But they are not. What we understand to be risk is embedded within social relations. Our knowledge is influenced by relations of power and of trust.[21] Power relations will influence both the knowledge that comes to your attention and the knowledge that you seek out. Corporations, as I discuss later in the chapter, often manipulate information about how risky their products are, and many of us are not well placed to seek other sources. Trust relations will influence what you make of that knowledge when it comes your way. Someone can tell you until they are blue in the face that cellular telephones represent a health risk, be they a Nobel prize-winning scientist or your neighbor next door. Yet if you do not trust that person's knowledge on this subject as being the truth, or if you do not trust the source from where they heard this information from, then you will likely not perceive cellular telephones as representing any particular risk.

I return to the relationships among risk, power, and trust at the end of the chapter. It is important to introduce them here, however, because they highlight the inherently social character of risk. And it is this social nature of risk that the rational choice perspective misses most.

The Culture of Risk

In response to the rational choice perspective's rather limited view of risk, centered on interest and utilities, other perspectives have been developed that give more consideration to values, worldviews, and culture. Led by anthropologists and cultural sociologists, a growing number of risk theorists suggest that perceptions of and responses to risk are fundamentally shaped by our cultural conditions. Enter the cultural perspective on risk.

Risk and Threats to the Group

Perhaps the most famous work to have come from this perspective is a book entitled *Risk and Culture,* written in 1982 by anthropologist Mary Douglas and political scientist Aaron Wildavsky. According to Douglas and Wildavsky, people tend to accept risks that help to reinforce the social solidarity of their institutions, and to reject those that do not. As one of many illustrations, the authors describe the belief of the Hima, a Ugandan pastoral people. According to the Hima people, cattle can die as a result of contact with women, or if someone from within their social group eats food produced by another group while drinking cow's milk. These beliefs, suggest Douglas and Wildavsky, function to reinforce the traditional sexual division of labor among the Hima as well as their separate identity from neighboring farming people. Risks, therefore, are not something that exist "out there," distinct from our cultural surround, but instead are artifacts of that surround that dialogically tend to reinforce it as well.

The sociologist Kai Erikson earlier made a related argument in *Wayward Puritans,* his

Figure 9.2   The Salem witch trials.

famous study of crime and deviance among the seventeenth-century Puritans of New England.[22] Erikson argued that at times of weakness and uncertainty in a group's social cohesion and sense of its boundaries, the perception of a threat can serve to draw the group together. Even more, Erikson argued that the experience of weak cohesion may lead people to perceive threats to begin with. What turned some old women in Salem into witches was not their practice of witchcraft. Rather, it was the people of Salem's practice of group cohesion in an uncertain time. As a new settlement in a new land, social order was very much in question. The discovery of witches of whatever kind "restates where the boundaries of the group are located," in Erikson's words, by clearly identifying a threat to those boundaries.[23] (See Figure 9.2.)

Perhaps as much could be said of the threat of terrorism today. Perhaps as much could be said

of the threat of meat-eating, or of cars, or of nuclear waste, or of any perception of risk that leads to the strengthening of group feeling, or the constitution of a new social group. As groups form in protest to a perceived risk or threat, they give the adherents a feeling of membership and order—a comforting feeling that, in an atomistic society whose rules of conduct seem so much up for grabs, can be hard to find.

Let me be quick to emphasize, though, that the implications of the perception of risk for group feeling does not necessarily imply that all risk is witchcraft, pure figments of an overwrought social imagination. People do die from Mad Cow Disease. People do die in car accidents. People do die from nuclear waste. The Twin Towers did fall. Life is often risky. But there is more to risk than the risky, and much of that more is the influence of group cohesion processes on our perception of the world and its worries.

Culture and Choice

There is also more to the perception of risk than the need for group cohesion. The work of Douglas, Wildavsky, and Erikson (from whom we will later hear again) provides a helpful corrective to the individualism and materialist confidence of rational risk assessment. However, we need to be careful not to overbalance the accounts and place too much emphasis on how larger cultural patterns and structures shape perceptions. We need to be wary of the problem of *functionalism*—that of seeing the functions of a larger whole as the only thing that controls the parts. It is people that make up society just as much as larger social structures and patterns do.

Recent cultural accounts of risk have been working on an understanding of culture that is not so top-down. Here, culture is something that both constrains and enables perceptions of risk, and the actions we take accordingly. Culture is both something that shapes us and something we shape within those constraints. Culture is something that influences our choices and gives us choices.

Let's consider, for example, the widely noted phenomenon that people are apparently more accepting of "voluntary risks" than "involuntary risks," which I mentioned a few pages back.[24] Recently scholars have argued that this distinction is too simplistic, since it ignores how culture shapes the choices we have before we even make a decision.[25] Take smoking. We may think that smoking represents a clear example of where the smoker has accepted a voluntary risk—the major risk ultimately being premature death. But smokers do not smoke simply for the sake of smoking. Smokers may, for instance, smoke to suppress their appetites in order to achieve that "ideal" body figure. Or they may smoke to fit in to a social group where smoking is considered "cool." Looking good and fitting in are culturally defined attributes of a person that are difficult to ignore in social life. There are, of course, other ways to look good and to fit in than through smoking. But for many people in many social contexts, those other ways may be less readily apparent to them or less available to them. When we consider the full context of a person's life, we discover him or her *taking* risks as much as choosing them.

Nevertheless, a person may not perceive smoking as an involuntary risk, depending on how they conceptualize the context in which they make their choices. Or they may see it in this way, at least in part. What is key, then, is how people themselves conceptualize the voluntariness or involuntariness of a risk—not how an outside observer may see it.

Closely linked to that perception is—going back to that phrase two paragraphs earlier—what is "readily apparent" to someone. Central to choice is knowledge. For example, tobacco companies knew the health consequences of smoking, yet kept much of that information from the public for decades, and carefully shaped people's knowledge environment through advertising and pressure on government officials. The public therefore "voluntarily" chose to smoke, but did so without a full and wide-awake awareness of the riskiness of smoking.

This brings us to what has been called "vertical" and "horizontal" knowledge gaps.[26] Because of the complexity of modern social life, knowledge gaps emerge among experts and also between experts and non-experts. We cannot possibly know everything there is to know, from how to rebuild a carburetor, to how to mend a hole in one's roof, to how subatomic particles react when they are exposed to high-intensity electromagnetic fields. The world has simply become too complex for that. It has become increasingly difficult to know all of the facts upon which to base one's actions.

Vertical knowledge gaps are those instances where information is not communicated across the levels of society's hierarchies. This lack of communication might be part of a deliberate effort to keep options off the table, as in the suppression of evidence about the health consequences of smoking. The evidence was in hand, but was not communicated from the "top" of society to the "bottom." Horizontal knowledge gaps, on the other hand, refer to those instances when knowledge exchange within a level in the social hierarchy breaks down, for example between scientists. To refer again to the smoking example, the suppression of evidence by tobacco corporations meant that corporate scientists and university scientists did not share the same pool of knowledge. Often, knowledge gaps can be both horizontal and vertical at the same time, as there was a dimension of the vertical in those different knowledge pools of corporate and university scientists. As a result, even "experts" can be in the dark.

In short, if someone were to offer you the last piece of chocolate cake on the table without informing you that it was moldy, could it be said that you voluntarily chose to eat a piece of moldy cake?

Rational Risk Assessment as Cultural Practice

Let's go back to the title of Douglas's and Wildavsky's book, *Risk and Culture*. What I have covered so far in this section on culture is a kind of "reining in" of risk, pointing out the limits of rationalism because of the cultural conditions under which we make decisions. Now I try to take a cultural perspective deeper, arguing that risk is itself a kind of culture. We might term this perspective as moving from "risk and culture" to "risk *as* culture."

Recall the questions from the beginning of this chapter: What is risk? Why are we suddenly all talking about it? As I discussed earlier in the chapter, it is probably not because we live in more perilous times. The people of the past surely faced worries and hazards equal to or greater than those of the current day. Among other things, they didn't live as long as people do today, as the technological optimist Julian Simon (see Chapter 4) was fond of pointing out. The people of the past also experienced much uncertainty in their lives, and they sought ways to deal with the unknown: religion, magic, charms

around the neck, and rituals performed under a full moon at midnight in a graveyard with a dead cat, such as Mark Twain so wonderfully described in *The Adventures of Tom Sawyer*. (See Figure 9.3.) Uncertainty is in part a matter of control. Through rituals with dead cats in the graveyard and sacrifices at the altar, the people of the past found ways to comprehend terror and the unknown and thus to gain a measure of power over it.

We are not so different today. We face much uncertainty—many worries, hazards, and scary possibilities that seem beyond our powers to control. Although lives in the modern, wealthy West are normally not so short, and perhaps not so brutish and nasty, there remains much that we cannot be sure about, many dark possibilities that we have to ponder. Living longer does not purge us of doubts and dangers. We still need ways to contend with them.

What is different about the worries of the present day is not the number of hazards we face or the degree of uncertainty we feel about our lives. Rather, it is the language we use to think and to talk about our worries, a language that, in keeping with the spirit of our time, is highly rationalistic. Consider the connotations of the very word we increasingly favor to talk about our troubles: *risk*. The term immediately conjures up numbers and calculations in a way that words like *hazard* and *concern* and *danger* do not. Risk is imbued with the image of science, of studies that have been done or could be done. Risk turns witchcraft into statistics. Risk turns subjective uncertainties into objective probabilities, sanctified by the iron laws of mathematical logic and scientific method. Along with the "iron cage" of rationalism, to use Max Weber's phrase (see Chapter 6), came the iron cage of risk.

This, then, is what *risk* is—a modern cultural means, a contemporary conceptual language, for confronting uncertainty. The people of the past did not think as much in this rationalist way. They had notions of numbers and chance and probability, of course. But the coming of a scientific and moneyed world order developed rationalism

"' LEMME SEE HIM, HUCK '"

Figure 9.3   Huck Finn's cure for warts, from *The Adventures of Tom Sawyer*.

into a defining feature of daily life. Indeed, the word *risk* is a relatively recent arrival in the English language, dating from the mid-seventeenth century—a time of greatly accelerating development of capitalism and its calculating spirit.[27] As the famous sociologist Georg Simmel observed a century ago,

> Gauging values in terms of money has taught us to determine and specify values down to the last farthing. . . . The ideal of numerical calculability has been made possible in practical, and perhaps even in intellectual, life only through the money economy.[28]

Risk (and its equivalents in other Western tongues, such as *risque, riesgo, risco, Risiko,* and риск) has come to be the word we most associate with the extension of rationalism into our outlook on danger and uncertainty.

Not that the people of the present have fully embraced the rationalization of risk. For example, a 1999 Gallup poll found that some 3 out of 4 Americans claim they pray daily.[29] A 2003 Harris Poll found that 84 percent of American adults believe God can perform miracles.[30] We remain fascinated by stories of the occult and by movies that weave magic and graveyard rituals into the plot. The New Age movement has drawn heavily on Wicca and other traditions in an often vigorously nonrationalistic way.[31]

The language of risk, however, has become—and remains—the most politically legitimate way for us to discuss and debate life's dangers and uncertainties. Part of the reason for the political legitimacy of rationalism is its implicit democratic appeal. There are some close ideological connections at work between rationalism and democracy. Rationalism appears democratic because of its universalist and objectivist claim that it represents the perspective of the entire demos, via the sanctity of the methods of science. Rational knowledge is knowledge that is supposed to be everybody's knowledge, at least potentially. It is unnamed, unidentified with a particular standpoint or culture, applying to all and representing all, and thus apparently democratic. Governmental agencies, not incoincidentally, typically defend their authority through such rationalist and implicitly democratic claims.

There may indeed be much democratic potential in rational risk assessment, given science's commitment to debate, as I come to at the end of the chapter. The point of a cultural perspective on risk is not to throw rationalism—and with it the material side of ecological dialogue—out the window. Rather, the point is to balance rationalism with the ideal side of the dialogue, showing the equal importance of how we socially construct our understanding of the material.

With that balance, we can recognize how rationalism can be a highly effective political tool for those who are able to wield its language to their advantage, often overriding its democratic potential. For rational risk assessment quickly leads to the rationalist claims of the state's regulatory authority. To speak of risk is not only to speak of control but also of power. It represents the extension of rationalism into our comprehension of the unknown, giving us a sense of control over uncertainty in a way that appeals to the modern mind. It as well represents the legal authority of expertise to order our lives in ways that may advantage the interests behind the experts more than those of us in front of the experts, down in the audience. Risk explains, and it also explains away. It gives control and it takes control, and therefore we often feel culturally trapped in the iron cage of risk.

The Sociology of Disasters

But life is indeed risky sometimes. It has its material worries and uncertainties. And sometimes, unfortunately, those worries and uncertainties become realities, disastrous realities. These disasters not only affect individual people, but can also threaten the social fabric that links us one to another. Sometimes the experience of disaster can bring people together, like the flight attendant discussed in Chapter 2 found, thereby allowing for both individual and collective recovery.[32] But sometimes disasters unfold in such a way that the fabric of human community is left in shreds, leaving its members flapping in the wind in shock, destitution, and alienation.[33] This social shredding is particularly true for disasters whose cause bears distinctly human fingerprints.

Take the common phrase "natural disaster." Scan a recent newspaper article describing a flood or a storm or a wildfire or an earthquake, and one is likely to find such phrases as "an act of God" and "Nature strikes again" strewn throughout the clipping. As long as we attribute the cause of a disaster to "natural" (or "supernatural") causes, it remains in the morally innocent realm of what earlier chapters termed the "natural conscience."

But consider. Much of the flooding that occurs today is the result of two centuries of human-induced landscape change: deforestation, the draining of wetlands, the channeling of rivers, the spread of roads and other impermeable surfaces, and the like. Global warming also affects rain patterns. Is flooding, then, a natural or "unnatural" act? The wildfires that rage in most years in the American West are in considerable measure the product of forest management practices, and the damage they cause must be attributed at least to some extent to the decisions of developers and governments to locate housing in vulnerable areas. We don't control earthquakes, of course. But the buildings that are most likely to fall are the shoddy ones built by unscrupulous contractors, sanctioned through payouts to equally unscrupulous government officials, as the residents of northwestern Turkey found in 1999.

Realizations like these anger people, understandably. But more than that, they undermine our trust, not just in the security of the world, but as well our trust in each other. This is a trauma that can be especially difficult to recover from.

A New Species of Trouble

The work of Kai Erikson has helped point sociologists' attention to this trauma. Erikson studied the devastating effects of a 1972 flood on the mining communities along Buffalo Creek in the West Virginia mountains.[34] The flood that literally wiped out these small towns, and the lives of 125 people, was not solely the result of an unusually heavy rain. The local mining company, which employed someone from most households in the valley, had constructed an earthen dam at the top of the valley, so as to form a settling pond for the murky waters pumped out of the lower reaches of the mines. The dam was poorly made and poorly maintained, and one February morning it simply gave way, unleashing a coal-dust-blackened tidal wave. In a matter of 3 hours, the water scoured the 17-mile valley of its 16 villages. As one witness of that terrible morning described,

> I cannot explain that water as being water. It looked like a black ocean where the ground had opened up and it was coming in big waves and it was coming in a rolling position. If you had thrown a milk carton out in the river—that's the way the homes went out, like they were nothing. The water seemed like the demon itself. It came, destroyed, and left.[35]

What Erikson discovered in the wake of that demon flood was not a "city of comrades," the term given by earlier disaster research to describe the renewed social solidarity that sometimes results after a disaster has subsided.[36] Instead, he found what has recently been termed a "corrosive community"—a place where community itself becomes soiled, ruined, and fractured, and people flounder in a deep, unshakable malaise.[37] Central to that corrosion was the sense of betrayal the residents felt. The coal company, and some misguided relief efforts, were supposed to provide a network of social trust, the looking-out-for-one-another that helps make us all safe. Instead, the people of Buffalo Creek were left bereft of the moorings of social support that, until they are gone, we often do not recognize as essential to the stability of a self.

"A profound difference [exists]," notes Erikson, "between those disasters that can be understood as the work of nature and those that need to be understood as the work of humankind."[38] Erikson calls these human-induced disasters a "new species of trouble," and they have several characteristic and interrelated features: (1) the crumbling of trust and the shredding of community ties; (2) a chronic social trauma that victims only slowly recover from, if at all; and (3) a pervasive sense of dread about what the future brings.[39] According to Erikson, these new troubles contaminate our minds as much as they may damage our bodies. Whereas "natural" disasters suggest a lack of control over processes beyond the reach of humans, techno-logical disasters suggest a perceived *loss* of con-trol over processes thought to be within the reach of humans and our commitment to care for one another. People find this loss deeply troubling.

The element of dread, Erikson notes, is partic-ularly characteristic of disasters caused by a toxic release, such as happened in Bhopal, or in Grassy Narrows, or as many fear is ongoing with regard to pesticides in our food. (See Chapter 5.) Instead of leaving easily noticed visible damage like col-lapsed bridges and devastated homes, toxics can be more insidious. They often lurk in a realm beyond the visible and can last for generations.[40] As has been said of the Chernobyl tragedy, most of its victims are yet to be born.[41] These new traumas do not take the form of broken windows and shattered bone. We should be so lucky. Rather, they manifest as a pervasive sense of threat from what may come: birth defects, lumps within the lungs, bleeding welts on the skin, premature death.

The dread associated with even the possibility of such harm numbs the spirit and clouds a person's sense of purpose and ability to navigate life. New species of trouble, then, do not exist merely in the here and now. Rather they are something we carry with us into the future—the unwanted baggage required for riding on the airline of modernity.

Normal Accidents

While society cannot fully prevent "natural" disasters, there is a general belief that we can at least anticipate and prepare for such events, and we find a certain degree of social and psycholog-ical comfort in this.[42] Technological disasters, on the other hand, are viewed in just the opposite manner—they are understood as preventable. But there is no way to fully anticipate and prepare for some technological disasters. As the sociologist Charles Perrow notes, many of our technological systems have become simply too complicated and involved.[43]

Perrow asks us to look at technologies as sys-tems, and from two dimensions, so as to under-stand their potential for catastrophic failure. The first is the extent to which a system's interactions are *linear* or *complex*, and the second is the extent to which a system is *loosely coupled* or *tightly coupled*.

In a linear system, components are spread out, easy to segregate, substitutable, and have little feedback between each other. An example might be automobile transportation. A complex system is the reverse: components are close together, hard to pull apart or substitute, and have a lot of feedback. The classic example would be a nuclear power plant.

Coupling refers to the degree of "slack or buffer or give between two items," writes Perrow.[44] A nuclear power plant is both complex and tightly coupled. If one component fails, it may very create considerable stress on several others. A university is a complex system that is loosely coupled. If one student fails, others are unlikely to fail because of it. Mining might be another. If one shaft caves in, others are unlikely to cave in because of it. Automobile transport may be linear, but it is tightly coupled. If one dri-ver makes an error, it is likely to have immediate consequences for several other drivers, but not the whole system of drivers. An elementary

INTERACTIONS

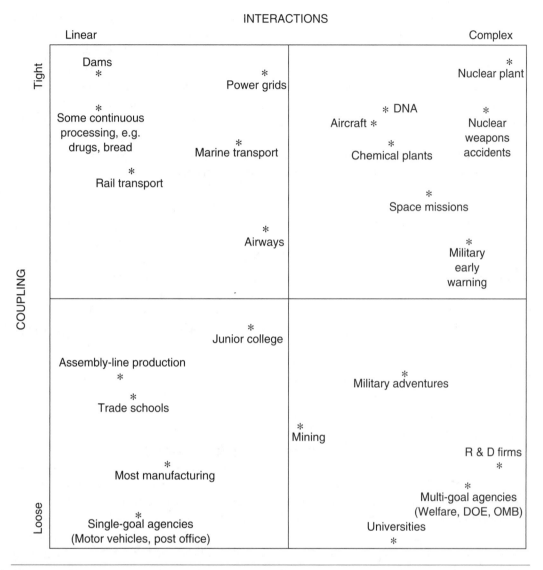

Figure 9.4   Perrow's theory of "normal accidents": Systems that are more complex and more tightly coupled will be more prone to unpredictable accidents with catastrophic potential.

school would be a linear system that is loosely coupled. It is similar to a university in its degree of coupling, but far less complex. (See Figure 9.4.)

Perrow uses this simple classification to make a profound observation. In systems that have complex and tightly coupled interactions, we should expect the occasional occurrence of a serious accident. Complex interactions confuse and confound those who try to deal with a breakdown in a system, and tight coupling gives them very little margin for error. The operators of a nuclear power plant, say, have very little time to figure out what is going on when meters start giving unusual readings, and there is little charity in the system for a mistaken interpretation. Perrow calls such events "normal accidents." Yes, they are accidental. But they are also, if not predictable, certainly unsurprising.

The fact is, no engineering manual of procedures can cover every eventuality. Even if a manual that large could be written, it would still have to be comprehended by those trying to respond to, say, two valves inadvertently left closed by a maintenance crew. A repair tag on the control panel that obscures the indicator saying the valves are closed. A pressure relief valve that subsequently fails to close when it should have. A faulty indicator that tells the control room that this valve did close when it didn't. A few operators who don't quite follow procedures.

These contingencies are precisely what let to the infamous accident at Three Mile Island. The two valves left closed prevented sufficient coolant from reaching the reactor core during a test. The operators shut down the backup cooling system too soon. The pressure relief valve left open allowed 32,000 gallons of overheated coolant to steam out of the core and into the air above the plant, carrying substantial radioactivity with it.

The governor of Pennsylvania soon made an announcement advising roughly 3,500 pregnant women and preschool children within 5 miles of the plant to evacuate the area. So what would you do, even if you weren't pregnant or a preschooler? Probably what 150,000 people did. Flee—an average of about 100 miles, apparently.[45] But that was either not far enough or not fast enough, for the region now has unusually high levels of several cancers. (See Figure 9.5.)

Perrow's reason for making this argument are several. Foremost, he wants to make a practical point: that complex, tightly coupled systems are risky. We now have a litany of examples to illustrate this point: Three Mile Island, Chernobyl, Bhopal, Toulouse, the *Challenger* accident, the *Columbia* accident, September 11. The last is a particularly troubling example from a systems theory point of view, because here we learned that two systems we thought of as separate— airplanes and skyskrapers—were not.

All of these normal accidents, and perhaps especially September 11, lead to a second observation Perrow wants us to recognize. We could use a good dose of humility with regard to our rationalist

confidence about technology. No amount of rational calculation of risk probabilities could have predicted any of these accidents. Rather than confidently calculating odds of the 1,000,000 to 1 variety in making decisions about riskiness, we need a more qualitative approach that understands accidents as a normal property of systems. Expect the unexpected, he tells us. And that should give us considerable pause with regard to systems with a high potential for catastrophic implications.

Finally, Perrow wants us to appreciate that technological systems are social systems. It is not human error on the part of operators that leads to technological disasters. Rather, it is forms of social organization—which is really what technology is, as Chapter 3 describes—that create situations where even highly trained, highly capable people are unlikely to be able to respond quickly enough, and correctly enough, to prevent a catastrophe. Thus, a technological disaster is really a *social* disaster, in two senses—a social disaster both in the organization of a dangerous situation and in its effects on us and our sense of confidence in each other.[46]

A Risk Society?

Like Dr. Frankenstein, we are in danger, so we seem increasingly to fear, of losing control of our own technological creations. We are as well losing the technological and rationalist confidence we once enjoyed, perhaps chastened by normal accidents, new species of trouble, risks that now seem less than voluntary, and other inadequacies of rational risk assessment. It is this Frankensteinian state of technological doubt and contention that the German environmental sociologist Ulrich Beck has termed a "risk society."[47]

Beck argues that Western societies are headed this way, and it is leading to a major reconfiguring of the basis of social conflict. Formerly, the central conflicts in society were class-based struggles over money and other resources. But in the risk society, conflict shifts to non-class-based struggles over pollution and other social and environmental bads.[48] In short, we in the West

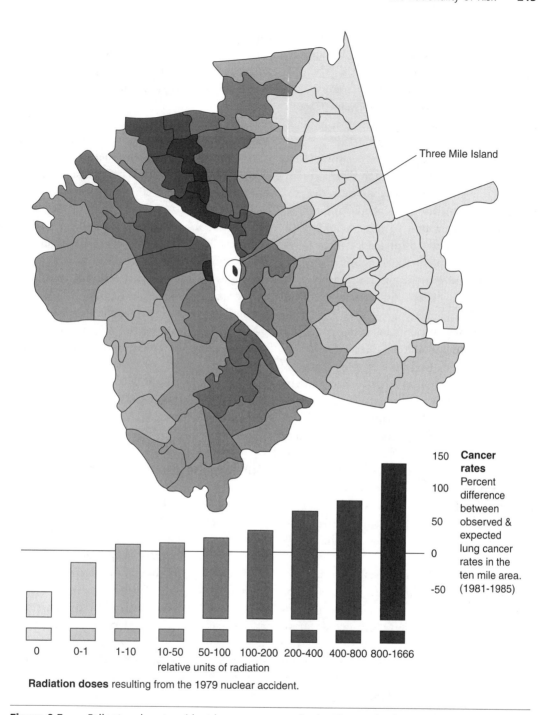

Three Mile Island

| | | | | | | | | | | 150 | **Cancer rates** |

Radiation doses resulting from the 1979 nuclear accident.

Cancer rates — Percent difference between observed & expected lung cancer rates in the ten mile area. (1981-1985)

| 0 | 0-1 | 1-10 | 10-50 | 50-100 | 100-200 | 200-400 | 400-800 | 800-1666 |

relative units of radiation

Figure 9.5   Fallout and post-accident lung cancer rates in the Three Mile Island region.

are moving, says Beck, from conflicts over the distribution of goods to conflicts over the distribution of bads.[49]

Significantly, many of the bads of modern society—pollution, technological hazards, ugly development—are hard to escape. They affect everyone. We are increasingly subject to a perverse new form of equality, an "equality of risk," as Beck calls it. In Beck's words, "The driving force in the class society can be summarized in the phrase: *I am hungry!* The movement set in motion by the risk society, on the other hand, is expressed in the statement: *I am afraid!*"[50]

Part of this fear is the public's pervasive sense that science is out of control, and that scientists are too. This sense, of course, increases the risk that people feel. It also leads people to question and doubt science. Our faith in the technological god has been shattered by pesticides in our food, by toxins in our water, by Chernobyls in our air, and by scientists in our news media who can't agree with each other. A risk society is not an optimistic society.

This shift from society's focus on "goods" to its focus on "bads" reflects a restructuring of social organization. In the words of Beck, in class society "being determines consciousness," and in risk society "consciousness (knowledge) determines being."[51] What he means is that in class society your material position—your income, your employment, your place of residence and upbringing—dominated your sense of who you were. In risk society, it is your ideas and beliefs that matter most, including worries you may have about the trustworthiness of the social and technological world. We are thus moving from a risky life to a life of risk.

Yet here Beck sees potential signs of hope. If ideas and beliefs now matter most, then maybe we can regain control over where science and technology are taking us. Maybe we can move from the modernization that was associated with class society to a new modernization, a "second modernization" that Beck terms *reflexive modernization*—a form of modernization in which we think critically and engage in democratic debate about science and technology. In Beck's words, the goal of reflexive modernization is "to break the dictatorship of laboratory science . . . by giving the public a say in science and publicly raising questions."[52] By *reflexive*, then, Beck does not mean "reflexes" or a mirror's "reflection," but

"self-confrontation" in which we collectively reflect on the meanings of modernity, science, and rationality.[53] And if we do not, we may plunge into a period of escalating fear and conflict over risk.

Indeed, risk is fast becoming global. "Risk society," says Beck, "means world risk society."[54] Yet it remains to be seen whether the global dimensions of risk result in new global coalitions or in new global conflict.

Beck's ideas have gained a lot of attention in recent years from environmental sociologists as well as political sociologists. His suggestion that risk is fundamentally reshaping the politics of our times has caused many scholars, and many politicians (at least within Germany, where Beck is from), to reconsider the significance of environmentalism. For many years, political commentators have generally viewed environmentalism as just another issue, one more demand on our political attention. If Beck is right, environmentalism is, or is fast becoming, the defining political issue of our time.

Questioning the Risk Society

Although the idea of risk society has been getting a lot of attention, it has also received considerable criticism.[55] Much of the criticism has focused on the notion of the perverse equality of risk society compared with the class inequalities of industrial society. "Poverty is hierarchic, smog democratic," Beck has written.[56] To be sure, smog affects everyone, rich and poor. So do global warming, the ozone hole, species loss, landscape destruction, pesticide residues in food, and the like. But we cannot doubt that the rich are in a far better position to avoid the worst consequences of all these threats, as Chapter 5 describes. The distribution of environmental bads (as well as environmental goods) is far from equal. It is true that even the wealthy must contend with environmental bads, and in this fact lies some hope for building political coalitions that cross the lines of race and class and nation. Still, that

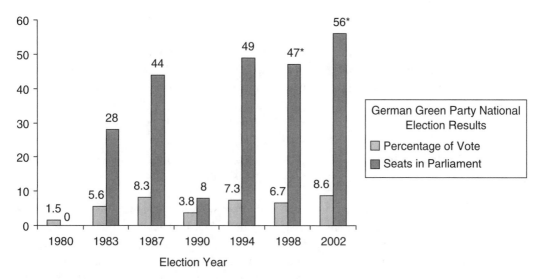

*Member of governing coalition with the Social Democratic Party

Figure 9.6   Growing strength of the German Greens: The Green Party has had a presence in the Bundestag since 1983, and has been part of the governing coalition since 1998.

doesn't mean the rich bear the risks equally with the poor. Wealth remains an important cleavage in environmental politics.[57]

Because of the way it understates this cleavage, the idea of a risk society is of little help in understanding the environmentalism of poor countries. One of the central driving forces of political conflict in poor countries originates very much from the feeling that "I am hungry." Yet poor countries nonetheless have vigorous environmental movements, as Chapter 7 discusses, just as the poor of rich countries have developed vigorous environmental movements. These movements are heavily based on class conflict— which is not to say that risk isn't involved. Disruptions in the environmental resources upon which you depend are particularly worrisome when you're poor.

Also, it may be that Beck's risk society theory fits his native Germany better than it fits most other wealthy countries.[58] The spectacular success of the German Green Party is, well, spectacular. No other country has seen the environmental agenda take such a central political role. (See Figure 9.6.) Meanwhile, environmental issues have a lower, in

some cases far lower, political profile in most other Western nations. Beck is right, though, to point to the frequent centrality of risk issues when green concerns do receive attention, such as the debate over Mad Cow Disease.

But the main difficulty with the risk society theory is that it overstates the degree to which we have overcome economic anxiety and economic conflict. In this Beck's ideas bear a close similarity with those of Inglehart and his theory of postmaterialism, also discussed in Chapter 7. Wealth creation remains the central political goal of every country in the world, rich and poor. Meanwhile, recent years have seen a great increase in economic inequality both between and within nations, reversing the equalizing trend that had prevailed during the middle decades of the twentieth century. In this, Beck seemingly ignores a persistent feature of contemporary times: People all over the world, in both rich countries and poor countries, still find themselves going to bed every night feeling "I am hungry."

But like many of the other theories discussed in the this book, the fact that risk society has attracted so much critical attention does not necessarily discredit it. Quite the reverse. Because Beck's work helps clarify so much, other scholars have worked out its implications with unusual care, sometimes uncovering problems. As I note later in the chapter, such is always the case with the best of science.

Risk and Democracy

One of the important implications of Beck's ideas is that, for all its problems, rationality is not irredeemable. It won't look the same any more if we do manage to redeem it. But there are aspects of the spirit of rationality that are not without merit. What we need is a subtler, wiser, less arrogant rationality. What we need is a rationality we can argue with, that respects the reasoning of others, and that takes those reasons into consideration when it answers with its own. What we need is, well, a *dialogic rationality.*

Part of the problem is that we long misunderstood what science was about. We thought science was about universal and permanent truths, consecrated through the perfection of method. We thought the point of science was to provide us with final answers. But final answers are the purpose of dogma, not science. Science does give us answers, but it does not give us final answers.

In other words, science is about debate and the willingness to continually refine and change one's views in the light of more observations, more experiences, and more good arguments. The truly dedicated scientist is not the one who wishes to make a discovery that will stand up for all time. If our understandings about something never changed again, this would only indicate that the topic of the "discovery" was so irrelevant to the human project that no one ever bothered to pursue the matter further. No, the most dedicated scientist is the one who most truly and fervently wants her or his research to be made out of date as quickly as possible. For if it does goes out of date, this is a sure indication that the topics and insights of the work were important enough to consider further.[59]

There is always something more to know, and something more to say. When we look to science to resolve the uncertainty of risk, we get the role of science exactly backward. Science *is* uncertainty. Thus, in a way science is risk itself. For science is a matter of answering every question and questioning every answer. It never stops. If this unfinalizable dialogue becomes what we mean by rationality, we can then perhaps recover the word from its high-handedness and exclusivity.

We have much work to do to attain that recovery, however. Currently, the all-too-common use of the language of science and rationality is to exclude others from the conversation. Science, we hear, is something that scientists do. If you are not a scientist, your views are not valid. Scientists use this rhetorical move to defend their authority, and government and business interests often call upon it too. Yet science is not something that scientists do. It is something that people do. But it is only science when they commit to engaging the views of others, to taking those views into consideration, to offering reasoned responses to them, and to being open to change in response to the evidence and arguments offered by others.

There can be *citizen scientists,* citizens who are scientists—citizens who offer reasoned evidence and arguments on scientific issues and who commit to changing their views in the face of the evidence and arguments of others.[60] Citizens can analyze evidence and even gather their own evidence in ways that avoid the known mishaps of method, a practice sometimes called "popular epidemiology."[61] There can be *scientist citizens,* scientists who are citizens—scientists who respect and respond to the reasoned views of the public, and who engage the concerns of the public in their work. And citizen scientists and scientist citizens can work together, and indeed increasingly do so through the practice of *participatory research* in which citizens and scientists form a common research team.[62]

It is here that the democratic potential of rationality lies. What might make risk assessment democratic is not the assumption of a universal perspective. Once again, it is the reverse. What might make risk assessment democratic is a willingness to engage a universe of *perspectives,* plural.

The Dialogue of Risk

But in order to get this dialogue of risk going, we're going to have to greatly improve our communication with one another. And unfortunately, there are powerful social interests who frequently and deliberately stand in the way.

Take the example of the famous *Oprah* episode on Mad Cow Disease, with which I began this chapter. Shortly after Oprah made her rather offhand remark about never eating another hamburger, she found herself served with a libel suit by the Texas Cattlemen's Association for defaming their product. The Cattlemen claimed that the bottom fell out of the cattle market immediately following Oprah's declaration about burgers, causing a 10 percent drop in cattle futures. Moreover, in 1995, Texas became one of an eventual 13 states to pass "food disparagement" statutes that provided restrictive libel standards for anyone stating in public that a particular food product was unsafe. Under such laws, it is not entirely clear that the first President Bush would have been clear of being libelous when he stated in 1990, "I'm President of the United States and I'm not going to eat any more broccoli."[63]

So the Cattlemen took Oprah to court, twice, and lost both times. Upon emerging from court victorious, Oprah declared, "Free speech not only lives, it rocks!"[64] But by the time it was all over in 2000, Oprah had spent more than $1 million defending herself.[65] The Cattlemen had made their point. If you're going to say anything bad about food in public, you had better have the funds at hand for a substantial legal battle. SLAPPs—strategic lawsuits against public participation—is what the environmental sociologist Penelope Canan and her colleague George Pring call this practice, and not without reason.[66] Such is increasingly the price of free speech.

Scientists researching environmental risk also sometimes have to face off with corporations in order to communicate their work to the public. Corporations can wield considerable influence in the government agencies that fund much scientific work, and have used that influence to suppress the publication of findings and to control the work that gets funded to begin with. James Zahn was an award-winning swine researcher at the U.S. Department of Agriculture's Agricultural Research Service, and worked in an Iowa lab on issues of pollution from hog confinements. Zahn's research found that air emissions from hog confinements contained antibiotic-resistant strains of bacteria that might threaten human health. Hog farming industry groups soon found about the research—Zahn wasn't trying to hide it—and put pressure on Zahn's superiors at the lab to put the findings in the deep freeze. They complied. They told Zahn he could not submit the work for publication in a scientific journal, nor could he speak in public about it. The results eventually did get around by word of mouth, and the story eventually hit the papers late in 2002. But by that time Zahn had quit the lab in frustration and had taken another job in another state. At this writing, the research still has not been published.[67]

During this controversy, it emerged that the U.S. Department of Agriculture for some time has been maintaining a list of "controversial" research topics that require permission from the department's Washington office before funding for them can be approved. (The department amended the list specially to include Zahn's work, he believes.) The *Des Moines Register,* the leading daily paper in Iowa, requested to see this list, and reported that it "appears to require special permission to study anything involving agricultural pollution of air, water or soil."[68] Such work can still be funded, but the delay of the special permission requirement makes it harder to meet grant application deadlines, and discourages scientists from investing time in a research topic that might not be approved. Scientists need to publish research to keep their jobs, and practices like these encourage them to choose safe topics—which in this day and age increasingly means topics that do not offend corporate interests.

Zahn's case was not an isolated incident, as other examples from agricultural and food research show. James Russell, a USDA researcher at Cornell University, had to abandon some of his research after his department was pressured by industry interests and by other researchers associated with those interests. And it was the mildest of findings. Russell had found that if cattle are fed hay instead of grain in the days before they are slaughtered, *E. coli* contamination in the meat was reduced. Such a finding suggests that *E. coli* contamination can occur in meat (which is widely documented) and that confinement feeding operations, which rely on grain for the feed, are part of the problem.[69] So the pressure for suppression was soon on.

Then there's the case of North Carolina State University professor JoAnn Burkholder, who found that hog confinement operations in North Carolina had polluted a stream with 15,000 times the legal limit of bacteria. That's *15,000* times the limit. In 1997 she publicized her findings so parents would know to keep their children from playing in the stream. Her university was soon flooded with requests from agricultural interests for her dismissal. She even received death threats.[70]

It only takes a few stories like this to scare researchers and thus have a far broader effect. But perhaps the most controversial is the "Pusztai affair," the case of the British scientist Arpád Pusztai, who lost his job in 1998 after speaking in public—with permission from his superiors—about his rat feeding studies of genetically modified potatoes. Using a specific kind of genetically modified potatoes (which had been modified with a gene from snowdrop flowers), he found that rats fed on them developed shrunken internal organs, had their immune system depressed, and grew more slowly.[71] Pusztai's research was eventually published in the respected British medical journal *Lancet,* but amid the storm of a parliamentary inquiry, a critical review of his work

by the British Royal Society, and reports of a threatening phone call to the editor of *Lancet* for having published the paper.[72] All this for some modest, tentative, preliminary findings that had negative implications for powerful corporate interests.

Dialogue and the Precautionary Principle

Censorship and intimidation are hardly conducive to dialogic rationality concerning risk. We need to encourage debate, but debate that engages each others' views, rather than ignoring them, silencing them, or shouting them down. This is particularly the case in situations of uncertainty and disagreement concerning potential harm.

The global debate over GMOs is a good example. Many people see the prospect of genetically modified crops with considerable alarm; many do not. Many find themselves somewhere in between, with concerns about transgenetic crops—that is, crops that involve genes from different species—but tolerable comfort with genetic modification that stays within a plant's hereditary genome. Some find studies like Pusztai's disquieting. Some find comfort in studies with GMO-friendly results. Some are puzzled over the contradictory findings and don't know what to think.

In response to situations like these, a number of scientists, government officials, environmental advocates, and even corporate executives have begun promoting the *precautionary principle.* In January 1998, 32 representatives from Canada, Europe, and the United States gathered at the Wingspread Conference Center in Racine, Wisconsin, to draft the Wingspread Statement on the Precautionary Principle. The statement defines the precautionary principle as follows:

> When an activity raises threats of harm to human health or the environment, precautionary measures should be taken even if some cause and effect relationships are not fully established scientifically.[73]

The British mathematician Peter Saunders, an advocate of the principle, puts it more plainly:

> All it actually amounts to is this: if one is embarking on something new, one should think very carefully about whether it is safe or not, and should not go ahead until reasonably convinced it is. It is just common sense.[74]

Look before you leap. Think before you act. And, most important, talk things out with others.

We'll need some time to do that, of course, which is the controversial aspect of the precautionary principle—especially for corporations eager to start getting a return on their investment in research and development. Some people will never be satisfied, critics of precaution respond. It's just a delaying tactic. Such an attitude, though, betrays the social commitment to dialogic rationality—to genuinely engaging the points brought up by others—for it implies that the impatient party has already made up her or his mind about who is right: me.

With regard to GMOs, many prominent scientific, professional, and governmental bodies have suggested that precaution is just what is needed. Has the debate proceeded far enough already? The journal *Lancet* in a 2002 editorial stated, no, "Consumers are probably right to be sceptical at present."[75] The British Medical Association advocates a moratorium on the introduction of genetically modified crops until more is known. The World Health Organization takes a more moderate position, stating that because "GM organisms contain different genes inserted in different ways," their "safety should be assessed on a case-by-case basis."[76]

Of course, at some point we have to make a decision before everything is known and everything is said. That's because everything will never be known and everything will never be said. And to this role we rightfully look to the decision-making power of government. But let's stop and talk about it first, at length, honestly, freely, and with respect for what others have to say.

Trust and the Dialogue of Risk

How do we get the dialogue of risk going? One thing is for sure, comments like the following from the U.S. Environmental Protection Agency's *Handbook for Environmental Risk Decision Making* don't help: "The bottom line is that our society is like a bunch of spoiled brats who want an affluent lifestyle based on a throwaway society, supplied by synthetic chemistry and risk free at the same time."[77] Nor does it help when the CEO of a mid-sized company proclaims the importance of "managing fear" and of "finding a way to help the public manage its growing anguish and still accomplish our business objectives."[78] Belittling the public is not the way to engage others in open, democratic dialogue.

No, what we need to repair most of all is a sense of *trust*, if we are to build a dialogic rationality of risk.[79] For knowledge is a social process. Most of what we know we learned, at least in part, from others. It has to be that way. Who has time in this life to experience the whole world? Do you need to eat a poisonous mushroom yourself to believe that it is bad for you? Do you need to do the lab tests yourself to suspect that dioxin is carcinogenic? Do you need to have lived in the deposition zone from Chernobyl or Three Mile Island or Bhopal to consider it awful to live with the dread of a chemical-time bomb ticking away inside you? No, you don't. But you need a basis for trusting the reports of others about all of these things.

The best way to build that trust is when people are open to questions that probe their reports of their experiences in the outdoors, in the lab, in their towns, in their families, in their own bodies—and when they are open to any considered reasons others might have for disagreeing. That doesn't mean we all have to agree. That doesn't mean that there cannot be uncertainty. For perfect agreement and certainty would lead us back to dogma, not science. And no one should trust dogma. Rather, trust should be about a willingness to disagree and debate and still retain a sense of social connection—a willingness to keep the conversation going, always open to further news, further ideas, further perspectives brought into our lives, and a confidence that others will have the same willingness.

Risk in the sense of uncertainty, then, can never be finally resolved. Nor should we try, for this is the paradox of risk: To seek its final resolution is to give up on the surest means we have for dealing with its consequences.

PART III

The Practical

CHAPTER 10

Organizing the Ecological Society

There is no wealth but life.

—John Ruskin, 1863

I own a car. I admit it. And I often use it. I live in an 1,850-square-foot house with four bedrooms, plus two bathrooms. It is not a solar house. We also own a share in a vacation house on the St. Lawrence River. My family owns a washing machine, a television, a stereo system, an answering machine, several phones, three clock radios, and two laptop computers. I own nine pairs of footwear of various sorts; nevertheless I just bought another pair. Our closet is filled with clothes we rarely wear, and yet we buy more. We have loads of books. I'm a semi-pro musician on the side, so we have a small orchestra of musical instruments, including a piano. We also have a range of shop and yard tools, bicycles for everyone in the family, a kitchen full of dishes and cookware, and a house worth of furniture. We moved to a new state recently, and the bill of lading from the moving company came to about 12,000 pounds. Plus, at the vacation home there is another houseful of furniture, another collection of tools, and another collection of dishes

and cookware—not to mention seven boats of various sorts, a pile of recreational gear, and a boathouse to fit them all during the summer and an old barn to store them all during the winter. That's a lot of stuff, an awful lot of stuff. And we have two children.

So how could I fancy to call myself an environmentalist—let alone an environmental sociologist?

There are a few things I could point to in my defense. My wife and I do own only one car, a 1995 used model. (We recently sold our previous car, an 18-year-old one. Reuse is as environmentally important as recycling and reduction.) We've been averaging 8,200 miles a year of late, 4,100 per driver, well below the U.S. average of 13,673 annual miles per driver.[1] We bicycle to work (it's about 2 miles each way for both of us), and we bike for most of our shopping, even in winter (which gets pretty forbidding in Wisconsin, where we now live). We made sure to buy a house in a location that was relatively convenient for bicycling, and also for getting around by bus when the weather is bad. Although we own a washing machine, we use a solar-powered clothes drier in the summer—a clothesline, that is— and a line strung across the basement in the winter. The television lives in the closet. It's just an old 17-inch model we picked up at a yard sale once. (You can't even hook cable to it.) We've watched it once in the past year, as far as I can recall. The kids can use the TV whenever they want to, but they're not much interested in it. As it's not out in a room, they don't think of it often. They easily enough find amusement in other ways.

Let's see . . . what else? We have no microwave oven, no cell phone, no VCR, no camcorder. There was a dishwasher already installed in our new house, but we hardly ever use it—once a month at most, if we've had a lot of company over. There was also central air conditioning installed, like almost every home in our neighborhood. But we've used it only once in the year and a half we've lived here, for about an hour, again when we had some company over. (It was a hot day and we were hosting a reception. Besides, we did think it a good idea to make sure it still works, should we ever decide to sell our house.) We keep no cupboard or closet full of household poisons. We grow some of our own vegetables during the summer, all organically, and we mow our small lawn, which is also organic, with a manual reel mower. We compost all our leaves, garden waste, and kitchen waste. The previous owners of the house installed a "rain garden" to promote infiltration and groundwater recharge, thus lessening the storm water and pollution load on the beleaguered lake in the park near our house. (The sewers for our neighborhood all dump into that poor little lake.) We use energy efficient light bulbs almost everywhere in the house, and we're very good about turning them off when a room's not in use. Our furnace is a high-efficiency model, and during the heating season we keep the thermostat at 62 degrees Fahrenheit for the day and 56 degrees Fahrenheit when we go to bed and when we're out, although we sometimes bump it up a degree or two in the evenings. All told, we use about 285 kilowatt hours of electricity a month, less than half of the 624 average for all households in Madison, Wisconsin, our city.[2] Considering that my household size is almost

double the Madison average of 2.19, we use about 25 percent as much electricity per person as the average local resident does. And we pay an extra fee with our local utility to support the small wind farm they've bought into. Our gas use is quite low; our local utility puts us in their "excellent" category in terms of BTUs of gas use per square foot. Although we do have a lot of books, as well as a few CDs, we've pretty much stopped buying them now. We use the library instead. (We pop down to our local branch several times a week.) We're avid recyclers too. We produce about a paper shopping bag of non-recyclable garbage a week, which isn't bad for an American family of four. And we aren't having any more kids.

I'm not a complete sinner, I think, but I'm certainly no environmental saint either. According to an online "ecological footprint" analysis I worked through once, my footprint is 16 biologically productive acres, in comparison with the U.S. average of 24. Not bad, huh? But according to footprint analysts, there are only 4.5 biologically productive acres per person on the planet. If everyone lived like I do, we'd need 3.6 planets, the site informed me.[3] So, am I just another environmental hypocrite, big on the guilt trip and fairly small on action, mostly talk and little walk?

From a certain political perspective, yes. As that is a perspective I share—the perspective of the committed environmental moralist—my environmental inadequacies often pain me deeply. Yet from a sociological perspective, my situation does not necessarily indicate some deep personal moral failing. In fact, to the extent that my situation is typical of others, it represents some important opportunities for social and environmental change. It suggests the possibility of collective action toward making a society that more closely resembles what we say we want it to be. And indeed, the overwhelming majority of the public in both rich nations and poor are concerned about the environment, even though very few could be said to have yet put that concern into full action. This concluding chapter considers these opportunities for change, closing the dialogic circle of the material and the ideal—or perhaps, better put, opening it up—with a focus on the practical implications of environmental sociology.

The A-B Split

Social psychologists have long noted that there is often a sharp disjunction between what people profess to value and believe and how they really act.[4] The *A-B split*, as it is sometimes called, standing for "attitude-behavior split," is a characteristic that probably all of us share, at least to some degree. Often people consciously recognize some of these inconsistencies. We work to adjust the behavior side to fit our attitudes, and sometimes, social psychologists find, we work to adjust our attitudes to fit our behaviors. These adjustments also go on unconsciously. One classic example of this process is the way 1960s radicals often became more conservative when they started raising families and entered the world of business. They found themselves taking on the very attitudes—and enacting the very behaviors—that they had been in the streets protesting a decade or two earlier.

But the point of the A-B split is not to suggest that these 1960s radicals are therefore hypocrites. Nor necessarily are all the rest of us who have adjusted what we believe to what we do, or who have gone on doing things that in fact do not fit what we believe. It is very hard to maintain a conscious sense of an A-B split. Such inconsistency strikes at the very core of our identity, our sense of who we are. Understandably, people tend to avoid conscious recognition of an ideological mismatch, if they can. But often they can't, and they try to adjust their lives and their thinking accordingly—which is also hard. In other words, an A-B split is a source of internal struggle and conflict. Contrary to the image of the complacent hypocrite, such a split is hardly something about which most people feel comfortable.

The sociological point here is that one of the main reasons people find their attitudes at odds with their behaviors (and often find themselves adjusting those attitudes to fit or putting the conflict out of their mind as much as possible) is social structure.[5] We do not have complete choice in what we do. Our lives are *socially organized,* with all the constraints that this implies. I own a car and use a car because the automobile-based planning of the past 50 years has led to the scattering of businesses, shopping, schools, parks, and homes. Our city has, for the United States, a pretty good system of bike paths, and an okay bus system. But they can't make up for the structured inconvenience of sprawl, so I often feel strongly pressured to use my car.

Social organization, however, also presents us with opportunities. When we as a community consider our collective attitudes and our collective behaviors—when we consider the ideal and the material implications of the current arrangement of our social and ecological lives—we have an opportunity to reconsider them as well. The social organization of our communities may be a large part of our problems, but the *social reorganization* of our communities can be a large part of the solutions. We can create new social structures, new constraining influences that shape and guide our lives.

Social structures are not necessarily bad things. It depends on what they guide us into doing. Social structures do not necessarily create the A-B split (or what is really an ideal-material split). Properly rearranged, properly reconsidered, social structures can help heal the splits in our communities—including that biggest community of all, the environment of which we are (thankfully, I say) an inescapable part.

Virtual Environmentalism

But it's never easy.[6] People are busy, terribly busy, caught as we are on the treadmills of production and consumption. Although we are surrounded by modernity's supposed inducements of choice and leisure, modernity equally induces us into a treadmill-driven rush from home to work to the point that work becomes home. And when we come home—late, probably—we're still in such a rush that what we do at home becomes work, as the sociologist Arlie Hochschild observes.[7] The supper has to be cooked, the dishes done, the children put to bed, the toys picked up, the floor swept, the clothes washed, and the bills paid.

When work becomes home and home becomes work, daily decisions have to be made fast. This isn't going to change soon. And if being an environmentalist means a lot of extra thought about the consequences of each act of consumption, if it means delaying buying decisions for days or weeks or months while you track down suppliers of environmentally friendly products, then daily decisions are unlikely to be made with the environment in mind. Environmentalism on these terms is unlikely to become a significant part of everyday life in a modern world. Our daily experience is too full already.

What we need, then, is what might be termed *virtual environmentalism*—environmentalism you don't have to think about because you just find yourself doing it anyway. Virtual environmentalism is environmentalism that lies behind and beneath our daily lives. Like environmentalism in the usual sense, virtual environmentalism is taking your bicycle to work, buying food produced with sustainable production methods, replacing old appliances with energy efficient ones, and using less heating, cooling, construction materials, and water. But virtual environmentalism means doing these things not because you've made a conscious decision to be environmentally good today, but because they were the cheapest and most convenient things to do. Virtual environmentalism is being environmentally good without having to be environmentally good.

I think it is safe to say that virtual environmentalism is a lot more likely to be popular with the general public than environmentalism by guilt, cajoling, shaming, issuing court summons, imposing fines, and locking offenders in jail. But it will only become popular if we change the structures of the cheap and the convenient by reorganizing the social organization of production and consumption. Environmental problems are problems of society, and problems of society require social solutions.

Social reorganization usually requires a terrific effort. But when you do reorganize society, you've really done something, something lasting and important—precisely *because* it is so hard to do. If social reorganization were easy, it probably wouldn't be social reorganization at all. But it can be done. And it is done, all the time. But you have to do it. We can become environmental without trying—but only if we try.

The Problem of Collective Action

What it takes is cooperation. One does not need to consider the matter closely, however, to recognize that human groups very often fail to act for the collective good.

The Tragedy of the Commons

The biologist Garret Hardin, in a famous 1968 article, "The Tragedy of the Commons," described the problem in stark terms. Imagine you are a shepherd grazing your sheep on your village's common pastureland, back in the hills above the village. As a member of the village, you have the right to graze your sheep there, just as every other village member does. You've got only 10 sheep, though, and after a while you think, "Well, I'd be a bit better off if I added a few more to my flock." Meanwhile, your fellow villagers are thinking the same thing about their own flocks. Pretty soon, as everyone adds a few more animals, there are a lot more sheep in the common pastureland.

The pastureland is only so big, though. Eventually overgrazing occurs. The grass cover gets thin, and the land starts to erode. Everybody's sheep start to die. You wind up with fewer sheep than you began with, and the eroded common land is no longer capable of supporting as many sheep as it originally could: economic and environmental disaster.

Here's how Hardin, rather melodramatically, described the situation:

> The inherent logic of the commons remorselessly generates tragedy. . . . The rational herdsman concludes that the only sensible course for him to pursue is to add another animal to his herd. And another; and another. . . . But this is the conclusion reached by each and every rational herdsman sharing a commons. Therein is the tragedy. Each man is locked into a system that compels him to increase his herd without limit—in a world that is limited. Ruin is the destination toward which all men rush, each pursuing his own best interest in a society that believes in the freedom of the commons.[8]

Hardin intended this parable as a master allegory for all environmental problems. Three examples he mentions in the article are traffic, pollution, and overfishing. Think of streets as a kind of commons, something we all collectively own—which, in fact, they are. As a member of the community, I am free to drive on my city's streets as much as I want. But what if everybody decides to get about this way? The result is traffic jams, smog, and the loss of alternatives as mass transit shuts down.

Or think of the lake where your summer cabin sits as a kind of commons. It's expensive to put in a good septic system, and it wouldn't hurt you much to flush into a shallow leaching field close to the water's edge where, as it happens, it would be the cheapest and easiest place to put the field. The lake is pretty big, and it can handle a little bit of pollution. Besides, it would be hard for anyone to determine that you're the one with the shallow leaching field close to the shoreline. Lots of cabins ring the lake. But what if everybody on the lake did what you're doing?

The oceans are a commons too. If I fish for a living, I might as well cast as big a net as I can.

What I do myself won't have that much effect on overall fish stocks. Anyway, the other fishers are probably going to do the same, right? And soon the fish are gone.

Hardin's analysis is far from perfect, as I come to in a moment. But it is hard to ignore the fact that traffic jams are on the rise. In 1996, for example, there was a spectacular traffic jam in central London—8 hours of gridlock, involving an estimated 250,000 cars.[9] Smog is also up worldwide, and mass transit is down. Many recreational lakes have been badly polluted by their users. Fishing stocks are in terrible shape in many parts of the oceans and have simply collapsed in the Grand Banks and Georges Bank, leaving hundreds of fishing communities from Newfoundland to New England economically devastated.

These are all examples of a more general class of circumstances, what social scientists call the *problem of collective action:* In a world of self-interested actors, how can we get people to cooperate for their own benefit? Individual actors pursuing their rational self-interest often lead us to irrational collective outcomes that in fact undermine the interests of those who enact them. The result is a striking paradox of social life: We often do not act in our own interests when we act in our own interests. Or, to put it another way, when we all do what we want, it often leads to outcomes nobody wants.

Why It Really Isn't as Bad as All That

Hardin's account of the "tragedy of the commons" remains one of the most discussed theories in environmental sociology, even 30 years after it was written. The phrase "tragedy of the commons" is familiar to many in the general populace. Academics regularly employ it in analyses. In a quick search of the databases at my university library, for example, I found dozens of recent academic articles that discussed the concept. In as specialized a realm as academia, this is a lot. Several of these articles extend the allegory of the commons far beyond environmental concerns, applying it to analyses of management-employee relations, prisons, and political action committees.[10]

Much of the reason for the continuing attention, though, is to point out how spectacularly oversimplified and overstated Hardin's allegory is and how it diverts attention from some fundamental social processes at work in environmental problems.[11]

To begin with, Hardin seemed to blame common ownership of resources for the tragedy. But in fact, we can find countless examples of highly successful use of commons for resource management. Grazing lands all across Africa, Asia, and South America; traditional systems of fisheries management in India and Brazil; even the private homes of modern families, which are a kind of commons in miniature and remain a highly popular form of social arrangement—these are just a few of the many examples of generally successful commons management.[12] Indeed, common ownership is the primary way that people have managed their affairs for centuries. And it has, at least until recent years, largely worked.[13]

Rather than the tragedy of the commons, Hardin's allegory is better characterized as the tragedy of individualism. For what breaks down Hardin's commons is not collective ownership itself but rather the inability (and perhaps unwillingness) of the herders to take a view wider than their own narrowly conceived self-interests.

Herders, in fact, are unlikely to conceive of their interests so narrowly, at least in traditional commons. For one thing, Hardin assumes that no one will notice the overgrazing until it is too late. But herders out there in the pasture every day with their sheep are likely very quickly to note the deteriorating condition of the grass. For another thing, Hardin assumes that the herders do not communicate with one another. More likely, as soon as the herders notice the beginnings of overgrazing, they will walk over to each other's houses in the village and have a few words about the situation. They will likely convene a gathering of some sort to try to work out an arrangement that restores the grass, while following local norms about the number of sheep each herder is fairly entitled to graze.

More significant, however, is the reliance of Hardin's allegory on a rational-choice view of human motivation. People are, simply put, more complex—and thankfully so. We are moved by more than our own narrowly conceived self-interests, as Chapters 2 and 9 described. Equally important are the sentiments—the norms, the feelings of affection and lack of affection for others—we have in social life. These sentiments are a crucial aspect not only of our humanity but, as we shall see, of our interests as well.

The Dialogue of Solidarities, or, Why the Lion Spared Androcles

Let's hear instead from Aesop, the ancient Greek storyteller, who used to tell quite a different allegory from that of the tragedy of the commons: the story of "Androcles and the Lion."[14] It's been a familiar tale to children from Western cultures for over two thousand years—I used to tell it to my own children when they were young—and with good reason, for it expresses some home truths that parents have long thought we would do well to recognize. In case you've forgotten this classic fable (or somehow never encountered it), let me retell it here.[15]

A slave named Androcles escapes from his cruel master and runs away into the forest. As he's walking through the woods, Androcles comes upon a lion, who is roaring loudly. Androcles is scared, but he notices that there's a nail stuck in one of the lion's paws. So he cautiously comes up to the lion, takes the lame paw in his hands, and pulls out the nail. And rather than eating him, the thankful lion suggests that they hunt together, using the lion's teeth and claws, and Androcles's hands and wit. The arrangement works well, and they grow fond of each other, living together for many years.

But they're a little careless one day, and some of the Emperor's men capture them both and lead them away to the Coliseum. In those days before television, people enjoyed going to the Coliseum to watch lions eat defenseless captives, and to watch other gruesome sports. Androcles and the lion are to be used for this unhappy purpose.

On the day of the event, great excitement fills the air. Even the Emperor is there. After all, it's good for your opinion poll numbers to be seen putting on a satisfyingly bloody Coliseum show. (OK, so that bit wasn't the way I used to tell it to my kids.) Tension mounts as the preliminary acts—foot races, weight lifting, gladiator fights—are held. Finally, Androcles is thrown into the ring, naked and unarmed. The lion, who has been starved for days, is also released into the ring. "With a terrible roar, he bounded toward the poor slave," is how our favorite version tells the story.[16]

At first, so hungry is the lion that he does not recognize Androcles. But as he approaches Androcles, he sees who it is. The lion lies down in front of Androcles and makes soft mewing sounds.

The Emperor is astonished. He asks to have Androcles brought over to his viewing platform so he can question him. Androcles explains the strange history of his friendship with the lion. The crowd roars its approval. The Emperor thinks for a moment, does a mental poll, and then proclaims, "Release him, and release the lion. Let them go free." The lion returns to the forest, and so does Androcles. After all, even though he is now free, Androcles has no education, money, relatives, or friends. Androcles and the lion live out the rest of their days together, the closest of companions.

As the story traditionally concludes, "And so we learn that no act of kindness is ever wasted."[17]

The above is not the usual sort of evidence that sociologists draw upon, but nonetheless let me try a bit of analysis of the home truths Aesop tries to get across to us. To begin with, why did the lion spare Androcles in the ring? At that moment the lion could have had no idea that refusing to eat his former partner would result in freedom. Indeed, the Coliseum operators might

have decided to kill this apparently hopeless lion for failing to put on a good show. (Coliseum operators were like that.)

And why did Androcles initially pull the nail from the lion's paw? At that moment Androcles could have had no idea that pulling the nail would result in his gaining a friend and hunting partner. (Hunting partnerships between humans and lions are, after all, rather unusual.) And neither could he know that they would eventually be able to return to the forest to live out their days together.

The reason was, according to Aesop, that the lion and Androcles were moved by more than narrow calculations of their own pure self-interest. They were moved as well by their sentiments: Androcles for a lion in pain, and the lion for a friend and former companion; Androcles for reasons of commitment to certain norms of behavior, and the lion for reasons of friendship, of affective commitment. These sentimental commitments in turn led—and this is a crucial point of criticism of the rational-actor model described in the tragedy of the commons—to the promotion of their interests, *although they could not know that at the time*. In other words, sentiments may promote interests but do not reduce to them.

At the same time, interests promote sentiments. A large part of the reason Androcles and the lion liked each other is that, beginning with Androcles's act of pulling the nail and extending through the lion's refusal to eat Androcles, they had learned to rely on each other to promote each other's interests. Because they helped each other out, they liked each other and shared a sense of commitment to common norms of social behavior. And because they liked each other and shared a commitment to common norms, they helped each other out. The story is thus another example of a dialogue, this time what I like to call the *dialogue of solidarities*. (See Figure 10.1.)

I use the plural because this dialogue is based on the interaction between two mutually supporting bases for social commitment: a *solidarity*

Figure 10.1   The dialogue of solidarities.

of interests and a *solidarity of sentiments*. The interests of both Androcles and the lion were served through their relationship. But as well, they sensed the existence of sentimental ties—affection and common norms—between them. And the one constantly shaped and maintained the other.

All this emphasis on sentiment may sound a little idealistic, the kind of rare altruism we sometimes hear about in stories, or, as in this case, in an ancient fable. But sentiment is actually quite common—and quite necessary—in social relationships, at least those that endure across time and space.

Consider, for example, a domestic union of some kind, two recent college graduates perhaps. They each have interests, such as careers. They support each other through graduate school. They make their job choices with the other partner's interests in mind. They manage their home

in ways that allow each to succeed at work. And thus they maintain a solidarity of interests.

However, there are always time delays involved in reciprocal and cooperative action. How does one partner know that the other will come through when it is the other partner's turn to make a career sacrifice? There are also always issues of space in reciprocal and cooperative action. The two domestic partners cannot keep each other under constant surveillance. How does each know that the other can be relied upon to coordinate shopping, to maintain monogamy (if the union is based on that understanding), to cover for each other when situations require it?

The answer is *trust*. This trust can exist because each believes the relationship to be based upon more than the narrow calculation of self-interests. Because each has affection for the other or because each has a sense of common commitment to common norms of interaction—or both—they can trust that the other will come through across the isolating reaches of time and space. Without this sense of trust that a solidarity of sentiments gives, no solidarity of interests can last long.

The process works the other way too. The persistence of a solidarity of interests is one of the principal ways that each partner comes to sense real affection and common normative commitment on the part of the other. If one partner violates that trust by not looking out for the other's interests, chances are, frankly, that pretty soon they won't like each other anymore, nor have faith that they share some crucial norms. Trust is the essential glue of both a solidarity of interests and a solidarity of sentiments.

So, to return finally to the tragedy of the commons, one of the main reasons why herders on a commons have usually managed to keep from overgrazing the pastures is that *they trust each other*. These are their neighbors, after all, and likely their kinfolk too. These are the people they relax with, dance with, worship with, and marry. Of course, villages sometimes fall into considerable internal conflict, and when they do, those sentimental ties may go. If so, the grass on the pastures will likely go too.[18]

The dialogue of solidarities is a kind of ecologic dialogue, a constant and mutually constituting interaction between the realm of the material (a solidarity of interests) and the realm of the ideal (a solidarity of sentiments). From this dialogue emerge solidarities of solidarities, if you will, within families, organizations, businesses, neighborhoods, villages, towns, cities, counties, provinces, states, nations, species, ecosystems, and all other kinds of commons. What I mean is, from this dialogue emerges *community*.

A Tale of Two Villages

Or so my colleague Peggy Petrzelka found in the Atlas Mountains of Morocco, home of the Imazighen people, who are more widely known as the Berber.[19] (*Imazighen* is the name they prefer.) Along the Imdrhas River Valley lie two villages, some 13 kilometers apart: Tilmi and M'semrir. It's not great cropland, and the Imazighen in the area have traditionally relied on grazing sheep and goats for income and sustenance. It's not great grazing land either, however. The land is steep and the climate is dry. So local villages use what they call the *agdal* system of collective management of the grazing lands, which have traditionally been held almost entirely in common.

Under *agdal*, grazing schedules and any disputes are worked out through a local representative council of herders, known as the *jemaa*. The head of the *jemaa* is called the *Amghrar*, and he (it is always a he) is elected by the local villagers. If signs of overgrazing start showing up, or if there's been a particularly dry spell, the *jemaa* will close certain areas of the commons to allow regeneration. The *nuadar*, two men from each village, are selected annually to keep watch on the commons to make sure that the guidelines of the *jemaa* are being followed. If someone violates the guidelines, they may be forced to pay an *izma*, a penalty. When fence repair, harvesting, or other work needs to be done, the villagers organize *touiza*—communal work teams. It's a system that has worked for centuries.

Has worked. Peggy, who speaks Arabic, got a chance to live for most of a year in the area, during the course of a fellowship. She soon noted what many in the area now frequently complain about: that in M'semrir, the *agdal* system is breaking down. The grass looks bad. Stocking rates are double what they should be. Violators are getting away without paying *izmas*. Much of the land has been privatized. Some people seem to be getting quite a bit richer, and satellite TV dishes have sprouted from a number of rooftops. *Touiza* is disappearing. People are scared of the *Amghrar*. The *jemaa* is increasingly an in-group who distribute grazing rights to each other and their friends. People are angry with each other.

But in Tilmi, the grass still looks good. Stocking rates are just what they should be. Very little of the traditional commons land has been privatized. The *jemaa* distributes grazing rights in ways that everyone Peggy spoke with found generally equitable. *Touiza* is still going strong. There are very few satellite dishes. When they disagree with him, Tilmi residents tell the *Amghrar* to his face. That's because they like him, and are confident that he likes them, even when there are disagreements. Which there aren't very often, because people in Tilmi still like each other.

In fact, the people in Tilmi like each so much that they dance together. A lot. It may sound romantic, but most evenings when the weather is fine and the work is done, a group of villagers gets together to sing and dance in the village center. When there are family celebrations—a wedding, a circumcision—virtually the entire village attends, and the dancing can go on for days, and until 2 or 3 in the morning. And they sing when they practice *touiza,* helping each other harvest their personal garden plots, or as they repair the road or clear snow. All this astounded Peggy. Yes, it may sound romantic, because it is romantic. But it is also what they really do.

In M'semrir, however, people don't dance much anymore. There may be a bit at family celebrations, but the whole village is no longer invited. Just close family and friends. In Tilmi, weddings are usually held together during the same season of the year, and the brides walk through the village together amid the throwing of dates, almonds, and figs from the roofs of the grooms' houses to the crowds below. But in M'semrir, weddings are individual and scattered throughout the year, and the rich and festive foods are thrown only to the guests.

Peggy went for a walk one day with Amina, a woman from M'semrir, up into the hills above the village. They paused for a rest on a high rock, overlooking M'semrir and the Imdrhas Valley below. They got to talking about changing traditions in M'semrir.

"We used to gather everyone and had one big party—now everyone has their own tradition," Amina remarked.

She pointed out what used to be the communal property, now divided into small private plots.

"*Nizha,*" she said to Peggy, "the words of today are not like the words of yesterday, and that which we did early is not that which we do today."

Why, then, this difference between the two villages? The Moroccan government has been working hard to "develop" the local economy, trying to increase the nation's productivity and also people's personal incomes. So they've developed regional market centers, and have begun promoting tourism. They have also promoted privatizing much of the communal land, figuring that production would go up. But in the rugged terrain of the Atlas Mountains, it's harder to bring "development" to the more remote villages. M'semrir is lower down the Imdrhas Valley, more accessible to the Jeeps of government officials and the delivery vans of the central Moroccan economy. Tilmi may be only 13 kilometers from M'semrir, but that 13 kilometers is up a twisty, rutted, dirt road, and the officials, tourists, and other bearers of "development" just don't make it up there so often.

People in Tilmi have heard of privatization, though. They aren't that isolated. After all, they often go to M'semrir for its bigger, more vibrant marketplace. And they've toyed with some the practices that the people of M'semrir have taken to. But thus far they've only toyed with them. Thus far they are still singing and dancing together. Thus far they still have a dialogue of solidarities. Thus far the grass is still green.

Dialogue, Democracy, and Environmental Problems

It's not just in the Atlas Mountains that the dialogue of solidarities is breaking down, of course, and not just in the Atlas Mountains that ecological dialogue is breaking down with it. We have considered these indications throughout the book—the challenges to sustainability, environmental justice, and the rights and beauty of nature. These challenges have material origins, such as the treadmills of production and consumption, technological somnambulism, and the interplay of population and inequality. They also have ideal origins, such as hierarchical and antidemocratic attitudes about society and the environment, and simplistic and uncritical conceptions of nature and a natural conscience. (There are, as well, important material bases to the "ideal" origins of our environmental challenges, and important ideal bases to the "material" origins, as earlier chapters discussed.) All these challenges relate issues of community to how we socially organize ourselves; to how we envision our relations with others, both human and non-human; and to how we dialogically organize our envisioning and envision our organizing.

Clearly, we need to be having a better dialogue about ecological dialogue.

Perhaps, in a perverse way, herein lies the value of Hardin's theory of the "tragedy of the commons." However historically inaccurate an allegory it may be, it does effectively portray what life might be like if we repudiate the lessons of dialogue. "Ruin is the destination toward which all men rush," Hardin gloomily wrote. If we all act individualistically, if we refuse to communicate with one another, and if we disregard the consequences for others (and thus for ourselves as well) of what we are doing, Hardin will surely be right. Such a logic, we cannot doubt, would indeed "remorselessly generate" environmental decline—as well as social inequality—which in turn would perpetuate a society desperate enough to follow such a logic to begin with.

We all know at some level that this possibility exists, it seems to me. This is why Hardin's allegory is, despite its inaccuracies, so frighteningly realistic. It reminds us of what we realize we could indeed become. This fright is a hopeful sign. It suggests that we recognize the value of broadening the dialogue of solidarities and the dialogue of ecology, even if we often fail to actually accomplish this broadness of conversation and consideration.

However, it must be said that a dialogic solidarity is not in itself a good thing: its value depends very much on the openness and inclusiveness of that dialogue. Solidarities that gain their social power from the exclusion of others can be very destructive. Nor is ecological dialogue in itself a good thing: Its value depends very much on the extent to which we have truly considered the potential interactions of the material and the ideal. The value of both forms of dialogue depends on the extent to which we have allowed these potential "voices" to be heard. What we want is not just dialogue, but broad and open dialogue.

Indeed, it could be said that the only true dialogue is a broad and open one. Otherwise, what we really have is what the theorist Mikhail Bakhtin called "monologue," people speaking without paying attention to the response of others, be those others people or the environment.[20] One important value of true dialogue is that it encourages us to take others into account and at the same time provides the means for doing so.[21] It is hard to establish a solidarity of interests unless we know what the interests of others are. We need to communicate and to have a sentimental commitment to the value of communication. We need to have what another theorist, Jürgen Habermas, has described as "an attitude oriented toward reaching understanding."[22]

Another important value of true dialogue is that, while promoting solidarities and the congruency of the material and the ideal, it also has an essential openness to change. True dialogue doesn't begin with a preconceived end point or a final solution but rather adjusts to new ideas and new material changes that emerge from the ongoing conversation of life. As Bakhtin once wrote, "There is neither a first word nor a last word and there are no limits to the dialogic context."[23] True social dialogue and true ecological dialogue encourage new possibilities and welcome critical evaluations of what is going on and what is being said, and of how we might reorganize our community life in ways more appropriate to our material conditions and our ideological orientations. Only in this way can we nourish what I take to be two of our most vital social and environmental joys: words and worlds without end.

The "Top" and "Bottom" of Social-Environmental Change

This is all rather abstract. Practically speaking, the message I've tried to convey is that environmental solutions depend fundamentally on participation. If we are to reorganize our communities in ways that endure, we need to encourage as many people as possible to be involved in the discussions.

How impractical, you may say. All this talk, and we never get anything done! *How impractical,* I may say right back. All this doing without any real talk about what we really want, and really need, to get done!

The problem of doing without talking is that effective doing requires cooperation. Changes that come only from on high encourage foot-dragging on the part of those down below and encourage authoritarianism on the part of those up above. Neither seems a good route to social change. Isolated individual changes that come only from below, on the other hand, tend not to be noticed when only a few are involved and tend to be actively ignored or actively restrained when many are involved. Again, neither of these seems a good route to social change.

We are coming to recognize, I think, that a "top-down" approach—"command and control" on the part of governments, corporations, and technologies—relies on unsatisfying means and produces unworkable ends. The top cannot keep the bottom under constant watch without intolerable levels of social intrusion, nor can it achieve effective policies if only the concerns of a powerful few have been taken into consideration. A "bottom-up" approach is now often advocated as the solution, and there is some wisdom in this suggestion.[24] A bottom-up approach is inherently based on the participation and willingness of those who enact any coordinated change, and thus obviates the need for intrusive surveillance

and encourages the formation of broadly based and broadly supported policies. But by itself, change coming from the bottom alone is unlikely to lead to lasting, substantial, and coordinated outcomes.

Rather, there is both a "top" and a "bottom" to effective social change, connected (yet again) by dialogue. The top represents our patterns of social organization based on government, the economy, technology, and other social structures. But without the participation and willingness of the bottom, these patterns of social organization cannot easily take hold. (Nor would they likely be fair.) The bottom represents social activism, the citizen pressure that indicates that change is desired and therefore ultimately possible. But without the participation of the top, the bottom will find it hard to coordinate its activities in the ways it desires. (See Figure 10.2.)

What I'm talking about here, of course, is *power.* For the bottom to have power, it needs the top. For the top to have power, it needs the bottom. And for effective social reorganization to occur, they both need dialogue. That is, they both need, as Anthony Giddens has termed it, "dialogic democracy"—a democracy in which all, including the environment, are taken into account.[25]

Reorganizing Communities

Perhaps, in fits and starts, stumbles and leaps, we're getting there. We *have* managed in recent years to coordinate some important social reorganization of environmental relations, generally through the cooperation of the bottom and the top.

Recycling in the United States

Recycling is a good example. Back in the early 1980s, some friends of mine in college lived in what they called Ecology House, a big old Victorian home owned by our university. These students lived there as a demonstration of urban

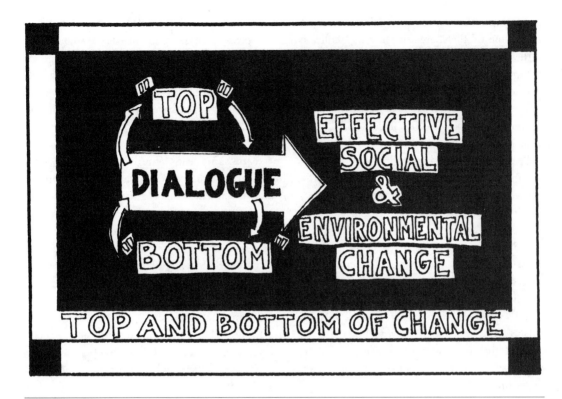

Figure 10.2   The "top" and "bottom" of social change.

environmental living. The students raised money for and installed a backyard compost bin, a composting toilet, energy efficient lighting, a solar greenhouse for heating, and other environmental improvements. But most impressive, I always thought, was the way these roughly 10 students, all of whom cooked and ate in the house, produced one lonely paper shopping bag of garbage a week. (About the same as my family of four does today.) Everything else was either precycled, recycled, or reused. They didn't generate much garbage to begin with, they returned to the production stream what they did generate, and they found other uses for a lot of stuff other people would have simply pitched.

Some people thought they were crazy, though. Unless you have that kind of young idealistic zeal, who could be bothered to sort paper, metal, and glass, or to compost food scraps (let alone personal manures)? "Recycling sounds like a great idea, but almost nobody will ever do it," they

were often told. The doubters had some statistics to back them up, too. As late as 1980, the recycling rate in the great throwaway society, the United States, was just 10 percent of all municipal solid waste.[26]

By 2001, the national rate was 30 percent and rising.[27] In 1988, there were just 600 curbside recycling programs in U.S. communities; by 1993, there were 3,700; by 2001, there were 9,700.[28] Waste reduction programs as of 2001 were removing some 55 million tons from ever entering the country's 230-million-ton waste stream—a vast improvement on the 0.6-million-ton figure for 1992.[29] The amount of solid waste sent to U.S. land fills every year is still high, some 161 million tons in 2001. But it's finally on the way down from the 1990 high-water mark of 172 million tons.[30]

For a while the main barrier to increased recycling was an embarrassment of recycled riches. The market was glutted, prices dropped, and a few communities were finding it necessary to send some of the materials they had collected to the landfill. But as more factories were set up to handle recycled materials, the situation rapidly reversed itself. Prices skyrocketed. In some cities, bundles of recycled newspapers were being stolen off the streets before official collection trucks could get to them.

Prices for recycled materials have dropped again since then and remain somewhat volatile, as is typical of raw materials markets. And recycling is now experiencing a political backlash—a sure sign, in a dialogic democracy, that an idea has hit prime time. Much of this backlash was unleashed in 1996 when Mayor Giuliani of New York sought to cut 38 percent from the city's recycling budget and the *New York Times* published a widely noticed (and, in my view, largely erroneous) piece criticizing recycling.[31] (At the time of this writing the political climate has moderated somewhat, although recycling remains under fire from some quarters.[32])

Nevertheless, community recycling in the United States must be considered an astonishing success story. And why? Because people demanded it be done. They were tired of having incinerators and waste dumps foisted on their neighborhoods. And they wanted to do something good for the environment. It was a matter of their interests and their sentiments. All that was needed were the social structures that could make it possible: government action, corporate investment, and technological changes. And it happened because the top and the bottom found they had something to talk about together.

Supplying Water in a Costa Rican Village

For years, international agencies have been drilling wells, planting trees, providing new crop varieties, building dams, and promoting tourism in "less-developed" communities across the world, hoping to spur economic development. Sometimes this form of international aid has worked, but very often it has not. Local people have often looked on with pleasant smiles while the dams were put up and have shaken hands in apparent thanks when given trees to plant, only to fail to maintain the dams and the trees later. Eventually—after the development reports were filed away back at the international aid agency's headquarters—the dams crumbled and the trees died.

Astonishing as it seems in retrospect, supporters of this 1970s-style approach to development rarely bothered to ask a crucial question of local people: What do you want? Such a top-down style of development assistance not only alienated the people it was supposed to help, but, because of the development officials' lack of knowledge of local conditions, top-down approaches often resulted in increased social inequality and environmental damage.

In the early 1990s, though, development agencies began to see both the practical and the democratic value of what has come to be called *participatory development*.[33] Involving local people as equal partners and leaders in development projects ensures a sense of ownership—of sentimental commitment—to a project. It also ensures that the project is more likely to do what people want, making the project fit their interests as well. This approach is so totally obvious in retrospect that it may seem incredible that development efforts ever took another course. But early development thinking often had little respect for the views of local people, seeing them as backward and incapable of understanding all the advantages of the modern techniques that were being offered to them, while assuming (rather contradictorily) that the modern way was what everyone wanted.

In 1994, I was fortunate enough to see firsthand the results of a more participatory approach to local development. An old friend lives in Platanillo, Costa Rica, a farming village of about 500 people in the foothills of the Talamanca Mountains. We had lost touch since meeting in the 1970s, but I happened to be in the country on university business. The village has no phone, and I wasn't even sure he was living there anymore. So I quite literally looked him up. I took the Platanillo bus up the dirt road into the mountains on a Saturday afternoon, got some directions from the barkeeper in the local tavern, and surprised my friend as he was returning from his fields for the day. He recognized me almost immediately, even after 17 years, and excitedly led me around his farm and the village.

One of the places he brought me to, with considerable pride, was the new water supply dam that he and some other villagers had installed earlier that year. The dam made a small impoundment on a stream up in the mountains above the village—not big enough to cause much damage should it give way some day, but large enough to supply all the houses on that side of the valley with running water. Before the dam was built, everyone was drawing water by hand from household wells, often dug dangerously close to outdoor toilets. Now everyone in the neighborhood had safe running water piped into their houses.

The people in Platanillo had some outside help in building the water system. My friend mentioned that several development agencies were involved, although he didn't mention which ones. That didn't seem important. Instead, he talked about the neighbors with whom he had worked on the project, about the way the sluice gate worked, about the way they arranged for the land where the dam sat, about the village committee that is maintaining the dam, and other local details. This clearly was the villagers' own water supply.

What really struck me, as my friend described the new system, was how much he knew about it—far, far more than I know about the water supply system in my own community. After all, my friend had helped build and design the one in his community. Should those pipes or that dam or the watershed up above or down below ever develop any problems, he and his neighbors would know what to do and would feel a sense of investment and responsibility for carrying out any repairs. Which was a good thing, I thought. In such a remote place, if the local people didn't

take care of a problem, it would be a long time before anyone else would.

As I took the bus back down the valley that evening, I passed a building in the next village down the road from Platanillo with a sign on it that said "U.S. Peace Corps." I don't know if Peace Corps volunteers were involved in Platanillo's dam—my friend never said. But if they were, I thought, they sure understood the value of participation.

Growing Local Knowledge in Honduras

Jeff Bentley is not your typical social scientist. I knew that as soon as I laid eyes on him in 1993, when he gave a seminar in my department. The title of his talk was suitably academic sounding—something like "Farmer-Scientists and Integrated Pest Management in Honduras," as I recall. But rarely, even in this informal age, is a seminar delivered by someone wearing old jeans whose bottom hems are frayed from continually catching beneath the wearer's construction-style boots. He did wear a sport coat, a tweed one, but it only made his jeans and uncombed hair seem that much more incongruous in a university seminar room.

And yet Bentley held the packed room (including several conservatively dressed scientists from the entomology department) absolutely spellbound. Bentley had been employed over the past few years in the Department of Crop Protection at the Escuela Agricola Panamericana in Zamorano, Honduras, trying out a radical new way of doing research on Honduras's farm problems, working with the country's poor peasant farmers. In collaboration with Werner Melara and others at Zamorano, Bentley had been going into Honduran villages and conducting entomology seminars with local farmers. "We don't tell them what to do to solve their pest problems," Bentley said. "We try to give them the intellectual tools for solving the problems themselves."[34]

Over the past 40 years, the typical approach of agricultural scientists working on the problems of tropical agriculture has been to encourage peasant farmers to adopt hybrid crop varieties developed by the scientists themselves. Such varieties generally yield more but also have fewer defenses against pests. The scientists have developed an answer for that problem too, though: pesticides. (It's a package deal.) But farmers have to buy the hybrid varieties and pesticides, rather than relying on seed saved from the previous crop and on lower-cost pest control practices. And if you're a poor Honduran farmer, money is something you don't have a lot of. Capital-intensive agriculture also promotes international economic inequality by draining scarce cash from the Honduran countryside. Plus, a high degree of literacy is required to read the label warnings on the safe and appropriate use of the pesticides. Thousands of people have been poisoned.[35]

Bentley's view is that any solutions farmers devise for themselves are far more likely to be relevant to their ecological, economic, cultural, and agricultural circumstances. Also, Bentley stresses the importance and validity of farmers' own knowledge about local conditions and local farming practices—their *local knowledge*.[36] Honduran peasant farmers are poor, not stupid, and they know a lot of relevant things that the scientists don't. After all, the peasant farmers live there.

University scientists do have a lot to offer local people, though, particularly concerning phenomena that are not easily observed. In Bentley's rural seminars, he helps the farmers see inconspicuous connections that the university scientists have figured out. Most local farmers don't understand insect life cycles, so he puts larvae in glass jars for several days so that people can watch caterpillars and grubs develop into adult insects. Local farmers almost never go out into their fields at night, so Bentley takes them out to watch insect activities by flashlight. And then he steps back and lets them apply the knowledge.

In one village, the local farmers had been spending quite a bit of money on pesticides to eradicate the fire ants that were infesting their fields, although they had no evidence that the ants were harming their yields. When Bentley took them out at night, though, they watched as the ants crawled up their corn plants and ate some other insects that were harming the crop. A local woman was very impressed with this observation and wondered how to encourage the ants. She recalled that ants were often attracted to the sugar in her kitchen, and she came up with the idea of mixing a dilute solution of sugar water and spraying it on infested plants to attract the ants.

This idea, suggested Bentley, has several advantages typical of local innovations. First, it's cheap, as sugar is relatively inexpensive. Second, it relies on easily accessible local materials— sugar and water. Third, it is something that the local people understand completely, which should allow them to refine the idea, generating further innovations. Fourth, it is safe, both for the environment and for the farmers. And fifth, as it is their own idea, local farmers feel a sense of ownership and are far more likely to be committed to making the idea work.

But does this idea from the bottom actually help control insect pests? Here's where the top— the scientists—can step in again, performing experiments and helping local people design their own experiments to assess the validity of the idea. With the Zamorano approach, scientists are still very important but, as Bentley and Melara explain, "We depend on farmers to help tell us what to study and to work with us in actually carrying out experiments in their fields, fine-tuning the technologies to their conditions."[37]

The point of participatory development, in other words, is not that local people always know best. Rather, the point is to get a dialogue going between local people and scientists, between local knowledge and expert knowledge. Such a dialogue encourages the respect and concern of each party for the other and perhaps even genuine friendships, as each comes to know the other better: solidarities of interests and sentiments. Participatory development is thus *dialogic development.*

Reorganizing Our Own Communities

Innovative ideas and cooperative social reorganizations are improving our ecological dialogue in communities all across the world. In this section, I discuss a few examples from the town I lived in until recently, Ames, Iowa, still the town I know best. These are not especially noteworthy social reorganizations. They have not attracted national and international attention, nor are they likely to do so. But their significance lies in the fact that they are *not* unique: Changes like these are happening in lots of places.[38]

A Bicycle-Powered Hauling and Delivery Business

Ames is a pleasant college town of about 50,000 residents. Its economy is based mainly on retail, government agencies, and Iowa State University, where I used to teach. (I teach at the University of Wisconsin-Madison now.) Despite the presence of a major university, Ames is not one of those funky college towns with a lot of alternative businesses run by aging, or New Age, hippies. It's a pretty ordinary place. "Ames—the center of it all" is the Chamber of Commerce's motto for the city, and they mean that both geographically and culturally. Still, new things happen even in ordinary places.

The sight of a bicycle hauling two trailers hooked up in tandem and loaded 5 feet high with recycling bins and loose cardboard is one of the striking sights of Ames. In 1992, Joan Stein and Jim Gregory began Fresh Aire Delivery, a bicycle-powered hauling and delivery service in Ames. Bicycle delivery services can be found in most major U.S. cities now. The hauling side of Fresh Aire is distinctive, though. Most of their hauls consist of recycled materials collected from households, businesses, and the university. Ames has a city-operated trash incinerator. With little need to put waste in landfills, the city has instituted only a rudimentary recycling program. Joan and Jim sought to correct the problem. Using trailers they design and build themselves, they expanded the business to the point where it employed 20 riders, including Jim and Joan. I used to see one of their riders almost every day.

"A lot of people just look, just stare," Joan explained to me one morning when I came over to interview them in their small but comfortable house. "And to be quite frank, it's worked to our advantage. It's kind of like a free form of advertising."

"I've hauled over a thousand pounds," said Jim. "You don't want to do that too much. You feel real tired!"

"And you thank the lord that Ames is flat," added Joan, laughing.

They both used to own cars, but neither does now. Joan's brother trashed hers some years ago. "I was thinking about getting rid of it anyway," she says. "So it worked out for the best.... It's been very liberating to live without one." Jim hasn't owned a car in 15 years, although in high school he used to fix up trucks and sell them. "When I finally got into college, I guess I kind of outgrew that stage," he says.

Why did they start this business? Not because they're anti-technology. They own a computer, a telephone, and a microwave oven. And I've watched Jim mow a lawn pushing a reel mower in one hand—they also used to run a non-power lawn mowing service—while holding a cell phone up to his ear with his other hand.

Eventually, Jim and Joan sold the recycling part of the business, so they could focus on making and selling the cargo trailers Jim had invented. (The trailers proved quite popular and can be seen in many American cities now.) Jim and Joan also make pedicabs and operate a holiday rickshaw service around town. And they still deliver furniture by bike. The new business is

Figure 10.3   Jim Gregory of Bikes at Work with his double-tandem bike trailers loaded up. Jim's trailers are a familiar sight in Ames, Iowa.

called Bikes at Work. (See Figure 10.3.) You can read all about it in Jim's book, *Cycling for Profit*.[39]

"People assume that doing things by bike is backward. I don't think it's that at all. I think it's just appropriate," Jim reasons.

And what makes bikes appropriate for Jim and Joan are their social and environmental consequences. "People view being inside the car as being inside their own body armor where they feel safe," Jim told me. "And I'm not sure that's the best way to go. You want to feel you're part of your environment as much as possible."

On a bike, Joan added, one stays "tuned in to the environment. And you don't abuse it so much if you're out there in the elements."

"Living this way for the past decade," agreed Jim, "I can't imagine not knowing there are kids playing, because you can hear them outside."

Maybe Joan put it best: "I just think our lifestyle keeps you accessible to other people. . . . It gives a feeling of openness."

It's the feeling of dialogue—social and ecological.

Community-Supported Agriculture

That same feeling of dialogue underlies another relatively new organization in Ames: the Magic Beanstalk CSA. The acronym "CSA" stands for "community-supported agriculture" projects, partnerships between farmers and consumers to support local agricultural production. Typically, consumers pay a set amount at the beginning of the season for a share in the farms' yield and get the produce directly from the farms. The idea began in Japan, where local food partnerships called *teikei* have existed since the 1960s. In Britain, they're called "box schemes," as the produce usually comes once a week in a big box. And since the late 1980s, about 1,000 CSAs have sprouted across the United States.[40] Iowa's first

CSAs started in 1995, and the Magic Beanstalk is one of the three that began that summer. As of 2003, some 15 local farms were producing vegetables, apples, strawberries, raspberries, honey, wool, pork, beef, chicken, lamb, turkey, eggs, goat cheese, herbs, whole grains, and cider—all following sustainable and humane farming methods—for about 100 Magic Beanstalk households.

Shelly Gradwell-Brenneman, then a graduate student at Iowa State University, was one of several people who were key to getting the Magic Beanstalk going. Sitting under a pine tree on Iowa State's central campus, she explained to me why.

"Our closest connection to the environment is through what we eat three times a day," Shelley pointed out. "That's our most close, direct, and intimate connection with the land. And that was totally missing in 1990s environmentalism."

Shelly used to work for the U.S. Park Service, doing environmental education, and she got frustrated with the contradictions she saw in some wilderness-preservation enthusiasts.

"They talk all about conservation and preservation of wilderness, jump in their Saabs on the weekends, and drive up into the mountains and bag peaks—and buy all that expensive gear and petroleum-based clothing," she observed. "It almost seemed to me like an extractive kind of use, even though they were total wilderness preservationists. They only seemed to think about the environment on the weekends."

CSAs, on the other hand, decrease energy use by promoting a local food supply. Typically, CSAs use sustainable (usually organic) and humane methods, and yet they deliver the food at a competitive price. The elimination of retailing allows farmers to claim a bigger share of the food dollar and still keep prices low, making sustainable, organic, and humane produce affordable. Thus, CSAs are not necessarily Saab-and-Gore-Tex environmentalism. Magic Beanstalk charges $285 for six months of vegetables enough for a hungry family of four or five. (Think about it. That's pretty cheap, especially for organic produce. And if you put in a few hours volunteering, the price is $250.) Also, Magic Beanstalk, like many CSAs,

has a special program to make food more affordable for lower-income households. CSAs provide a way for people to connect symbolically with the land, as Shelly described, and a way for people to connect with each other, rich and poor, rural and urban. CSAs are about more than food. They are also about community, social and ecological. (See Figure 10.4.)

A CSA clearly depends in part upon a solidarity of interests. By committing to a price up front, consumers share in the risk of agricultural production. Farmers have guaranteed sales, which is a great comfort when you are about to sink a lot of money and time into the ground. Consumers' interests are served by getting a good product at a good price. Each side gets something they are interested in.

The success of a CSA depends as well upon a solidarity of sentiments—at least the Magic Beanstalk does. Both producers and consumers share a commitment to a common norm: promoting sustainable community. This common desire is central to the group. Producers and consumers interact socially through harvest festivals, field days, kids' days, cooking and canning classes, short chitchats when the produce is delivered, and more. They *like* each other, and the group wouldn't operate so smoothly if that weren't the case.

All of these solidarities were severely threatened during the Magic Beanstalk's first year, though. The spring of 1995 was very wet and cold in Iowa. People had signed up expecting weekly vegetable deliveries to start in mid-May, but the main producer's fields were under several inches of water. By mid-June, not a leaf of lettuce had been delivered—a rather inauspicious beginning. The organizers were panicked, convinced the CSA was about to collapse before it had really even begun. But no customer called to complain. The producers sent out letters offering a full refund to anyone who wanted out. No one did. Because of normative and affective commitments, the solidarity held across this trustbusting moment. And when regular vegetable deliveries finally began in the first week of July, a loud collective whoop could be heard in central

Figure 10.4   Picking peas and weeding onions at the Magic Beanstalk CSA. Members of a community-supported agriculture project sometimes help out with the chores on a volunteer basis.

Iowa. They had done it. They had created a lasting community.

Here's how one Iowa CSA producer described the dialogical bonds a CSA depends upon: "My shareholders are friends of mine; they trust me." Shareholders and friends; interests and sentiments.

Here's another producer: "Before we started working together in the CSA, we didn't know each other at all. . . . [Now] we respect each other and know that we will help each other." Respect and helping each other; sentiments and interests.

Here's a CSA member: "We became members because we enjoy fresh vegetables and because we really believe in the philosophies behind CSA." Fresh vegetables and philosophies; interests and sentiments.[41]

The Magic Beanstalk takes its name from the traditional story "Jack and the Beanstalk," in which Jack, a poor starving farm boy, grows a huge beanstalk from a magic bean in order to steal some food from the airborne castle of a giant. For the Magic Beanstalk CSA, the giant represents modern agriculture and its efforts to take away the market of small, local farms. Jack represents the courage of local farms trying to get back some of that market.

As Shelly explained, "In the version that we have, the giant gets his head cut off. The beanstalk doesn't get cut down. It's the victory of local agriculture over the military-agricultural complex."

That image of a "military-agricultural complex" describes a depressingly frequent feature of market developments: social and environmental fragmentation. But markets do not have to develop in that way. Instead of being a site of pure competitive individualism, a production and consumption treadmill, a market can be a place of cooperation and connection. It all depends on whether a market is conceived of as a solidarity or as a "solo"-darity. The Magic Beanstalk CSA demonstrates that the former is possible—and preferable.[42]

Smart Growth

Suburban sprawl isn't as bad in Ames as it is in a lot of places. Because of the farm crisis of the 1980s, the population of Iowa actually dropped during that decade of explosive suburbanization in much of the United States. Money was tight, so there wasn't a lot of development then, and there isn't much compared to most of the rest of the country. "We have a real opportunity to avoid some of the mistakes that were made elsewhere," says Joe Lynch, a local Ames activist for sound urban planning.

But sprawl is nevertheless well under way in Ames, promoting automobile dependency, isolating people and neighborhoods, and leading to what Joe calls "retail strip mines"—strip developments of huge stores that close down local businesses, mine a community's economy, and ship the profits to an out-of-town corporation. Ames has a couple of big strip malls now, and a controversial regional mall is soon to be built there. Plus, recent residential development has followed the standard separationist model in which housing types are segregated and kept far removed from commercial development, forcing people to drive to work and shops. This approach has come to be what people in town generally expect now. Commercial development today always seems to bring cars, traffic, and parking lots, so understandably no one wants that near their homes—which only promotes greater use of cars and more ugly "retail strip mines."

Joe has been one of a number of Ames residents who in the past few years have tried to change the town's vision of development. He goes to city council meetings, he writes occasional guest columns in a local paper, he reads up on what is going on in other communities, and—perhaps most important—he talks to people. Time and again he engages townspeople in conversation, describing the importance of what he calls "relationships" and the need to "look at systems in comprehensive ways." He stops them in the streets. He goes into local stores and chats with the owners and workers. His principal message is, as he explained to me one afternoon on the deck of his self-built solar home, "You don't solve pollution problems by worrying about what comes out at the end. You solve pollution problems by looking at the system and redesigning what people need."

The vision that Joe and other activists in town are advocating is what is often called *smart growth*. The basic idea of smart growth is to reject the standard polarization between anti-growth naysayers and pro-growth yea-sayers, familiar to development controversies across the country. Smart growth says, yes, there are serious problems with how development usually goes on in the United States. But we can use the power of development forces to "grow out of" sprawl. Pressures for growth provide the capital to reshape what we have done and give us the opportunity to rethink what we might do. Besides, there are good economic reasons for reshaping what we've done and might do—let alone the environmental reasons. It's expensive to construct and maintain the necessary roads, sewer lines, and power lines and to provide police, fire, and emergency services to spread-out developments. Although sprawl is often defended for adding tax base to a community, the cost of providing for it can easily be more than the added government revenue.

Smart growth is often coupled with an architectural style and approach to planning called *new urbanism*.[43] The basic idea of new urbanism is to model new developments on the kind of traditional neighborhoods that cities routinely turn into historic districts. If we think such areas are nice enough to make special efforts to preserve them and to visit them as tourists, new urbanists ask, why not design all our neighborhoods that

Figure 10.5   A street in Kentlands, Maryland, the best-known "new urbanism" development. Note the space-saving, close-together houses with small front yards and the community-building presence of porches. Although this view shows single-family homes, Kentlands has a wide variety of housing types—as is characteristic of "smart growth" initiatives.

way? New urbanism is thus in many ways the traditional urbanism, the urbanism of a time when cities were built for people rather than cars. And if we build with people first in mind instead of cars, the result will be not only pleasing to the eye but pleasing to the balance sheets of local governments, because of new urbanism's efficient land use. That's the smart growth part. But also, new urbanism advocates argue that such an approach helps reduce the impact of development on community in the ecological sense and helps promote more interactiveness in the community in the social sense. (See Figure 10.5.)

New urbanism designers typically recommend the following guidelines for people-friendly development: Build houses up, not out, so lots can be narrower and land use efficiency can go up. Bring back the front porch, the sidewalk, and the alleyway, all zones of interaction between neighbors. Make most streets through-streets so all the traffic doesn't get channeled onto a few trunk roads, causing traffic jams even in suburbs. Bring back the corner shop. Provide a diversity of housing types within a neighborhood so that people with all kinds of household situations can live there, from singles, to families with children, to the elderly. Locate stores and schools and workplaces near homes—and without the traffic and oversized parking lots that make most commercial life so unappealing and environmentally unsound today. Don't mix stores and housing types higgledy-piggledy, but instead institute far more detailed zoning plans than the current big-blob style of zoning with huge areas devoted to a single type of use. Increase density, so walking and public transit are more realistic options. (See Figure 10.6.)

Figure 10.6   A street in Providence, Rhode Island, developed in the 1890s. New urbanism takes as its model "old urbanism" developments like this one. Note here too the close-together houses, the small yards, the front porches. Also note the mixing of single-family homes with the duplex in the foreground.

Ames's developers and city planners thought these ideas were completely unrealistic at first. Also, they interpreted Joe and other planning activists as anti-business, applying the standard naysayer/yea-sayer model to public debate. "I'm not against commercial activity," responds Joe, who is a small business person himself. (He and his wife, Lonna Nachtigal, operate a small vegetable farm just outside of town, among other activities.) "That's not the issue. The issue is how can we design commercial activity so that it doesn't destroy our communities and our neighborhoods."

Through a long series of meetings and discussions over several years, often heated, and finally culminating in a one-day seminar at which some of the United States' leading new urbanism designers spoke, local developers and city officials and activists began to see that they had a lot in common. Some developers and officials, it turned out, didn't particularly like putting in the same old sprawling developments. They realized sprawl was a financial drain on a community. Moreover, some members of the local business community were worried about the problem of retail strip mining too. They just thought that's what people wanted.

The result is that one of Ames's new developments, its biggest in years, is following many features of the new urbanism approach. Lot sizes are smaller. There are front porches, sidewalks on both sides of the streets, and some alleyways. Builders are putting in a wide range of housing types, from apartments to townhouses to detached single-family homes. And there's a small main street with multistory commercial buildings that front directly on the sidewalk, instead of having a big parking lot in front. If it works, it will be the kind of place where parents feel safe sending their children to the corner store for milk, where people walk to work or to the bus stop, where neighbors know each other a little bit better, and where fewer resources are demanded from the environment.[44]

In other words, the activists and developers and city officials built a solidarity of solidarities, across interests and sentiments, from bottom to top, and made a change. The process was not without conflict. The parties still don't always trust one another, and the plan does not follow the new urbanism model in some ways that the activists and the designer hired by the developers regard as crucial. (The designer was upset enough to ask to have his name removed from the project.) And there have been a few charges that the developers were slow to build the project in order to wrest a few extra financial concessions from a nervous Ames City Council, which was anxious about the success of this novel development. Yet they still managed to make enough connections, social and environmental, to achieve a small but significant reorganization of the pattern of life in Ames.

As Joe says, "It's a matter of relationships, all these relationships. That's what nature teaches us." He paused and then asked me, nodding toward my tape recorder, "Did you turn that thing off?" I shook my head, and he repeated with a grin, leaning toward the machine, and saying in a dramatic voice, "That's what nature teaches us—the value of relationships! I hope that's what your book teaches."

I hope so too.

Reorganizing Societies

Finally, we need to reorganize the larger societies of which we are all a part. Here too there is a "top" and a "bottom" to social change, as well as interests and sentiments that must be gathered together into the interactive solidarities of dialogic democracy.

To begin with, we need better sources of communication about the environment so that we will better understand what our interests really are. The basic political thermometer of social health remains growth in GDP (Gross Domestic Product).[45] But as the environmental economist Herman Daly has noted, GDP is often a perverse measure of environmental health.[46] For example, under current accounting, a disaster like the *Exxon Valdez* oil spill shows up as a positive contribution to GDP because it stimulates so much economic activity in cleaning up the spill. So, too, for cleaning up hazardous waste sites, removing asbestos and lead paint from old buildings, and paying any medical costs incurred from environmental contamination. Moreover, depletion of nonrenewable resources shows up as income under GDP calculations instead of what it really is: an irreplaceable withdrawal from our ecological bank account. In other words, as far GDP is concerned, environmental degradation is good for the economy because, at least in the short run—and the short run is all GDP measures—it creates jobs and gives us spending money.

Daly's ideas have recently been used to devise a new thermometer, the GPI—the genuine progress indicator, a complex index of more than 20 different economic factors. These factors include measures of environmental health such as pollution, resource depletion, and long-term environmental damage, as well as measures of social health such as crime and income distribution. The GPI gives a very different picture of how we're doing than does GDP. For example, in the United States GDP per capita has shown continuous gains since World War II, whereas GPI steadily declined for most of this period. The GPI dropped 1 percent in the 1970s, 2 percent in the 1980s, and 6 percent in the 1990s through to 1995.[47] Things ticked up during the last half of the 1990s, though, growing 3.3 percent from 1994 to 2000, largely because of gains in wealth and in income equality during the go-go years of the booming '90s. All told, the GDP rose 125 percent from 1974 to 2000, while the GPI rose just 25 percent during this period—which is still something, but a lot less rosy a record than we usually think of.[48] Unfortunately, a lot more of us have heard of GDP than have yet heard of the GPI.

Another way to increase environmental communication is by putting the environment right where we're all sure to notice: in costs. Currently, many environmental consequences of our economic activity are external to the costs of goods and services. One way to internalize the environment in our economic thinking is through *green taxes*, sometimes called "Pigouvian taxes" after Nicholas Pigou, the English economist who proposed the idea in the early 1900s. Green taxes are an attempt to make the price of goods and services reflect their true costs and to shift the burden of government revenue generation away from regressive taxation schemes like sales taxes and value-added taxes. Finland, for example, now has a carbon tax aimed at internalizing the costs of global warming and other pollution issues associated with fossil fuel use. Britain has a landfill tax. The Netherlands and several Scandinavian countries now have energy taxes.

Green taxes offer a lot of possibilities, but like any taxation scheme they have to be handled with great care. Taxes are perhaps the most hotly contested of any issue these days. If they are not supported by public sentiment, and if they harm public interests, perhaps by being instituted in regressive ways, green taxes will be a political disaster. Also, powerful interests often get the upper hand in taxation debates, as when Belgium instituted a pesticide tax that exempted farmers and when the early versions of energy taxes in Scandinavia exempted some energy-intensive industries. But perhaps we can learn the lessons of these early experiments and use green taxes to help build an economy that reflects what things really cost.

There is also increasing excitement these days among business leaders about *industrial ecology*, as Chapter 8 discussed—about treating industry as a part of ecologic systems as opposed to a means of dominating ecologic systems.[49] The key principle of industrial ecology is regarding pollution as a sign of inefficiency in an industry. Waste products should be regarded as wasted opportunities, not leftovers to be gotten rid of in the cheapest and faster and least conspicuous way possible. "Closing the loop" is the way advocates of industrial ecology often describe the greener approach. By greening business, we can prevent environmental problems instead of having to ameliorate them. Environmental standards such as ISO 14000 alert industry to places where the loop is perhaps not yet closed and opportunities are being wasted. Industrial ecology thus advises business to see environmental standards and environmental regulation as business opportunities rather than obstructions to be fought or dodged.

This is the process environmental sociologists refer to as "ecological modernization," as Chapter 7 also described. Rather than the old big-smokestacks-and-big-technology-that-nobody-controls vision of modernity, ecological modernization takes a greener view of modernity's potential. Is ecological modernization a contradiction in terms? It is perhaps too soon to tell. But without a more participatory and dialogic vision of modernization—a vision that includes the participation of the "top," the "bottom," and the environment itself—we may never get a chance to find out. (See Figure 10.7.)

And to get that chance we need to recognize that, among other things, there is still a crucially important place for law and good government in organizing the ecological society. We need regulation and regulatory agencies; we need laws and legislatures; we need international treaties and international treaty organizations. But we also need them to be more participatory than they have generally been in the past. As the political scientist Elinor Ostrom has observed, "In contemporary conceptions of social order, the 'government' often is seen as an external agent whose behavior is exogenous to the situation."[50] This conception of an external government has, of late, been equally characteristic of some elected officials and some of those who elected them, or have chosen not to participate in the electoral

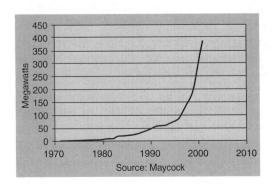 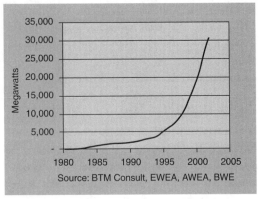

Figure 10.7   Ecological modernization: World wind energy generating capacity (left panel) and world production of photovoltaic cells (right panel). With technologies such as these, industrialism can become more a source of environmental solutions and less a source of environmental problems, argue ecological modernization advocates.

process. The us-versus-them view of the relationship between the government and the people will have to be repaired. For the government is, or rather should be, us.

Reorganizing Ourselves

In all these ways, we can achieve virtual environmentalism—the virtue of being environmental without being virtuous. And, I believe, we not only can. We must. For in the end, there is nothing virtual about virtual environmentalism. It's the real thing.

We are, however, unlikely to work to change our local communities and the bigger communities that whole societies represent unless we have personally committed to change. Reorganizing our communities also involves reorganizing ourselves. It's going to take some virtue to become virtual environmentalists.

It's important to recognize the interaction, the dialogue, between reorganizing community and reorganizing ourselves. We are more likely to regard the environment in environmentally appropriate ways when our community life is organized to encourage such regard. But we can't simply wait around for that community reorganization to

happen. We need to make it happen. Individuals are the agents of community change as much as communities are the agents of individual change.

In other words, our personal values and actions do matter. There is a crucial ethical dimension to our ecological dialogues. Our virtues, at least, need to be more than virtual.

Which brings us back to community, for ethical ideas are always ideas about community relationships. Aldo Leopold put it well in "The Land Ethic," probably the twentieth century's most influential essay on environmental ethics: "All ethics so far evolved rest upon a single premise: that the individual is a member of a community of interdependent parts."[51] But how we draw the boundary of community membership shapes (and is shaped by) our sense of with whom we feel interdependent, and thus for whom we feel a sense of moral concern. (Moral concern and interdependent parts—it's the interplay of sentiments and interests again.) Our fellowship with others implies that they are entitled to our moral concern, just as we are entitled to their moral concern.

My point is that in the idea of community is the idea of equality—and the idea of inequality. There is a constant tension between community and inequality, between commitment to those included within the community's boundaries and lack of commitment, and consequent inattention, to the troubles of those excluded from the community. Ideas of community, inequality, and the boundaries of moral concern are thus closely intertwined.

Each of the three central issues of environmentalism—sustainability, environmental justice, and the rights and beauty of nature—challenges a different dimension of these boundaries of concern. Sustainability considers how we draw boundaries of concern between present and future generations. Environmental justice considers how we draw boundaries of concern between human groups. The rights and beauty of nature considers how we draw boundaries of concern between humans and the rest of creation.

This last boundary is perhaps the most difficult. How can we form a sense of community with the ecosystem, something we're not even sure is an intentional actor? How can we form a solidarity of interests and sentiments with something we're not even sure has interests and sentiments? Would not such an "ethical extension," as Leopold termed it, be mere anthropomorphism—treating the inherently nonhuman as the human—and therefore highly unstable?

Environmental sociology can help us here, I think. We must begin by recognizing that all communities are imagined.[52] This is why trust is so important. We cannot get into the mind of the other, so we are always guessing, trusting, and closely watching for the signs of solidarity.

The same may be the case for human-environmental interactions. We need to imagine this form of community too. And this imagination is what the environmental movement has long promoted, at least as I interpret the two sides of what has long been the main debate in environmental ethics: anthropocentric environmentalism versus ecocentric environmentalism.

Anthropocentric environmentalism suggests that we consider our own interests first in our interactions with the environment—interests in sustainability and environmental justice—and also that we need to consider the environment's interests in

order to gain our own. (That last clause, I should point out, is what distinguishes anthropocentric environmentalism from mere anthropocentrism.) In other words, anthropocentric environmentalism says, Treat the environment well and it will treat us well in return: hence, a solidarity of interests.

Ecocentric environmentalism, on the other hand, suggests that we consider the environment as a moral entity in its own right and with its own beauty and that we see ourselves as a part of that moral entity. It argues that we need to go beyond questions of calculated human interest and recognize the importance of what the environmental philosopher Paul Taylor, for example, termed "respect for nature."[53] But we are part of that beautiful nature for which respect is due: hence, a solidarity of sentiments.

As with purely human communities, the solidarity-of-sentiments side of environmental ethics is the harder argument to make. This difficulty stems, we cannot doubt, from the individual and instrumental thinking so characteristic of our time and place. The challenge of imagination is particularly hard here because the environment does not speak, at least not directly. Which may in part be why anthropomorphism, as in the story of Androcles and the lion, is such a popular way to think about the environment: It helps us imagine the voice of the other in the ecological dialogue.

But I believe the environmental movement is right to try to make the case for a solidarity of environmental sentiments. Even though it is a hard case to make, the evidence suggests to me that it is a vital case. Moments that threaten to bust the glue of trust are too frequent. Also, we can't always wait to figure out what part of the ecosystem is crucial to our interests before we act, and sentiments may add some efficiency here. If for no other reason than they are good for our interests, we need to have sentimental bonds with the ecosystem as well. But the bonds of sentiment are unlikely to last unless they are also good for our interests—which, I believe, they are. Thus, the wise anthropocentrist is also an ecocentrist and vice versa, not one or the other.

If the paradox of collective action is that people often do not act in their own interests when they act in their own interests, the solution is clear: Also act on your sentiments. But consider those sentiments and those interests broadly and openly. We need each to participate in the maintenance of the dialogue, the ecological dialogue, over what our sentiments and interests—our ideals and our material conditions—in fact are.

Maintaining this dialogue is the basic work of the democratic community, from the smallest to that biggest community of all. It is also the sustainable, just, right, and beautiful thing to do.

Notes

Chapter 1

1. For an introduction to the literature on the realist-constructionist debate, see, on the realist side, Benton (1994, 2001a, 2001b); Dickens (1996); Dunlap and Catton (1994); Martell (1994); and Murphy (1994a, 1994b); and, on the constructionist side, Burningham and Cooper (1999); Cronon (1995b); Dupuis and Vandergeest (1996); Hajer (1995); Hannigan (1995); Mjoset (2001); and Yearley (1991, 1996). Within the United States, there was considerable debate over whether the position of Buttel, a leading figure in the field, is constructionist (for example, Buttel [1992] and Taylor and Buttel [1992]; see the discussion and critique in Dunlap and Catton [1994]). Recently, however, there have been a number of attempts to reconcile the two sides; for example, Bell (1999); Buttel (1996); Lidskog (2001); Metzner (1997); and Woodgate and Redclift (1998). Burningham and Cooper (1999) can also be read as such an endeavor. In the past few years, there has also been much excitement among many environmental sociologists for the work of the French theorist Bruno Latour (1987, 1993, 1999) and his "actor-network" approach as a way to resolve the realist-constructionist debate. See Chapter 8 for a discussion of Latour.

2. The conceptual language of dialogue—or, more properly, of *dialogics*—is not common in sociology, although it is now common in the humanities. For an introduction to the concept of dialogics for the human sciences, including sociology, see Bell and Gardiner (1998), which introduces the dialogic perspective of the Russian theorist Mikhail Bakhtin(1981, 1984, 1986). The approach to environmental sociology I develop in the present book is heavily based on the work of Bakhtin, as well as that of the Brazilian dialogic theorist, Paulo Freire (1993).

3 For an example, see Seidman (1994).

4. I mean *responsible* here in the sense of what I have elsewhere termed "response ability"—a world that encourages responses from others by giving those responses careful consideration (Bell, 2004).

5. They are, in order, 1998, 2002, 2003, 2001, 1997, 1995, 1990 (tied with 1995), 1999, 1991 (tied with 1999), 2000. Worldwatch Institute (2003: 40); National Institute of Water and Atmospheric Research (2003); and World Meteorological Organization (2003a, 2003b, 2003c).

6. Ibid.

7. Worldwatch Institute (2002: 51).

8. Oulan Tarmo (2003).

9.   Bell (1985), 168.

10.   Worldwatch (2003), 84; a considerably smaller figure than was estimated a few years ago, but still quite significant.

11.   Ibid.

12.   Bullard (1997).

13.   Paul (2003); Long and Ort (2002).

14.   For example, the same study that found a 17 percent boost in soybean yields found a 20 percent drop due to ozone pollution, as discussed following.

15.   Buie (1995); Funk (1995); MacKenzie (1995); Klinenberg (2002: 9).

16.   World Meteorological Organization (2003b).

17.   The Canadian Press (2003); Tagliabue (2003); Associated Press (2003); CBS (2003).

18.   Worldwatch Institute (2003: 93).

19.   Ibid.

20.   Ibid.

21.   Figures from ibid. and Brown, Renner, and Flavin (1997), 17–18. Linden (1994) writes that "according to Franklin Nutter, the president of the Reinsurance Association of America, 'global warming could bankrupt the industry.'" Also see Stix (1996).

22.   National Snow and Ice Data Center (2002).

23.   Gibbs (2001).

24.   Wilford (2001).

25.   Gibbs (2001).

26.   Hileman (1995).

27.   Ziska and Caulfield (2000).

28.   Stevens (1997).

29.   The standard reference in the field is the third report of the Intergovernmental Panel on Climate Change of the United Nations (2002a), an unusually accessible document that summarizes the views of climatologists as a whole. One prominent skeptic is Richard S. Lindzen, a climatologist at MIT who argues that the computer models used in global warming predictions are not accurate enough and that scientists have not taken adequate account of the role of atmospheric water vapor. For example, see his concept of a climate "iris" of cloud cover that increases as warming increases, leading to greater reflectivity and, in turn, cooling (Lindzen et al., 2001).

30.   Revkin (2002).

31.   There is still skepticism even here, however. This skepticism is based mostly on the argument that recent measurements are biased by the increased "heat-island" effect of expanding urban areas, where most weather stations are situated. Rural weather stations do show less of a warming trend. However, there is also abundant evidence of glacial retreat in mountain systems across the world, indicating global warming in even these most rural and remote of regions, as well as satellite data showing earlier springs and later falls in northern climates. See Stevens (1997).

32.   Second report of the Intergovernmental Panel on Climate Change (1996).

33.   Intergovernmental Panel on Climate Change (2002a: 5).

34.   Goddard Space Flight Center (2002).

35.   Hansen and Nazarenko (2004).

36.   Ibid.

37.   Intergovernmental Panel on Climate Change (2002a: 5).

38.   Kalnay and Cai (2003).

39.   Imbrie and Imbrie (1979), 178.

40.   Unless, of course, your local utility uses nuclear or hydroelectric power. But these have problems of their own.

41. National Weather Service (2003).

42. On cancer rates, see Intergovernmental Panel on Climate Change (2002b: 12.7.1). My children experienced the sun health classes when they attended school in New Zealand in 2001.

43. Worldwatch Institute (2002: 54).

44. On increases in ultraviolet radiation, see Stevens (1995).

45. Worldwatch Institute (2002: 54).

46. Greenpeace (2003).

47. Kerr (1995b); Worldwatch (2002: 54).

48. Miller (1994), 581.

49. Ibid., 232.

50. Paul (2003); Chameides et al. (1994).

51. Karmel and FitzGibbon (2002), citing an EPA study.

52. See Natural Resources Defense Council ([NRDC], 2003b) for an online overview of the 1996 study. For the EPA study, see Suplee (1995).

53. Suplee (1995). See also Samet et al. (2000) in the *New England Journal of Medicine*, which found a similar result.

54. Pearce (1995) for percentage of forests damaged, and European Commission (2000) for figures on defoliation.

55. European Commission (2000).

56. General Accounting Office (2000).

57. Ibid.

58. *China Times* (2000).

59. Environment Canada (2003).

60. Freemantle (1995).

61. Environment Canada (2003).

62. Miller (1994), 324.

63. My calculations based on figures from Pimentel et al. (1995).

64. Brown, Lenssen, and Kane (1995), 118–119.

65. Miller (1994), 332.

66. World Bank (2002), 3.

67. All figures from United Nations Environment Programme ([UNEP], 2003), Table 28.

68. Anderson (1995).

69. Worldwatch (2002), 134.

70. Anderson (1995) gives a figure of one-quarter; WWF Australia (2003) gives a figure of 21 percent.

71. Jones (2003); Miller (1994), 347.

72. Dubash (2002).

73. Brown, Lenssen, and Kane (1995), 123.

74. Miller (1994), 351; UNEP (2003).

75. Brown, Renner, and Halweil (2000), 122.

76. UNEP (2003), 19.

77. Brown, Lenssen, and Kane (1995), 123.

78. UNESCO (2004).

79. Ibid., 122.

80. Ibid., 123.

81. UNEP (2003), 89.

82. Meadows et al. (1992), 56.

83. Ibid., 54-56.

84. Miller (1994), 362; Brown, Lenssen, and Kane (1995), 41; Fresco (2003).

85. U.S. Environmental Protection Agency (2003).

86. American Farmland Trust (2002). I am, however, no longer as confident about these numbers as I was in the first edition of this book, as American Farmland Trust now reports substantially different figures than it did in American Farmland Trust (1994), my earlier source.

87. Worldwatch (2003), 29.

88. Ibid. Growing conditions weren't the best in 2002, and this 294 kilogram per person figure is listed by Worldwatch as preliminary. Nevertheless, 2001 wasn't much better, at 308 kilograms; nor was 2000, at 307 kilograms.

89. Vidal (1995); Essential Action and Global Exchange (2000).

90. Sachs (1996).

91. Ibid.

92. Ibid.

93. Johansen (forthcoming).

94. Shell Oil, belatedly, also agrees and has now modified its statement of business principles to include specific reference to human rights (Beavis and Brown, 1996). However, it has only a spotty record of following through on its human rights commitment, such as the way it handled the April 29 oil blow-out, taking days to stop it and months to even begin to clean it up.

95. Here I am following, in modified form, the distinction Beck (1996) makes between "goods" and "bads." Beck's emphasis, however, is actually on the increasing equality he sees in the distribution of "bads," which is a central feature of what he terms the "risk society" of late modern societies. I critique this conclusion in Chapter 9.

96. Hilz (1992).

97. Institute for Agriculture and Trade Policy (1995).

98. *Financial Times* (2002); Grieder (2001).

99. There is a voluminous literature on this topic. For an introduction, particularly to the debate over whether race is a factor over and beyond class, see Anderton et al. (1994); Boerner and Lambert (1995); Bullard (1994a); Commission for Racial Justice (1987); Goldman (1996); Goldman and Fitton (1994); Heiman (1996); Krieg (1995); Mohai and Bryant (1992); and Chapter 5.

100. For an account of this pain, see Erikson (1994)

101. World Bank (2002), Table 1.

102. Ibid., based on the figures for "purchasing power parity."

103. United Nations Development Programme ([UNDP], 1994), Fig. 2.6.

104. UNDP (1999), 3.

105. The UNDP (1999) gives a figure of 74 to 1 for 1997, the last year for which they have reported this item. I calculated it myself based on 2001 figures from the World Bank (2002), and came up with a figure of about 68 to 1, but my methodology may have differed in a few respects. I derived my figure by first ranking countries by gross domestic product (GDP) per capita and then adding up their populations from the top and bottom until I arrived at one-fifth of the world's population in 2001, and then adding together the GDP of each fifth. (This required taking in only a portion of the population of India, as it lies precisely at the cusp of the lowest 20 percent, and taking in its entire population would well exceed 20 percent of the world's population. Here I added in the same proportion of the Indian GDP as the proportion of the population included.) I suspect that the UNDP figures reported higher inequality as they were based on gross national product (GNP, which includes overseas earnings) rather than GDP (which does not), as GDP tends to lower the income of wealthy nations and to increase the income of poor nations, relative to GNP.

106. UNDP (2003), Table 13, gives the figures for 107 countries around the world, and 48 of those round to 6 to 1 or less, and 60 to 7 to 1 or less.

107.   Ibid.

108.   Wolff (1995), 21. The figures Wolff gives for the 1920s are for inequality in wealth, rather than income, presenting some problems of comparability with the figures I cite for the 1990s. In general, wealth inequalities are greater than income inequalities. However, the societies that are high in one are almost always high in the other, allowing the historical comparison to be made.

109.   Ibid.

110.   Korten (1995), 108; UNDP (1992). This is an extremely difficult number to gauge with any certainty.

111.   World Bank (2002).

112.   World Bank (2000), 23; Worldwatch (2002), 149. But note how these two sources choose slightly different comparison years. The World Bank's choice of 1980 allows it to say that world poverty is "declining," while the Worldwatch's choice of 1987 allows it to say that poverty "persists."

113.   Korten (1995), 39.

114.   UNDP, 2000: 82.

115.   UNDP, 1999: 3.

116.   Durning (1992), 50, Table 4-1.

117.   To use the economic term, the demand for some of these items is "inelastic"—that is, there are limits to how much it can fluctuate, and it probably does not increase at the same rate as wealth.

118.   UNDP (2003), 10.

119.   UNDP (2003), using the year 2000 percentages from Table 7 and the year 2001 population figures from Table 5.

120.   Brown, Lenssen, and Kane (1995), 146–147.

121.   On shelter, see Brown, Lenssen, and Kane (1995), 142; on population, see Brown, Flavin, and Kane (1996), 88.

122.   UNDP (2003), Table 6; figure for 2000.

123.   Ibid.

124.   World Health Organization ([WHO], 2003).

125.   Comptroller and Auditor General (2001).

126.   Freid et al. (2003), Table 68.

127.   WHO (2003).

128.   UNDP (2003), Table 1, comparing the "least developed countries" with the "high income OECD" countries.

129.   Ibid., Table 3.

130.   Ibid., Table 8.

131.   National Coalition for the Homeless (2002).

132.   Lowe et al. (2001).

133.   Edgar et al. (2002).

134.   Hunger and food insecurity figures from Nord et al. (2002).

135.   Kim et al. (2001).

136.   Ibid.

137.   Anthanasiou (1996).

138.   Leopold (1966 [1949]), 262.

139.   Miller (1994), 421.

140.   Worldwatch (2003), 82.

141.   Ibid.

142.   Worthy and Holdaway (2002).

143.   World Conservation Union ([IUCN], n.d.).

144. Leakey and Lewin (1996).
145. Miller (1994), 421.
146. Worldwatch (2002), 104, citing World Resource Institute estimates.
147. Ibid., citing an FAO study.
148. Ibid.
149. Ibid.
150. Ibid.
151. Bell and Laine (1985).

Chapter 2

1. Kearney (1995).
2. Cited in Guha (1995).
3. Marx (1972 [1844]), 58; emphasis in the original.
4. Ibid., 4.
5. In his more considered moments, Karl Marx recognized this interplay as well, offering the term *dialectics* to describe it. Drawing on Hegel, Marx described dialectics as an endless cycle of movement from thesis to antithesis to synthesis, with any synthesis becoming the thesis to which the next antithesis responds. Such an account, however, over-polarizes the explanation of social change. The concept of dialogue, which I take from the writings of the Russian social theorist Mikhail Bakhtin (1981, 1984 [1996], 1986), is an improvement because it emphasizes the mutual conditioning of social factors—a process that is not necessarily oppositional and polarized. For a more detailed critique of the concept of dialectics and a fuller explanation of the analytical advantages of dialogue, see Gardiner (1992). See also the closely related views of Weber (1958 [1904–1905], 277, n. 84).
6. For a review, see Parker (1996).
7. Maslow (1970 [1943]).
8. Ibid., 38.
9. Ibid., 100.
10. This point is also made by Inglehart (1977, 1990). For a detailed critique of Inglehart's particular application of this point, however, see Chapter 6.
11. Sahlins (1972).
12. Ibid., 11.
13. Ibid., 4.
14. Ibid., 27.
15. Gusinde (1961), 86–87; cited in ibid., 13. The Yahgan called themselves the "Yamana," but have now virtually disappeared from the world. As of 1990, there remained only four native speakers of their language, four women living on Navarino Island in Chile's section of the Cape Horn region. For an excellent video on the subject, see *Homage to the Yahgans* (1990).
16. Sahlins (1972), 11.
17. Ibid., 37.
18. For more on the social creation of the concept of being poor, see Norberg-Hodge (1991).
19. Veblen (1967 [1899]).
20. Ibid., 83.
21. Hirsch (1977), 20.
22. Twain (1991 [1876]), 20.
23. See Katz (1994); Wilson and Yaro (1988).
24. Fickling (2003).

25.   On the illegal trade in rhino horns, including a spectacular 1996 bust of a garage in Kensington, England, with 107 horns, see Streeter (1996). On current numbers of rhinos, see SOS Rhino (2002).

26.   SOS Rhino (2002) and World Conservation Union (IUCN) (n.d.)

27.   For a discussion of the relationship among the ideas of Durkheim, Weber, and Tönnies on these points, see Bell (1998a).

28.   Csikzentmihalyi and Rochberg-Halton (1981).

29.   I take this and the following three paragraphs, in modified form, from Bell (1998a).

30.   Bell (1998a).

31.   I draw much of the section that follows from Bell (1997).

32.   I take this quotation (which also appears in Bell [1997]) from Mauss (1990 [1950]), 11. I have also translated into English a few words left in Maori in the original, and put back into Maori one word originally left in English.

33.   Mauss (1990 [1950]), 20.

34.   Douglas and Isherwood (1979).

35.   There is a huge debate on just how effective ads are and how they are interpreted by the public. The classic work that refutes a Pavlovian response to ads is Schudson (1984).

36.   Schudson (1984).

37.   I quote this ad from an issue of the *International Herald Tribune* from sometime in the fall of 1996.

38.   Prices and products all from the Gaiam Web site, www.gaiam.com, and retrieved on January 20, 2004.

39.   For example, see Anthanasiou (1996).

40.   Wachtel (1983), 62, 64.

41.   Schor (1992), 45.

42.   Ibid.; on other industrialized countries, see "Traffic" (1996).

43.   Schor (1992), 29.

44.   Ibid., 32, 82; Table 3.2.

45.   Figures from the U.S. Bureau of Labor Statistics Web site.

46.   See Durning (1992), 131–132, on rise in time spent shopping. Durning at the time listed television watching as the fastest growing category, but television watching in the United States has been declining in recent years due to increases in Internet use.

47.   For the figures on these, see Durning (1992), 43 and 132, citing surveys by others, and Putnam (2000).

48.   On work time, see "Traffic" (1996); for the rest, see Knight and Stokes (1996).

49.   Schor (1992), 2.

50.   For example, Douglas and Isherwood (1979).

51.   Douglas and Isherwood (1979).

52.   For an account of class-bounded patterns of fellowship in Britain, see Bell (1994a); for the United States, see Rubin (1994).

53.   Warr and Payne (1982), cited in Argyle (1987), 92.

54.   Argyle (1987), 93, summarizing several studies.

55.   Schor (1992), 115, summarizing many surveys.

56.   I take the widely used metaphor of a treadmill from Wachtel (1983); Durning (1992), 39; and Schor (1992), 125; the phrase "the treadmill of consumption," however, is original with me, as far as I know.

57.   Gallup (1989), cited in Schor (1992), 126.

58.   Unpublished research, Department of Sociology, Iowa State University.

59.   Erikson (1976).

60.   Ibid.

Chapter 3

1. Hill (1988), cited in Irwin (1995), 2.
2. Schudson (1984) is the best account of our resistance to advertising, although he overstates our ability to resist because he concentrates on resistance to individual ads as opposed to the cumulative impact of being surrounded by ads constantly.
3. Korten (1995), 37.
4. Jacobs (1991).
5. Merton (1973 [1968]).
6. Douthwaite (1992), 18.
7. Closely related ideas can be found in the work of Schnaiberg (1980); Schnaiberg and Gould (1994); Galbraith (1958); Cochrane (1958); O'Connor (1973), and others.
8. See Chapter 1 for a discussion of growing inequality. During the late 1990s, income for most workers in the United States, at least, did indeed pick up for a time—only to be reversed in the early 2000s.
9. On the rate of corporate profit, see Morin and Berry (1996).
10. Logan and Molotch (1987).
11. Ibid.
12. Novek (1995).
13. Jacobs (1991), 25.
14. U. S. Department of Agriculture (1994), Table 393; figure for 1993.
15. This is the Sac County facility owned by Iowa Select (Hupp 2003), which is the biggest that I have heard of in Iowa.
16. Becker (2002).
17. Hupp (2003).
18. See Otto and Lawrence (2002).
19. For a review, see "New Deals" (1995).
20. Mellon et al. (2001).
21. Ibid.
22. D'Aoust et al. (1992), for example, found "disturbing" levels of antibiotic-resistant salmonella in the food chain.
23. Jensen and Hayes (2003).
24. Yepson (1995).
25. For a review of the current status of the legal debate in Iowa, see Babcock et al. (2003).
26. Lowe (1995).
27. Fischer and Dornbusch (1983), 14.
28. I ask this question along with my colleague Philip Lowe in Bell and Lowe (2000). The argument in this section is mainly drawn from that paper.
29. Berlin (1969 [1958]).
30. Including Berlin himself.
31. Bell and Lowe (2000).
32. I got these figures directly from the Office of the Federal Registrar.
33. Bell (1995).
34. For example, see Cochrane (1958) and Rifkin (1995).
35. Warner and England (1995).
36. Worldwatch (2003), 56; 2002 figures.
37. Bureau of Transportation Statistics (2003).
38. Ibid.
39. Durning (1992), 80–81.

40. Brown, Renner, and Flavin (1997), 74; Brown, Flavin, and Kane (1996), 84; Jianhua (2003).

41. Brown, Flavin, and Kane (1996), 84; Asiaweek (2001).

42. Centers for Disease Control (1998).

43. The specific figures for 2002 were 42,850 killed and 2,914,000 injured. Trends in death are up, and trends in injuries are down. National Highway Traffic Safety Administration (2003).

44. Brown, Kane, and Roodman (1994), 132–133; National Safety Council figures; and International Road Traffic and Accident Database ([IRTAD] 2003).

45. World Health Organization ([WHO] 2003); 1998 figures.

46. Ibid.

47. "Roads Claim" (1996); Chris Mead, British Ecological Society, personal communication. Mead estimates the road deaths of British birds to be between 3 and 60 million, but with the likely total somewhere in the upper half of that range.

48. Royal Commission on Environmental Pollution study, cited in "Traffic" (1996).

49. Cited in Fischlowitz-Roberts (2002).

50. Ibid.

51. Brown, Renner, and Flavin (1997), 74.

52. Chris Mead, British Ecological Society, personal communication; Reijnen et al. (1995).

53. There was a spate of these studies in the 1990s. I cite the figures from perhaps the most comprehensive, albeit not the one with the biggest numbers: MacKensie et al. (1992).

54. Ibid., here and for the subsidy numbers in the following paragraphs.

55. Trips figure from Bureau of Transportation Statistics (2003); parking spaces figure from MacKensie et al (1992).

56. For recent reviews, see Kay (1998); Duany et al. (2001); and Alvord (2000).

57. I calculated the per car figure by dividing the $300 billion by the 190 million size of the U.S. car fleet at the time of the MacKensie et al. (1992) study, yielding $1,578.95 per car. I calculated the per gallon figure by dividing the 2 trillion miles Americans annually drove at that time by the fleet size, yielding 10,526.3 miles a year. Dividing this figure by a generous 25 (the mileage per gallon of the U.S. car fleet is actually around the 22–23 mark) yields an average annual fuel use of 421.1 gallons. Dividing 421.1 into $1,578.95 yields $3.7496.

58. Hart and Spivak (1993).

59. Yago (1984), 56–69.

60. Ibid., 60.

61. Merton (1957 [1949]).

62. Winner (1986), 10.

63. Feder and Revkin (2000).

64. Mumford (1934), 365.

65. Ibid., 6.

Chapter 4

1. Malthus (1993 [1798]).

2. Engels (1987 [1844]), 104.

3. For example, Wichterich (1988), cited in Duden (1992), 157. See discussion following.

4. Becker (1986). Similar views have been expressed by Simon (1981, 1995); Boserup (1965) represents a more moderate position. See later discussion in this chapter.

5. See, for example, Brown and Kane (1995); Meadows et al. (1992).

6. Brown, Flavin, and Kane (1996), 89; Independent Commission on Population and Quality of Life (1996), 11.

7. Worldwatch (2003), 66.

8. Ibid., 67.

9. Independent Commission on Population and Quality of Life (1996), frontispiece.

10. Brown and Kane (1995), 51. Because of annual fluctuations, a more precise figure is not possible.

11. United Nations Development Programme ([UNDP] 2003), Table 5, based on projections for the period 2001–2015.

12. Ibid.

13. United Nations Population Division (2003).

14. I thank my son Sam for help with these calculations.

15. Ibid.

16. UNDP (2003), Table 5.

17. United Nations Population Division (2001).

18. See Chapter 3.

19. Lappé and Schurman (1988).

20. Independent Commission on Population and Quality of Life (1996), 15. See that report for a more extensive discussion on this issue.

21. Stein (1995), 133.

22. Barraclough (1982), 102; McEvedy (1995).

23. For a more cynical, and I believe less accurate, interpretation, see Sachs (1992).

24. For example, see Lipset (1959, 1981 [1960]).

25. Quoted in Esteva (1992), 6.

26. Brown, Lenssen, and Kane (1995), 72.

27. UNDP (2003), Table 16.

28. For details, see Chapter 1.

29. UNDP (2003), Table 12.

30. Ibid.

31. World Resources Institute (1996), 162.

32. George and Sabelli (1994), 14.

33. Total debt from Worldwatch (2003), 47; percentage of GDP from UNDP (2003), Table 16.

34. UNDP (2003), Table 16; figure "low human development" countries for 2001.

35. Ibid.

36. Ibid.

37. Worldwatch (2002).

38. For an introduction, see Hopkins and Wallerstein (1982) and Frank (1969). For a recent summary, see Hall (1996).

39. Hewitt and Wield (1992), 57.

40. George and Sabelli (1994), 55.

41. Brown, Lenssen, and Kane (1995), 72.

42. Walton (1994).

43. Herbert (1997).

44. Stiglitz (2002). See also Bruno and Squire (1996), an op-ed article by two high-ranking members of the World Bank's staff, arguing that inequality slows economic growth.

45. Lappé and Shurman (1988), 12, Table 1.

46. Lappé, writing in 1977, used the figure of 2 pounds of grain or 3,000 calories a day, but things have changed since then. See following. I use a ratio of grain to calories derived from Brown, Renner, and Flavin (1997), 27. Current grain production per person is from Worldwatch (2003), 29.

47. Brown and Kane (1994), 66–67.
48. Ibid., Table 4-1.
49. Lappé and Schurman (1988), 14.
50. Ibid., 21.
51. Sen (1981).
52. Sen engages in a little sleight of hand here, in my judgment. Because the third rice harvest, the *aman* harvest, lasts from November to January, it is difficult to decide how to divide its production between the two years. This is an important issue because Sen bases his food-availability figures on annual grain production. Unaccountably, however, Sen includes the *aman* crop entirely in the year in which the January part of the harvest falls, despite the fact that two-thirds of the harvest period is in the previous year. (See Sen [1981], 137.) This allows him to effectively extend the size of the 1974 harvest by including the entire 1973–1974 *aman* crop in 1974 and displacing the entire 1974–1975 *aman* crop, which was badly damaged by the floods, into 1975. As a result, his figures for food availability in 1974 are suspiciously high.
53. Kinealy (1996).
54. Sen (1981), 129.
55. For example, see Devereux (1993); Sarre and Blunden (1995); and even such well-known neo-Malthusians as Meadows et al. (1992).
56. Brown and Kane (1994), 56; 1993 figures.
57. See Devereux (1993), 76–82, for an overview.
58. Stewert (1982), cited in Devereux (1993), 79.
59. Ehrlich (1968).
60. See Sarre and Blunden (1995), 70–71, for a full account.
61. Simon (1981). See also Simon and Kahn (1984); Simon (1995).
62. See Simon (1995).
63. See Chapter 1 for details.
64. As James Scott (1976) has argued, the poor tend to be adverse to risk because their margin is already so tight to begin with.
65. Boserup (1965).
66. Boserup (1981), 3.
67. See Scott (1986) for a study of the displacement of labor and subsequent impoverishment through agricultural intensification in Malaysia.
68. Boserup (1965), 118.
69. Devereux (1993) makes this point very well.
70. Moore (1996).
71. Brown and Kane (1995), 22.
72. Ibid., 38.
73. The following account is drawn from Visser (1986).
74. Scott (1986).
75. Ibid.
76. Brown and Kane (1995), 136.
77. Ibid., Figure 10-3.
78. Brown, Renner, and Flavin (1997), 27.
79. Brown, Flavin, and Kane (1996), 24.
80. Goodno (1995).
81. For example, bioengineer Donald Duvick, cited in Brown and Kane (1995), 139–140; see also the skeptical view of the *Financial Times* in Green (1996).
82. Notestein (1945).
83. Schultz (1981).

84. Stein (1995), 10.
85. Teitelbaum (1987), 31.
86. For a more detailed account of all of these, see ibid.
87. Sachs (1992), 3–4.
88. Norberg-Hodge (1991).
89. For a similar conclusion, see Teitelbaum (1987); Sarre and Blunden (1995).
90. Pietila and Vickers (1994), 14.
91. Ibid., 15.
92. Boserup (1989 [1970]), 35.
93. UNDP (2003), Table 26.
94. Lappé and Schurman (1988), 25–26.
95. Stein (1995).
96. Walby (1996).
97. Moghadam (1996), 1.
98. Joekes (1987) and Standing (1989), cited in Moghadam (1996), 1.
99. Stein (1995); Moghadam (1996); Pietila and Vickers (1994).
100. Stein (1995), 46; Lappé and Schurman (1988), 27.
101. I take this history from Stein (1995), 129–146, who should be consulted for a more detailed account.
102. Wichterich (1988), cited in Duden (1992), 157.
103. Ehrlich and Ehrlich (1990), 17. A similar emphasis on birth control can be found in Ehrlich (1968).
104. For examples of this critique, see Mamdani (1972) and Hartmann, (1987), cited in Duden (1992), 156.
105. I take this account from Stein (1995), 20.
106. Cottrel (1955), 2. I have paraphrased Cottrel to eliminate his gender-specific usage.

Chapter 5

1. I give this account of the Bhopal tragedy based on Chauban (1996); Delhi Science Forum (1984); Morehouse and Subramaniam (1986); and Weir (1986).
2. Timings from Morehouse and Subramaniam (1986).
3. Delhi Science Forum (1984) said a "conservative" figure was 5,000. Morehouse and Subramaniam agree, but report that some estimates put the figure at 10,000. Kurzman (1987) says 8,000. Web sites say if those who died years afterward from the effects are included, the figure rises to 20,000–30,000.
4. The standard figure reported by almost everyone is 200,000, but some sources like Kurzman (1987) put the figure at 300,000.
5. I take the following quotations from Eklavya (1984).
6. Anon. (2001).
7. In February 2001, Union Carbide merged with Dow Chemical Company. Dow and Union Carbide now both claim that because of the merger, Dow has no liability in regard to what happened in Bhopal on December 3, 1984.
8. Klinenberg (2002: 11) goes on to note, "We can collectively unmake them, too, but only once we recognize and scrutinize the cracks in our social foundations that we customarily take for granted and put out of sight."
9. For more on this topic, see the discussion in Chapter 6 of Bakhtin's concept of the "classical body."
10. The term *invironment* was first suggested in Bell and van Koppen (1998).

11. Steingraber (1997).

12. Quoted in Erikson (1994), 38.

13. Erikson (1994).

14. Ibid., 39.

15. For recent studies that show a clear negative association between who gets the bads and who gets the goods, see Edwards and Ladd (2000); Evans and Kantrowitz (2002); Mennis (2002); Morello-Frosch et al. (2001); Pastor et al. (2001, 2002); Pellow et al. (2001); and Pine et al. (2002). More ambiguous results are found in Cassidy et al. (2001), who find effects of race and not of class; Denq et al. (2000), who find effects of class but not of race; and Taquino et al. (2002), who find that the unit of analysis has a strong impact on the results.

16. Erikson (1994), 34.

17. Ibid., 36.

18. Ibid., 56.

19. U.S. Chemical Safety and Hazard Investigation Board ([CSB] 2002) and United Nations Environment Programme (2001) report far lower numbers—4,000 residences damaged and 500 left uninhabitable. The higher numbers come from a Toulouse government Web site (Mairie de Toulouse, 2003).

20. CSB (2002).

21. Arens and Thull (2001).

22. CSB (2002).

23. Goldman and Fitton (1994).

24. Mohai and Bryant (1992).

25. Boerner and Lambert (1995).

26. Heiman (1996); Goldman (1996).

27. Anderton et al. (1994).

28. Davidson and Anderton (2000).

29. Cf. Downey (1998); Weinberg (1998).

30. Cassidy et al. (2001); Daniels and Friedman (1999); Stretesky and Hogan (1998); plus Hines (2001); Pastor et al. (2001, 2002); Pine et al. (2002). Note that the last four did not study the question of class explicitly.

31. Denq (2000); Stretesky and Lynch (1999); and Taquino et al. (2002); plus Evans and Kantrowitz (2002) and Mennis (2002). Note that the last two did not study race explicitly.

32. Davidson and Anderton (2000); Downey (1998); Edwards and Ladd (2000); Krieg (1998); Mitchell et al. (1999); and Morello-Frosch et al. (2001). Note that Davidson and Anderton (2000) found that class was far more significant, and the association they found with African Americans living in non-metropolitan areas was not statistically significant at the 95 percent confidence level statisticians typically require to feel sure about their findings.

33. Pastor et al. (2002).

34. Pine et al. (2002).

35. Downey (1998).

36. Taquino et al. (2002).

37. Evans and Kantrowitz (2002). It is sometimes asked which came first: Do the disadvantaged move into communities that are already contaminated, or are contaminants disproportionately sited in disadvantaged communities? There is, as yet, little research on this question, aside from Pastor et al. (2001), which found that disproportionate siting matters more than disproportionate move-in.

38. Environmental Protection Agency ([EPA] n.d.), figure for 1999.

39. Tomlin (1997).

40. World Health Organization ([WHO] 1998).

41. I take all of the examples of pesticides and their links to birth defects from Steingraber (2001).

42. Oliva, Spira, and Multigner (2001).

43. Swan et al. (2003).

44. Abell et al. (1994).

45. Greenlee et al. (2003).

46. Nelson et al. (2000).

47. Bosma et al. (2000).

48. Stallones and Besser (2001).

49. Charlier et al. (2003).

50. Alavanja et al. (2003).

51. Natural Resources Defense Council (2003).

52. Zheng et al. (1999).

53. Brasher (2003).

54. EPA (2003a). The EPA also notes that some 75 percent of the U.S. field corn acreage is treated with atrazine.

55. Organic Monitor (2003).

56. Organic Trade Association (2003), citing a 2002 study by the Natural Marketing Institute.

57. Wargo (1998).

58. EPA (2003b).

59. Steingraber (2001), 252.

60. Ibid., 251.

61. Cited in Ibid., 251–252.

62. Ibid., 253.

63. Bentham (1996 [1779]).

64. The origin of this phrase is also often attributed to Bentham, and he did use a similar version of it, but apparently borrowed it from elsewhere.

65. Many contemporary utilitarians agree with me here, in fact. They argue that simply raising GNP per capita does not necessarily result in the greatest possible increase in total happiness if that rise in GNP per capita is badly distributed, and thus will not constitute the *greatest* good for the greatest number. However, all utilitarians are united by the idea that sometimes the minority must accept an unpleasant sacrifice to benefit the majority. I thank Jamie Mayerfeld for this observation.

66. Strictly speaking, Rawls did not himself see his theory as appealing to selfishness, however. His argument is that we should leave the whole question aside and start from the "original position" and see what principles of justice we would come up with then. His argument is, if we do so, we will be obliged to plan as if we were the worst off person. But in my view, this nevertheless amounts to an appeal to our selfish concern that we might be wind up among the disadvantaged. I again thank Jamie Mayerfeld for helping me think through this issue.

67. Rawls (1971), 60.

68. Ibid., 62.

69. Ibid.

70. I depart from calling Rawls's theory "liberalism," as is conventionally done, because the term *liberalism* is so easily confused by those unfamiliar with its complexities as a political commitment, as opposed to a theory of justice—arenas that are closely connected but distinct.

71. Sen (1992, 1999).

72. United Nations Development Programme ([UNDP] 1999).

73. Dworkin (2000).

74. For example, Rawls (1995).

75. The definition of social power has been debated long and contentiously within sociology. The definition I offer here is drawn from pragmatism and from Weber, with a hint of Foucault.

76. De Tocqueville (1988 [1835–1840]).

77. For more on isodemocracy, see Bell (2003), from which I derive much of the argument here.

78. Dupuis (2000).

Chapter 6

1. Guha (1999).

2. Weber (1958 [1904–1905]), 60.

3. Italy has the tenth highest per capita GDP in Western Europe, and France the fourteenth highest, as of 2001 (United Nations Development Programme, 2003).

4. Weber (1958 [1904–1905]), 181.

5. Ibid.

6. White (1967), 1207.

7. Ibid., 1204.

8. Ibid., 1205.

9. Ibid.

10. For examples, see Northcott (1996) and Van Dyke (1996).

11. Fung (1966 [1948]).

12. Merton (1965), 65; my emphasis.

13. Ibid., 136.

14. Bellah (1969).

15. The following account is largely drawn from Bell (1994b) and Gardiner (1993).

16. Bakhtin (1984 [1965]).

17. Rabelais (1931 [1532–1552]).

18. Bakhtin (1984 [1965]).

19. Ibid., 12.

20. Ibid., 28, 38.

21. On this point, see both Bell (1994b) and Cresswell (1996), 128.

22. Bakhtin (1984 [1965]), 474.

23. For these quotations, see Plumwood (1994a), 19, citing Morgan (1989).

24. Quoted in Menard (2001), 86–87.

25. For a recent review, see Warren (1996).

26. Plumwood (1994a), 13.

27. Quoted in Seager (1993), 221.

28. Quoted in ibid.

29. The leading male ecofeminist writer is Jim Cheney. See, for example, Cheney (1994).

30. Plumwood (1994a), 9.

31. Ibid., 43.

32. Plumwood (1994b), 74.

33. Bell (1994a), 210–224.

34. Ibid., 218.

35. Ibid., 219–220.

36. Seager (1993), 9.

37. Shiva (1988). In recent writings, Shiva remains unrepentant for her much-criticized idea of the "feminine principle."

38. For examples, see Plant (1989); Diamond and Orenstein (1990).

39. See Seager (1993); Plumwood (1994b); Biehl (1991); and Slicer (1994). Biehl has been a strong critic from outside ecofeminism. The other three are from within ecofeminism. Buege (1994) is a critique of Biehl for tarring all ecofeminist writers with the same essentialist brush.

40. Slicer (1994).

41. Hierarchical categories also dialogically promote a hierarchical frame of mind. See Bell (1998a).

42. Goldman and Schurman (2000).

43. I have had a hand in this one, I confess. See Banerjee and Bell (2001).

Chapter 7

1. Carson (1962), 261–262.

2. Ibid., 97.

3. See, for example, Guha (1999). Guha also notes that *Silent Spring* stayed on the *New York Times* best-seller list for 31 weeks, sold a half-million copies in hardback alone, and was soon published in a dozen countries.

4. Gallup International (n.d.).

5. Inglehart (1995). See also the similar findings in Mertig and Dunlap (2001).

6. Horace (1983), 215–216; Epistle I, 10.

7. Clare (1993), 48.

8. In making this argument, I draw heavily upon the analysis contained in Bell (1994a) and Bell (1999).

9. See Bell (1994a) for more detail.

10. See Bell (1994a) and almost anything Michel Foucault ever wrote.

11. Collingwood (1960 [1945]), 45.

12. Lovejoy and Boas (1935), 104.

13. Finley (1963), 55. Burenhult (1994), 152, gives a figure of only 75,000 for the fifth century B.C.E., and 250,000 for Athens and its hinterlands, which is still a remarkable total.

14. Plato (1952), 483.

15. Plato (1985), 338e and 343b.

16. Rommen (1947 [1936]).

17. See Lovejoy and Boas (1935).

18. Plato (1952), 483.

19. Plato (1965); *Timaeus* sec. 4, 29.

20. See Aristotle (1987); *Parts of Animals,* 1.1, 639b:20, and *Politics* 1.1, 1252a: 0–5.

21. Bartlett (1980), 3.

22. Ibid.

23. Lao Tzu (1963), v. 23.

24. Ibid., v. 156.

25. Ibid., v. 185a.

26. Ibid., vv. 43a and 81.

27. Lieh Tzu (1960), 135–136.

28. Fung (1966 [1948]), 18–19.

29. Merton (1965), 115.

30. Chuang Tzu (1968), 32–33.
31. Lao Tzu (1963), ch. 54; 126.
32. Ibid., ch. 56; 117.
33. Ibid., ch. 81; 143.
34. Fung (1966 [1948]), 177, 284. For a contrasting view, see Peerenboom (1991).
35. Fung (1966 [1948]), 101.
36. Thoreau (1975 [1862]), 164.
37. Ibid., 176.
38. Ibid., 170–171.
39. Ibid., 185.
40. See Bell (1994a).
41. See *Defense of Socrates:* 21a–23c (Plato, 1997). It should be noted that, ever since his own time, there has been a vigorous debate as to whether it is appropriate to consider Socrates a Sophist or not.
42. Thoreau (1975 [1862]), 203–204.
43. Ibid., 200–201.
44. Bell (1994a), 147.
45. Inglehart (1995).
46. Downs (1972).
47. Dunlap (2002).
48. Downs (1972).
49. Dunlap (2002).
50. Cotgrove (1982).
51. Jones and Dunlap (1992).
52. Mertig and Dunlap (2001).
53. Public Agenda On-line (2003) reporting on an April 2000 ABC News/*Washington Post* poll.
54. Kalof et al. (2002).
55. Ibid.
56. Guha (1999).
57. For examples, see Bullard (1993, 1994a, 1994b); Hofrichter (1993); and Taylor (1989).
58. Cited in Guha (1999).
59. Abramson and Inglehart (1995), 1.
60. Inglehart (1977), 10.
61. Inglehart modifies Maslow, however, arguing that there is no particular order to the salience of the needs above the physical; see Inglehart (1990).
62. For simplicity's sake, I have reproduced here only the reduced version of Inglehart's scale, which contains three such sets of four choices. Postmaterialism researchers use the full scale whenever possible. But the single set of four choices I have included is the most widely used.
63. Abramson and Inglehart (1995), 19; Table 2-2.
64. Inglehart (1995), Fig. 5.
65. Ibid., 68.
66. For a summary, see Inglehart (1990, 1995).
67. Guha (1999) and the debate over the application of postmaterialism to global environmentalism in the Spring 1997 issue of *Social Science Quarterly.*
68. Inglehart (1995).
69. Catton and Dunlap (1980); Cotgrove (1982); Dunlap (1980); Dunlap and Van Liere (1978, 1984); Milbrath (1984). See Dunlap et al. (2000) for a revised version of the NEP scale, plus a review of studies using the older version of the scale.

70. Not to mention the "transindustrial paradigm," the "metaindustrial paradigm," and the "ecological paradigm." See Olsen et al. (1992) for a complete review.

71. Olsen et al. (1992).

72. Ibid., 137.

73. For an example of research in this general tradition that uses a far more complex array of categories, in this case in relation to attitudes toward animals, see Kellert and Berry (1982).

74. Dunlap et al. (2000). Paradigm shift researchers have sometimes broken survey responses into different dimensions, although without any great consistency of results, as Dunlap et al. describe. Dunlap et al. argue that this lack of consistency is a sign that "multi-dimensionality" is not significant, however, and that overall the NEP hangs together in the public mind as a single, relatively unified construct. They also suggest that some of the phrasing of the original scale may have obscured the unity of the NEP. I confess to remaining dubious that the revised scale improves the validity of the single construct view, although it may well increase the reliability of it.

75. Beus and Dunlap (1991); Dunlap and Van Liere (1978); and Dunlap et al. (2000).

76. Dunlap et al. (2000) report the differences between 1976 and 1990 surveys of the state of Washington. The other example is Arcury and Christianson (1990).

77. Mol (2001), 59.

78. Mol (1996), 303.

79. Mol and Spaargaren (2000), 27.

80. Pianin (2003).

81. Mol (2001).

82. International Organization for Standards ([ISO] 2003).

83. For example, see Blowers (1997); Blühdorn (2000); Hannigan (1995); and Leroy and Tatenhove (2000).

84. Mol (1996), 309.

85. Hannigan (1995), 184.

86. Hajer (1995).

87. On "weak" versus "strong" ecological modernization, see Christoff (1996); "thin" and "thick" are my own suggestions.

88. Buttel (2003).

89. Socioeconomic Data and Applications Center ([SEDAC] 2003).

90. See Mol and Spaargaren (2000).

91. Thomas (1983), 16. Throughout this section I draw heavily on Thomas's argument, but I depart in arguing for the importance not only of material comforts to the new sensibility of nature but also new democratic feelings toward human social relations.

92. Guha (1999); Mol (1995).

93. I depart here from what may appear to be the superficially similar argument of Nash (1989). My argument is not for a history of ethical extension through various social boundaries and thence into the natural world, but rather of the interactive development of both. Indeed, in many cases extension of rights into nature preceded extension of rights into society. For example, the Royal Society for the Prevention of Cruelty to Animals was founded some 100 years before the foundation of the Royal Society for the Prevention of Cruelty to Children. It is, yet again, a matter of dialogic causality.

94. Engels (1973 [1845]), 89–92.

95. Marsh (1965 [1864]), 3, 465.

96. Inglehart (1990).

97. Bridges and Bridges (1996).

98. Guha (1999).

99. Ibid.

Chapter 8

1. Rolston (1979), 9.

2. Bell (1994a, 1997). The distinction I am drawing has some parallels in what Rolston (1979) describes as "following nature in an absolute sense" versus "following nature in an artifactual sense" but differs in that Rolston does not consider issues of power and interest.

3. Erikson (1966).

4. The solution Rolston (1979), 12, offers is what he calls the "relative" sense of following nature, in which "we may conduct ourselves more or less continuously or receptively with nature as it is proceeding upon our entrance." I have elsewhere (Bell 1994a) described this as the "pastoral" solution, which places human ways on a gradient between the natural and the unnatural.

5. Aristotle (1987); *Physics* 185b: 15–25.

6. In Aristotle's words, "A thing is due to nature, if it arrives, by a continuous process of change, starting from some principle in itself, at some end." Aristotle's *Physics* II.8, 199b: 15–20.

7. Kuo Hsiang's writings are intermingled with those of Chuang Tzu in the *Chuang Tzu*, which Kuo Hsiang edited and augmented with his own commentaries around 300 B.C.E. I take this version from Fung (1953 [1934]: 216–217). Note that in the original in Fung, he gives "non-activity" where I have given the Chinese term, *wu wei*.

8. I thank a colleague from Hong Kong whose name I do not recall for this observation, made over beer at an Oxford pub.

9. See, for example, Beck (1996a); Bell (1996); Cantrill and Oravec (1996); Cronon (1995b); Dupuis and Vandergeest (1996); Eder (1996); Ellen and Fuhui (1996); Evernden (1992); Greider and Garcovich (1994); Hannigan (1995); Haraway (1991); Latour (1993); Soper (1995); and Yearley (1991). There is also a large older, largely nonsociological, literature that discusses the social construction of nature; for example, Collingwood (1960 [1945]); Hubbard (1982); Lovejoy (1936); Lovejoy and Boas (1935); Mill (1961 [1874]); and Williams (1980 [1972]), 70–71. This older literature is often ignored by more recent writers, but I have found it enormously clarifying.

10. Williams (1980 [1972]), 70–71.

11. Bell (1989, 1996).

12. The standard sources for this version of New England are Allport (1990); Black (1950); Raup (1967); and Wilson (1967 [1936]), among hundreds of others.

13. Haystead and Fite (1955), 29. Even environmental historians have accepted this view; for example, Merchant (1989).

14. The few sources that have include Barron (1984); Destler (1973); French (1911); and Higbee (1958).

15. See Bell (1996) for the sources for these.

16. Bell (1996).

17. Bell (1996), 41–44, Tables 2-1 and 2-4.

18. Ibid., 43, Tables 2-2 and 2-3.

19. Barron (1984).

20. Bell (1996), 50.

21. Bell (1996).

22. Bell (1989); Bell (1996), 50–53.

23. Meek (1971), 195.

24. Darwin (1958), 42–43; cited in Hubbard (1981), 24.

25. Hubbard (1981), 24.

26. Cited in Schmidt (1971), 47; see also Engels (1940 [1898]), 208.

27. Herrnstein and Murray (1994).

28. For example, Fraser (1995).

29. Cited in Gould (1996 [1981]).

30. Gould (1996 [1981]), Table 2.1.

31. Ibid., 97.

32. Ibid.

33. Ibid., 93.

34. Huntington (1915).

35. Ibid.

36. Scott (1990).

37. Guha (1989, 1997).

38. Guha (1997), 15.

39. Peluso (1996).

40. Ibid.

41. Cronon (1995), 81.

42. Urry (1990, 1995).

43. Greider and Garcovich (1994), 1.

44. Bell (1997).

45. For extensive critiques of heritage tourism, see Lowenthal (1997, 1985).

46. Hinrichs (1996), 259.

47. Barrett (1994), 256.

48. The letter also lists Linus Pauling, the two-time Nobel Prize winner, and Stewart Udall, former U. S. Secretary of the Interior, as members of the National Advisory Board of Population-Environment Balance.

49. Hardin (1977).

50. Latour (1993).

51. Freudenburg et al. (1995).

52. This story is also sometimes told in a way that is more flattering to Canute, namely that he ordered the tide to stop as a deliberate lesson in the limits of the power of kings compared to the power of God.

53. See Bell (1994a), ch. 1.

Chapter 9

1. I base the following on the verbatim transcript of the April 16, 1996, *Oprah Winfrey Show* from http://www.mcspotlight.org/media/television/oprah_transcript.html (retrieved October 24, 2003).

2. The nineteenth-century German philosopher Georg Wilhelm Friedrich Hegel believed that periods in history could be identified by a certain "spirit" that represents their age, a particular theme that captures the essence of an era. Eugene A. Rosa (2000) in particular has referred to "risk" as representing the spirit of our age.

3. Beck (1992 [1986], 1996a).

4. The U.K. Department of Health monthly report for January 2004 gives the figure of 145 for the United Kingdom (retrieved January 31, 2004, from http://www.doh.gov.uk/cjd/stats/jan04.htm). The number worldwide figure of 155 is from a National Cattleman's Beef Association site (retrieved January 31, 2004, from http://www.bseinfo.org/dsp/dsp_locationContent.cfm?locationId=1259).

5. The U.K. Department of Health monthly reports list three deaths from nvCJD for 1995 and 10 for 1996 in the United Kingdom (retrieved January 31, 2004, from http://www.doh.gov.uk/cjd/stats/jan04.htm). I was unable to find yearly information for nvCJD deaths in other countries, but given that there have been only 10 nvCJD deaths ever in all outside of the United Kingdom, the world figure at the time of Oprah's show is unlikely to have been more than 15.

6. In 1998, Oprah again stated publicly her intention to swear off hamburgers.

7. Although he is acknowledged on the title page and in the preface for his contributions to this second edition, I want to specifically thank Michael Carolan here for his suggestion of the distinction between *risk* and *risky.*

8. See Freudenburg (2000) for further discussion. Also see Perrow (1984) on "normal accidents"; Luhmann (1994) on "structural differentiation"; Giddens (1990) on "system complexity"; and Parsons (1951) on "disembedding of social systems."

9. This is an example of a "normal accident" (Perrow, 1984), which is explained in more detail later in the chapter.

10. Maynard Haskins was my father's occasional penname. AutoBAN is as well a fictitious group.

11. Haskins is, of course, best known for his other fictitious book, *The Frangibility of Change* (London: Soncino Press, 1972).

12. On U.S. traffic fatalities and injuries, see National Highway Traffic Safety Administration (2003). On worldwide traffic fatalities, see World Health Organization ([WHO] 2003). On U.S. AIDS deaths, see Centers for Disease Control (2003). On worldwide AIDS deaths, see Gouede (2003). For the figure on U.S. deaths from automotive air pollution, we divided the figure for U.S. air pollution deaths in half, based on the similar results of a study of air pollution in France, Switzerland, and Austria published in *Lancet* and cited in Fischlowitz-Roberts (2002). The WHO figure also comes from Fischlowitz-Roberts (2002).

13. Elster (1989b), 37.

14. See, for example, Coleman (1990); Hardin (1991, 1993).

15. Rosa (2000).

16. Kleim and Ludin (1997).

17. For example, see Elster (1989a).

18. Carolan (2002).

19. For example, see Elster (1989a).

20. See, for example, Douglas and Wildavsky (1982); Perrow (1984); Slovic (1987); Kunreuther (1992); Kleinhesselink and Rosa (1994); and Erikson (1994).

21. French philosopher Michel Foucault argues that the social relations of power and knowledge are inseparably constituted, and thereby refers to them as "power/knowledge." Michael Carolan and I build upon Foucault's (1969) notion of power/knowledge to include both "identity" and "trust." See Carolan and Bell (2003a, 2003b); Carolan (2002); and Bell (forthcoming) for a more detailed discussion.

22. Erikson (1966).

23. Ibid., 13.

24. Starr (1969) is credited with being the first to conceptually develop this distinction between "voluntary" and "involuntary" risk.

25. Purcell et al. (2000).

26. Ibid.; Freudenburg (2000).

27. Onions (1955) dates the word *risk* from 1661, when it was borrowed from the French *risque*—which was also at one time a common way "risk" was spelled in English.

28. Simmel (1990 [1900]), 444–445.

29. Gallup (1999).

30. Taylor (2003).

31. The continuing appeal of traditional institutions for dealing with uncertainty is largely effect of the failure of rationalism to answer the question of *who* will get cancer and *when*. For a detailed critique of the limits of rationalism, see the next section.

32. See, for example, Barton (1969).

33. Erikson (1994); Edelstein (2000); Couch et al. (2000).

34. Erikson (1976).

35. Ibid., 30.

36. Prince (1920).

37. Freudenburg and Jones (1991).

38. Erikson (1994), 19.

39. Erikson (1994). Human-induced disasters are not exclusively new, however. During the early decades of the nineteenth century, the northeastern section of the United States experienced an unprecedented series of "natural" disasters, mainly in the form of flash floods, which wiped out mills and towns in numerous river valleys. It was only later that these floods were linked to deforestation and agriculture settlement (Lowenthal, 2000).

40. Indeed, recent studies have indicated that even the fourth generation of people (or the great-grandchildren of people) exposed to radiation could inherit unstable genomes, which was cited as a possible explanation for the leukemia cluster around Britain's Sellafield nuclear plant. See Dubrova et al. (2000). Childhood leukemia is around 10 times as common in Seascale in Cumbria, where many Sellafield workers live, as in Britain overall, although epidemiological studies have not conclusively linked this to the parents' exposure. See Muir (2002).

41. Beck (1996b).

42. Picou and Gill (2000).

43. Perrow (1984).

44. Ibid., 90.

45. Erikson (1994), 139–140.

46. Steinberg (2002) makes this argument very well for the Chicago heat wave of 1995.

47. The imagery of the Frankenstein monster is best captured in what Beck (1992 [1986]), 37, calls the "boomerang effect": "The formerly 'latent side effects' strike back even at the center of their production. The agents of modernization themselves are emphatically caught in the maelstrom of hazards that they unleash and profit from."

48. See, for example, Beck (1992 [1986]), 1994, 1997, 1999.

49. Beck (1996a), 6. The distinction between "environmental goods" and "environmental bads," which has been used throughout the book, is drawn from Beck.

50. Beck (1992 [1986]), 49.

51. Ibid., 53; in the original, the second phrase is in italics.

52. Beck (1995), 16.

53. Beck (1994), 5.

54. Beck (1992 [1986]), 1. This is also made in direct reference to Karl Marx. Thus, whereas Marx stands Hegel "on his head," here Beck does the same with Marx.

55. Buttel (1997); Renn (1997); Alexander (1996); Freudenburg (2000).

56. Beck (1992 [1986]), 36.

57. Beck (1992 [1986]), 35–36, and (1999) does see that risk is unequally distributed, but he does not take into account the political significance of this inequality. The risk society framework seems of little help in illuminating this aspect of our environmental condition.

58. Buttel (1997).

59. For more on such a conception of science, see Bell (2004). Some of the lines on science I include here are closely based on what appears there.

60. Irwin (1995).

61. Brown (1990).

62. For a study of participatory research in agriculture, see Bell (2004). For a study of participatory research in air pollution issues, see Yearley et al. (2003).

63. Reported in Nestle (2002), 163.

64. LaMotte and Davis (1998).

65. Nestle (2002), 164.

66. Pring and Canan (1996).

67. Beeman (2002).

68. Ibid.

69. Ibid.

70. Ibid.

71. Scottish researchers fed the same potatoes to aphids and then fed the aphids to ladybugs. They found that the female ladybugs had their life spans cut in half, and also suffered reproduction problems (Kirby, 1999).

72. Pusztai's *Lancet* article is Ewen and Pusztai (1999).

73. Science and Environmental Health Network (2004).

74. Saunders (2000).

75. "How Safe" (2002).

76. WHO (2003c).

77. W. Cooper (1996), 9.

78. Lukaszewski (1992).

79. See Carolan (2002); Carolan and Bell (2003a, 2003b).

Chapter 10

1. U.S. Department of Energy (2003), based on 2001 data. Men drive about 60 percent more than women, 16,749 miles versus 10,174 miles per year.

2. I got these figures from our electric utility on October 6, 2003.

3. The site is www.earthday.net/footprint /index.asp. I took the survey on October 6, 2003.

4. In this paragraph, I am passing at great speed over an enormous amount of scholarly work. The "attitude-behavior relationship," or "A-B split" as I am terming it here, is assuredly one of the most researched topics in social science. For a review, see Kraus (1995).

5. This is a point that most of the scholarly literature on the relationship between attitudes and behaviors misses. Social psychological theories like Festinger's (1962 [1957]) "cognitive dissonance" and Ajzen's and Fishbein's (1980) "reasoned action" tend to individualize the question, to see it as a "micro" issue rather than placing it within a wider social context. For an environmental account of the attitude-behavior split as an effect of social structure, see Ungar (1994); my argument parallels his in several regards.

6. I take the following section, virtually verbatim, from Bell (2001).

7. Hochschild (1997).

8. Hardin (1968).

9. See G. Cooper (1996). The tie-up was caused when a truck became stuck after trying to go under a bridge that was too low. For the driver's safety, the morning papers the next day declined to give his name.

10. See Burton and Dunn (1996); Conybeare and Squire (1994); Polakowski and Gottfredson (1996).

11. For example, see Argyle (1991); Bromley (1992); Feeny et al. (1996); Hinde and Groebel (1992); Ostrom (1990); Roberts and Emel (1992); Stevenson (1991); Thompson and Wilson (1994).

12. On grazing land, see Thompson and Wilson (1994) and Mearns (1996); on fisheries in India, see Gadgil and Guha (1995), 81–84; on fisheries in Brazil, Begossi (1995).

13. See Argyle (1991); Ostrom (1990).

14. This section is largely drawn from Bell (1998a).

15. I base my own telling of the story of "Androcles and the Lion" on Black (1991) and Bartlett (1980). A very similar Aesop fable is "The Lion and the Mouse."

16. Black (1991, 23).

17. This moral is actually from the telling of "The Lion and the Mouse" version of the story in Bartlett (1980, 66). Black (1991, 24) offers this conclusion instead: "And so this story teaches us that a good deed never goes unrewarded," which is a little too instrumental for my tastes.

18. For empirical support of this argument in actual commons, see Begossi (1995) on the role of kinship in the management of Brazilian fisheries, and Petrzelka and Bell (2000) on the importance of collective events like daily communal dancing for herders in the Atlas Mountains of Morocco, discussed in detail following.

19. The following account is drawn from Petrzelka and Bell (2000).

20. Bakhtin (1986). For an insightful application of the concepts of dialogue and mono-logue to our environmental condition, see Gardiner (1993).

21. On the notion of dialogue as "taking others into account," see Bell (1998b).

22. Originally Habermas (1984); my citation, however, is from Habermas (1989), 157. Although I cite Habermas, and my argument is informed by him, I depart from Habermas in some significant ways here. Most notably, Habermas's argument is rooted in a purely rational model in which "communicative action," as Habermas terms it, is one of two types of ratio-nal social action, the other being "strategic action." Communication, for Habermas, is a ratio-nal motivation in itself. Rather, I see communication as a means of achieving the ends of both a solidarity of interests and a solidarity of sentiments, instead of a rational end in itself. I also view social action as equally "rational," that is, oriented toward interests, and "nonrational," that is, oriented toward sentiments. The two, interests and sentiments, constitute each other. See Bell (1998a, 1998b) for more detailed explanations.

23. Bakhtin (1986), 170.

24. See, for example, Brecher (1994); Johnson (1992); Whitley (1992).

25. On "dialogic democracy," see Giddens (1994); on the process of "taking into account," see Bell (1998b).

26. Environmental Protection Agency ([EPA] 2003c).

27. Ibid. To be precise, it was 29.7 percent in 2001.

28. Earlier figures from Easterbrook (1995); 2001 figure from EPA (2003c).

29. EPA (2003c), Table ES-6. In 2000, the country's municipal waste stream was 232 million tons; in 2001 it was 229 million tons. So I have used a figure of 230 million tons as a more general total.

30. Ibid.

31. The *New York Times* piece is by Tierney (1996). Several news organizations pub-lished copycat pieces in the months that followed; for example, Budiansky (1996); Seligman (1996).

32. See, for example, DiConsiglio (1997) or Weinberg et al.'s (2000) and Schnaiberg's and Gould's (1994) argument that recycling is working out to be a government gift to the treadmill of production.

33. For a sample of the extensive literature on participatory development, Brohman (1996); Ghai and Vivian (1992); Hobley (1996); Stiefel (1994).

34. See Bentley and Andrews (1991); Bentley and Melara (1991); Bentley (1994); Bentley et al. (1994).

35. For a compelling history of agricultural poisoning in Latin America, see Wright (1990).

36. There is a huge, and growing, literature on local knowledge. For useful introductions, see Brush and Stabinsky (1996); Campbell and Manicom (1995); Geertz (1983); Hassanein and Kloppenburg (1995); Nazarea-Sandoval (1995).

37. Bentley and Melara (1991), 43.

38. The interviews for this section were conducted in July 1997.

39. You can find out more about Jim's and Joan's bicycle-based enterprises at their Web site, www.bikesatwork.com.

40. Gradwell et al. (1997), 1–2.

41. All quotations from ibid.

42. You can learn more about CSAs and other forms of local agriculture, as well as locate the CSAs and farmers' markets across the United States nearest you, at www.localharvest.org.

43. See Katz (1994); Kunstler (1993, 1996); Langdon (1994).

44. You can find out more about this development, which is called Somerset, at the following Web site, maintained by local developers: www.ames-somerset.com.

45. There has recently been a switch from GNP (Gross National Product) to GDP (Gross Domestic Product). GNP counts the earnings a domestic company makes abroad as income; GDP does not. But GDP counts the earnings made by foreign companies as income, even though the profit goes elsewhere, a common occurrence in poor countries. Thus, GDP tends to overstate the national income of a poor country and correspondingly understate the national income of a rich country.

46. See Daly and Cobb (1989); Daly (1991).

47. Cobb et al. (1995a, 1995b).

48. Cobb et al. (2001).

49. For an introduction, see Ayres and Ayres (1996); Graedel and Allenby (1995); or the *Journal of Industrial Ecology.*

50. Ostrom (1990), 215.

51. Leopold (1961 [1949]), 239.

52. This point was famously made by Anderson (1991 [1983]).

53. Taylor (1986).

References

Abell, Annette, Ernst, Erik, & Bonde, Jens Peter. 1994. "High Sperm Density among Members of Organic Farmers' Associations." *Lancet* 343(1):498.

Abramson, Paul R., & Inglehart, Ronald. 1995. *Value Change in Global Perspective.* Ann Arbor: University of Michigan Press.

Ajzen, Icek, & Fishbein, Martin. 1980. *Understanding Attitudes and Predicting Social Behavior.* Englewood Cliffs, NJ: Prentice-Hall.

Alavanja, Michael C. R., & 12 others. 2003. "Use of Agricultural Pesticides and Prostate Cancer Risk in the Agricultural Health Study Cohort." *American Journal of Epidemiology* 157:800–814.

Alejandro, Oliva, Spira, Alfred, & Multigner, Luc. 2001. "Contribution of Environmental Factors to the Risk of Male Infertility." *Human Reproduction* 16(8):1768–1776.

Alexander, Jeffery C. 1996. "Reflexive Modernization: Politics, Tradition and Aesthetics in the Modern Social Order." *Theory, Culture and Society* 13(4):133–138.

Allport, Susan. 1990. *Sermons in Stone: The Stone Walls of New England and New York.* New York and London: Norton.

Alvord, Katie. 2000. *Divorce Your Car! Ending the Love Affair with the Automobile.* Gabriola Island, BC: New Society Press.

American Farmland Trust. 1994. *Farming on the Edge: A New Look at the Importance and Vulnerability of Agriculture Near American Cities.* Washington, DC: American Farmland Trust.

American Farmland Trust. 2002. *Farming on the Edge: Sprawling Development Threatens America's Best Farmland.* Washington, DC: American Farmland Trust. Retrieved August 24, 2003, from http://www.farmland.org/farmingontheedge/

Anderson, Benedict. 1991 (1983). *Imagined Communities: Reflections on the Origin and Spread of Nationalism,* Rev. ed. London and New York: Verso.

Anderson, Ian. 1995. "Australia's Growing Disaster." *New Scientist* 147:12–13.

Anderton, Douglas L., Anderson, Andy B., Oakes, John Michael, & Fraser, Michael R. 1994. "Environmental Equity: The Demographics of Dumping." *Demography* 31(2):229–248.

Anon. 2001. *Union Carbide's Factory in India: Still a Potential Killer.* Retrieved October 12, 2003, from http://www.bhopal.net/oldsite/contamination.html

Anthanasiou, Tom. 1996. *Divided Planet: The Ecology of Rich and Poor.* Boston: Little, Brown.

Arcury, T. A., & Christianson, E. H. 1990. "Environmental Worldview in Response to Environmental Problems." *Environment and Behavior* 22:387–407.

Arens, Marianne, & Thull, François. 2001. "Chemical Explosion in Toulouse, France Leaves at Least 29 Dead." *World Socialist Web Site.* Retrieved October 23, 2003 from http://www.wsws.org/articles/2001/sep2001/toul-s25.shtml

Argyle, Michael. 1987. *The Psychology of Happiness*. New York and London: Methuen.

Argyle, Michael. 1991. *Cooperation: The Basis of Sociability*. London: Routledge.

Aristotle. 1987. *A New Aristotle Reader*. Edited by J. L. Ackrill. Princeton, NJ: Princeton University.

Asiaweek. 2001 "Numerology: Asians Hit the Road." *Asiaweek*. Retrieved January 21, 2004, from http://www.asiaweek.com/asiaweek/magazine/nations/0,8782,165900,00.html

Associated Press. 2003. "French Minister Predicts More Heat Wave Deaths." *CTV*. Aug. 31, 2003. Retrieved September 1, 2003, from http: //www.ctv.ca/servlet/ArticleNews/story/CTVNews/1062344615564_61/?hub=health

Ayres, Robert U., & Ayres, Leslie W. 1996. *Industrial Ecology: Towards Closing the Materials Cycle*. Cheltenham, UK: Edward Elgar.

Babcock, Bruce, Herriges, Joseph A., & Secchi, Silvia. 2003. "Living with Hogs in Rural Iowa." *Iowa Ag Review* 9(3):1–3.

Bailey, Ronald, ed. 1995. *The True State of the Planet*. New York: Free Press.

Bakhtin, Mikhail. 1981. *The Dialogic Imagination: Four Essays*. Austin: University of Texas.

Bakhtin, Mikhail. 1984 (1965). *Rabelais and His World*. Bloomington: Indiana University Press.

Bakhtin, Mikhail. 1986. *Speech Genres and Other Late Essays*. Trans. Vern W. McGee. Minneapolis: University of Minnesota Press.

Banerjee, Damayanti, & Bell, Michael M. 2001. "Ecogender: Locating Gender in Environmental Sociology," paper presented at the annual meeting of the Rural Sociological Society, Albuquerque, New Mexico, August 16.

Barraclough, Geoffrey, ed. 1982. *The Times Concise Atlas of World History*. London: Times Books.

Barrett, Stanley R. 1994. *Paradise: Class, Commuters, and Ethnicity in Rural Ontario*. Toronto: University of Toronto Press.

Barron, Hal S. 1984. *Those Who Stayed Behind*. Cambridge: Cambridge University Press.

Bartlett, John. 1980 (1855). *Familiar Quotations*. Ed. Emily Morison Beck. Boston: Little, Brown.

Barton, A. 1969. *Communities in Disaster: A Sociological Analysis of Collective Stress Situations*. Garden City, NY: Doubleday.

Beavis, Simon, & Brown, Paul. 1996. "Shell Oil Has Human Rights Rethink." *Guardian*, Nov. 8, p. 1.

Beck, Ulrich. 1992 (1986). *Risk Society: Toward a New Modernity*. London: Sage.

Beck, Ulrich. 1994. "The Reinvention of Politics: Towards a Theory of Reflexive Modernization." In *Reflexive Modernization Politics, Tradition and Aesthetics in the Modern Social Order*, ed. U. Beck, A. Giddens, & S. Lash, pp. 1–55. Cambridge: Polity Press.

Beck, Ulrich. 1995. *Ecological Politics in an Age of Risk*. Cambridge: Polity Press.

Beck, Ulrich. 1996a. "World Risk Society as Cosmopolitan Society? Ecological Questions in a Framework of Manufactured Uncertainties." *Theory, Culture, and Society* 13(4):1–32.

Beck, Ulrich. 1996b. "Risk Society and the Provident State." In *Risk, Environment, and Modernity: Towards a New Ecology*, ed. S. Lash, B. Szerszynski, & B. Wynne, pp. 27–43. London: Sage.

Beck, Ulrich. 1997. *The Reinvention of Politics: Rethinking Modernity in the Global Social Order*. Cambridge: Polity Press.

Beck, Ulrich. 1999. *World Risk Society*. Cambridge: Polity Press.

Becker, Elizabeth. 2002. "Big Farms Making a Mess of U.S. Waters, Cities Say," *New York Times*, Feb. 10. Retrieved January 13, 2002, from http://www.nytimes.com/2002/02/10/politics/10FARM.html

Becker, Gary S. 1986. "The Prophets of Doom Have a Dismal Record." *Business Week,* Jan. 27, p. 22.

Beeman, Perry. 2002. "Ag Scientists Feel the Heat." *Des Moines Register,* Dec. 1. Retrieved October 30, 2003, from http://desmoinesregister.com/business/stories/c4789013/19874144.html

Begossi, Alpina. 1995. "Fishing Spots and Sea Tenure: Incipient Forms of Local Management in Atlantic Forest Coastal Communities," *Human Ecology* 23:387–406.

Bell, Michael M. 1985. *The Face of Connecticut: People, Geology, and the Land.* Hartford, CT: State Geological and Natural History Survey of Connecticut.

Bell, Michael M. 1989. "Did New England Go Downhill?" *Geographical Review,* 79(4):451–467.

Bell, Michael M. 1994a. *Childerley: Nature and Morality in a Country Village.* Chicago: University of Chicago Press.

Bell, Michael M. 1994b. "Deep Fecology: Mikhail Bakhtin and the Call of Nature." *Capitalism, Nature, Socialism* 5(4):65–84.

Bell, Michael M. 1995. "The Dialectic of Technology: Commentary on Warner and England." *Rural Sociology* 60(4):623–632.

Bell, Michael M. 1996. "Stone Age New England: A Geology of Morals." In *Creating the Countryside: The Politics of Rural and Environmental Discourse,* ed. Melanie Dupuis & Peter Vandergeest, pp. 29–64. Philadelphia, PA: Temple University Press.

Bell, Michael M. 1997. "The Ghosts of Place." *Theory and Society* 26:813–836.

Bell, Michael M. 1998a. "Culture as Dialog." In *Bakhtin and the Human Sciences: No Last Words,* ed. Michael M. Bell & Michael Gardiner, pp. 49–62. London: Sage.

Bell, Michael M. 1998b. "The Dialogue of Solidarities, or Why the Lion Spared Androcles," *Sociological Focus* 31(2):181–199.

Bell, Michael M. 1999. "Natural Conscience: Environmental Morality and the Constructionism-Realism Debate." In *Sociological Theory and the Environment: Proceedings of the Second Woudschoten Conference,* Vol. 2., ed. Auguus Gijswijt, Frederick Buttel, Peter Dickens, Riley Dunlap, Authur Mol, & Gert Spaargaren. Amsterdam: Research Committee 24 (Environment and Society) of the International Sociological Association and the University of Amsterdam.

Bell, Michael M. 2001. "Can the World Develop and Sustain Its Environment?" In *Sociology for a New Century,* ed. York Bradshaw, Joseph Healey, & Rebecca Smith, pp. 440–459. Thousand Oaks, CA: Pine Forge Press.

Bell, Michael M. 2003. "Dialogue and Isodemocracy: Creating the Social Conditions of Good Talk." In *Walking Towards Justice: Democratization in Rural Life,* ed. Michael M. Bell & Frederick Hendricks, with Azril Bacal. Research in Rural Sociology and Development book series. Amsterdam and New York: JAI/Elsevier.

Bell, Michael M.; with Bauer, Donna, Jarnagin, Sue, & Peter, Greg. (Forthcoming, 2004). *Farming for Us All: Practical Agriculture and the Cultivation of Sustainability.* Rural Studies Series of the Rural Sociological Society. College Station, PA: Penn State University Press.

Bell, Michael M., & Gardiner, Michael, eds. 1998. *Bakhtin and the Human Sciences: No Last Words.* London: Sage.

Bell, Michael, & Laine, Edward. 1985. "Erosion of the Laurentide Region of North America by Glacial and Glacio-fluvial Processes." *Quaternary Research* 23:154–174.

Bell, Michael M., & Lowe, Philip. 2000. "Regulated Freedoms: The Market and the State, Agriculture and the Environment." *Journal of Rural Studies* 16:285–294.

Bell, Michael M., & van Koppen, Kris. 1998. "Coming to Our Senses: (In Search of) the Body in Environmental Social Theory," XII Congress of the International Sociological Association, Montreal, Canada, July.

Bellah, Robert. 1969. *Tokugawa Religion: The Values of Preindustrial Japan.* New York: Free Press.

Bentham, Jeremy. 1996 (1779). *Introduction to the Principles of Morals and Legislation.* Oxford: Clarendon Press.

Bentley, Jeffery W. 1994. "Facts, Fantasies, and Failures of Farmer Participatory Research." *Agriculture and Human Values* 11(2/3):140–150.

Bentley, Jeffery W., & Andrews, Keith L. 1991. "Pests, Peasants, and Publications: Anthropological and Entomological Views of an Integrated Pest Management Program for Small-Scale Honduran Farmers." *Human Organization* 50:113–24.

Bentley, Jeffery W., & Melara, Werner. 1991. "Experimenting with Honduran Farmer-Experimenters." *Overseas Development Institute Newsletter* 24:31-48.

Bentley, Jeffery W., Rodriguez, G., & Gonzalez, A. 1994. "Science and People: Honduran Campesinos and Natural Pest Control Inventions." *Agriculture and Human Values* 11(2/3):178–182.

Benton, Ted. 1994. "Biology and Social Theory in the Environmental Debate." In *Social Theory and the Global Environment*, ed. Michael Redclift & Ted Benton. London: Routledge.

Benton, Ted. 2001a. "Environmental Sociology: Controversy and Continuity." *Sosiologisk Tidsskrift* 9(1–2):5–48.

Benton, Ted. 2001b. "Theory and Metatheory in Environmental Sociology. A Reply to Lars Mjoset." *Sosiologisk Tidsskrift* 9(1–2):198–207.

Berlin, Isaiah, Sir. (1969 [1958]) "Two Concepts of Liberty." In *Four Essays on Liberty.* London and New York: Oxford University Press.

Beus, Curtis E., & Dunlap, Riley E. 1991. "Measuring Adherence to Alternative vs. Conventional Agricultural Paradigms: A Proposed Scale." *Rural Sociology* 56(3):432–460.

Biehl, Janet. 1991. *Rethinking Ecofeminist Politics.* Boston: South End Press.

Black, Fiona. 1991. *Aesop's Fables.* Kansas City: Andrews and McMeel.

Black, John D. 1950. *The Rural Economy of New England.* Cambridge, MA: Harvard University Press.

Blowers, Andrew. 1997. "Ecological Modernization or the Risk Society?" *Urban Studies* 34:845–871.

Blühdorn, Ingolfur. 2000. "Ecological Modernization and Post Ecological Politics." In *Environment and Global Modernity*, ed. Gert Spaargaren, Arthur P. J. Mol, & Fredrik H. Buttel, pp. 209–228. London: Sage Studies in International Sociology.

Boerner, Christopher, & Lambert, Thomas. 1995. "Environmental Injustice." *Public Interest* 95(118):61–82.

Boserup, Ester. 1965. *The Conditions of Agricultural Growth: The Economics of Agrarian Change Under Population Pressure.* London: George Allen & Unwin.

Boserup, Ester. 1981. *Population and Technology.* Oxford: Basil Blackwell.

Boserup, Ester. 1989 (1970). *Woman's Role in Economic Development.* London: Earthscan.

Bosma, M. P. J., van Boxtel, R. W., Ponds, H. M., Houx, P. J., & Jolles, J. 2000. "Pesticide Exposure and Risk of Mild Cognitive Dysfunction." *Lancet* 356(9233).

Brasher, Philip. 2003. "Study Finds No Atrazine-Cancer Link." *Des Moines Register,* July 18. Retrieved October 24, 2003, from http://desmoinesregister.com/business/stories/c4789013/21775812.html

Brecher, Jeremy. 1994. *Global Village or Global Pillage: Economic Reconstruction from the Bottom Up.* Boston: South End Press.

Bridges, Olga, & Bridges, Jim. 1996. *Losing Hope: The Environment and Health in Russia.* Aldershot, UK: Avebury.

British Broadcasting Corporation (BBC). 2000. "Parkinson's Linked to Insecticide Use." *BBC News*. Retrieved February 2, 2004, from http://news.bbc.co.uk/1/hi/health/738020.stm

Brohman, John. 1996. *Popular Development: Rethinking the Theory and Practice of Development*. Oxford, UK, and Cambridge, MA: Blackwell.

Bromley, Daniel W., ed. 1992. *Making the Commons Work: Theory, Practice, and Policy*. San Francisco: ICS Press.

Brown, Lester R., Flavin, Christopher, & Kane, Hale. 1996. *Vital Signs, 1996: The Trends That Are Shaping Our Future*. New York and London: Norton.

Brown, Lester R., Lenssen, Nicholas, & Kane, Hale. 1995. *Vital Signs, 1995: The Trends That Are Shaping Our Future*. New York and London: Norton.

Brown, Lester R., & Kane, Hale. 1995. *Full House: Reassessing the Earth's Population Carrying Capacity*. New York: Norton.

Brown, Lester R., Kane, Hale, & Roodman, David Malin. 1994. *Vital Signs, 1994: The Trends That Are Shaping Our Future*. New York and London: Norton.

Brown, Lester R., Renner, Michael, & Flavin, Christopher. 1997. *Vital Signs 1997: The Environmental Trends That Are Shaping Our Future*. New York and London: Norton.

Brown, Lester R., Renner, Michael, & Halweil, Brian. 2000. *Vital Signs 2000: The Environmental Trends That Are Shaping Our Future*. New York and London: Norton.

Brown, Philip. 1990. "Popular Epidemiology: Community Response to Toxic Waste-Induced Disease." In *The Sociology of Health and Illness in Critical Perspective*, ed. P. Conrad & R. Kern, pp. 77–85s. New York: St. Martin's Press.

Bruno, Michael, & Squire, Lyn. 1996. "The Less Equal the Asset Distribution, the Slower the Growth." *International Herald Tribune*, Sept. 30, p. 12.

Brush, Stephen B., & Stabinsky, Doreen. 1996. *Valuing Local Knowledge: Indigenous People and Intellectual Property Rights*. Washington, DC: Island Press.

Budiansky, Stephen. 1996. "Being Green Isn't Always What It Seems," *U.S. News and World Report* 121:42.

Buege, Douglas J. 1994. "Rethinking Again: A Defense of Ecofeminist Philosophy." In *Ecological Feminism*, ed. Karen Warren, pp. 42–63. London and New York: Routledge.

Buie, Elizabeth. 1995. "Global Warming Question Has Scientists Under High Pressure." *Herald (Glasgow)*, Aug. 2, p. 6.

Bullard, Charles. 1997. "Study Seeks Cut in Carbon Dioxide." *Des Moines Register*, Apr. 28, pp. 1M, 5M.

Bullard, Robert D. 1993. *Confronting Environmental Racism: Voices from the Grassroots*. Boston: South End Press.

Bullard, Robert D. 1994a. *Dumping in Dixie: Race, Class, and Environmental Quality*, 2nd ed. Boulder, CO: Westview Press.

Bullard, Robert D., ed. 1994b. *Unequal Protection: Environmental Justice and Communities of Color*. San Francisco: Sierra Club Books.

Bureau of Transportation Statistics (2003). *2001 National Household Travel Survey*. Washington, DC: U.S. Department of Transportation.

Burenhult, Goran, ed. 1994. *Old World Civilizations: The Rise of Cities and States*. San Francisco: HarperCollins.

Burningham, Kate, & Cooper, Geoff. 1999. "Being Constructive: Social Constructionism and the Environment." *Sociology* 33(2):297–316.

Burton, Brian K., & Dunn, Craig P. 1996. "Collaborative Control and the Commons: Safeguarding Employee Rights." *Business Ethics Quarterly* 6:277–288.

Buttel, Frederick H. 1992. "Environmentalization: Origins, Processes, and Implications for Rural Social Change." *Rural Sociology* 57:1–27.

Buttel, Frederick H. 1996. "Environmental and Resource Sociology: Theoretical Issues and Opportunities for Synthesis." *Rural Sociology* 61:56–76.

Buttel, Frederick H. 1997. "Classical and Contemporary Theoretical Perspectives and the Environment." Paper presented at Social Theory and the Environment conference of the International Sociological Association, Zeist, The Netherlands.

Buttel, Frederick H. 2003. "The Political Economy of Environmental Flows: Globalization, Unipolarity, and the Need to Reinvent the National-State, Some More Than Others." *Governing Environmental Flows: Conference Proceedings.* CD. Research Committee 24 (Environment and Society) of the International Sociological Association, Wageningen, The Netherlands, June 13–14.

CBS. (2003). "France Ups Heat Toll." *CBS News.* Retrieved January 8, 2004, from http://www.cbsnews.com/stories/2003/08/29/world/main570810.shtml

Campbell, Marie, & Manicom, Ann. 1995. *Knowledge, Experience, and Ruling Relations: Studies in the Social Organization of Knowledge.* Toronto and Buffalo: University of Toronto Press.

Canadian Press. 2003. "Death Toll From Heat Wave in France Likely to Reach 10,000, Minister Says." Retrieved August 21, 2003, from http://www.canada.com/news/world/story.asp?id=6CBDED10-289E-42AB-AD88-51C7C4E7BDDA

Cantrill, James G., & Oravec, Christine L., eds. 1996. *The Symbolic Earth: Discourse and Our Creation of the Environment.* Lexington: University Press of Kentucky.

Carolan, Michael S. 2002. *Trust and Sustainable Agriculture: The Construction and Application of an Integrative Theory.* Unpublished doctoral thesis, Iowa State University, Department of Sociology.

Carolan, Michael S., & Bell, Michael M. 2003. "In Truth We Trust: Discourse, Phenomenology, and the Social Relations of Knowledge in an Environmental Dispute." *Environmental Values* 12(2):225–245.

Carolan, Michael S., & Bell, Michael M. 2004, forthcoming. "No Fence Can Stop It: Debating Dioxin Drift from a Small U.S. Town to Arctic Canada." In *Science and Politics in the International Environment,* ed. Neil Harrison & Gary Bryner. Boulder: Rowman & Littlefield.

Carson, Rachel. 1962. *Silent Spring.* Greenwich, CT: Fawcett Crest.

Cassidy, Elizabeth A., Judge, Rebecca P., & Sommers, Paul M. 2000. "The Distribution of Environmental Justice: A Comment." *Social Science Quarterly* 81(3):877–878.

Catton, William R., & Dunlap, Riley E. 1980. "A New Ecological Paradigm for Post-Exuberant Sociology." *American Behavioral Scientist* 24:15–47.

Centers for Disease Control (CDC). 1998. *National Mortality Data, 1997.* Hyattsville, MD: National Center for Health Statistics.

Centers for Disease Control (CDC). 2003. *AIDS Cases in Adolescents and Adults by Age: United States, 1994–2000.* HIV/AIDS Surveillance Supplemental Report 9(1). Retrieved October 30, 2003, from http://www.cdc.gov/hiv/stats/hasrsuppVol9No1.htm

Chameides, W. L., Kasibhatla, P. S., Yienger, J., & Levi, H. 1994. "Growth of Continental-Scale Metro-Agro-Plexes, Regional Ozone Pollution, and World Food Production." *Science* 264:74.

Charlier, C., Albert, A., Herman, P., Hamoir, E., Gaspard, U., Meurisse, M., & Plomteux, G. 2003. "Breast Cancer and Serum Organochlorine Residues." *Occupational and Environmental Medicine* 60:348–351.

Chauhan, P. S. 1996. *Bhopal Tragedy: Socio-Legal Implications.* Jaipur and New Delhi: Rawat Publications.

Cheney, Jim. 1994. "Nature/Theory/Difference: Ecofeminism and the Reconstruction of Environmental Ethics." In *Ecological Feminism,* ed. Karen Warren. London and New York: Routledge.

China Times. 2000. "Acid Rain Problem Getting Worse." *Taiwan Headlines*. Retrieved August 22, 2003, from http://www.taiwanheadlines.gov.tw/20001128/20001128s2.html

Christoff, P. 1996. "Ecological Modernisation, Ecological Modernities." *Environmental Politics* 5(3):476–500.

Chuang Tzu. 1968. *The Complete Works of Chuang Tzu*. Trans. Burton Watson. New York: Columbia University.

Clare, John D., ed. 1993. *Classical Rome*. San Diego and New York: Harcourt Brace.

Cobb, Clifford, Glickman, Mark, & Cheslog, Craig. 2001. *The Genuine Progress Indicator: 2000 Update*. Oakland, CA: Redefining Progress.

Cobb, Clifford, Halstead, Ted, & Rowe, Jonathan. 1995a. "If the GDP Is Up, Why Is America Down?" *Atlantic Monthly* 276 (Oct.):59–78.

Cobb, Clifford, Halstead, Ted, & Rowe, Jonathan. 1995b. *The Genuine Progress Indicator: Summary of Data and Methodology*. San Francisco: Redefining Progress.

Cochrane, W. 1958. *Farm Prices: Myth and Reality*. Minnesota: University of Minnesota Press.

Coleman, James C. 1990. *Foundations of Social Theory*. Cambridge, MA: MIT Press.

Collingwood, R. 1960 (1945). *The Idea of Nature*. London: Oxford University Press.

Commission for Racial Justice. 1987. *Toxic Waste and Race in the United States: A National Report on the Racial and Socioeconomic Characteristics of Communities with Hazardous Waste Sites*. New York: United Church of Christ.

Comptroller and Auditor General. 2001. *Tackling Obesity in England*. HC 220, Session 2000–2001. London: The Stationery Office.

Conybeare, John A. C., & Squire, Peverill. 1994. "Political Action Committees and the Tragedy of the Commons: The Case of Nonconnected PACs." *American Politics Quarterly* 22:154–174.

Cooper, Glenda. 1996. "An Undying Love That Is Driving Us to Distraction," *Independent* (UK), Dec. 12, p. 5.

Cooper, William. 1996. "Values and Value Judgments in Ecological Health Assessments." In *Handbook for Environmental Risk Decision Making: Values, Perceptions and Ethics*, ed. C. Richard Cothern, pp. 3–10. Boca Raton, FL: Lewis Publishers.

Cotgrove, Stephen F. 1982. *Catastrophe or Cornucopia: The Environment, Politics, and the Future*. Chichester, UK, and New York: Wiley.

Cottrel, Fred. 1955. *Energy and Society: The Relation Between Energy, Social Change, and Economic Development*. New York: McGraw-Hill.

Couch, Stephen R., Kroll-Smith, Steve, & Kindler, Jeffery. 2000. "Discovering and Inventing Hazardous Environments: Sociological Knowledge and Publics at Risk." In *Risk in the Modern Age: Social Theory, Science, and Environmental Decision-Making*, ed. Maurie J. Cohen, pp. 173–195. New York: St. Martin's Press.

Cresswell, Tim. 1996. *In Place/Out of Place: Geography, Ideology, and Transgression*. Minneapolis and London: University of Minnesota Press.

Cronon, William. 1995a. "The Trouble with Wilderness, or, Getting Back to the Wrong Nature." In *Uncommon Ground: Toward Reinventing Nature*, ed. William Cronon. New York: Norton.

Cronon, William, ed. 1995b. *Uncommon Ground: Toward Reinventing Nature*. New York: Norton.

Csikzentmihalyi, Mihaly, & Rochberg-Halton, Eugene. 1981. *The Meaning of Things: Domestic Symbols and the Self*. Cambridge: Cambridge University Press.

Daly, Herman E. 1991. *Steady-State Economics*, 2nd ed. Washington, DC: Island Press.

Daly, Herman, & Cobb, John B. 1989. *For the Common Good: Redirecting the Economy Toward Community, the Environment, and a Sustainable Future*. Boston: Beacon.

Daniels, Glynis, & Friedman, Samantha. 1999. "Spatial Inequality and the Distribution of Industrial Toxic Releases: Evidence from the 1990 TRI." *Social Science Quarterly* 80(2):244–262.

D'Aoust, J. Y., Sewell, A. M., Daley, E., & Greco, P. 1992. "Antibiotic Resistance of Agricultural and Foodborne Salmonella Isolates in Canada: 1986-1989." *Journal of Food Protection* 55(6):428–434.

Darwin, Charles. 1958. *The Autobiography of Charles Darwin.* Ed. Frances Darwin. New York: Dover Publications.

Davidson, Pamela, & Anderton, Douglas L. 2000. "Demographics of Dumping II: A National Environmental Equity Survey and the Distribution of Hazardous Materials Handlers." *Demography* 37(4):461–466.

Delhi Science Forum. 1984. *Bhopal Gas Tragedy.* New Delhi: Delhi Science Forum.

Denq, Furjen, Constance, Douglas H., Joung, Su-Shiow. 2000. "The Role of Class, Status, and Power in the Distribution of Toxic Superfund Sites in Texas and Louisiana." *Journal of Poverty* 4(4):81–100.

Destler, Chester M. 1973. *Connecticut: The Provisions State.* Chester, CT: Pequot Press.

de Tocqueville, Alexis. 1988 (1835–1840). *Democracy in America.* Vols. I and II. New York: Harper & Row.

Devereux, Stephen. 1993. *Theories of Famine.* New York and London: Harvester/Wheatsheaf.

Diamond, Irene, & Orenstein, Gloria E., eds. 1990. *Reweaving the World: The Emergence of Ecofeminism.* San Francisco: Sierra Club Books.

Dickens, Peter. 1996. *Reconstructing Nature: Alienation, Emancipation and the Division of Labour.* London: Routledge.

DiConsiglio, John M. 1997. "Rethinking Recycling," *Scholastic Update* 129:10–11.

Douglas, Mary, & Isherwood, Baron. 1979. *The World of Goods: Towards an Anthropology of Consumption.* New York: Basic.

Douglas, Mary, & Wildavsky, Aaron. 1982. *Risk and Culture: An Essay on the Selection of Technological and Environmental Dangers.* Berkeley, CA: University of California Press.

Douthwaite, Richard. 1992. *The Growth Illusion: How Economic Growth Has Enriched the Few, Impoverished the Many, and Endangered the Planet.* Devon, UK: Green Books.

Downey, Liam. 1999. "Environmental Injustice: Is Race or Income a Better Predictor?" *Social Science Quarterly* 79(4):766–778.

Downs, Anthony. 1972. "Up and Down with Ecology: The Issue-Attention Cycle." *Public Interest* 28:38–50.

Duany, Andres, Plater-Zyberk, Elizabeth, & Speck, Jeff. 2001. *Suburban Nation: The Rise of Sprawl and the Decline of the American Dream.* New York: North Point Press.

Dubash, Navroz K. 2002. *Tubewell Capitalism: Groundwater Development and Agrarian Change in Gujarat.* Oxford: Oxford University Press.

Dubrova, Yuri E., Plum, Mark, Gutierrez, Bruno, Boulton, Emma, & Jeffreys, Alec J. 2000. "Genome Stability: Transgenerational Mutation by Radiation." *Nature* 405(37):37.

Duden, Barbara. 1992. "Population." In *The Development Dictionary: A Guide to Knowledge as Power,* ed. Wolfgang Sachs, pp. 146–157. London and Atlantic Highlands, NJ: Zed Books.

Dunlap, Riley E. 1980. "Paradigmatic Change in Social Science: From Human Exemptionalism to an Ecological Paradigm." *American Behavioral Scientist* 24:5–14.

Dunlap, Riley E. 1992. "Trends in Public Opinion Toward Environmental Issues: 1965-1990." In *American Environmentalism: The U.S. Environmental Movement, 1970-1990,* ed. Riley E. Dunlap & Angela G. Mertig. Philadelphia: Taylor and Francis.

Dunlap, Riley E. 2002. "An Enduring Concern: Light Stays Green for Environmental Protection." *Public Perspective* Sept/Oct, pp. 10–14.

Dunlap, Riley E., & Catton, William R. 1994. "Struggling with Human Exemptionalism: The Rise, Decline, and Revitalization of Environmental Sociology." *American Sociologist* 25:113–135.

Dunlap, Riley E., & Van Liere, Kent D. 1978. "The New Environmental Paradigm: A Proposed Measuring Instrument and Preliminary Results." *Journal of Environmental Education* 9:10–19.

Dunlap, Riley E., & Van Liere, Kent D. 1984. "Commitment to the Dominant Social Paradigm and Concern for Environmental Quality: An Empirical Examination." *Social Science Quarterly* 65:1013–1028.

Dunlap, Riley E., Van Liere, Kent, Mertig, Angela, & Jones, Robert Emmet. 2000. "Measuring Endorsement of the New Ecological Paradigm." *Journal of Social Issues* 56(3): 425–442.

Dupuis, Melanie. 2000. "Not in My Body: rBGH and the Rise of Organic Milk." *Agriculture and Human Values* 17:285–295.

Dupuis, Melanie, & Peter Vandergeest, eds. 1996. *Creating the Countryside: The Politics of Rural and Environmental Discourse.* Philadelphia, PA: Temple University Press.

Durkheim, Emile. 1964 (1893). *The Division of Labor in Society.* Trans. George Simpson. New York: Free Press.

Durning, Alan T. 1992. *How Much Is Enough? The Consumer Society and the Future of the Earth.* New York: Norton.

Dworkin, Ronald. 2000. *Sovereign Virtue: The Theory and Practice of Equality.* Selections. Cambridge, MA, and London: Harvard University Press.

Easterbrook, Gregg. 1995. "Good News from Planet Earth;" *USA Weekend,* Apr. 14-16, pp. 4–6.

Edelstein, Michael R. 1988. *Contaminated Communities: The Social and Psychological Impacts of Residential Toxic Exposure.* Boulder, CO: Westview Press.

Eder, Klaus. 1996. *The Social Construction of Nature: A Sociology of Ecological Enlightenment.* London and Thousand Oaks, CA: Sage.

Edgar, Bill, Doherty, Joe, & Meert, Henk. 2002. *European Observatory on Homelessness: Review of Statistics on Homelessness in Europe.* European Federation of National Organizations Working with the Homeless. Retrieved September 1, 2003, from http://www.feantsa.org/obs/obs_archive_1.htm

Edwards, Bob, & Ladd, Anthony E. 2000. "Environmental Justice, Swine Production and Farm Loss in North Carolina." *Sociological Spectrum* 20(3):263–290.

Ehrlich, Paul R. 1968. *The Population Bomb.* New York: Ballantine Books.

Ehrlich, Paul R., & Ehrlich, Anne H. 1990. *The Population Explosion.* London: Hutchinson.

Eklavya. 1984. *Bhopal: A People's View of Death, Their Right to Know and Live.* Bhopal, India: Eklavya.

Ellen, Roy, & Fuhui, Katsuyoshi. 1996. *Redefining Nature: Ecology, Culture and Domestication.* Oxford, UK, and Washington, DC: Berg.

Elster, Jon. 1989a. *Nuts and Bolts for the Social Sciences.* Cambridge: Cambridge University Press.

Elster, Jon. 1989b. *Solomonic Judgements.* Cambridge: Cambridge University Press.

Engels, Friedrich. 1940 (1898). *The Dialectics of Nature.* Trans. Clemens Dutt. New York: International Publishers.

Engels, Friedrich. 1973 (1845). *The Condition of the Working Class in England, from Personal Observations and Authentic Sources.* Moscow: Progress Publishers.

Engels, Friedrich. 1987 (1844). "Outlines of a Critique of Political Economy." In *Perspectives on Population: An Introduction to Concepts and Issues,* ed. Scott W. Menard & Elizabeth W. Moen, pp. 104–105. New York and Oxford: Oxford University Press.

Environment Canada. 2003. *Acid Rain and Water.* Retrieved August 22, 2003, from http://www.ec.gc.ca/acidrain/acidwater.html

Environmental Protection Agency (EPA). (n.d.). "1998–1999 Pesticide Market Estimates: Sales." *About Pesticides.* Retrieved October 22, 2003, from http://www.epa.gov/oppbead1/pestsales/99pestsales/sales1999.html

Environmental Protection Agency (EPA). 2003a. "Atrazine Background." *Pesticides: Topical and Chemical Fact Sheets.* Retrieved January 27, 2004, from http://www.epa.gov/pesticides/factsheets/atrazine_background.htm

Environmental Protection Agency (EPA). 2003b. *Pesticides and Food: Why Children May Be Especially Sensitive to Pesticides.* Retrieved October 22, 2003, from http://www.epa.gov/pesticides/food/pest.htm

Environmental Protection Agency (EPA). 2003c. *Municipal Solid Waste in the United States: 2001 Facts and Figures.* Washington, DC: Office of Solid Waste and Emergency Response.

Erikson, Kai T. 1966. *Wayward Puritans: A Study in the Sociology of Deviance.* New York: John Wiley.

Erikson, Kai T. 1976. *Everything in Its Path: Destruction of Community in the Buffalo Creek Flood.* New York: Simon & Schuster.

Erikson, Kai. T. 1994. *A New Species of Trouble: Explorations in Disaster, Trauma, and Community.* New York: Norton.

Essential Action and Global Exchange. 2000. *Oil For Nothing: Multinational Corporations, Environmental Destruction, Death and Impunity in the Niger Delta.* Retrieved September 1, 2003, from http://www.essentialaction.org/shell/report/

Esteva, Gustavo. 1992. "Development." In *The Development Dictionary: A Guide to Knowledge as Power,* ed. Wolfgang Sachs, pp. 6–25. London and Atlantic Highlands, NJ: Zed Books.

European Commission. 2000. *2000 Report on the Forest Condition in Europe.* Press release only. Retrieved August 22, 2003, from http://www.dk2002.dk/euidag/rapid/19/

Evans, Gary W., & Kantrowitz, Elyse. 2002. "Socioeconomic Status and Health: The Potential Role of Environmental Risk Exposure." *Annual Review of Public Health* 23:303–331.

Evernden, Neil. 1992. *The Social Creation of Nature.* Baltimore: Johns Hopkins University Press.

Ewen, Stanley W. B., & Pusztai, Arpád. 1999. "Effect of Diets Containing Genetically Modified Potatoes." *Lancet* 354(9187).

Feder, Barnaby J., & Revkin, Andrew C. 2000. "Vast Effort to Fix Computers Defended (and It's Not Over)," *New York Times,* Jan. 1. Retrieved February 1, 2004, from http://www.greenspun.com/bboard/q-and-a-fetch-msg.tcl?msg_id=002COM

Feeny, David, Hanna, Susan, & McEvoy, Arthur E. 1996. "Questioning the Assumptions of the 'Tragedy of the Commons' Model of Fisheries." *Land Economics* 72:187–205.

Festinger, Leon. 1962 (1957). *A Theory of Cognitive Dissonance.* Stanford, CA: Stanford University Press.

Fickling, David. 2003. "Toothfish 'Poachers' Arrested After 7000km Antarctic Chase." *Guardian Weekly,* Sept. 4–10, p. 3.

Financial Times. 2002. "Mexican Nightmare." *Foreign Direct Investment,* Apr. 2. Retrieved August 28, 2003, from http://www.fdimagazine.com

Finley, Moses I. 1963. *The Ancient Greeks.* New York: Viking.

Fischer, Stanley, & Dornbusch, Rudiger. (1983). *Economics.* New York: McGraw-Hill.

Fischlowitz-Roberts, Bernie. 2002. "Air Pollution Fatalities Now Exceed Traffic Fatalities by 3 to 1." *Earth Policy Institute.* Retrieved October 8, 2003, from http://www.earth-policy.org/Updates/Update17.htm

Flegal K. M., Carroll, M. D., Ogden, C. L., & Johnson, C. L. 2002. "Prevalence and Trends in Obesity among U.S. Adults, 1999–2000." *JAMA* 288:1723–1727.

Foucault, Michel. 1969. *The Archaeology of Knowledge and the Discourse of Language.* New York: Harper Colophon.

Frank, Andre Gundar. 1969. "The Development of Underdevelopment." In *Latin America: Underdevelopment or Revolution.* New York and London: Monthly Review.

Fraser, Steven, ed. 1995. *The Bell Curve Wars: Race, Intelligence, and the Future of America.* New York: Basic Books.

Freemantle, Michael. 1995. "The Acid Test for Europe." *Chemical and Engineering News* 73(18):10–17.

Freid, V. M., Prager, K., MacKay, A. P., & Xia, H. 2003. *Health, United States, 2003, and Chartbook on Trends in the Health of Americans.* Hyattsville, MD: National Center for Health Statistics.

Freire, Paulo. 1993 (1970). *Pedagogy of the Oppressed.* New York: Continuum.

French, George. 1911. *New England: What It Is and What It Is to Be.* Boston: Boston Chamber of Commerce.

Fresco, Louise. 2003. "Fertilizer and the Future." *Agriculture 21.* Food and Agriculture Organization of the United Nations. Retrieved August 24, 2003, from http://www.fao.org/ag/magazine/0306sp1.htm

Freudenburg, William R. 2000. "Social Constructions and Social Constrictions: Toward Analyzing the Social Construction of 'The Naturalized' as Well as 'The Natural.'" In *Environment and Global Modernity,* ed. Gert Spaargaren, Arthur P. J. Mol, & Frederick Buttel, pp. 103–119. London: Sage.

Freudenburg, William R., Frickel, Scott, & Gramling, Robert. 1995. "Beyond the Nature/Society Divide: Learning to Think About a Mountain." *Sociological Forum* 10:361-392.

Freudenburg, William R., & Jones, Timothy R. 1991. "Attitudes and Stress in the Presence of Technological Risk: A Test of the Supreme Court Hypothesis." *Social Forces* 69:1143–1168.

Fung, Yu-Lan. 1953 (1934). *A History of Chinese Philosophy.* Vol. II. Trans. Derk Bodde. Princeton, NJ: Princeton University Press.

Fung, Yu-Lan. 1966 (1948). *A Short History of Chinese Philosophy.* Ed. Derk Bodde. New York: Free Press.

Fung, Yu-Lan. 1989 (1931). *Chuang-Tzu: A New Selected Translation with an Exposition of the Philosophy of Kuo Hsiang.* Beijing: Foreign Languages Press.

Funk, John. 1995. "Summer Chills Out: Season Had It All: Hot, Wet, Dry—But It's Fall Now." *Plain Dealer,* Sept. 23, p. 1a.

Gadgil, Madhav, & Guha, Ramachandra. 1995. *This Fissured Land: An Ecological History of India.* Delhi: Oxford University Press.

Galbraith, John Kenneth. 1958. *The Affluent Society.* New York: New American Library.

Gallup International. (n.d.) "World Opinion: Governments Care Too Little about the Environment." *Recent International Surveys.* Retrieved March 21, 2003, from http://www.gallup-international.com/survey11.htm

Gallup Organization. 1999. "As Nation Observes National Day of Prayer, 9 in 10 Pray—3 in 4 Daily." *Poll Analyses.* Retrieved January 30, 2004, from http://www.gallup.com/subscription/?m=f&c_id=10494

Gardiner, Michael. 1992. *The Dialogics of Critique: M. M. Bakhtin and the Theory of Ideology.* London: Routledge.

Gardiner, Michael. 1993. "Ecology and Carnival: Traces of a 'Green' Social Theory in the Writings of M. M. Bakhtin." *Theory and Society* 22(6):765–812.

Geertz, Clifford. 1983. *Local Knowledge: Further Essays in Interpretive Anthropology.* New York: Basic Books.

General Accounting Office. 2000. *Acid Rain: Emission Trends and Effects in the Eastern United States.* GAO/RCED-00-47. Washington, DC: U.S. Government Printing Office.

George, Susan, & Sabelli, Fabrizio. 1994. *Faith and Credit: The World Bank's Secular Empire.* Harmondsworth, UK: Penguin.

Ghai, Dharam, & Vivian, Jessica M., eds. 1992. *Grassroots Environmental Action: People's Participation in Sustainable Development.* London and New York: Routledge.

Gibbs, Walter. 2001. "Research Predicts Summer Doom for Northern Ice Cap." *New York Times,* July 11. Retrieved February 1, 2004, from http://www.nytimes.com/library/national/science/071100sci-environ-climate.html

Giddens, Anthony. 1984. *The Constitution of Society: Outline of the Theory of Structuration.* Cambridge, UK: Polity Press.

Giddens, Anthony. 1990. *The Consequences of Modernity.* Cambridge, UK: Polity Press.

Giddens, Anthony. 1994. *Beyond Left and Right: The Future of Radical Politics.* Cambridge, UK: Polity Press.

Glacken, Clarence. 1967. *Traces on the Rhodian Shore.* Berkeley: University of California Press.

Goddard Space Flight Center. 2002. "Greenhouse Emissions Growth Slowed Over Past Decade." *Top Story,* Jan. 14. Retrieved August 21, 2003, from http://www.gsfc.nasa.gov/topstory/20020103greenhouse.html#press

Goldman, Benjamin A. 1996. "What Is the Future of Environmental Justice?" *Antipode* 28(2):122–142.

Goldman, Benjamin, & Fitton, L. J. 1994. *Toxic Wastes and Race Revisited.* Washington, DC: United Church of Christ Commission for Racial Justice.

Goldman, Michael, & Schurman, Rachel A. 2000. "Closing the 'Great Divide': New Social Theory on Society and Nature." *Annual Review of Sociology* 26:563–584.

Goodno, James B. 1995. "A Job for Super Rice." *Technology Review,* Aug./Sept., pp. 20-22.

Gouede, Nicholas. 2003. "World AIDS Day: New Priorities Needed to Reverse Spread of Disease." *Choices: The Human Development Magazine.* Retrieved October 30, 2003, from http://www.undp.org/dpa/choices/2003/march/hiv.html

Gould, Stephen Jay. 1996 (1981). *The Mismeasure of Man,* 2nd ed. New York: Norton.

Gradwell, Shelly, DeWitt, Jerry, Salvador, Ricardo, & Mayerfeld, Diane. 1997. *Iowa Community Supported Agriculture: Resource Guide for Producers and Organizations.* Ames: Iowa State University Extension.

Graedel, T. E., & Allenby, B. R. 1995. *Industrial Ecology.* Englewood Cliffs, NJ: Prentice-Hall.

Green, Daniel. 1996. "Biotechnology: Long Way from Maturity in Spite of the Promises." *Financial Times,* Nov. 26, Special Section, p. 1.

Greenlee, A. R., Arbuckle, T. E., & Chyou, P. H. 2003. "Risk Factors for Female Infertility in an Agricultural Region." *Epidemiology* 14:429–436.

Greenpeace. 2003. *Greenfreeze: A Revolution in Domestic Refrigeration.* Retrieved August 22, 2003, from archive.greenpeace.org/ozone/greenfreeze/

Greider, Thomas, & Garkovich, Lorraine. 1994. "Landscapes: The Social Construction of Nature and the Environment," *Rural Sociology* 59(1):1–24.

Grieder, William. 2001. "Sovereign Corporations." *Nation,* Apr. 30. Retrieved August 28, 2003, from http://www.thenation.com/issue.mhtml?i=20010430

Guha, Ramachandra. 1989. "Radical American Environmentalism and Wilderness Preservation: A Third-World Critique." *Environmental Ethics* 11:71–83.

Guha, Ramachandra. 1995. "Mahatma Gandhi and the Environmental Movement in India." *Capitalism, Nature, Socialism* 6(3):47-61.

Guha, Ramachandra. 1997. "The Authoritarian Biologist and the Arrogance of Anti-humanism: Wildlife Conservation in the Third World." *Ecologist* 27(1):14-19.

Guha, Ramachandra. 1999. *Environmentalism: A Global History.* Boston: Addison-Wesley.

Gusinde, Martin. 1961 (1937). *The Yamana: The Life and Thought of the Water Nomads of Cape Horn,* 5 vols. New Haven, CT: Human Relations Area Files.

Habermas, Jürgen. 1984. *The Theory of Communicative Action.* 2 vols. Boston: Beacon Press.

Habermas, Jürgen. 1989. *Jürgen Habermas on Society and Politics: A Reader*. Ed. Steven Seidman. Boston: Beacon Press.

Hajer, Martin. 1995. *The Politics of Environmental Discourse*. New York: Oxford University Press.

Hall, Thomas D. 1996. "The World-System Perspective: A Small Sample from a Large Universe." *Sociological Inquiry* 66(4):440–454.

Hannigan, John A. 1995. *Environmental Sociology: A Social Constructionist Perspective*. London and New York: Routledge.

Hansen, James., & Nazarenko, Larissa. 2004. "Soot Climate Forcing via Snow and Ice Albedos." *Proceedings of the National Academy of Science* 101:423–428.

Haraway, Donna Jeanne. 1991. *Simians, Cyborgs, and Women: The Reinvention of Nature*. New York: Routledge.

Hardin, Garrett. 1968. "The Tragedy of the Commons." *Science* 162:1243–1248.

Hardin, Garrett. 1977. *The Limits of Altruism: An Ecologist's View of Survival*. Bloomington: Indiana University Press.

Hardin, Russel. 1991. "Trusting Persons, Trusting Institutions." In *Strategy and Choice*, ed. R. Zeckhauser, pp. 185–209. Cambridge, MA: MIT Press.

Hardin, Russel. 1993. "The Street-Level Epistemology of Trust." *Politics and Society* 21:505–529.

Hart, Stanley I., & Spivak, Alvin L. 1993. *The Elephant in the Bedroom: Automobile Dependence and Denial: Impacts on the Economy and Environment*. Pasadena, CA: Hope Publishing House.

Hartmann, Betsy. 1987. *Reproductive Rights and Wrongs: The Global Politics of Population Control and Contraceptive Choice*. New York: Harper.

Hassanein, Neva, & Kloppenburg, Jack R., Jr. 1995. "Where the Grass Grows Again: Knowledge Exchange in the Sustainable Agriculture Movement." *Rural Sociology* 60:721–740.

Haystead, Ladd, & Fite, Gilbert C.. 1955. *The Agricultural Regions of the United States*. Norman: University of Oklahoma Press.

Heiman, Michael K. 1996. "Race, Waste, and Class: New Perspectives on Environmental Justice." *Antipode* 28(2):111–121.

Hemingway, Ernest M. 1976 (1941). *For Whom the Bell Tolls*. London: Grafton.

Herbert, Bob. 1997. "Nike's Boot Camps:" *New York Times*, Mar. 31.

Herrnstein, Richard, & Murray, Charles. 1994. *The Bell Curve: Intelligence and Class Structure in American Life*. New York: Free Press.

Hewitt, Tom, & Wield, David. 1992. *Industrialization and Development*. Oxford: Oxford University Press.

Higbee, Edward. 1958. *American Agriculture: Geography, Resources, and Conservation*. New York: Wiley.

Hileman, Bette. 1995. "Scientists Warn That Disease Threats Increase as Earth Warms Up." *Chemical and Engineering News* 73(40):19–20.

Hilz, Christoph. 1992. *The International Toxic Waste Trade*. New York: Van Nostrand Reinhold.

Hinde, Robert A., & Groebel, Jo, eds. 1992. *Cooperation and Prosocial Behavior*. Cambridge: Cambridge University Press.

Hines, Revathi I. 2001. "African Americans' Struggle for Environmental Justice and the Case of the Shintech Plant: Lessons Learned from a War Waged." *Journal of Black Studies* 31(6):777–789.

Hinrichs, C. Clare. 1996. "Consuming Images: Making and Marketing Vermont as Distinctive Rural Place." In *Creating the Countryside: The Politics of Rural and Environmental*

Discourse, ed. Melanie DuPuis & Peter Vandergeest, pp. 259–278. Philadelphia: Temple University Press.

Hirsch, Fred. 1977. *Social Limits to Growth.* London: Routledge.

Hobley, Mary. 1996. *Participatory Forestry: The Process of Change in India and Nepal.* London: Overseas Development Institute.

Hofrichter, Richard, ed. 1993. *Toxic Struggles: The Theory and Practice of Environmental Justice.* Philadelphia: New Society Publishers.

Hopkins, Terence K., & Wallerstein, Immanuel. 1982. *World Systems Analysis: Theory and Methodology.* Beverly Hills, CA: Sage.

Horace. 1983. (c. 20 B.C.E.) *The Essential Horace.* Trans. Burton Raffel. San Francisco: North Point Press.

"How Safe Is GM Food?" 2002. *Lancet* 360(9342).

Hubbard, Ruth. 1982. "Have Only Men Evolved?" In *Biological Woman: The Convenient Myth,* ed. Ruth Hubburd, Mary Sue Henifin, & Barbara Fried. Cambridge, MA: Schenkman.

Huntington, Ellsworth. 1915. *Civilization and Climate.* New Haven, CT: Yale University Press.

Hupp, Staci. 2003. "ISU Livestock Study Draws Fire," *Des Moines Register,* Aug. 29. Retrieved October 8, 2003, from desmoinesregister.com/news/stories/c5903220/22119060.html

Imbrie, John, & Imbrie, Katherine Palmer. 1979. *Ice Ages: Solving the Mystery.* Short Hills, NJ: Enslow.

Independent Commission on Population and Quality of Life. 1996. *Caring for the Future: Making the Next Decades Provide a Life Worth Living.* Oxford, UK, and New York: Oxford University Press.

"Inequality: For Richer, for Poorer." 1994. *Economist.* Nov. 5, pp. 19–21.

Inglehart, Ronald. 1977. *The Silent Revolution: Changing Values and Political Styles Among Western Publics.* Princeton, NJ: Princeton University Press.

Inglehart, Ronald. 1990. *Culture Shift in Advanced Industrial Society.* Princeton, NJ: Princeton University Press.

Inglehart, Ronald. 1995. "Public Support for Environmental Protection: Objective Problems and Subjective Values in 43 Societies." *PS: Political Science and Politics* 28(1):57–72.

Institute for Agriculture and Trade Policy. 1995. "Hazardous Waste Dump Plans Attacked." *NAFTA and Inter-American Trade Monitor* 2(27), Oct. 20.

Intergovernmental Panel on Climate Change. 1996. *Climate Change 1995.* 3 vols. Cambridge and New York: Cambridge University Press.

Intergovernmental Panel on Climate Change. 2002a. *Climate Change 2001: Synthesis Report: Third Assessment Report of the Intergovernmental Panel on Climate Change.* Cambridge and New York: Cambridge University Press.

Intergovernmental Panel on Climate Change. 2002b. *Climate Change 2001: Working Group II: Impacts, Adaptation, and Vulnerability.* Retrieved August 22, 2003, from http://www.unep.no/climate/ipcc_tar/wg2/481.htm

International Organization for Standards (ISO). 2003. *The ISO Survey of ISO 9000 and ISO 14001 Certificates: Twelfth Cycle, 2002.* Retrieved January 28, 2004, from http://www.iso.ch/iso/en/iso9000-14000/iso14000/iso14000index.html

International Road Traffic and Accident Database (IRTAD). 2003. *Selected Risk Values for the Year 2001.* Retrieved October 8, 2003, from http://www.bast.de/htdocs/fachthemen/irtad/english/we2.html

Irwin, Alan. 1995. *Citizen Science: A Study of People, Expertise, and Sustainable Development.* London: Routledge.

Jacobs, Michael. 1991. *The Green Economy: Environment, Sustainable Development, and the Politics of the Future.* London and Concord, MA: Pluto.

Jensen, Helen H., & Hayes, Dermot J. 2003. "Antibiotics Resistance: Taking Stock of Denmark's Experience." *Iowa Ag Review* 9(3):4–5.

Jianhua, Feng. 2003. "Parking Strife Frustrates China's Auto Ambitions." *China Today.* Retrieved January 21, 2004, from http://www.chinatoday.com.cn/English/p20.htm

Joekes, Susan. 1987. *Women in the World Economy: An INSTRAW Study.* New York: Oxford University Press.

Johansen, Bruce E. (Forthcoming). "Nigeria: The Ogoni: Oil, Blood, and the Death of a Homeland." In *Indigenous Peoples and Environmental Issues: An Encyclopedia.* Greenwood Press. Retrieved September 1, 2003, from http://www.ratical.org/ratville/IPEIE/

Johnson, H. Thomas. 1992. *Relevance Regained: From Top-Down Control to Bottom-Up Empowerment.* New York: Free Press.

Jones, Nicola. 2003. "South Aral Sea Gone in Fifteen Years." *New Scientist,* July 21. Retrieved August 22, 2003, from http://www.ecology.com/ecology-news-links/2003/articles/7-2003/7-21-03/south-aral-sea.htm

Jones, Robert Emmet, & Dunlap, Riley E. 1992. "The Social Bases of Environmental Concern: Have They Changed Over Time?" *Rural Sociology* 57(1):28–47.

Kalnay, Eugenia, & Cai, Ming. 2003. "Impact of Urbanization and Land-Use Change on Climate." *Nature* 423:528–531.

Kalof, Linda, Dietz, Thomas, & Guagnano, Gregory. 2002. "Race, Gender and Environmentalism: The Atypical Values and Beliefs of White Men." *Race, Class, Gender* 9(2):1–19.

Karmel, Philip E., & FitzGibbon, Thomas M.; Bryan Cave, LLP. 2002. "PM2.5: Federal and California Regulation of Fine Particulate Air Pollution." *California Environmental Law Reporter.* Retrieved August 22, 2003, from http://www.bryancave.com

Katz, Peter. 1994. *The New Urbanism: Toward an Architecture of Community.* New York: McGraw-Hill.

Kay, Jane Holtz. 1998. *Asphalt Nation: How the Automobile Took over America, and How We Can Take It Back.* Reprint ed. Berkeley: University of California Press.

Kearney, Syd. 1995. "Liberace Museum Is Delivering the Glitz." *Des Moines Register,* Oct. 6, p. 2t.

Kellert, Stephen R., & Berry, Joyce K. 1982. *Knowledge, Affection and Basic Attitudes Toward Animals in American Society.* Washington, DC: U.S. Government Printing Office.

Kerr, Richard, A. 1995. "Scientists See Greenhouse, Semiofficially." *Science* 269:1667.

Kim, Myoung, Ohls, Jim, & Cohen, Rhoda. 2001. *Hunger in America 2001: National Report.* Chicago, IL: America's Second Harvest. Retrieved August 28, 2003, from http://www.hungerinamerica.org/

Kinealy, Christine. 1996. "How Politics Fed the Famine." *Natural History* 105(1):33–35.

Kirby, Alex. 1999. "Sci/Tech Parliament Ponders GM Potatoes." *British Broadcasting Corporation,* Mar. 8. Retrieved October 30, 2003, from http://news.bbc.co.uk/2/hi/science/nature/291105.stm

Kleim R., & Lubin, I. 1997. *Reducing Project Risk.* Aldershot: Gower.

Kleinhesselink, R. R., & Rosa, Eugene. 1994. "Nuclear Trees in a Forest of Hazards: A Comparison of Risk Perceptions Between American and Japanese Students." In *Nuclear Power at the Crossroads: Challenges and Prospects for the Twenty-First Century,* ed. T. C. Lowinger & G. W. Hinman, pp. 101–119. Boulder, CO: International Research Center for Energy and Economic Development.

Kleyman, Paul. 2001. "Scientists Link Parkinson's and Pesticides in Search for Cure." *Aging Today* 12(3). Retrieved February 12, 2004, from http://www.asaging.org/at/home/archives/cfm

Klinenberg, Eric. 2002. *Heat Wave: A Social Autopsy of Disaster in Chicago.* Chicago: University of Chicago Press.

Knight, Barry, & Stokes, Peter. 1996. *The Deficit in Civil Society in the United Kingdom.* Birmingham, UK: Foundation for Civil Society.

Korten, David. 1995. *When Corporations Rule the World.* West Hartford, CT: Kumarian.

Kraus, Stephen J. 1995. "Attitudes and the Prediction of Behavior: A Meta-Analysis of the Empirical Literature." *Personality and Social Psychology Bulletin* 21:58–75.

Krieg, Eric J. 1998. "The Two Faces of Toxic Waste: Trends in the Spread of Environmental Hazards." *Sociological Forum* 13(1):3–20.

Krieg, Eric L. 1995. "A Socio-Historical Interpretation of Toxic Waste Sites: The Case of Greater Boston." *American Journal of Economics and Sociology* 54(1):1–14.

Kunreuther, Howard. 1992. "A Conceptual Framework for Managing Low-Probability Events." In *Social Theories of Risk*, ed. Sheldon Krimsky & Dominic Golding, pp. 301–320. Westport, CT: Praeger.

Kunstler, James Howard. 1993. *The Geography of Nowhere: The Rise and Decline of America's Man-Made Landscape.* New York: Simon & Schuster.

Kunstler, James Howard. 1996. *Home from Nowhere: Remaking Our Everyday World for the Twenty-First Century.* New York: Simon & Schuster.

Kurzman, Dan. 1987. *A Killing Wind: Inside Union Carbide and the Bhopal Catastrophe.* New York: McGraw-Hill.

LaMotte, Greg, & Davis, Patty. 1998. "Oprah: Free Speech Rocks: Texas Cattlemen Lose Defamation Suit." *CNN Interactive.* Retrieved January 31, 2004, from http://www.cnn.com/US/9802/26/oprah.verdict/

Langdon, Philip. 1994. *A Better Place to Live: Reshaping the American Suburb.* Amherst: University of Massachusetts.

Lao Tzu. 1963. *Lao Tzu: Tao Te Ching.* Trans. D. C. Lau. Harmondsworth, UK: Penguin.

Lappé, Frances Moore. 1980 (1977). *Food First: The Myth of Food Scarcity.* London: Souvenir Press.

Lappé, Frances Moore, & Schurman, Rachel. 1988. *Taking Population Seriously.* London: Earthscan Publications.

Latour, Bruno. 1987. *Science in Action.* Cambridge, MA: Harvard University Press.

Latour, Bruno. 1993. *We Have Never Been Modern.* London: Harvester/Wheatsheaf.

Latour, Bruno. 1999. *Pandora's Hope: Essays on the Reality of Science Studies.* Cambridge, MA: Harvard University Press.

Leakey, Richard, & Lewin, Roger. 1996. *The Sixth Extinction: Patterns of Life and the Future of Humankind.* New York: Anchor.

Lieh Tzu. 1960. *The Book of Lieh-Tzu.* Trans. A. C. Graham. London: John Murray.

Leopold, Aldo. 1961 (1949). "The Land Ethic." In *A Sand County Almanac*, pp. 237-264. San Francisco: Sierra Club Books.

Leopold, Aldo. 1966 (1949). *A Sand County Almanac, with Essays on Conservation from Round River.* New York: Sierra Club/Ballantine.

Leroy, P., & van Tatenhove, J. 2000. "New Policy Arrangements in Environmental Politics: The Relevance of Political and Ecological Modernization." In *Environment, Sociology and Global Modernity*, ed. Gert Spaargaren, Arthur P.J. Mol, & Fred Buttel, pp. 187–209. London: Sage.

Lertzman, Renee. 1997. "Home and the World: A Conversation with Yi-fu Tuan." *Terra Nova* 2(1):85–95.

Lidskog, Rolf. 2001. "The Re-Naturalization of Society? Environmental Challenges for Sociology." *Current Sociology/Sociologie Contemporaine* 49(1):113–136.

Linden, Eugene. 1994. "Burned by Warming: Big Losses from Violent Storms Make Insurers Take Global Climate Change Seriously." *Time*, Mar. 14.

Lindzen, R. S., Chou, M. D., & Hou, A. Y. 2001. "Does the Earth Have an Adaptive Infrared Iris?" *Bulletin of the American Meteorological Society* 82:417–432.

Lipset, Seymour M. 1959. "Some Social Requisites of Democracy: Economic Development and Political Legitimacy." *American Political Science Review* 53 (Mar.): 69–105.

Lipset, Seymour M. 1981 (1960). *Political Man: The Social Bases of Politics.* Baltimore: Johns Hopkins University Press.

Logan, John, & Molotch, Harvey. 1987. *Urban Fortunes: The Political Economy of Place.* Berkeley: University of California Press.

Long, Steven, & Ort, Donald. 2002. *SoyFACE: A Changing Environment for Agriculture.* Retrieved August 22, 2003, from http://www.soyface.uiuc.edu/news.htm

Lovejoy, Arthur O. 1936. *The Great Chain of Being.* Cambridge, MA: Harvard University Press.

Lovejoy, Arthur O., & Boas, George. 1935. *Primitivism and Related Ideas in Antiquity.* Baltimore: Johns Hopkins Press.

Lowe, Eugene T., with Slater, Art, Welfley, James, & Hardie, Doreen. 2001. *A Status Report on Hunger and Homelessness in America's Cities: A 27-City Survey.* U.S. Conference of Mayors. Retrieved August 28, 2003, from http://www.usmayors.org/USCM/home.asp

Lowe, Philip. 1995. "Social Issues and Animal Waste: A European Perspective." In *New Knowledge in Livestock Odor Proceedings of the International Livestock Odor Conference '95*, pp. 168-171. Ames: Iowa State University.

Lowenthal, David. 1985. *The Past Is a Foreign Country.* Cambridge and New York: Cambridge University Press.

Lowenthal, David. 1997. *The Heritage Crusade and the Spoils of History.* London: Penguin.

Lowenthal, David. 2000. "A Historical Perspective on Risk." In *Risk in the Modern Age: Social Theory, Science, and Environmental Decision-Making*, ed. Maurie J. Cohen, pp. 251–257. New York: St. Martin's Press.

Luhmann, Niklas. 1994. *Risk: A Sociological Theory.* New York: Aldine de Gruyter.

Lukaszewski, James E. 1992. "Managing Fear: Taking the Risk Out of Risk Communication." *Vital Speeches of the Day* 58:238–241.

Lynch, Eamon. 1995. "What Price Pigs? Waste Lagoon Collapses at North Carolina Hog Farm." *Audubon* 97 (Sept./Oct.):14.

MacKensie, Debora. 1995. "Deadly Face of Summer in the City." *New Scientist* 147, Sept. 9, p. 4.

MacKensie, James J., Dower, Roger C., & Chen, Donald D. T. 1992. *The Going Rate: What It Really Costs to Drive.* Washington, DC: World Resources Institute.

Mairie de Toulouse. 2003. "Sinistre AZF: le point sur la reconstruction des quartier sinistrés." Mairie de Toulouse. Retrieved October 22, 2003, from http: //www.mairietoulouse.fr/ Actualite/Dossiers_Actualites /AZF/AZF_reconstruction.htm

Malthus, Thomas. 1993 (1798). *An Essay on the Principle of Population.* Ed. Geoffrey Gilbert. Oxford and London: Oxford University Press.

Mamdani, Mahmood. 1972. *The Myth of Population Control: Family, Caste, and Class in an Indian Village.* New York: Monthly Review Press.

Marsh, George Perkins. 1965 (1864). *Man and Nature.* Cambridge, MA: Belknap Press of Harvard University Press.

Martell, Luke. 1994. *Ecology and Society: An Introduction.* Cambridge, MA: Polity Press.

Marx, Karl. 1972 (1844). "Economic and Philosophic Manuscripts of 1844: Selections." In *The Marx-Engels Reader,* ed. Robert C. Tucker. New York: Norton.

Marx, Karl. 1972 (1859). "Preface to a Contribution to the Critique of Political Economy." In *The Marx-Engels Reader,* ed. Robert C. Tucker. New York: Norton.

Maslow, Abraham. 1970 (1943). "A Theory of Human Motivation." In *Motivation and Personality,* 2nd ed, pp. 80–106. New York: Harper & Row.

Mauss, Marcel. 1990 (1950). *The Gift: The Form and Reason for Exchange in Archaic Societies.* Trans. W. D. Hall. New York and London: Norton.

McEvedy, Colin. 1995. *The Penguin Atlas of African History.* Harmondsworth, UK, and New York: Penguin Books.

Meadows, Donella H., Meadows, Dennis L., & Randers, Jorgen. 1992. *Beyond the Limits: Confronting Global Collapse, Envisioning a Sustainable Future.* Post Mills, VT: Chelsea Green.

Mearns, Robin. 1996. "Community, Collective Action and Common Grazing: The Case of Post-Socialist Mongolia." *Journal of Development Studies* 32:297–339.

Meek, Ronald L., ed. 1971. *Marx and Engels on the Population Bomb.* Berkeley: Ramparts.

Mellor, Mary. 1994. "Varieties of Ecofeminism." *Capitalism, Nature, Socialism* 5(4):117–125.

Mellon, Margaret, Benbrook, Charles, & Benbrook, Karen Lutz. 2001. *Hogging It: Estimates of Antimicrobial Abuse in Livestock.* Cambridge, MA: Union of Concerned Scientists.

Menard, Louis. 2001. *The Metaphysical Club: A Story of Ideas in America.* New York: Farrar Straus & Giroux.

Mennis, Jeremy. 2002. "Using Geographic Information Systems to Create and Analyze Statistical Surfaces of Population and Risk for Environmental Justice Analysis." *Social Science Quarterly* 83(1):281–297.

Merchant, Carolyn. 1989. *Ecological Revolutions: Nature, Gender, and Science in New England.* Chapel Hill: University of North Carolina Press.

Merleau-Ponty, Maurice. 1970. *Themes from the Lectures at the College de France 1952–1960.* Evanston, IL: Northwestern University Press.

Mertig, Angela G., & Dunlap, Riley E. 2001. "Environmentalism, New Social Movements, and the New Class: A Cross-National Investigation." *Rural Sociology* 66:113–136.

Merton, Robert K. 1957 (1949). "The Self-Fulfilling Prophecy." In *Social Theory and Social Structure.* Glencoe, IL: Free Press.

Merton, Robert K. 1973 (1968). "The Matthew Effect in Science." In The *Sociology of Science: Theoretical and Empirical Investigations.* Chicago: University of Chicago Press.

Merton, Thomas. 1965. *The Way of Chuang Tzu.* New York: New Directions.

Metzner, Andreas. 1997. "Constructivism and Realism (Re)Considered." Paper presented at Social Theory and the Environment conference of the International Sociological Association, Zeist, The Netherlands.

Milbrath, Lester W. 1984. *Environmentalists: Vanguard for a New Society.* Albany: State University of New York Press.

Mill, John Stuart. 1961 (1874). "Nature." In *The Philosophy of John Stuart Mill,* ed. Marshall Cohen. New York: Modern.

Miller, G. Tyler, Jr. 1994. *Living in the Environment,* 8th ed. Belmont: Wadsworth.

Mitchell, Jerry T., Thomas, Deborah S. K., & Cutter, Susan L. 1999. "Dumping in Dixie Revisited: The Evolution of Environmental Injustices in South Carolina." *Social Science Quarterly* 80(2):229–243.

Mjoset, Lars. 2001. "Realisms, Constructivisms and Environmental Sociology: A Comment on Ted Benton's 'Environmental Sociology: Controversy and Continuity.'" *Sosiologisk Tidsskrift* 9(1–2):180–197.

Moghadam, Valentine M., ed. 1996. *Patriarchy and Development: Women's Positions at the End of the Twentieth Century.* Oxford: Clarendon Press.

Mohai, Paul, & Bryant, Bunyan. 1992. "Environmental Racism: Reviewing the Evidence:" In *Race and the Incidence of Environmental Hazards: A Time for Discourse,* ed. Bunyan Bryant & Paul Mohai. Boulder, CO: Westview.

Mol, Arthur P. J. 1995. *The Refinement of Production: Ecological Modernization Theory and the Chemical Industry.* Utrecht, Netherlands: Van Arkel.

Mol, Arthur P. J. 1996. "Ecological Modernisation and Institutional Reflexivity: Environmental Reform in the Late Modern Age." *Environmental Politics* 5:302–323.

Mol, Arthur P. J. 2001. *Globalization and Environmental Reform. The Ecological Modernization of the Global Economy.* Cambridge, MA: MIT Press.

Mol, Arthur P. J., & Spaargaren, Gert. 2000. "Ecological Modernization Theory in Debate: A Review." In *Ecological Modernization Around the World,* ed. Arthur P. J. Mol & D. A. Sonnenfeld, pp. 17–49. London: Cass.

Moore, Molly. 1996. "If Possible, the Air in Mexico City Just Gets Worse." *International Herald Tribune,* Nov. 26, pp. 1, 10.

Morehouse, Ward, & Subramaniam, M. Arun. 1986. *The Bhopal Tragedy: What Really Happened and What It Means for American Workers and Communities at Risk.* A Report of the Citizens Commission on Bhopal. New York: Council on International and Public Affairs.

Morello-Frosch, Rachel, Pastor, Manuel, & Sadd, James. 2001. "Environmental Justice and Southern California's 'Riskscape': The Distribution of Air Toxics Exposures and Health Risks among Diverse Communities." *Urban Affairs Review* 36(4):551–578.

Morgan, Fidelis, ed. 1989. *A Misogynist's Source Book.* London: Jonathan Cape.

Morin, Richard, & Berry, John M. 1996. "As for the Economy Public Sees Thorns: Survey Finds Americans Gloomy." *International Herald Tribune,* Oct. 14, pp. 1, 6.

Muir, Hazel. 2002. "Suffer the Children: The Effects of Radiation Don't Stop with the People Exposed to it." *New Scientist* May 11 (2342), p. 5.

Mumford, Lewis. 1934. *Technics and Civilization.* London: Routledge & Kegan Paul.

Murphy, Ray. 1994a. *Rationality and Nature.* Boulder, CO: Westview.

Murphy, Ray. 1994b. "The Sociological Construction of Science without Nature." *Sociology* 28(4):957–974.

Nash, Roderick. 1989. *The Rights of Nature: A History of Environmental Ethics.* Madison: University of Wisconsin Press.

National Coalition for the Homeless. 2002. *Who Is Homeless?* Fact Sheet #3. Washington, DC: National Coalition for the Homeless. Retrieved August 28, 2003, from http://www.nationalhomeless.org/facts.html

National Highway Traffic Safety Administration (NHTSA). 2003. *Motor Vehicle Traffic Crash Fatality and Injury Estimates for 2002.* National Center for Statistics and Analysis. Retrieved October 8, 2003, from http://www-nrd.nhtsa.dot.gov/departments/nrd-30/ncsa/AvailInf.html

National Institute of Water and Atmospheric Research. 2003. *Global Temperatures in 2002: 2nd Warmest Year on Record.* Retrieved August 20, 2003, from http://www.niwa.cri.nz/pubs/mr/archive/2003-02-07

National Snow and Ice Data Center. 2002. *Larsen B Ice Shelf Collapses in Antarctica.* Retrieved August 22, 2003, from nsidc.org/iceshelves/larsenb2002/

National Weather Service. 2003. *Stratosphere: Southern Hemisphere Ozone Hole Size.* Retrieved August 22, 2003, from http://www.cpc.ncep.noaa.gov/products/stratosphere/sbuv2to/ozone_hole.html

Natural Resources Defense Council (NRDC). 2003a. "Toxic Herbicide Atrazine Contaminating Water Supplies, While EPA Cuts Special Deal with Manufacturer." *Toxic Chemicals & Health: Pesticides: In Brief: News.* Retrieved October 24, 2003, from http://www.nrdc.org/health/pesticides/natrazine.asp

Natural Resources Defense Council (NRDC). 2003b. *Danger in the Air: Thousands of Early Deaths Could Be Averted with Cleaner Air Standards.* Retrieved August 22, 2003, from http://www.nrdc.org/air/pollution/nbreath.asp

Nazarea-Sandoval, Virginia D. 1995. *Local Knowledge and Agricultural Decision Making in the Philippines: Class, Gender, and Resistance.* Ithaca: Cornell University Press.

Nestle, Marion. 2002. *Food Politics: How the Food Industry Influences Nutrition and Health.* Berkeley: University of California Press.

"New Deals at the Packaging Plants." 1995. *Successful Farming* 93 (Mar.):22.

Norberg-Hodge, Helena. 1991. *Ancient Futures: Learning from Ladakh.* San Francisco: Sierra Club.

Nord, Mark, Andrews, Margaret, & Carlson, Steven. 2002. *Household Food Security in the United States, 2001.* Washington, DC: USDA Economic Research Service.

Northcott, Michael S. 1996. *The Environment and Christian Ethics.* Cambridge, UK, and New York: Cambridge University Press.

Notestein, Frank W. 1945. "Population: The Long View." In *Food for the World,* ed. Theodore W. Schultz. Chicago: University of Chicago Press.

Novek, Joel. 1995. "Environmental Impact Assessment and Sustainable Development Case Studies of Environmental Conflict." *Society and Natural Resources* 8:145–159.

O'Connor, James. 1973. *The Fiscal Crisis of the State.* New York: St Martin's Press.

Olsen, Marvin E., Lodwick, Dora G., & Dunlap, Riley E. 1992. *Viewing the World Ecologically.* Boulder, CO: Westview.

Onions, C. T. 1955 (1933). *The Oxford Universal Dictionary on Historical Principles.* 3rd ed. Oxford: Oxford at the Clarendon Press.

Organic Monitor. 2003. *The Global Market for Organic Food and Drink.* Abstract of report 7001–40. Retrieved October 24, 2003 from http: //www.organicmonitor.com/700140.htm

Organic Trade Association. 2003. "Industry Statistics and Projected Growth." *Organic Trade Association.* Retrieved October 24, 2003 from http://www.ota.com/organic/mt/business.html

Ostrom, Elinor. 1990. *Governing the Commons: The Evolution of Institutions for Collective Action.* Cambridge and New York: Cambridge University Press.

Otto, Dan, & Lawrence, John. 2002. *The Iowa Pork Industry 2000: Trends and Economic Performance.* Department of Economics, Iowa State University. Retrieved May 21, 2002, from http://www.econ.iastate.edu/faculty/Lawrence/Acrobat/iowa%20hogs2002.pdf

Oulan Tarmo. (2003). *Pikaluistelun Historia: From the Dutch Canals to the Frozen Gulf of Bothnia.* Retrieved August 20, 2003, from http://www.ouluntarmo.fi/lupy/pikaluistelu/historia/H/historia.htm

Parker, Barry R. 1996. *Chaos in the Cosmos: The Stunning Complexity of the Universe.* New York: Plenum Press.

Parsons, Talcott. 1951. *The Social System.* New York: Free Press.

Pastor, Manuel, Jr., Sadd, James L., & Morello-Frosch, Rachel. 2002. "Who's Minding the Kids? Pollution, Public Schools, and Environmental Justice in Los Angeles." *Social Science Quarterly* 83(1):263–280.

Pastor, Manuel, Jr., Sadd, Jim, & Hipp, John. 2001. "Which Came First? Toxic Facilities, Minority Move-In, and Environmental Justice." *Journal of Urban Affairs* 23(1):1–21.

Paul, Jim. 2003. "Warming, Smog Tested on Crops." *MSNBC.* Retrieved August 22, 2003, from stacks.msnbc.com:80/news/938545.asp?cp1=1

Pearce, Fred. 1995. "Acid Fallout Hits Europe's Sensitive Spots." *New Scientist* 147, July 8, p. 6.

Peerenboom, R. E. 1991. "Beyond Naturalism: A Reconstruction of Daoist Environmental Ethics." *Environmental Ethics* 13(1):3–22.

Pellow, David N., Weinberg, Adam, & Schnaiberg, Alan. 2001. "The Environmental Justice Movement: Equitable Allocation of the Costs and Benefits of Environmental Management Outcomes." *Social Justice Research* 14(4):423–439.

Peluso, Nancy Lee. 1996. "Reserving Value: Conservation Ideology and State Protection of Resources." in *Creating the Countryside: The Politics of Rural and Environmental Discourse,* Melanie Dupuis & Peter Vandergeest, eds. Pp. 135–165. Philadelphia: Temple University Press.

Perrow, Charles. 1984. *Normal Accidents: Living with High-Risk Technologies*. New York: Basic Books.

Petrzelka, Peggy, & Bell, Michael M. 2000. "Rationality and Solidarity: The Social Organization of Common Property Resources in the Imdrhas Valley of Morocco." *Human Organization* 59(3):343–352.

Pew Research Center. 1998. "Pew Values Update: American Social Beliefs 1997–1987." Retrieved March 19, 1999, from http://www.people-press.org/valuetop.htm

Pianin, Eric. 2003. "Study Finds Net Gain From Pollution Rules: OMB Overturns Past Findings on Benefits." *Washington Post*, Sept. 27, p. A1.

Picou, Steven J., &. Gill, Duane A. 2000. "The *Exxon Valdez* Disaster as Localized Environmental Catastrophe: Dissimilarities to Risk Society Theory." In *Risk in the Modern Age: Social Theory, Science, and Environmental Decision-Making*, ed. Maurie J. Cohen, pp. 143–170. New York: St. Martin's Press.

Pietila, Hillcka, & Vickers, Jeanne. 1994. *Making Women Matter: The Role of the United Nations*. London and Atlantic Highlights, NJ: Zed Books.

Pimentel, David, Harvey, C., Resosudarmo, P., Sinclair, K., Kurz, D., McNair, M., Crist, S., Shpritz, L., Fitton, L., Saffouri, R., & Blair, R. 1995. "Environmental and Economic Costs of Soil Erosion and Conservation Benefits." *Science* 267:1117–1123.

Pine, John C., Marx, Brian D., & Lakshmanan, Aruna. 2002. "An Examination of Accidental-Release Scenarios from Chemical-Processing Sites: The Relation of Race to Distance." *Social Science Quarterly* 83(1):317–331.

Plant, Judith, ed. 1989. *Healing the Wounds: The Promise of Ecofeminism*. Philadelphia: New Society.

Plato. 1952 (c. 399 B.C.E.) *Plato's Gorgias*. Trans. W. C. Helmbold. New York: Liberal Arts Press.

Plato. 1965 (c. 360 B.C.E.). *Timaeus and Critias*. London: Penguin.

Plato. 1985 (c. 399 B.C.E.). *The Republic*. Trans. Richard W. Sterling & William C. Scott. New York: Norton.

Plato. 1997 (c. 399 B.C.E.) *Defence of Socrates, Euthyphro, Crito*. Trans. David Gallup. Oxford: Oxford University Press.

Plumwood, Val. 1994a. *Feminism and the Mastery of Nature*. London and New York: Routledge.

Plumwood, Val. 1994b. "The Ecopolitics Debate and the Politics of Nature." In *Ecological Feminism*, ed. Karen Warren, pp. 64–87. London and New York: Routledge.

Polakowski, Michael, & Gottfredson, Michael R. 1996. "The Use of Prisons as a Commons Problem: An Exploratory Study." *Journal of Research in Crime and Delinquency* 33:70–93.

Prince, S. H. 1920. *Catastrophe and Social Change*. New York: Columbia University Press.

Pring, George W., & Canan, Penelope. 1996. *SLAPPs: Getting Sued for Speaking Out*. Philadelphia: Temple University Press.

Public Agenda On-Line. 2003. "Environment: A Nation Divided?" *Environment*. Retrieved January 28, 2004, from http: /www.publicagenda.org/issues/nation_divided_detail.cfm?issue_type=environment&list=1

Purcell, Kristen, Clark, Lee, & Renzulli, Linda. 2000. "Menus of Choice: The Social Embeddedness of Decisions." In *Risk in the Modern Age: Social Theory, Science, and Environmental Decision-Making*, ed. Maurie J. Cohen, pp. 62–79. New York: St. Martin's Press.

Putnam, Robert. 2000. *Bowling Alone: The Collapse and Revival of American Community*. New York: Simon & Schuster.

Rabelais, Francis. 1931 (1532–1552). *The Works of Francis Rabelais*. Ed. Albert J. Nock & Catherine Rose Wilson. New York: Harcourt, Brace.

Raup, Hugh M. 1967. "The View from John Sanderson's Farm: A Perspective for the Use of the Land." *Forest History* 10:1–11.

Rawls, John. 1971. *A Theory of Justice.* Cambridge, MA: Belknap Press of Harvard University Press.

Rawls, John. 1995. *Political Liberalism.* New York: Columbia University Press.

Reijnen, Rien, Foppen, Rudd, & Braak, Cajo-Ter. 1995. "The Effects of Car Traffic on Breeding Bird Populations in Woodland. III. Reduction of Density in Relation to the Proximity of Main Roads." *Journal of Applied Ecology* 32:187–202.

Renn, Ortwin. 1997. "The Demise of the Risk Society." Paper presented at the Annual Meeting of the American Sociological Association, Toronto, Canada.

Revkin, Andrew C. 2002. "Climate Changing, U.S. Says in Report." *New York Times*, June 3. Retrieved June 3, 2002, from http://www.nytimes.com/2002/06/03/science/03CLIM.html

Rifkin, Jeremy. 1995. *The End of Work: The Decline of the Global Labor Force and the Dawn of the Post-Market Era.* New York: Putnam.

"Roads Claim Up to 60 Million Birds a Year." 1996. *Times* (London), Sept. 10, p. 8.

Roberts, Rebecca S., & Emel, Jacque. 1992. "Uneven Development and the Tragedy of the Commons: Competing Images for Nature-Society Analysis." *Economic Geography* 68:249–271.

Rolston, Holmes, Ill. 1979. "Can and Ought We to Follow Nature?" *Environmental Ethics* 1(1):7–30.

Rommen, Heinrich A. 1947 (1936). *The Natural Law.* Trans. Thomas R. Hanley. St. Louis, MO: B. Herder.

Rosa, Eugene A. 2000. "Modern Theories of Society and the Environment: The Risk Society." In *Environment and Global Modernity*, ed. Gert Spaargaren, Arthur P. J. Mol, & Frederick Buttel, pp. 73–101. London: Sage.

Rubin, Lillian. 1994. *Families on the Fault Line: America's Working Class Speaks about the Family, the Economy, Race, and Ethnicity.* New York: HarperCollins.

Ruskin, John. 1967 (1863). *Unto This Last: Four Essays on the First Principles of Political Economy.* Ed. Lloyd J. Hubenka. Lincoln: University of Nebraska Press.

Sachs, Aaron. 1996. "Dying for Oil." *Worldwatch* 9(3):10–21.

Sachs, Wolfgang, ed. 1992. *The Development Dictionary: A Guide to Knowledge as Power.* London and Atlantic Highlands, NJ: Zed Books.

Sahlins, Marshall. 1972. "The Original Affluent Society." In *Stone Age Economics.* New York: Aldine, pp. 1–39.

Samet, Jonathan M., Dominici, Francesca, Curriero, Frank C., Coursac, Ivan, & Zeger, Scott L. 2000. "Fine Particulate Air Pollution and Mortality in 20 U.S. Cities, 1987–1994." *New England Journal of Medicine* 343(24):1742–1749.

Sarre, Philip, & Blunden, John. 1995. *An Overcrowded World? Population, Resources, and the Environment.* Oxford and New York: Oxford University Press and the Open University.

Saunders, Peter. 2000. "Use and Abuse of the Precautionary Principle." *Third World Network.* Retrieved January 31, 2004, from http://www.twnside.org.sg/title/saunders.htm

Schmidt, Alfred. 1971. *The Concept of Nature in Marx.* Trans. Ben Foukes. London: New Left Books.

Schnaiberg, Alan, & Gould, Kenneth Alan. 1994. *Environment and Society: The Enduring Conflict.* New York: St. Martin's Press.

Schnaiberg, Alan. 1980. *The Environment, from Surplus to Scarcity.* New York and Oxford: Oxford University Press.

Schor, Juliet B. 1992. *The Overworked American: The Unexpected Decline of Leisure.* New York: Basic.

Schudson, Michael. 1984. *Advertizing: The Uneasy Persuasion.* New York: Basic.

Schultz, T. Paul. 1981. *Economics of Population.* Reading, MA: Addison-Wesley.

Schumpeter, Joseph A. 1949. *The Theory of Economic Development: An Inquiry into Profits, Capital, Credit, Interest, and the Business Cycle.* Cambridge, MA: Harvard University Press; London: Oxford University Press.

Science and Environmental Health Network. 2004. *Precautionary Principle.* Retrieved January 31, 2004, from http://www.sehn.org/precaution.html

Scott, James C. 1976. *The Moral Economy of the Peasant: Rebellion and Subsistence in Southeast Asia.* New Haven, CT: Yale University Press.

Scott, James C. 1986. *Weapons of the Weak: Everyday Forms of Peasant Resistance.* New Haven, CT: Yale University Press.

Scott, James C. 1990. *Domination and the Arts of Resistance: Hidden Transcripts.* New Haven, CT: Yale University Press.

Seager, Joni. 1993. *Earth Follies: Feminism, Politics, and the Environment.* London: Earthscan.

Seidman, Steven. 1994. *Contested Knowledge: Social Theory in the Post-Modern Era.* Oxford, UK, and Cambridge, MA: Blackwell.

Seligman, Daniel. 1996. "Too Much Recycling?" *Fortune* 134:155–156.

Sen, Amartya. 1981. *Poverty and Famines: An Essay on Entitlement and Deprivation.* New York and Oxford: Oxford University Press.

Sen, Amartya. 1992. *Inequality Reexamined.* Cambridge, MA: Harvard University Press.

Sen, Amartya. 1999. *Development as Freedom.* New York: Anchor Books.

Shanna H. Swan, & 9 others. 2003. "Geographic Differences in Semen Quality of Fertile U.S. Males." *Environmental Health Perspectives* 111(4).

Shiva, Vandana. 1988. *Staying Alive: Women, Ecology and Development.* London: Zed Books.

Simmel, Georg. 1990 (1900). *The Philosophy of Money.* Ed. David Frisby; Trans. Tom Bottomore and David Frisby, 2nd enl. ed. London and New York: Routledge.

Simon, Julian, ed. 1995. *The State of Humanity.* Oxford, UK, and Cambridge, MA: Blackwell.

Simon, Julian. 1981. *The Ultimate Resource.* Princeton, NJ: Princeton University Press.

Simon, Julian, & Kahn, Herman. 1984. *The Resourceful Earth: A Response to Global 2000.* Oxford and New York: Basil Blackwell.

Singer, Peter. 1996 (1975). "Animal Liberation." In *Animal Rights: The Changing Debate,* ed. Robert Garner. New York: New York University Press.

Slicer, Deborah. 1994. "Wrongs of Passage: Three Challenges to the Maturing of Ecofeminism." In *Ecological Feminism,* ed. Karen Warren, pp. 29–41. London and New York: Routledge.

Slovic, Paul. 1987. "Perception of Risk." *Science* 236:280–285.

Socioeconomic Data and Applications Center (SEDAC). 2003. "Treaty Texts." *Environmental Treaties and Resource Indicators.* Retrieved January 27, 2004, from http://sedac.ciesin.columbia.edu/entri/TextsToc.jsp

Soper, Kate. 1995. *What Is Nature? Culture, Politics and the Non-Human.* Oxford, UK, Cambridge, MA: Blackwell.

SOS Rhino. 2002. "African Rhinos Edge Back from the Brink." *In the News.* Retrieved September 9, 2003, from http://www.sosrhino.org/news/rhinonews061202b.php

Stallones, Lorann, & Beseler, Cheryl. 2001. "Pesticide Poisoning and Depressive Symptoms Among Farm Residents." *Annals of Epidemiology* 12(6):389–394.

Standing, Guy. 1989. "Global Feminization Through Flexible Labour." *World Development* 17(7):1077–1095.

Starr, Chauncey. 1969. "Social Benefit versus Technological Risk: What Is Our Society Willing to Pay for Safety?" *Science* 165:1232–1238.

Stein, Dorothy. 1995. *People Who Count: Population and Politics, Women and Children.* London: Earthscan.

Steingraber, Sandra. 1997. *Living Downstream: An Ecologist Looks at Cancer and the Environment.* New York: Addison-Wesley.

Steingraber, Sandra. 2001. *Having Faith: An Ecologist's Journey to Motherhood.* New York: Berkley Books.

Stetkiewicz, Chris. 2003 "Ultra-Green Seattle Sorts Through Recycling Options." *Reuters News Service,* Jan. 14. Retrieved October 8, 2003, from http://www.planetark.org/dailynewsstory.cfm/newsid/19406/story.htm

Stevens, Wallace K. 1995. "Study of Cloud Patterns Points to Many Areas Exposed to Big Rises in Ultraviolet Radiation." *New York Times,* Nov. 21, p. C4.

Stevens, Wallace K. 1997. "A Greener Green Belt Bears Witness to a Warming Trend." *New York Times,* Apr. 22, p. B10.

Stevenson, Glenn G. 1991. *Common Property Economics: A General Theory and Land Use Applications.* Cambridge and New York: Cambridge University Press.

Stewart, F. 1982. "Poverty and Famines: Book Review." *Disasters* 6(2).

Stiefel, Matthias. 1994. *A Voice for the Excluded: Popular Participation in Development: Utopia or Necessity?* London and Atlantic Highlands, NJ: Zed Books.

Stiglitz, Joseph E. 2002. *Globalization and Its Discontents.* New York: Norton.

Stix, Gary. 1996. "Green Policies: Insurers Cope with Global Warming." *Scientific American* 274:27–28.

Streeter, Michael. 1996. "Record Haul of Rhino Horn Is Seized." *Independent,* Sept. 4, p. 1.

Stretskey, Paul, & Hogan, Michael J. 1998. "Environmental Justice: An Analysis of Superfund Sites in Florida." *Social Problems* 45(2):268–287.

Stretesky, Paul, & Lynch, Michael J. 1999. "Environmental Justice and the Predictions of Distance to Accidental Chemical Releases in Hillsborough County, Florida." *Social Science Quarterly* 80(4):830–846.

Suplee, Curt. 1995. "Dirty Air Can Shorten Your Life, Study Says: Death Rate Higher in Worst Cities." *Washington Post,* Mar. 10, p. A1.

Tagliabue, John. 2003. "Death Toll in Europe's Heat Wave Is Continuing to Climb." *New York Times,* Aug. 14, 2003. Retrieved August 21, 2003, from http://www.nytimes.com/2003/08/14/international/europe/14CND-EURO.html

Taquino, Michael, Parisi, Domenico, & Gill, Duane A. 2002. "Units of Analysis and the Environmental Justice Hypothesis: The Case of Industrial Hog Farms." *Social Science Quarterly* 83(1):298–316.

Taylor, Dorceta E. 1989. "Blacks and the Environment: Toward an Explanation of the Concern and Action Gap Between Blacks and Whites." *Environment and Behavior* 21(2):175–205.

Taylor, Humphrey. 2003. "The Religious and Other Beliefs of Americans 2003." *Harris Poll Library.* Retrieved January 30, 2003, from http://www.harrisinteractive.com/harris_poll/index.asp?PID=359

Taylor, Paul W. 1986. *Respect for Nature: A Theory of Environmental Ethics.* Princeton, NJ: Princeton University Press.

Taylor, Peter J., & Buttel, Frederick H. 1992. "How Do We Know We Have Global Environmental Problems? Science and the Globalization of Environmental Discourse." *Geoforum* 23:405–416.

Teitelbaum, Michael S. 1987. "Relevance of Demographic Transition Theory for Developing Countries." In *Perspectives on Population: An Introduction to Concepts and Issues,* ed. Scott W. Menard & Elizabeth W. Moen, pp. 29–36. New York and Oxford: Oxford University Press.

Thomas, Keith. 1983. *Man and the Natural World: Changing Attitudes in England, 1500–1800.* London: Allen Lane.

Thompson, Gary D., & Wilson, Paul N. 1994. "Common Property as an Institutional Response to Environmental Variability." *Contemporary Economic Policy* 12:12–21.

Thoreau, Henry David. 1962 (1854). *The Variorum Walden*. New York: Washington Square Press.

Thoreau, Henry David. 1975 (1862). "Walking." In *Excursions*. Gloucester, MA: Peter Smith.

Thurow, Lester C. 1996. *The Future of Capitalism: How Today's Economic Forces Shape Tomorrow's World*. New York: William Morrow.

Tierney, John. 1996. "Recycling Is Garbage." *New York Times Magazine*, June 30, pp. 24–29.

Tomlin, C. D. S. 1997. *The Pesticide Manual: A World Compendium*, 11th ed., British Crop Protection Council.

"Traffic: Not Bothered." 1996. *Economist*. Sept. 7, pp. 25–26.

Twain, Mark. 1991 (1876). *The Adventures of Tom Sawyer*. Philadelphia and London: Running Press.

UNESCO. 2004. "Threats: Disturbed Balance of the Lagoon." *Venice, Safeguarding Campaign*. Retrieved January 14, 2004, from http: //www.unesco.org/culture/heritage/tangible/venice/html_eng/menacelag.shtml

Ungar, Sheldon. 1994. "Apples and Oranges: Probing the Attitude-Behavior Relationship for the Environment." *Canadian Review of Sociology and Anthropology* 31:288–304.

United Nations Development Programme (UNDP). 1992. *Human Development Report 1992*. New York: Oxford University Press.

United Nations Development Programme (UNDP). 1994. *Human Development Report 1994*. New York: Oxford University Press.

United Nations Development Programme (UNDP). 1996. *Urban Agriculture: Food, Jobs and Sustainable Cities*. New York: United Nations Development Programme.

United Nations Development Programme (UNDP). 1999. *Human Development Report 1999*. New York and Oxford: Oxford University Press.

United Nations Development Programme (UNDP). 2000. *Human Development Report 2000*. New York and Oxford: Oxford University Press.

United Nations Development Programme (UNDP). 2003. *Human Development Report 2003*. New York and Oxford: Oxford University Press.

United Nations Environment Programme. 2001. "Ammonium Nitrate Explosion in Toulouse–France: 21 September 2001." *Awareness and Preparedness for Emergencies on a Local Level*. Retrieved October 22, 2003, from http://www.uneptie.org/pc/apell/disasters/toulouse/home.html

United Nations Environment Programme (UNEP). 2003. *Groundwater and Its Susceptibility to Degradation: A Global Assessment of the Problem and Options for Management*. Nairobi, Kenya: United Nations Environment Programme.

United Nations Population Division. 2001. *World Population Prospects: The 2000 Revision: Highlights*. New York: United Nations.

United Nations Population Division. 2003. *World Population 2002*. Excel spread sheet. Department of Economic and Social Affairs. Retrieved August 18, 2003, from http://www.un.org/esa/population/

Urry, John. 1990. *The Tourist Gaze: Leisure and Travel in Contemporary Societies*. London: Sage.

Urry, John. 1995. *Consuming Places*. London and New York: Routledge.

United States Department of Agriculture. 1994. *Agricultural Statistics 1994*. Washington, DC: United States Government Printing Office.

U.S. Chemical Safety and Hazard Investigation Board (CSB). 2002. "French Chemical Plant That Exploded in Southern France Not to Reopen." *CSB Incident News Reports*. Retrieved October 22, 2003, from http://www.chemsafety.gov/circ/post.cfm?incident_id=5247

U.S. Department of Energy. 2003. "Men versus Women: Average Annual Miles per Driver." *FreedomCAR and Vehicle Technologies Program: Fact of the Week.* Retrieved February 1, 2004, from http://www.eere.energy.gov/vehiclesandfuels/facts/2003/fcvt_fotw255.shtml

U.S. Environmental Protection Agency. 2003. "1998–1999 Pesticide Market Estimates: Historical Data." *About Pesticides.* Retrieved August 24, 2003, from http://www.epa.gov/oppbead1/pestsales/99pestsales/historical_data1999_3.html

Van Dyke, Fred. 1996. *Redeeming Creation: The Biblical Basis for Environmental Stewardship.* Downers Grove, IL: InterVarsity Press.

Veblen, Thorstein. 1967 (1899). *The Theory of the Leisure Class.* New York: Funk & Wagnalls.

Vidal, John. 1995. "Black Gold Claims a High Price." *Guardian Weekly,* Jan. 15, 1995, p. 7.

Visser, Margaret. 1986. *Much Depends on Dinner: The Extraordinary History and Mythology, Allure and Obsessions, Perils and Taboos, of an Ordinary Meal.* Toronto: McClelland & Stewart.

Wachtel, Paul. 1983. *The Poverty of Affluence: A Psychological Portrait of the American Way of Life.* New York: Free Press.

Walby, Sylvia. 1996. "The 'Declining Significance' or the 'Changing Forms' of Patriarchy?" In *Patriarchy and Development: Women's Positions at the End of the Twentieth Century,* ed. Valentine M. Moghadam, pp. 19–33. Oxford: Clarendon Press.

Walton, John. 1994. *Free Markets and Food Riots: The Politics of Global Adjustment.* Oxford, UK, and Cambridge, MA: Blackwell.

Wargo, John. 1998. *Our Children's Toxic Legacy: How Science and Law Fail to Protect Us from Pesticides,* 2nd ed. New Haven, CT: Yale University Press.

Warner, W. Keith, & England, J. Lynn. 1995. "A Technological Science Perspective for Sociology." *Rural Sociology* 60:607–622.

Warr, P., & Payne, R. 1982. "Experience of Strain and Pleasure among British Adults." *Social Science and Medicine* 16:1691–1697.

Warren, Karen, ed. 1994. *Ecological Feminism.* London and New York: Routledge.

Warren, Karen. 1996. "Ecological Feminist Philosophies: An Overview of the Issues." In *Ecological Feminist Philosophies,* ed. Karen Warren, pp. ix–xxvi. Bloomington and Indianapolis: Indiana University Press.

Weber, Max. 1958 (1904–1905). *The Protestant Ethic and the Spirit of Capitalism.* New York: Charles Scribner.

Weber, Max. 1967 (1922). *Economy and Society.* Ed. Guenther Roth & Claus Wittich. Vol. 1. Berkeley: University of California.

Weber, Max. 1988 (1909). *The Agrarian Sociology of Ancient Civilizations.* London: Verso.

Weinberg, Adam S. 1998. "The Environmental Justice Debate: A Commentary on Methodological Issues and Practical Concerns." *Sociological Forum* 13(1):25–32.

Weinberg, Adam S., Pellow, David N., & Schnaiberg, Alan. 2000. *Urban Recycling and the Search for Sustainable Community Development.* Princeton, NJ: Princeton University Press.

Weir, David. 1986. *The Bhopal Syndrome: Pesticide Manufacturing and the Third World.* Penang, Malaysia: International Office of Consumers Unions.

White, Lynn. 1967. "The Historical Roots of Our Ecological Crises." *Science* 155:1203–1207.

Whitley, Richard. 1992. "Changing Organizational Forms: From the Bottom Up." In *Rethinking Organization: New Directions in Organization Theory and Analysis,* ed. Michael Reed & Michael Hughes. London and Newberry Park, CA: Sage.

Wichterich, Christa. 1988. "From the Struggle against 'Overpopulation' to the Industrialization of Human Production." *Reproductive and Genetic Engineering* 1(1):21–30.

Wilford, John Noble. 2000. "Open Water at Pole Not Surprising, Experts Say." *New York Times,* Aug. 29. Retrieved February 2, 2004, from http://www.climateark.org/articles/2000/3rd/opwapole.htm

Williams, Raymond. 1980 (1972). "Ideas of Nature." In *Problems in Materialism and Culture*, pp. 67–85. London: Verso.

Wilson, Harold Fisher. 1967 (1936). *The Hill Country of Northern New England*. New York: AMS Press.

Wilson, Randall, & Yaro, Robert D. 1988. *Dealing with Change in the Connecticut River Valley: A Design Manual for Conservation and Development*. Amherst: Center for Rural Massachusetts, University of Massachusetts.

Winner, Langdon. 1986. *The Whale and the Reactor: A Search for Limits in an Age of High Technology*. Chicago and London: University of Chicago Press.

Wolff, Edward N. 1995. *Top Heavy: A Study of the Increasing Inequality of Wealth in America*. New York: Twentieth-Century Fund Press.

Woodgate, Graham, & Redclift, Michael. 1998. "From a 'Sociology of Nature' to Environmental Sociology: Beyond Social Construction." *Environmental Values* 7:3–24.

World Bank. 1994. *World Development Report 1994*. Oxford: Oxford University.

World Bank. 2000. *World Development Report 2000/2001*. New York: Oxford University Press.

World Bank. 2002. *World Development Report 2003: Sustainable Development in a Dynamic World*. New York: Oxford University Press.

World Conservation Union (IUCN). (n.d.). "Summary Statistics for Globally Threatened Species." *2003 IUCN Red List of Threatened Species*. Retrieved January 15, 2004, from http://www.redlist.org/

World Health Organization (WHO). 1998. *The WHO Recommended Classification of Pesticides by Hazard, and Guidelines to Classification, 1998–1999*. WHO/PCS/98.21. Geneva: International Programme on Chemical Safety.

World Health Organization (WHO). 2003a. *Obesity and Overweight*. Global Strategy on Diet, Physical Activity, and Health fact sheet. World Health Organization. Retrieved February 2, 2004, from http://www.who.int/hpr/gs.fs.obesity.shtml

World Health Organization (WHO). 2003b. *Road Traffic Injuries*. Fact Sheet. Retrieved September 12, 2003, from http://www.who.int/world-health-day/2004/en/

World Health Organization (WHO). 2003c. *20 Questions on Genetically Modified (GM) Foods*. Retrieved October 30, 2003, from http://www.who.int/foodsafety/publications/biotech/20questions/en/

World Meteorological Organization. 2003a. "The Global Climate in 2002." *World Climate News* 23:4–5.

World Meteorological Organization. 2003b. *WMO Statement on the Status of the Global Climate in 2002*. WMO report 949. Geneva, Switzerland: World Meteorological Organization.

World Meteorological Organization. 2003c. *WMO Statement on the Status of the Global Climate in 2003*. WMO press release no. 702. Geneva, Switzerland: World Meteorological Organization.

World Resources Institute. 1996. *World Resources, 1996–1997*. New York and Oxford: Oxford University Press.

Worldwatch Institute. 2002. *Vital Signs 2002*. New York and London: Norton.

Worldwatch Institute. 2003. *Vital Signs 2003*. New York and London: Norton.

Worthy, Trevor H., & Holdaway, Richard N. 2002. *The Lost World of the Moa: Prehistoric Life of New Zealand*. Bloomington: Indiana University Press.

Wright, Angus Lindsay. 1990. *The Death of Ramon Gonzalez: The Modern Agricultural Dilemma*. Austin: University of Texas Press.

WWF Australia. 2003. *Murray Darling Basin*. Retrieved August 28, 2003, from http://www.wwf.org.au/default.asp?p=MDB.htm

Yago, Glenn. 1984. *The Decline of Transit: Urban Transportation in German and U.S. Cities, 1900–1970.* Cambridge, MA, and London: Cambridge University Press.

Yearley, Steven. 1991. *The Green Case: A Sociology of Environmental Issues, Arguments, and Politics.* London: HarperCollins.

Yearley, Steven. 1996. *Sociology, Environmentalism, Globalization.* London: Sage.

Yearley, Steve, Cinderby, Steve, Forrester, John, Bailey, Peter, & Rosen, Paul. 2003. "Participatory Modeling and the Local Governance of the Politics of Air Pollution: A Three-City Case Study." *Environmental Values* 12(2).

Yepson, David. 1995. "What about the Big Hog Lots?" *Des Moines Register,* Nov. 27, p. 9.

Zheng, T., Holford, T. R., Mayne, S. T., Ward, B., Carter, D., Owens, P. H., Dubrow, R., Zahm, S. H., Boyle, P., Archibeque, S., & Tessari, J. 1999. "DDE and DDT in Breast Adipose Tissue and Risk of Female Breast Cancer." *American Journal of Epidemiology* 150:453–458.

Ziska, Lewis H., & Caulfield, Frances. 2000. "The Potential Influence of Rising Atmospheric Carbon Dioxide (CO2) on Public Health: Pollen Production of Common Ragweed as a Test Case." *World Resource Review* 12(3):449.

Index

Sources of Illustrations

Where not indicated, the source is the author.

Cover art
Marc Chagall, *I and the Village*, 1911, Museum of Modern Art. Used with permission of the Museum of Modern Art and the Chagall Estate.

Chapter 1: Environmental Problems and Society

Figure 1.2 Courtesy of the World Meteorological Organization.
Figure 1.3 From Worldwatch Institute, 2003, *Signposts, 2003*, CD-ROM, Washington, DC: Worldwatch Institute. Used with permission of the Worldwatch Institute.
Figure 1.4 Courtesy of the Goddard Space Flight Center.
Figure 1.5 Courtesy of the Goddard Space Flight Center.
Figure 1.7 Based on Korten, David, 1995, *When Corporations Rule the World*, West Hartford, CT: Kumarian; and on United Nations Development Programme (UNDP), 2003, *Human Development Report 2003*, New York and Oxford: Oxford University Press.
Figure 1.8 Courtesy of the United Nations Environment Programme.
Figure 1.9 From Brown, Lester R.; Renner, Michael; and Flavin, Christopher, 1997, *Vital Signs 1997: The Environmental Trends That Are Shaping Our Future*, New York and London: Norton. Used with permission of the Worldwatch Institute.

Chapter 2: Consumption and Materialism

Figure 2.2 Hewitt Associates. Used with permission of Hewitt Associates.
Figure 2.3 Reprinted with the permission of Simon & Schuster from *Bowling Alone: The Collapse and Revival of American Community* by Robert D. Putnam. Copyright © 2000 by Robert D. Putnam.
Figure 2.4 Based on Veenhoven, R., *Average Happiness in 68 nations in the 1990s*, World Database of Happiness, Rank Report 2002/1, www.eur.nl/fsw/research/happiness; and United Nations Development Programme (UNDP), 2000, *Human Development Report 2000*, New York and Oxford: Oxford University Press.

Figure 2.6   From Durning, Alan T., 1992, *How Much Is Enough? The Consumer Society and the Future of the Earth,* New York: Norton. Used with permission of the Worldwatch Institute.

Chapter 3: Money and Machines

Figure 3.2   Photo by Helen D. Gunderson. Used with permission of Helen D. Gunderson.

Figure 3.4   From Worldwatch Institute, 2003, *Vital Signs 2003,* New York and London: Norton. Used with permission of the Worldwatch Institute.

Chapter 4: Population and Development

Figure 4.1   Based on information from Independent Commission on Population and Quality of Life, 1996, *Caring for the Future: Making the Next Decades Provide a Life Worth Living,* Oxford, UK, and New York: Oxford University Press; and United Nations Population Division, 2003, *World Population 2002,* Excel spread sheet, Department of Economic and Social Affairs; retrieved August 18, 2003, from http://www. un.org/esa/population/.

Figure 4.2   Based on information from Freeman-Grenville, G. S. P., 1991, *The New Atlas of African History,* New York: Prentice Hall.

Figure 4.3   From Worldwatch Institute, 2003, *Vital Signs 2003,* New York and London: Norton. Used with permission of the Worldwatch Institute.

Figure 4.4   Based on information from Sarre, Philip, and Blunden, John, 1995, *An Overcrowded World? Population, Resources, and the Environment,* Oxford and New York: Oxford University Press and the Open University.

Chapter 5: Body and Health

Figure 5.1   Used with permission of Corbis.

Figure 5.2   Adapted from Pastor, Manuel, Jr., Sadd, Jim, & Hipp, John, 2001, "Which Came First? Toxic Facilities, Minority Move-In, and Environmental Justice," *Journal of Urban Affairs* 23(1):1–21.

Figure 5.3   Based on information from World Health Organization (WHO), 1998, *The WHO Recommended Classification of Pesticides by Hazard, and Guidelines to Classification, 1998-1999,* WHO/PCS/98.21, Geneva: International Programme on Chemical Safety.

Chapter 6: The Ideology of Environmental Domination

Figure 6.2   Used with permission of Bibliothèque Publique et Universitaire de Genève.

Figure 6.3   By permission of the Folger Shakespeare Library.

Figure 6.4   Used with permission of the Worcester Art Museum, Worcester, Massachusetts.

Chapter 7: The Ideology of Environmental Concern

Figure 7.1   Used with permission of the Rachel Carson History Project.

Figure 7.2   Photo by David Gradwohl. Used with permission of David Gradwohl.

Figure 7.4   From Dunlap, Riley, 2002, "An Enduring Concern: Light Stays Green for Environmental Protection," *Public Perspective*, Sept/Oct, 10–14.

Figure 7.5   Based on figure 4.1 in Gurr, Ted Robert, and Marshall, Monty, 2003, *Peace and Conflict 2003: A Global Survey of Armed Conflicts, Self-Determination Movements, and Democracy*, College Park, MD: Center for International Development and Conflict Management. Used with permission of the Center for International Development and Conflict Management.

Chapter 8: The Human Nature of Nature

Figure 8.1   Fisher Museum Dioramas, Harvard Forest, Petersham, MA. Used with permission of the Fisher Museum.

Figure 8.2   Fisher Museum Dioramas, Harvard Forest, Petersham, MA. Used with permission of the Fisher Museum.

Figure 8.3   Fisher Museum Dioramas, Harvard Forest, Petersham, MA. Used with permission of the Fisher Museum.

Figure 8.4   Based on the US Census of Agriculture, various years.

Figure 8.5a and 8.5b   From Huntington, Ellsworth, 1915, *Civilization and Climate*, New Haven, CT: Yale University Press.

Figure 8.6   Lawren S. Harris, *Lake and Mountains*, 1927–1928. Used with permission of the Art Gallery of Ontario.

Chapter 9: The Rationality of Risk

Figure 9.1   Based on information from the US Meat Export Federation.

Figure 9.2   Used with permission of Corbis.

Figure 9.3   From Twain, Mark, 1904, *The Adventures of Tom Sawyer*, New York: Harper and Brothers.

Figure 9.4   Adapted from Perrow, Charles; *Normal Accidents*. Copyright © 1999 by Princeton University Press. Reprinted by permission of Princeton University Press.

Figure 9.5   From Wing, Steve; Richardson, David; Armstrong, Donna; and Crawford-Brown, Douglas, 1997, "A Reevaluation of Cancer Incidence Near the Three Mile Island Nuclear Plant: The Collision of Evidence and Assumptions," *Environmental Health Perspectives*, 105, (1), 52-57.

Chapter 10: Organizing the Ecological Society

Figure 10.3   Photo by Joe Lynch. Used with permission of Joe Lynch.

Figure 10.4   Photo by Shelly Gradwell-Brenneman. Used with permission of Shelly Gradwell-Brenneman.

Figure 10.7   From Worldwatch Institute, 2003, Signposts, 2003, CD-ROM, Washington, DC: Worldwatch Institute. Used with permission of the Worldwatch Institute.

Page 250   Photo by Shelly Gradwell-Brenneman. Used with permission of Shelly Gradwell-Brenneman.

About the Author

Michael Mayerfeld Bell is an associate professor of rural sociology at the University of Wisconsin-Madison. Mike is principally an environmental sociologist, but he also conducts research on culture, economic sociology, sustainable agriculture, community, place, rural society, inequality, gender, the body, democracy, and social theory. Two central themes can be heard in all of his work: dialogics and the sociology of "nature," broadly conceived. Mike is the author of *Childerley: Nature and Morality in a Country Village* (University of Chicago Press, 1994), which was co-winner of the 1995 Outstanding Book Award of the Sociology of Culture Section of the American Sociological Association. He is the author, along with Gregory Peter, Susan Jarnagin, and Donna Bauer, of *Farming for Us All: Practical Agriculture and the Cultivation of Sustainability* (Pennsylvania State University Press, 2004). Mike has also worked as a geologist and is the author of *The Face of Connecticut: People, Geology, and the Land* (State of Connecticut, 1985), which won an American Library Association award.

Mike continues to have a second life as a part-time composer of new music and folk music, and as a folk musician. Mike plays mandolin in the Barn Owl Band, and appeared with them on the National Public Radio show *A Prairie Home Companion* in 2002. In the area of new music, Mike has recently completed a string quartet, a string trio, and several pieces for piano, and is at work on a symphonic poem.

You can learn more about Mike's work and passions at http://www.michaelmbell.net.